Understanding
Major Mental Disorder:
The Contribution of Family Interaction Research

Understanding Major Mental Disorder

The Contribution of Family Interaction Research

EDITED BY

KURT HAHLWEG

Max Planck Institute of Psychiatry
Munich, West Germany

MICHAEL J. GOLDSTEIN

Department of Psychology
University of California, Los Angeles

FAMILY PROCESS PRESS
New York
1987

149 East 78th Street, New York NY 10021

All correspondence and inquiries should be directed to Family Process Press, a Division of Family Process Inc., 149 East 78th Street, New York, NY 10021.

The text of this book was typeset in English Times. Composition was done by Bytheway Typesetting Services. Printing was done by Science Press. Binding was done by Short Run Bindery Inc.

Printed in the United States of America.

Library of Congress Cataloging-in-Publication Data

Understanding major mental disorder.

(The Family Process Press monograph series)
Includes bibliographies and indexes.
1. Mentally ill—Family relationships. I. Hahlweg, Kurt. II. Goldstein, Michael J. (Michael Joseph), 1930- . III. Series. [DNLM: 1. Family. 2. Mental Disorders. WM 100 U52]
RC455.4.F3U53 1987 616.89 87-6858
ISBN 0-9615519-4-1
ISBN 0-9615519-5-X (soft)

Contributors

Cheri Adrian, Ph.D.
Department of Psychology
University of California
Los Angeles, California

Robert F. Asarnow, Ph.D.
Department of Psychiatry and Biobehavioral Sciences
University of California
Los Angeles, California

Joan R. Asarnow, Ph.D.
Department of Psychiatry and Biobehavioral Sciences
University of California
Los Angeles, California

Donald H. Baucom, Ph.D.
Department of Psychology
University of North Carolina at Chapel Hill
Chapel Hill, North Carolina

Sharon L. Ben-Meir, M.A.
Department of Psychology
University of California
Los Angeles, California

Dorli Burge, M.A.
Department of Psychology
University of California
Los Angeles, California

Andrew Christensen, Ph.D.
Department of Psychology
University of California
Los Angeles, California

Jeri A. Doane, Ph.D.
Yale Psychiatric Institute
Yale University School of Medicine
New Haven, Connecticut

S. Wayne Duncan, Ph.D.
Department of Psychology
University of Denver
Center for Marital and Family Studies
Denver, Colorado

Kristin Ø. Ernø, Cand. Psychol.
Department of Behavioral Sciences in Medicine
University of Oslo
Oslo, Norway

Tamara Goldman Sher, B.A.
Department of Psychology
University of North Carolina at Chapel Hill
Chapel Hill, North Carolina

Michael J. Goldstein, Ph.D.
Department of Psychology
University of California
Los Angeles, California

David Gordon, Ph.D.
Department of Psychology
University of California
Los Angeles, California

Kurt Hahlweg, Ph.D.
Max Planck Institute of Psychiatry
Munich, West Germany

Constance Hammen, Ph.D.
Department of Psychology
University of California
Los Angeles, California

Donald Hiroto, Ph.D.
Veterans Administration Medical Center
Brentwood, California

Arne Holte, *Associate Professor*
Department of Behavioral Sciences in Medicine
University of Oslo
Oslo, Norway

Jill M. Hooley, Ph.D.
Department of Psychology and Social Relations
Harvard University
Cambridge, Massachusetts

Paul Howes, M.A.
Department of Psychology
University of Denver
Center for Marital and Family Studies
Denver, Colorado

Theodore Jacob, Ph.D.
Division of Child Development and Family Relations
University of Arizona
Tucson, Arizona

Carol Jaenicke, Ph.D.
Department of Psychology
University of California
Los Angeles, California

Kristin Kveseth, Cand. Psychol.
Department of Behavioral Sciences in Medicine
University of Oslo
Oslo, Norway

Ilpo Lahti, M.D.
Department of Psychiatry
University of Turku
Turku, Finland

Ana Magaña, M.A.
Department of Psychology
University of California
Los Angeles, California

Howard J. Markman, Ph.D.
Department of Psychology
University of Denver
Center for Marital and Family Studies
Denver, Colorado

David J. Miklowitz, Ph.D.
Department of Psychology
University of California
Los Angeles, California

Juha Moring, M.D.
Department of Psychiatry
University of Oulu
Oulu, Finland

Mikko Naarala, M.D.
Department of Psychiatry
University of Oulu
Oulu, Finland

Clifford I. Notarius, Ph.D.
Department of Psychology
Catholic University of America
Washington, D.C.

Keith H. Nuechterlein, Ph.D.
Department of Psychiatry and Biobehavioral Sciences
University of California
Los Angeles, California

David S. Pellegrini, Ph.D.
Department of Psychology
Catholic University of America
Washington, D.C.

John Richters, Ph.D.
Laboratory of Developmental Psychology
National Institutes of Health
Bethesda, Maryland

Tuula Rönkkö, M.D.
Department of Psychiatry
University of Oulu
Oulu, Finland

Karen S. Snyder, M.A.
Department of Psychology
University of California
Los Angeles, California

Anneli Sorri, M.D.
Department of Psychiatry
University of Oulu
Oulu, Finland

Ragnar Storaasli, M.A.
Department of Psychology
University of Denver
Center for Marital and Family Studies
Denver, Colorado

Pekka Tienari, M.D.
Department of Psychiatry
University of Oulu
Oulu, Finland

Karl-Erik Wahlberg, Ph.D.
Department of Psychiatry
University of Oulu
Oulu, Finland

Lars Wichstrøm, *Research Fellow*
Department of Behavioral Sciences in Medicine
University of Oslo
Oslo, Norway

Lyman C. Wynne, M.D., Ph.D.
Department of Psychiatry
University of Rochester School of Medicine and Dentistry
Rochester, New York

Contents

PART II. STUDIES OF PSYCHOPATHOLOGICAL GROUPS

PART III. MARITAL INTERACTION RESEARCH

Introduction

ALTHOUGH clinical and conceptual studies of families and family therapy have proliferated ever since the mid-1950s, systematic research on intrafamilial processes in families with a psychiatrically ill member has developed much more slowly throughout these years. Starting in the late 1960s, research activity and interest in this area shifted from cross-sectional studies of families with a member who was already ill to prospective studies of families with children at risk for later illness. During the last ten years, interest has shifted again, with an emphasis on family factors in the course and outcome of psychiatric illness. This volume is a collection of articles, by leading family researchers, which illustrate the new and exciting methods and findings that are having a major impact on how we think about and intervene in the major mental disorders.

Does this recent work represent real change in the way modern family researchers conceptualize and carry out their studies? We think that the answer is affirmative.

In the cross-sectional studies of the 1950s and 1960s, family interaction was studied after a mental disorder had been present for some time. It was assumed that by comparing families with relatives who had different forms of mental disorder (and families free of psychiatric disorder), patterns would emerge that discriminated normal families from those containing a mentally disordered person, and, further, that each form of mental disorder would have a distinctive form of family transaction. This earlier research was guided by ambitious family-system theories positing that disturbance in family dynamics was a major, but not the sole etiological agent for mental disorders, and that each disorder had discriminable patterns of family dynamics.

It is ironic that despite the family-system orientation of most investigators during the 1950s and 1960s, there was only partial recognition that these cross-sectional family interaction data reflected a complex amalgam of family processes, some of which antedated the onset of disorder in the ill family member and others that reflected diverse forms of accommodation to the presence of disorder. Undoubtedly, the great difficulties in replicating findings across studies, so characteristic of that earlier period (see 2, 3, 5), were due in part to the fact that each sample varied to some degree in the patterns of pre- and post-onset family adaptations. Other factors that limited the possibilities of replication were wide variations from sample to sample in the criteria used to diagnose offspring, the methods for eliciting interactional data, and the coding systems used to reduce data to quantifiable units. Gradually, there was increasing recognition that cross-sectional studies, carried out *after* a mental disorder had been present for some time, were quite limited in revealing etiological processes.

We believe, however, that the shift in focus in family research on major mental disorders from the mid-sixties to mid-seventies was not due solely to the difficulties in replication across samples. During this same period, convincing evidence appeared that there was a strong genetic predisposition to a number of major mental disorders such as schizophrenia, bipolar disorder, and alcoholism. These findings, combined with powerful evidence of the efficacy of psychopharmacology for a number of these disorders, challenged the underlying paradigm of previous family studies in which intrafamilial transactions were hypothesized to be the predominant etiological agents. A more sophisticated model was necessary to guide the next era of research on the family.

The model that has emerged to guide this wave of family research, reflected in this volume, has been called the *vulnerability-stress* model, a model originally articulated by David Rosenthal in 1970 (7) and more recently modified by Zubin and Spring (12). According to this model, a predisposition to a disorder, such as schizophrenia, is inherited and forms the basis for various indices of vulnerability to the disorder. This vulnerability is modified by all life events that increase or decrease the likelihood that a major psychiatric disorder, such as schizophrenia, will emerge in early adulthood. The stress-vulnerability model is also applicable to the post-onset stage of psychiatric disorder because vulnerability continues to be modified in association with variations in remission from the acute phase of the disorder, and this vulnerability interacts with various intercurrent life events, within and outside of the family, to modify the risk for subsequent episodes of the disorder.

The implications of the vulnerability-stress model for family interaction research are profound. Most importantly, they imply that researchers need to investigate the interaction between intrafamilial relationships and indices of vulnerability to a particular psychiatric disorder. Ideally, researchers should have available an established vulnerability marker that can be investigated in the context of different family environments, some of which may be deemed protective and others adversive.

Unfortunately, despite numerous efforts to define such vulnerability markers—and there are some promising leads at the present time (with regard to schizophrenia, see 6)—none have a secure status as yet. The best risk marker for most major mental disorders is still the rather crude index of being an offspring of a parent with that disorder. Nevertheless, recognition of the vulnerability-stress model has stimulated a new sense of purpose and vigor among family researchers in the last twenty years. They have recognized that tests of this model, from a family perspective, require longitudinal, prospective designs in which family relations are evaluated prior to the onset of a disorder, either in its prodromal or active forms, followed by careful evaluations of targeted offspring over subsequent years as they pass through the risk period for the disorder. Studies using the "high-risk" paradigm have re-invigorated the field of family research.

In the present volume, there are several examples of research in this general paradigm. The studies by Goldstein; Hammen et al.; Jacob; Richters; Tienari et al.; and Wynne (see chapters 1–4, 6, 12) all reflect this tradition. In each of these studies some measure of risk, usually but not always a family history of a disorder, is used to define populations at higher or lower risk for a particular disorder, and family relationships are intensively analyzed in order to understand the current and future studies of offspring. It is interesting to note that those studies also represent a broader range of interest because they go beyond schizophrenia and investigate factors involved in the intergenerational transmission of depression and alcoholism.

A second limitation in the family research of the 1950s and 1960s was the lack of generally agreed-upon measures of significant intrafamilial processes. Other than the notion of communication deviance, originally proposed by Wynne and Singer in the mid-1960s (8, 9, 10), few of the variables studied earlier revealed consistent and significant intergroup comparisons. During the last ten years, researchers have been stimulated by British research oriented to predicting the course of the major mental psychiatric disorders, particularly schizophrenia. The concept of high expressed emotion (4) defined a set of attitudinal attributes of key relatives about mentally ill family members, particularly involving high rates of criticism and/or emotional overinvolvement that were associated with a marked probability of relapse in the nine-month period after a patient was discharged from the hospital. Research on expressed emotion (EE) energized the field of family research as it seemed to specify a potent intrafamilial stress factor that interacted with the remitted schizophrenic's vulnerability to relapse.

Whereas the original EE studies were provocative, many questions about the construct remain unanswered. First, does this measure, which is derived from an interview with a relative, reflect ongoing family transactions? Work in this particular area is presented in another book that we edited (1), and it indicates that when one aggregates data over a total interaction, high-EE and low-EE relatives behave in distinctly different ways that are congruent with their expressed attitude. However, such aggregate data summed across a total interaction do not identify the micro-processes by which family members reach these states of high or low criticism. As a result, family researchers have turned to methods such as sequential analysis in order to analyze the details of these reciprocal interaction cycles. In the present volume, Hahlweg et al. (see Chapter 9) demonstrate how one model of sequential analysis can elucidate the nature of interaction patterns in high- and low-EE families.

A second unresolved question with regard to EE has to do with its specificity as a risk marker for schizophrenic relapse. Are such attitudes also present in relatives living with family members who manifest other major mental disorders? Do they serve as risk markers for relapse in the other groups? Similar questions can be asked about the communication deviance concept of Wynne and Singer that was originally hypothesized and later shown (11) to occur along a continuum of frequency from the parents of schizophrenics to parents of "borderline" patients, neurotics, and normals.

One chapter by J. Asarnow et al. (see Chapter 7) and one by Miklowitz et al. (see Chapter 11) deal with this issue of specificity in studying family interaction patterns of recent-onset manics, childhood-onset schizophrenics and depressives, and major depressive disorders in adults. These studies indicate that high-EE attitudes, or alternative variations of this construct, are clearly *not* specific to schizophrenia. Where follow-up data are available, as in Chapter 12, measures of EE or variants thereof are also predictive of the short-term course of mania and major depressive disorder.

Despite the predictive value of the EE measure, it is still unclear how family attitudes relate to variations in patient behavior over time. Hooley (see Chapter 10) analyzes the EE contruct from the point of view of what is termed attribution theory, and she finds this theory helpful in providing links among EE attitudes, the quality of the marital relationship, and variations in the form of a relative's symptoms over time.

Many of the chapters may seem to be largely atheoretical. They investigate the validity of constructs about family processes but are largely devoid of broad-gauge theorizing. There are some exceptions to this, however. The chapter by Holte and his associates (see Chapter 8) reflects a different tradition. Strongly influenced by family-system theory, these investigators have developed a methodology for studying family processes implicated by this theoretical model as significant for psychopathology, and they have created viable coding systems to capture these processes in a form appropriate for sophisticated data analyses. Their studies raise important questions for future research concerning the relationship between theoretically driven measures and the more empirically derived constructs such as communication deviance and expressed emotion. Do we, in fact, end up in the same place when we start from these quite different research traditions, or are there unique insights available from each that enrich our understanding of intrafamilial processes?

Another important theoretical issue is also dealt with in the chapter by R. Asarnow (see Chapter 5). Although many researchers have been stimulated by the vulnerability-stress model, few investigate the links between measures of vulnerability in offspring and measures of intrafamilial processes. R. Asarnow indcates how, when both classes of measures are collected in a study, one can examine the cross-generational transmission of key elements of a particular psychopathological condition such as schizophrenia. He suggests how a measure, such as parental communication deviance, can be related to vulnerability markers, such as deficits in information processing in parents as well as in their schizophrenic offspring.

In some of the family-system theories of the 1950s and 1960s, a major hypothesis was that disturbances in the family system derived from underlying difficulties in the marital relationship. Despite these clinical observations, few family researchers included measures of marital relationships in their family interaction studies. Intead, most of the research on marital distress and discord took place in studies conducted by researchers and clinicians who approached marital therapy from a behavioral perspective. These investigators studied marital interaction in order to understand how distressed couples differed from nondistressed ones, and how behavioral marital therapy altered the processes observed in distressed couples. However, these marital researchers did not focus on issues of psychopathology. In fact, there was an initial tendency to shy away from viewing marital discord from this perspective. Furthermore, there was no study of the full family system in order to trace the impact of marital distress on other family members.

As editors, we concluded that there was a need to stimulate a dialogue between family and marital researchers. The last section of this book is devoted to a series of chapters from clinical researchers who study healthy and distressed marriages. Chapter 13 by Notarius and Chapter 14 by Christensen describe methods for defining patterns of marital interaction. Chapter 15 by Markman et al. deals with two issues: first, whether these measures, obtained before marriage, are valid predictors of the short-term course of a marriage, and, second, whether a premarital preventive intervention program can alter this course in a more favorable direction. The final chapter by Baucom and Goldman Sher (see Chapter 16) raises questions at a methodological level and attempts to provide solutions to problems that plague both family and marital research, namely, how to integrate data from different family members into composite indices that reflect the status of the marriage or the whole family system. The fact that Baucaum and Goldman Sher use the expressed emotion construct as a key example indicates that the process of communication between the two groups of researchers has begun. We hope that the inclusion of chapters by leading researchers on marital quality and therapy will point the way to methods and concepts that can be incorporated into the next generation of family interaction studies and that, reciprocally, future studies of marriage will also focus on issues of psychopathology.

Some chapters in this volume are revisions of papers originally written for a conference sponsored by the Max Planck Institute of Psychiatry, Munich, West Germany, held in Schloss-Ringberg, Bavaria, from September 1 to 6, 1985. The editors and authors are deeply indebted to the Max Planck Society for its support. The conference was deemed an enormous success by all participants, and we hope that the vitality of the field of family interaction research, so apparent at that conference, is communicated by this collection of articles. We also express our gratitude to Margaret Toohey for her extensive efforts in editing and preparing the chapters in this volume for publication.

January 21, 1987

KURT HAHLWEG
MICHAEL J. GOLDSTEIN
Editors

REFERENCES

1. Goldstein, M. J., Hand, I., & Hahlweg, K. *Treatment of schizophrenia: Family assessment and intervention*. Heidelberg: Springer-Verlag, 1986.

2. Helmersen, P. *Family interaction and communication in psychopathology: An evaluation in recent perspectives*. London: Academic Press, 1983.

3. Jacob, T. Family interaction in disturbed and normal families: A methodological and substantive review. *Psychological Bulletin 82*: 33–65, 1975.

4. Leff, J., & Vaughn, C. E. *Expressed emotion in families*. New York: Guilford Press, 1985.

5. Liem, J. H. Family studies in schizophrenia: An update and a commentary. *Schizophrenia Bulletin 6*: 429–459, 1980.

6. Nuechterlein, K. H., & Dawson, M. E. A heuristic vulnerability/stress model of schizophrenic episodes. *Schizophrenia Bulletin 10*: 300–312.

7. Rosenthal, D. *Genetic theory and abnormal behavior*. New York: McGraw-Hill, 1970.

8. Singer, M. T., & Wynne, L. C. Thought disorder and family relations of schizophrenics: III. Methodology using projective techniques. *Archives of General Psychiatry 12*: 187–200, 1965.

9. ______, & Wynne, L. C. Communication styles in parents of normal, neurotics and schizophrenics: Some findings using a new Rorschach scoring manual. In I. M. Cohen (ed.), *Family structure, dynamics and therapy*. Washington DC: American Psychiatric Association (Research Report No. 20), 1966.

10. Wynne, L. C., & Singer, M. T. Thought disorder and family relations of schizophrenics: I. A research strategy. *Archives of General Psychiatry 9*: 191–198, 1963.

11. ______, Singer, M. T., Bartko, J. J., & Toohey, M. L. Schizophrenics and their families: Research on parental communication. In J. M. Tanner (ed.), *Developments in psychiatric research*. London: Hodder & Stoughton, 1977.

12. Zubin, J., & Spring, B. J. Vulnerability—A new view of schizophrenia. *Journal of Abnormal Psychology 86*: 103–126, 1977.

I

High-Risk Studies

1

FAMILY INTERACTION PATTERNS THAT ANTEDATE THE ONSET OF SCHIZOPHRENIA AND RELATED DISORDERS:

A Further Analysis of Data from a Longitudinal, Prospective Study*

MICHAEL J. GOLDSTEIN
University of California, Los Angeles

DESPITE frequent reports in the literature of disordered relationship systems in families containing a schizophrenic relative, it has proved difficult to separate those relationships reactive to the psychotic relative from those antedating the onset of the disorder. Unless we can demonstrate that such relationship patterns precede the onset of the disorder, either in its prodromal or full-blown state, it is difficult to conclude that disturbed family relationships play a contributory role in the development of the disorder. The purpose of the present paper is to report further on the results of a longitudinal-prospective study designed to establish whether or not

*The research described in this paper was supported by NIMH Grant MH08744 and by a research project grant from the John D. and Catherine T. MacArthur Foundation. Michael J. Goldstein is a member of the MacArthur Mental Health Research Network on Risk and Protective Factors in the Major Mental Disorders. The author would like to thank a number of people who played a very important role in this project: Eliot H. Rodnick, the original co-investigator on the study who played a major role in the design and implementation of the study for many years, Sigrid McPherson, Kathryn West, and Jeri Doane who served consecutively in the vital role of project coordinator, and our many graduate students whose ideas and energy replenished the aging principal investigator.

certain characteristic patterns of family relationships antedate the onset of schizophrenia and related disorders such as schizotypal, paranoid, and borderline personality disorders.

The study began over twenty years ago with a cohort of 64 families, each of whom contained a mildly to moderately disturbed teenager. Each family had applied for help for their teenager from a university-based psychology clinic. The cohort was believed to contain a number of individuals at risk for subsequent schizophrenia and schizophrenia-linked disorders because we hypothesized that disturbances in adolescence increased the likelihood of more severe psychopathology in adulthood.

Design of the Study

All families studied were intact at the time of the initial assessment. The families were predominantly Caucasian, of middle- to upper-middle-class status, and above average in intelligence. None of the adolescents were considered psychotic at the time of admission. Within this heterogeneous sample, we subdivided the adolescent cases into four groups on the basis of the nature of their presenting problem. Further, hypotheses concerning relative risk for schizophrenia were articulated, based on our review of various follow-back and follow-up studies, such that two of these groups (active family conflict and withdrawn) were hypothesized to be at higher than average risk, while the other two groups (aggressive antisocial and passive negative) were hypothesized to be at much lower risk.

All families agreed to participate in a six-session series of family assessment procedures designed to reveal characteristic patterns of family interaction. The family assessment consisted of two main elements, individual assessment of the parents and index case, and family assessment in which the family was observed discussing a series of conflictual family problems. (See 3 for details of the rationale for the study and the assessment procedures.)

Our working hypothesis was that early signs of maladjustment in an adolescent, coupled with the presence of disturbances in communicational and affective climate within the family, would increase the risk for schizophrenia or schizophrenia-spectrum disorders in the offspring.

The Dimensions of Family Behavior Used in this Study

There are obviously many aspects of family behavior that have been hypothesized as relevant to the development of schizophrenia. We have relied on measures that have been well operationalized and have been found empirically valid in systematic studies of families containing a schizophrenic offspring. These measures are: *communication deviance* (CD), *expressed emotion* (EE), and *affective style* (AS). All of these measures are derived from parental behavior in one context or another (see Table 1).

Communication deviance (CD) is derived from the work of Wynne and Singer (13) and refers to an inability of a parent or parents to establish and maintain a shared focus of attention during transactions with another person. In a series of cross-sectional studies, these investigators have found high CD strongly associated with schizophrenia in an offspring. Typically, this measure is derived from transactions between a parent and a tester during the administration of a projective technique, usually the Rorschach or Thematic Apperception Test (TAT).

In our study, we used the individual TATs administered to each parent to rate CD. Using a factor analytic solution and scoring rules developed by Jones (4), parental units were classified into three levels of CD as follows: *High CD* — based on one of two criteria: *both* parents show at least one CD factor score greater than T = 60 or *one* parent shows an elevation above T = 60 on one of two selected factors scores—misperceptions or major closure problems. These two patterns were found associated with offspring schizophrenia in a cross-sectional study done by Jones. *Intermediate CD* — defined as a pattern in which only one parent shows an elevation greater

TABLE 1
Glossary of Terms

Parent Measure	Definition	Data Source
Communication Deviance (CD)	Parental communication style in which difficulties are observed in maintaining a clear focus of attention and meaning	Coded from transcripts of parents' responses to a standard series of 7 TAT cards
Affective Style (AS)	Parental verbal behaviors observed in family interaction, involving either personal criticism, guilt induction, or intrusiveness	Coded from transcripts of parental speech in actual interactions with index child while focused on a family problem
Expressed Emotion (EE)	Negative parental attitudes of criticism and/or emotional overinvolvement directed at a specific family member	Coded from audiotapes of individual interview with each parent

than a T score of 60 on other than the critical factors cited above, and the second parent shows no elevations above 60 on any factor. *Low CD* — defined as a pattern in which neither parent has an elevation greater than a T score of 60 on any CD factor. Congruent with the original model outlined by Wynne and Singer, we hypothesized that all cases of schizophrenia and schizophrenia-spectrum disorders noted at follow-up would be noted in high CD family units.

Affective attitudes have been suggested as important to the course of schizophrenia once the disorder develops (7). The relationship of negative attitudes toward an offspring to the course of schizophrenia has been established. However, the present study deals with the course of psychiatric disorders from adolescence to adulthood, and it was hypothesized that similar attitudes might be related to this life course as well. Specifically, we hypothesized that negative affective attitudes might serve as potentiators of a psychopathological process and would increase the likelihood of schizophrenic development in a vulnerable offspring from a high CD home environment.

Two measures of affective attitude were used in this study, a measure of what is termed expressive emotion (EE) and a measure of affective style (AS).

Note that among the predictor variables, two of the three (AS and EE) had considerable overlap on a conceptual level as both measured affective attitudes toward the index adolescent. However, EE is a measure of attitude and AS of actual interactional behavior, and we were interested in which was a better predictor of the offspring's subsequent diagnostic status. The working hypothesis was that a combination of CD and *some* measure of the affective climate of the family would optimize the identification of schizophrenia-spectrum cases.

Expressed emotion is a construct derived from the previously cited British work and reflects attitudes of criticisms and/or emotional overinvolvement expressed during a tape-recorded interview with an examiner. While the original assessment involved a special interview, the Camberwell Family Interview (11), similar assessments were done on parents in our study from a parent interview administered at the time of the original family assessment. Parents are categorized as high or low EE, based largely on the criticism criterion (greater than 6 criticisms expressed = high EE), and then formed into parental groups as follows: *Dual high EE*, both parents high; *Mixed*, one parent high, the other low; and *Dual low EE*, both parents low. The second measure of affective attitudes was termed *negative affective style* and is derived from directly observed interactions during which family members discussed conflictual problems. These interactions were coded with measures that resembled the EE dimension as they might be expressed transactionally. Special attention was given to certain low frequency behavior by the parents such as personal criticism, guilt induction, critical intrusiveness, and excessive noncritical intrusiveness. A full description of this system is contained in an article by Doane et al. (1) in which the originator of the system, Jeri Doane, describes the rationale and details of the codes. Families were classified as negative, intermediate, or benign in affective style, based on profile criteria originally developed by Doane and her colleagues. Other studies by our group have revealed that high EE attitudes and negative affective style behaviors co-exist in a number of persons (8, 10). However, the relationship is far from perfect, and so we have included both measures as predictors in this study.

Affective style (AS) was also trichotomized using the original criteria used by Doane et al. (1). Note that in that 1981 paper only a dichotomy on AS was used; but with the larger number of outcomes now available, we were able to use the original three-way categorization of benign, intermediate, or negative AS. Negative AS was defined as an interaction characterized by either one harsh criticism or guilt-inducing statements, or by six or more intrusive statements in the absence of any statement of support for the teenager. Intermediate AS was defined by the same behavioral criteria, but where at least one support statement is present. Benign AS describes a family interaction lacking in harsh criticism, guilt inducement or excessive intrusiveness on the part of the parents when talking with the teenager.

Follow-Up Procedures

Five years after the initial contact, the now young adult index cases were sought and, if located and amenable, interviewed with a structured psychiatric interview and diagnosed by the RDC system by a clinician blind as to any data on the case. Independent parent interviews were also done to corroborate data from the offspring, and any relevant hospital records were sought. At a point 10 years after this diagnostic assessment, the process was repeated again, although the data from the 15-year assessment were categorized according to DSM-III. The earlier RDC diagnoses were converted to the closest DSM-III equivalent. The number of cases seen at each point is presented in Table 2.

We see that a substantial percentage of the cases had data that covered the full 15-year period. For cases that were not available or refused the 5-year follow-up, the 15-year contact was used to assess the psychiatric status at that point in time as well as for the intervening period. Thus, there was little problem including these cases in the analysis. However, there was a problem concerning the eleven cases with only a 5-year contact. As seen in Table 1, only seven survived this period, and extensive data are available on the psychiatric status of the four deceased cases. Of the seven who survived,

TABLE 2

Follow-up Status of Sample of 64 Cases Over 15-Year Period

Status of Case	n
5- and 15-year data available	38
15 year only	8
5 year only	11*
Unable to locate at both contact points	5
Refused both contacts	2
Total	64

*Four cases deceased between 5- and 15-year contact. Data on life course sought from parents when possible.

only three failed to reveal any diagnosable mental disorder at the 5-year contact. Because our concern was with the lifetime prevalence of the most severe mental disorders in this sample, cases were included in the analysis reported here if such a disorder was evident at the 5-year point. One possible bias in this procedure is an underestimation of the severity of disorder. However, in a number of instances the disorder observable at 5 years was quite severe as there was 1 case of probable schizophrenia, 1 schizoid personality, 4 cases of severe substance abuse with associated antisocial personality disorder, and 1 borderline personality disorder. Thus, it is unlikely that more severe diagnoses would have been substituted on the basis of a later contact. Therefore, those cases with diagnosable mental disorders who only had a 5-year assessment were included in the follow-up analysis.

If during the follow-up interview either the index case or the parents indicated that another sibling had manifested a pattern of severe psychopathology, that sibling (or siblings) was contacted, interviewed, and diagnosed using the same procedures used with the index case. Eight siblings from seven families were so assessed. Three siblings were diagnosed as schizophrenic (two from the same family), two were diagnosed schizotypal personality disorder, one as a major depressive disorder, possibly bipolar, and one received no psychiatric diagnosis. Because some of the family predictors discussed below were not linked to a particular child in the family, these sibling diagnoses could also be utilized as outcome criteria. In these analyses, the most severe outcome among the different offspring was used as an alternative outcome measure to test the predictive validity of selected family measures.

Was there a notable bias in the family measures used for the sample with psychiatric outcomes at fifteen years? It is always possible that the sample available for longitudinal analysis was not typical of the original cohort of 64. Generalizations concerning the predictive validity of the family attributes would be very questionable if the subset of 54 were atypical in terms of parental CD, EE, or AS. Fortunately, this did not prove to be the case. For CD, the percentage of the original 64 cases in the three CD categories were: 28% low, 37% intermediate, and 41% high; within the sample with diagnostic outcomes the comparable percentages were: 23% low, 38% intermediate, and 40% high. Thus, the cases available for analysis were not atypical on CD. Similarly, with regard to AS, the percentages for the total sample were: 47% benign, 16% intermediate, and 37% negative; the percentages for the subsample available for longitudinal analyses were 44%, 17%, and 38%, respectively. A similar pattern was observable for EE as well. Thus, there is little evidence that the sample available for longitudinal analysis was different on these parental attitudes from the original sample that had entered the study almost 20 years ago.

Diagnostic Procedures at Five- and Fifteen-Year Follow-Ups

Slight differences existed in procedures for the 5- and 15-year follow-up contacts. At both times, two separate contacts were made, one with the index case and one with the parents.

At the time of the 15-year contact, a special interview was constructed that was coded to DSM-III. It was thus possible to use it to make most Axes I and II diagnoses. These interviews with the young adult were videotaped whenever possible, but at least audiotaped if staff had to travel to a distant site to do the interview. The great majority of these interviews were carried out by our colleague Jeri Doane, who was blind as to the prior psychiatric status of each case. The original set of 7 cards of the TAT, administered at the time of the original assessment, were readministered at this time. In addition, separate, two-part interviews were held with the parents; one part reviewed data similar to that in the 5-year parent interview (covering symptomatic and social-role functioning), and a second part used the RDC procedure for evaluating the Family History of Mental Illness. This interview was administered to each parent separately when possible, and the psychiatric history of the parent and the spouse was evaluated. In addition, the incidence of mental illness in all relatives was investigated and pedigrees were drawn up by a judge blind as to any data on the index young adult or any prior data on family interaction.

The interviews at the 15-year follow-up were reviewed by at least two raters, the interviewer and a blind rater who had had no prior contact with the cases or any of the family data before viewing the videotape or listening to the audiotape. All diagnoses were placed in DSM-III format for Axes I, II, and III, and evidence from the interview was documented in detail to justify any diagnosis. The blind rater also provided a written diagnostic report describing the person in narrative terms. The blind and nonblind raters' diagnostic impressions were then compared, and where any significant discrepancy existed, a second blind rater reviewed the tape and made independent diagnoses. The three sets of diagnoses were then reconciled at a case conference and a consensus diagnosis made. In fact, in only 4 of 46 cases assessed at the 15-year contact was a second blind rating required. In 42 cases, the agreement was extremely close.

In order to follow procedures used in recent psychiatric epidemiology studies, diagnoses were classified as definite, probable, and possible, using criteria developed by the Weissman group at Yale.

Because DSM-III can yield a plethora of diagnoses, it was necessary to establish some hierarchy for ordering diagnoses, so we followed the procedure used by the Weissman group and established our hierarchy according to the purpose of the study—to identify cases at risk for schizophrenia and schizophrenia-spectrum disorders. The hierarchy established was 1) schizophrenia; 2) schizotypal personality; 3) paranoid personality; 4) schizoid personality; and 5) borderline personality disorders. Beyond this sequence of diagnoses, all others were given a primary diagnosis based on the syndrome with the greatest impact on social-role functioning. What this hierarchy implies is that certain Axis II diagnoses (2–5 above) would take precedence over some on Axis I. For example, a patient with a schizotypal personality disorder and a history of substance abuse would receive a primary diagnosis of the former.

At the time of the final diagnostic appraisal, covering the 15-year period, the most severe primary diagnosis over that period was used as the criterion disorder for predictive purposes. For example, if a person received a diagnosis of simple phobia at 5 years but schizotypal personality at 15 years, the latter was used as the main outcome criteria.

Results

Table 3 presents the number and percentages of cases in each primary diagnosis category for the sample of 54 index cases originally selected as disturbed adolescents. In order to establish the predictive validity of the three family measures, it was necessary to group these diagnoses into clusters. As with the family predictors, a trichotomy was used. The key to the use of this trichotomy is the notion of the extended schizophrenia spectrum suggested originally in the Danish Adoption Studies (6). These studies re-

TABLE 3

Primary Lifetime Diagnosis for Index Case Observed During Follow-up Period

	n	%
No mental illness	16	30
Major depressive disorder*	6	11
Antisocial personality/substance abuse	11	20
Mixed personality disorders	6	11
Borderline personality disorder	6	19
Schizoid personality disorder	3	6
Paranoid personality disorder	1	2
Schizotypal	1	2
Schizophrenia	4	7
Total	54	100

*Includes one obsessive-compulsive disorder with marked depressive features and dysthymic disorder.

vealed that the biological relatives of adopted-away schizophrenics manifested a spectrum of psychiatric disorders ranging from schizophrenia or borderline schizophrenia to schizoid, paranoid, and what was then termed inadequate personality. This clustering of disorders, termed the extended schizophrenia spectrum, was far less frequently found in the biological relatives of nonpsychiatric adoptees.

Recent analyses of the Danish Adoption cases by Kendler and Gruenberg (5), using the more recent DSM-III criteria, revealed an aggregation of cases with diagnoses of schizophrenia, schizotypal, and paranoid personality disorder in this same sample of biological relatives of schizophrenics. The status of the borderline and schizoid personality disorders was more questionable in the Kendler and Gruenberg analysis. However, given the ambiguity in the literature concerning the association or borderline personality disorder and the extended schizophrenia spectrum, we utilized two spectrum categories as outcome criteria: a *broad* schizophrenia spectrum that included borderline and schizoid personality disorder along with those disorders identified by Kendler and Gruenberg as part of the spectrum, and a narrow one that excluded the borderline and schizoid categories. In addition, the trichotomy included two other categories: no mental illness (NMI) over the 15-year period, and the "Other" psychiatric disorder (other), which includes all cases of DSM-III diagnoses not classified in the broad or narrow schizophrenia spectrum. The Other group was particularly important theoretically as it provided an opportunity to test whether factors such as high CD are indeed specific to schizophrenia or merely identify intrafamilial stressors that increase the liability among the offspring for psychiatric disorders in general.

Initially, we tested the association between our three family variables and the trichotomy of outcomes using the broad-band schizophrenia-spectrum outcome grouping. Subsequently, we investigated the utility of the three predictors to segregate the narrow spectrum of disorders. In these analyses, borderline and schizoid personality disorders were grouped in the Other psychiatric disorder category, leaving only schizophrenia, schizotypal, and paranoid personality disorders in the extended schizophrenia-spectrum group.

The three predictors then were entered into a log linear analysis to evaluate how they related to the three outcome categories as independent factors and how well they related when the variance in the other two predictors was partialed out. The distributions of outcomes are presented first for each predictor taken by itself, as shown in Table 4.

When the log linear procedure was used to test the contribution of each variable with overlapping variance with the others removed, probabilities for the partial association were .002 for CD, .001 for AS, but a clearly nonsignificant .789 for EE. Thus, when both affective measures are in the log linear analysis, EE no longer reaches significance as a contributor to the prediction of outcome.

Next, a similar log linear analysis tested the relative contribution of CD and AS only. Here each variable still made a significant contribution to the

TABLE 4

Distribution of Outcome

	CD*			**AS***			**EE***		
	NMI	Other	Spec.	NMI	Other	Spec.	NMI	Other	Spec.
*Low***	8	2	1	11	11	1	5	12	1
Intermed.	3	11	5	1	6	2	6	5	6
High	3	7	10	4	4	12	1	4	7
	($p<.002$)			($p<.0008$)			($p<.04$)		

Note: NMI = no mental illness; Other = other psychiatric disorder than schizophrenia spectrum; Spec. = extended schizophrenia spectrum, broad grouping.

*The number of cases out of 54, with usable data and available outcome ratings were: CD = 50; AS = 52; EE = 47.

**For AS, comparable categories are benign, intermediate, and negative; for EE, dual-low, mixed, and dual-high EE.

placement of subjects in the three outcome groups; CD had a partial chi-square of 17.90, $p<.001$, and AS, 22.94, $p<.0001$.

Another approach to the analysis of these data utilized a discriminant function procedure in which CD, AS, and EE were used as variables in order to classify cases into the three outcome groups. The actual number of cases correctly classified were 45.5% no mental illness, 71.47% nonspectrum psychiatric, and 71.4% spectrum diagnoses. Only CD and AS contributed significantly to the classification. The classification rules were then tested using the Jackknife procedure in which each case was dropped from the sample and the classification process was repeated. The relationship between the original prediction and those derived from the Jackknifed procedure is shown in Table 5. The similarity in the two matrices indicates that the combination of CD and AS lead to stable assignment of cases to their respective outcome groups.

The results of this type of analysis can be pursued in more detail to determine whether CD and AS have utility because they segregate the non-

TABLE 5

Classification Matrix

Group	**%Correct**	**Number of Cases Classified into Group**		
		NMI	Nonspectrum	Spectrum
NMI	45.4	5	6	0
Nonspec.	71.4	2	15	4
Spectrum	71.4	0	4	10
Total	65.2	7	25	14

Jacknifed Classification

Group	**%Correct**	**Number of Cases Classified into Group**		
		NMI	Nonspectrum	Spectrum
NMI	45.4	5	6	0
Nonspec.	66.7	3	14	4
Spectrum	71.4	0	4	10
Total	63.0	8	24	14

mental illness cases from all others, or whether they actually distinguish those families with spectrum disorders from those containing offspring with some other form of psychiatric disorder. This is an issue of considerable theoretical significance as it relates to the *specificity* of these family factors to discrete forms of psychiatric disorders. When the matrix from the original log linear analyses was subdivided into sub-matrices and specific chi-square tests run, it was revealed that the most reliable separation of groups was between the spectrum cases and all others ($p < .003$); the segregation between the NMI and nonspectrum cases was only marginally significant ($p < .054$). Thus, the combination of high CD and negative AS specifically identifies a subset of families with a higher probability of spectrum disorders in particular, and not psychiatric cases in general.

It may be helpful for the reader to see the actual number of cases assigned to the three psychiatric outcome groups according to the three levels of CD and AS. These data are presented in Table 6. They clearly indicate that the overwhelming number of schizophrenia-spectrum cases occur when high CD and a negative AS profile were present at the time of the original family assessment. The other notable clustering of spectrum cases is present when a negative AS profile and an intermediate CD pattern coexisted at the original assessment. It is also important to note the apparent

TABLE 6

The Combination of CD and AS as Predictors of Psychiatric Outcome Status at 15 Years

	AS Group			**Outcome Group**
	Benign	**Intermediate**	**Negative**	
	4	1	3	NMI
Low	1	1	1	OPD
	0	0	1	Spec
	2	0	1	NMI
CD Int.	6	4	2	OPD
	0	1	3	Spec
	4	0	0	NMI
High	4	1	1	OPD
	1	1	8	Spec

Note: NMI = no mental illness; OPD = other psychiatric disorder; Spec = extended schizophrenic-spectrum disorders, broad criterion.

protective role of low parental CD because the overwhelming majority of cases from those families have had no further mental disorder since the time of their original adolescent difficulties.

Up to this point, we have relied on the broad concept of the extended schizophrenia-spectrum, which included borderline and schizoid personality disorders as well as paranoid, schizotypal, and schizophrenic disorders. Next, we organized the third outcome group by diagnoses found by Kendler and Gruenberg to be present in the biological relatives of adopted-away schizophrenics.

The restriction of the spectrum category to this narrower range of diagnoses posed one problem as it reduced the N in the third diagnostic category to 6, limiting the possibilities for group segregation. Despite the obvious limitation, we reran the log linear analyses with the new, narrower spectrum grouping. The results were much poorer than previously and the chi-square barely bordered on statistical significance. Thus, the combination of high CD and negative AS do not isolate a group of individuals with specific disorders in this narrow schizophrenia spectrum. One of two conclusions can be drawn from these analyses—either the high-CD, negative-AS family is associated with more severe forms of offspring psychopathology that do not possess a specific link to schizophrenia, *or* the borderline and schizoid personality disorders share some common precursors with schizophrenia that have not been articulated in prior adoption studies.

The inclusion of data from the siblings: If at any point during the 5- or 15-year follow-up the index case or respondent provided information suggestive of a severe psychiatric disorder in another offspring in the family, that sibling was contacted, interviewed, and diagnosed using similar instruments and procedures as were used with the index cases. Siblings were interviewed if reports suggested any of the broad spectrum of disorders in our third diagnostic group as these were the disorders of particular interest to our hypothesis. Eight siblings from seven families qualified for intensive assessment. Three siblings were diagnosed as schizophrenic (two from the same family), two were diagnosed schizotypal personality disorders, one was diagnosed borderline personality disorder, one major depressive disorder, possibly bipolar, and the last received no psychiatric diagnosis.

These data were included in a subsequent analysis that relied on another method for estimating risk for schizophrenia-spectrum disorders. The measure of CD is not linked to any one child in the family. Therefore, we can ask whether high-CD families as a *unit* are at risk for these disorders. By substituting the most severe disorder in any one sibling as the outcome for a family unit, we can examine whether CD is associated with a high likelihood of schizophrenia-spectrum disorder. This substitution of outcomes was done so that the most severe outcome in the family was the outcome diagnosis for that family. Once again, only one outcome diagnosis was assigned per family unit, so that there were still 54 outcome diagnoses. The substitution process was as follows: schizophrenia would replace schizotypal or another spectrum diagnosis; schizotypal would replace any other personality disorder diagnosis, and so on, using our previously identified hierarchy of diagnoses. These new outcomes for each family unit were then related to the three levels of CD. (Note that a similar process could not be done for AS and EE as these were directed at a specific offspring in the family, our target child.)

We then examined the number of schizophrenia-spectrum disorders using the "worst" outcome in the family as the criterion variable (see Figure 1). These results can be contrasted with the results when the outcome diagnosis of the index case was used (see Figure 2). It can be seen that there is a stronger association between CD level and the number of schizophrenia-spectrum disorders when the "worst" case was used as the dependent variable than when the index case was used. In fact, 14 of 19 high-CD families

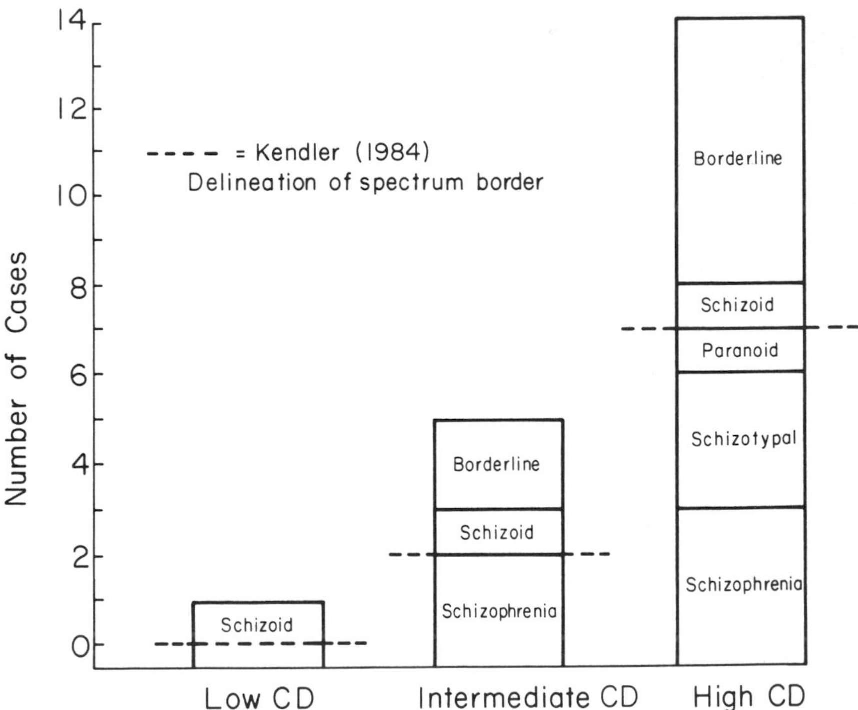

Fig. 1. Number of cases (index or sibling as most severe) diagnosed as schizophrenia-spectrum at follow-up, by parental CD group.

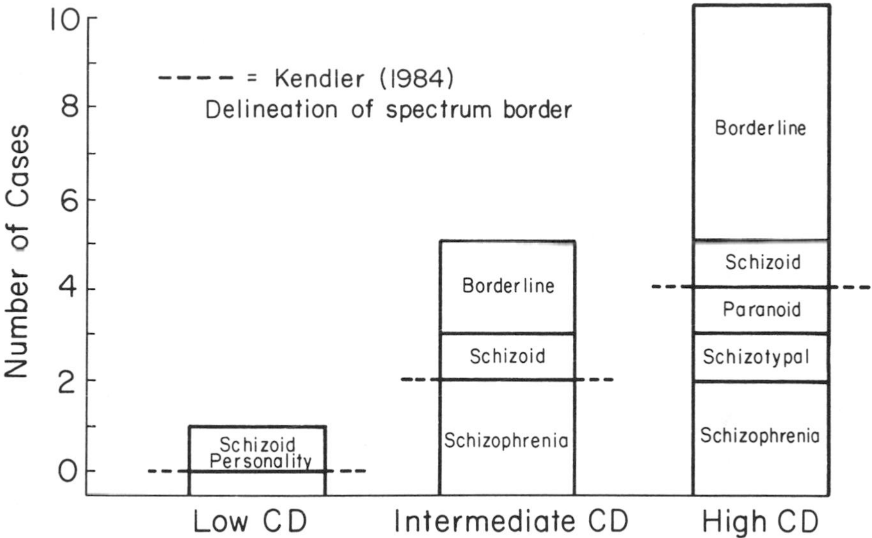

Fig. 2. Number of index cases diagnosed as extended schizophrenia-spectrum, by parental CD group.

have at least one broad-spectrum case in the families, whereas only 10 broad-spectrum diagnoses were found in the sample of index offspring. Note also that for the narrow-spectrum diagnoses, as defined by Kendler and Gruenberg (5), 7 of 19 (37%) high-CD cases fit into this category, while in the sample of index cases only 4 of 19 (22%) manifested narrow-spectrum cases. Thus it appears that the CD level of the parents serves as a familial risk marker for schizophrenia-spectrum disorder for *some* offspring in the family, but does not permit one to target the specific offspring. Possibly, if we had AS data as directed toward each offspring in the family, this would permit us to identify the high-risk child (children) in the family.

Form of the adolescent behavior problem as a predictor of long-term psychiatric status: While most of this chapter has dealt with the predictive value of parental attributes assessed at the time of the target adolescent's difficulties, we did, in fact, hypothesize that certain patterns of adolescent psychopathology were more likely than others to be precursors of subsequent schizophrenia-spectrum disorders in adulthood. Specifically, in our 1968 article (3), we hypothesized that two groups, the withdrawn and what we termed as the active family conflict forms of adolescent behavior problems, were at higher risk for schizophrenia-spectrum disorders than members of the other two groups termed aggressive antisocial and passive negative. The relationship between problem group and the three-category system of primary psychiatric diagnoses used in previous analyses are presented in Table 7. These data fail to support the hypothesis for groups identified as 2 and 4 in Table 7. In fact, the only significant finding is the markedly lower rate of spectrum disorders in group 3, the passive negative group characterized by a covert oppositional style in relationship to teachers and parents. If we dimensionalize these problem groups, as suggested in our earlier writings, into an inside- (groups 2 and 4) and outside-home locus group, there is a statistically significant association with outcome category, with the outside-home group receiving a lower rate of spectrum diagnoses ($p<.05$). However, the effect is carried entirely by the passive negative group (group 3).

Do the parental attributes of CD and AS predict outcome when problem group is factored into the equation? Using the log linear model once again, but entering problem groups as a two-level predictor—inside- versus outside-home problems in addition to CD and AS—revealed that problem group no longer predicted the rate of spectrum outcomes when CD and AS were present. Both CD ($p<.01$) and AS ($p<.0002$) were still significant predictors of outcome status in the young adult when the variance predictable by problem group was partialed out. Thus, the major predictors of offspring psychiatric status are parental or intrafamilial attributes. It should be pointed out that categorization of adolescent psychopathology by form is but one way to test hypotheses concerning behavioral precursors of schizophrenia. There may be other measures of the severity of adolescent psychopathology that can be estimated by more subtle measures than were available to us in the mid-1960s, which may indeed reveal important associations between parental and offspring risk markers that interact over time to increase the likelihood of a schizophrenia-spectrum disorder.

TABLE 7

Association between Adolescent Problem Group and Psychiatric Status at 15-Year Follow-up

		Outcome Category		
	n (54)	**NMI**	**Other**	**Spectrum**
Group				
1. Aggressive, antisocial	13	4	5	4
2. Active family	16	3	9	4
3. Passive, negative	12	6	5	1
4. Withdrawn, socially isolated	13	3	4	6

Family Mental Illness and CD as Predictors of Outcome

As indicated previously, we have carried out interviews concerning the history of mental illness in the parents, siblings, and other second-degree relatives. This phase of our research is not complete, but about half of the sample has been studied and analyzed. One way that we have looked at these data is to consider whether there is any evidence of a severe mental disorder in any first- or second-degree relatives. Severe mental disorder was defined by RDC Family History criteria as one of the following: psychosis, schizophrenia, or severe recurrent mood disorder, either unipolar or bipolar. Families were considered family-history positive if one of the above were present, and negative when none were present. This represents only one approach to classifying families with regard to family history, and we plan others that will take into account whether the relative was first- or second-degree, and also the number of generations in which disorders were present.

For the purpose of this volume, we examined the relationship between CD level and the presence of a positive or negative history for severe mental disorder. With 31 families studied to date, there is no association. Approximately half of the families with a positive history are high CD and the rest intermediate or low. So, they are not equivalent markers of risk. Next, we examined whether within the context of a stress-diathesis theory, a combination of high CD and a positive family history increased the risk for schizophrenia-spectrum disorder in any offspring in the family. Here we used the worst-case diagnosis, described above as the outcome variable. Of 12 high-CD families studied to date, 5 had a negative family history and 7 a positive one. The rates for broad- and narrow-spectrum disorders as a function of CD and family history status are presented in Table 8. We can see that the combination of a positive family history for severe psychopathology and high CD is a high-risk indicator because 86% of these families have at least

TABLE 8

Rate of Broad- and Narrow-Spectrum Disorders in High-CD Families as a Function of Family History of Mental Illness

	Broad Spectrum Outcomes		**Narrow Spectrum Outcomes**	
	n	**%**	**n**	**%**
Postitive Family History (n = 7)	6	86	5	71
Negative Family History (n = 5)	1	20	1	20

one offspring who later manifested a broad-spectrum disorder and 71% a narrow-spectrum one, while high-CD families with a negative history have a 20% offspring rate for both broad- and narrow-spectrum disorders. We recognize that a positive family history does not imply a genetic, as contrasted to a psychosocial, mode of transmission. However one may interpret these data, it does point to an important combination of predictors. Further analysis will examine specific family pedigrees to determine whether, in families with positive histories, high-CD status in a parent is associated with the positive family line or not. We hope to determine whether CD and family history co-segregate or whether they are totally independent risk markers.

One other finding, wholly unexpected, has emerged in these preliminary studies with CD and family history. Earlier in this paper we indicated that high-CD status was defined by one of two criteria, both parents high or one parent high on *only* certain specific factors: 2 (misperceptions) or 6 (major closure problems.) We then examined whether either high-CD pattern interacted with family history of mental illness. Of the 12 families studied thus far with high CD, 4 were defined as high by the dual-parent pattern and 8 by the single-parent one. Of the 4 with the dual-parent pattern, 3 had a negative family history and 1 a positive one, while in the single-parent criteria group, 6 had a positive family history and 2 a negative one. These numbers are too small for statistical analyses, but they do suggest the possibility that certain types of CD are linked to the family history criteria, while others are not. Interestingly, all broad-spectrum outcomes (6/6) occurred in high-CD families defined by the single-parent criterion and (5/6) narrow-spectrum outcomes were from the same group. These data suggest that certain patterns of CD may be more valid markers of the risk for offspring schizophrenia than others.

The latter findings are particularly interesting in light of the results of a recent study carried out by Robert Asarnow, myself, and two colleagues at Pittsburgh, Diane Wagener and Gerard Hogarty (12). We examined the relationship among maternal CD patterns, maternal attention test performance on the CPT and span of apperception (SAT) tests, and comparable attention test performance in their schizophrenic offspring. Elevations on either factor 2 or 6 in the parent were associated with poor attention test performance in both the parental and offspring data, but other CD factors were not. It appeared that those parents with poor attentional functioning are likely to have schizophrenic offspring with comparably poor attentional performance. The link between the two sets of attention test data seems to be CD patterns of elevated factor 2 or 6. Thus, it appears that elevations on these factors mark deficits in attentional functioning that are transmitted cross-generationally, either experientially or genetically. Further studies of specific components of the aggregate CD measures seem warranted in order to define discrete parental risk markers for schizophrenia.

Discussion

In an early publication from our research group (1), we concluded that parent CD was a significant marker of the potential for subsequent offspring schizophrenia or schizophrenia-spectrum disorders. The longer period of our follow-up has only strengthened this conclusion. In fact, when we expand our analysis beyond the original index cases (who were the focus of intensive study) to include their siblings, the high-CD parental pattern shows a strong association with the subsequent appearance of a schizophrenia-spectrum disorder in *some* offspring in the family. In retrospect, it was obviously a tactical error not to obtain attitudinal and interactive behavior samples with the other siblings at the time of our original contact. For while we can use CD level as a generic marker for the family unit, the measures of affective attitude are specifically linked to the original index cases. Thus, it is not possible to extend the analysis of the interactive effects of CD, EE, and AS to the other siblings in the family, some of whom were obviously at risk for schizophrenia-spectrum disorders.

Despite these limitations, the second conclusion from our earlier report, which covered the significant interaction between CD level and affective attitude in influencing the course of psychiatric disorder from adolescence to adulthood, is even more strongly confirmed with data from the extended follow-up. The adolescent at risk for schizophrenia-spectrum disorders comes from a home environment characterized by high CD and a strongly negative affective climate. The behavioral indicator of affective attitude, AS type, proved to be a better addition to CD than the attitudinal measure of EE. Previously, we drew a different conclusion as we found that all of the narrow-spectrum outcomes, in addition to high CD, had *both* negative-AS and high EE (see 2). However, in that report we treated AS as a dichotomy because we grouped the intermediate and negative AS cases together. In the present report we utilized the trichotomy originally suggested by Doane, and in this instance the overlap between the EE and AS grouping is considerable. Thus, EE had less to add to prediction when we segregated the extreme, negative AS group from the intermediate one.

It is interesting to note that the only difference between the intermediate and negative AS profiles was the presence of a minimum of one support statement in the context of the critical AS behaviors. While it is hard to envision that one such remark could make such a notable difference in a ten-minute, emotionally laden interaction, it may reflect tendencies toward compromise or a latent positive attitude toward the adolescent largely masked by the conflict of the moment, a quality that may be totally lacking in the negative-AS profile family. We often talk in family research about the power of low frequency behaviors in influencing the tone of a larger stream of interaction behavior. The impact of one such support statement in the course of a largely negative interaction may be an example of that principle.

Up to this point, we have not related these findings to issues concerning the etiology of schizophrenia. We can assume that patterns of disordered family relationships precede the onset of schizophrenia and related disorders by a considerable period of time. Further, there seems to be a moderate degree of specificity to this prediction as the combination of parental high CD and negative affective attitudes relate more closely to one group of disorders, which consists of schizophrenia and what we have termed as the broad spectrum of related disorders, than to other psychiatric disorders. However, we do not have any bipolar disorders in our sample thus far, so it is difficult to know whether the specificity is to certain classes of *severe* psychiatric disorders or to schizophrenia in particular. In one study currently underway in our laboratory, we are attempting to answer this question with a cross-sectional study contrasting the CD level and affective attitudes of parents of young, recent onset schizophrenics with those of young, recent onset manic patients (see Chapter 11). That study suggests, in fact, that CD may be a marker of the potential for offspring psychosis but not specifically for schizophrenia.

The present analyses have proved most powerful when we have used the broad-spectrum concept as one of our criterion groups. When we have attempted to use the narrow-spectrum grouping of Kendler and Gruenberg, derived from their reanalysis of the Danish Adoption Study sample, our predictions were less successful. One of two conclusions can be drawn from their findings: either the high-CD, negative-AS family pattern is associated with very severe forms of psychopathology in adulthood but bears no specific link to schizophrenia per se, *or* the borderline and schizoid personality disorders share some common precursors with schizophrenia, which have not been articulated in the prior adoption studies.

One way to approach this issue is to use the family genetic load for schizophrenia, as estimated by a family history of the disorder, to determine whether interactional variables such as high CD and negative AS influence the probability of expression of schizophrenia and narrowly defined schizophrenia-spectrum disorders in the offspring. We have not yet subdivided our family pedigrees into those with a family history of schizophrenia or narrowly defined schizophrenia-spectrum disorders versus those with severe affective disorders; but, in fact, most of the cases described previously with a positive family history of mental disorder have histories in the schizophrenia cluster. Thus, while we are speculating beyond our data, the previously presented findings support a special type of diathesis-stress theory in which the predisposition toward schizophrenia and closely associated disorders, as estimated from family history, is modified in a major way by the particular patterns of stressful family relationships. Note that it does not appear to be stressful family relationships in general that interact with the predisposition to this disorder because the families of our substance abuse, depressed, and antisocial cases are very stressful and conflictual; however, they are not characterized by the combination of high CD and negative AS. It appears that schizophrenia and narrowly defined schizophrenia-spectrum disorders arise in families with a *specific* diathesis and a *specific* type of family stress. It is very gratifying to see that these conclusions parallel the preliminary findings of the Finnish Adoption Study (see Chapter 2), a study that is more favorably poised to evaluate the relative contributions of genetic and environmental factors to schizophrenia.

One other point before concluding this chapter. We have relied extensively on two or three measures of family functioning as predictors of outcome. We view these measures as marker variables that index very complex transactional processes among family members. However, the marker variables cannot reveal these complex and subtle processes. There is still a need for detailed micro-analyses of the interactional data available from this project. Previously (see 9), we indicated a number of analyses that we have carried out along these lines, and a tentative model for interpreting the marker variables and their process analyses as they may relate to the development of schizophrenia. Obviously, we hope to gain more insights from detailed microanalyses of the interactional data base available from this study so that a richer understanding of these complex family processes can be achieved. Thus far we have only analyzed parental behavior in the family interaction task. Recently, we have developed a coding algorithm for adolescent interactional behavior, termed the coping style system, which we believe captures the various maneuvers available to a teenager when confronted with parental messages and pressures. Clearly, our understanding of family processes related to the development of schizophrenia will only be complete when we understand the role of offspring in triggering and reacting to variations in parental communication and affective styles. Hopefully, various analytic procedures for the explication of sequential patterns in these data can clarify these subtle interactional processes and their relation to the subsequent expression of schizophrenia and related disorders in offspring.

REFERENCES

1. Doane, J. A., West, K. L., Goldstein, M. J., Rodnick, E. H., & Jones, J. E. Parental communication deviance and affective style: Predictors of subsequent schizophrenia-spectrum disorders in vulnerable adolescents. *Archives of General Psychiatry 38*: 679–685, 1981.

2. Goldstein, M. J. Family factors that antedate the onset of schizophrenia and related disorders: The results of a fifteen year prospective longitudinal study. *Acta Psychiatrica Scandinavica 71* (Suppl. 319): 7–18, 1985.

3. ______, Judd, L. L., Rodnick, E. H., Alkire, A., & Gould, E. A method for studying social influence and coping patterns within families of disturbed adolescents. *Journal of Nervous and Mental Disease 147*: 233–251, 1968.

4. Jones, J. E. Patterns of transactional style deviance in the TAT's of parents of schizophrenics. *Family Process 16*: 327–337, 1977.

5. Kendler, K. S., & Gruenberg, A. M. An independent analysis of the Danish Adoption Study of schizophrenia: VI. The relationship between psychiatric disorder as defined by DSM-III in the relatives and adoptees. *Archives of General Psychiatry 41*: 555–564, 1984.

6. Kety, S. S., Rosenthal, D., Wender, P. H., & Schulsinger, F. The types and prevalence of mental illness in the biological and adoptive families of adopted schizophrenics. In D. Rosenthal & S. S. Kety (eds.), *The transmission of schizophrenia*. Oxford: Pergamon Press, 1968.

7. Leff, J. P. Schizophrenia and sensitivity to the family environment. *Schizophrenia Bulletin 2*: 566–574, 1976.

8. Miklowitz, D. J., Goldstein, M. J., Falloon, I. R. H., & Doane, J. A. Interactional correlates of expressed emotion in the families of schizophrenics. *British Journal of Psychiatry 144*: 482–487, 1984.

9. Rodnick, E. H., Goldstein, M. J., Lewis, J. M., & Doane, J. A. Parental communication style, affect, and role as precursors of offspring schizophrenia-spectrum disorders. In N. F. Watt, E. J. Anthony, L. C. Wynne, & J. E. Rolf (eds.), *Children at risk for schizophrenia: A longitudinal perspective*. Cambridge: Cambridge University Press, 1984.

10. Valone, K., Norton, J. P., Goldstein, M. J., & Doane, J. A. Parental expressed emotion and affective style in an adolescent sample at risk for schizophrenia-spectrum disorders. *Journal of Abnormal Psychology 92*: 399–407, 1983.

11. Vaughn, C. E., & Leff, J. P. The influence of family and social factors on the course of psychiatric illness: A comparison of schizophrenic and depressed neurotic patients. *British Journal of Psychiatry 129*: 125–137, 1976.

12. Wagener, D. K., Hogarty, G. E., Goldstein, M., Asarnow, R. F., & Brown, A. Information processing and communication deviance in schizophrenic patients and their mothers. *Psychiatry Research 18*: 365–377, 1986.

13. Wynne, L. C., Singer, M. T., Bartko, J. J., & Toohey, M. L. Schizophrenics and their families: Research on parental communication. In J. M. Tanner (ed.), *Developments in Psychiatric Research*. London: Hodder & Stoughton, 1977.

2

THE FINNISH ADOPTIVE FAMILY STUDY OF SCHIZOPHRENIA: Possible Joint Effects of Genetic Vulnerability and Family Interaction*

PEKKA TIENARI, ILPO LAHTI, ANNELI SORRI, MIKKO NAARALA, KARL-ERIK WAHLBERG, TUULA RÖNKKÖ, JUHA MORING
University of Oulu, Finland

LYMAN C. WYNNE
University of Rochester
Rochester, New York

THE FAMILY has always been an issue in the etiology, pathogenesis, and course of schizophrenia. The prevalence of schizophrenia and other psychopathology among the relatives of schizophrenic patients is higher than in the general population (1). In all studies, the concordance figures for schizophrenia in monozygotic twins have been higher than those in dizygotic twins (1, 15). Observations of monozygotic twin pairs discordant for schizophrenia have revealed consistent differences in personality development and in relationships to significant others (13, 14, 23). Both genetic and environmental interpretations can be given for all of these observations (27).

The notion that disordered family relationships or communicational

*This research study is supported by the Finish National Medical Research Council and the National Institute of Mental Health, U.S.A. (Grant 1RO1-MH39663).

patterns may be a significant factor in the development of schizophrenia is not new. Most research, however, has focused on family interaction only after the diagnosis of schizophrenia in an offspring and, in many instances, following treatment. Only a limited number of studies have employed control groups that could establish a distinctive linkage of family variables with schizophrenia as opposed to other forms of psychopathology. And many of these did not involve observations of family interaction but, rather, made inferences about interaction on the basis of observations of the behavior of family members in individual test situations (7). In contrast, by studying direct family interaction before the onset of schizophrenia, the investigator attempts to control for the effects of schizophrenia in the child on the family system.

Prospective, longitudinal research designs may help rule out the responsivity hypothesis, that is, the hypothesis that disordered parental interaction or communicational patterns have arisen in response to schizophrenia in the offspring. Such designs offer many advantages for examining the relationship between the characteristics of family interaction and the development of schizophrenia in offspring (24). As Reiss (10) pointed out, however, in order to establish an etiologic role for the family in the development of schizophrenia, it is not enough to demonstrate that deviant family interaction precedes the onset of the disorder in the child. It must also be shown that family variables and psychopathology in children are not spuriously related. For example, it has been suggested that the relationship between parental communication and the presence of schizophrenia in an offspring may be genetically determined; that is, both parental communication difficulties and the risk for schizophrenia in the child may be products of a common genetic heritage.

In seeking to assess and to separate the effects of hereditary and family dynamic factors, psychiatric research is faced with the difficulty that disordered parents who have transmitted genetic factors to their offspring have generally also brought them up. In a study of children adopted away at an early age, discrimination between these two sets of factors is possible. The biologic parents have given to the child their genetic characteristics and sometimes the very early environment; the adoptive parents have provided the more enduring family environment and rearing.

Some well-known adoption studies of schizophrenia have been carried out. The study of Kety, Rosenthal, and Wender (4) examined the genetic hypothesis, beginning with adopted schizophrenics and studying the types and prevalence of mental illness in their biologic relatives and adoptive family members. That study was not designed to analyze the family rearing environment. Heston (2) reported a high, age-corrected rate (16.6%) for schizophrenia in the offspring of schizophrenic mothers reared in foundling homes and eventually adopted or reared in foster homes, usually by paternal relatives. There were methodological problems with Heston's study, however. Rosenthal et al.'s (12) Danish study corrected some of these weaknesses. The offspring were all formally adopted by a nonrelative, and the interviewer and raters were blind as to whether the adoptees were index or control offspring. A major diagnostic uncertainty in the data analyzed by Rosenthal et al. arose because the Danish biologic index parents were not interviewed. The parental diagnoses were based upon the hospital-record summaries, translated into English, from which American researchers made the diagnoses.

In all of these reports of adoptive samples, rearing variables were studied in a very limited way by focusing mainly upon the hypothesis that the diagnosis of rearing parent is a rearing variable. Rosenthal et al. (11) correlated the degree of psychopathology in adoptees with their recall of the quality of their relationship with their adoptive parents. Wynne and Singer (28) measured parental communication more directly, using an index of communication deviance (CD), scored blindly on Wender et al.'s (25) Rorschach protocols from individual adoptive parents. They found no differences in CD between two groups of rearing parents, biologic parents, and adoptive parents who had reared schizophrenic offspring, but both groups of parents had significantly more CD than did a control group of parents who had reared normal adoptees. In none of these studies has interaction between family members been observed directly.

The major goal of the Finnish adoptive family study is to re-assess genetic contributions to schizophrenia and to add measures of the adoptive family rearing environment. That is, we are interested in joint effects of genetic and family environmental variables and in their possible contribution to both psychopathology and healthy functioning of adoptees during development. This approach includes new attention to the possibility that healthy, possibly protective, rearing family environment may reduce genetic risk. During the course of this study, we also shall consider whether the direction of effects between genetic and family environmental factors can be clarified through prospective, longitudinal study of adoptees at risk.

Sampling

A nationwide sample has been collected in Finland of women who were hospitalized because of schizophrenia. The sample includes all women resident in psychiatric hospitals in 1960 as well as later consecutive admissions, making a total of 19,447 schizophrenic women (17, 22). Through the use of registers, it has been found that 289 offspring of 263 schizophrenic women have been officially adopted away. Of these 289 offspring, 196 have been placed in nonrelative families in Finland before the age of five years (143 or 73% before the age of two years). The adoptees studied thus far were born in 1970 or earlier, and thus have now entered the age of risk for schizophrenia.

These index offspring and their adoptive families have been blindly compared with matched controls, that is, adoptive families with adopted-away offspring of biological parents who were not hospitalized because of psychosis. The matching was carried out independently case by case by persons who were given the matching criteria but did not otherwise participate in the study. The criteria for pairs of the control and index cases were as follows:

- age difference, <1 year, between index and control adoptee
- age difference, <10 years, between adoptive versus control parents
- index and control adoptees matched for sex
- nine groupings according to age of placement in family: (<6 months, 6–11 months, 12–17 months, 18–23 months, 24–29 months, 30–35 months, 36–41 months, 42–47 months, and 48–60 months
- family residence, town or country
- family structure, adoptee living with adoptive mother and father versus only father or only mother
- social class (in Finland, classified by occupation)

Biologic control parents have been excluded only if they have been treated for psychosis. Hence, some of the biologic parents in the control series have received psychiatric help for reasons other than psychosis. The adoptive index and control series were numbered randomly so that four psychiatrists conducting the personal interviews with the adoptive rearing families were blind as to whether each case was an index or a control (17, 22).

Procedures

Adoptive Families

Adoptive and control families have been investigated in their homes, directly and intensively, with tape-recorded procedures that usually take two days – 14 to 16 hours (17, 21).

1. *Joint interviews with the whole family* particularly elucidate the interaction and relationships between children and parents, the general fam-

ily climate, the family's isolation from or contact with the broader environment, and the ability of the family members to cope socially and occupationally. Separate lists of questions were developed for the family interview and for the couple interview. These questions and the interviewing technique were developed over the course of several years by using the knowledge obtained from the family literature and our own clinical experience. All four interviewers are psychiatrists and have had a long psychotherapeutic and clinical training. They were able to encourage free communication within the semistructured framework of the interviews.

2. *Joint interviews with the parental couples* were designed to assess with a separate set of questions the marital relationship, the marital communication patterns, the factors that led to the adoption, and the experiences of the adopting parents with one another and the adoptee beginning at the early stages of adoption.

3. *Consensus Rorschach*: The tape-recorded Couple Rorschach is the first part of the Consensus Rorschach (8, 9). The couple is asked to look at Rorschach cards I and III and to try to reach a consensus as to what the inkblots represent. The Couple Rorschach is useful for examining the relations of the spouses without the effect of the child's presence. In the second part of the Consensus Rorschach, the Family Rorschach, the spouses begin by instructing the child about the task. This provides an impression of how parents transmit information to the child. The family as a unit then looks at Rorschach cards I and III and a new card, VIII. The tape recordings of the Consensus Rorschach have been evaluated independently by blind raters using the Beavers-Timberlawn Family Rating Scales (6), and they also will be rated for communication deviance, healthy communication, acknowledgment, and other indices of family interaction.

4. The *Interpersonal Perception Method (IPM)* was developed by Laing, Phillipson, and Lee (5). In their original procedure, 60 issues were identified that arise in dyadic relationships, for each of which 12 questions had to be answered. The issues are presented as phrases that refer to the relationship or experience of the individual subject in the relationship between the subject and another person. This method differs from other experimental methods in that even though individual subjects are asked in the IPM to think about their interaction with another family member, their replies are first obtained individually; later, the investigator compares each person's responses with those of the other family members. During the test administration, the individual is asked to rate his or her view of each issue, to postulate the way in which the partner may experience the same issue, and to conjecture what he or she thinks the other person believes he or she has answered. We have used an abbreviated version of this method. Instead of

using all 60 questions, we used only the 30 items that have proved to have the highest reliability and validity.

Individual Members of Adoptive Families

After the conjoint interviewing and testing, the adoptive parents and adoptees each were given an individual, semistructured interview and individual Rorschachs. In addition, the adoptive parents were given four subtests (information, similarities, picture completion, and digit symbol) of the Wechsler Intelligence Test (WAIS). The offspring were given these subtests as well as the arithmetic and block design subtests; they also were given the MMPI. All interviews and test examinations were tape-recorded. This has made it possible later to carry out blind ratings and independent reclassifications by other investigations.

Biological Parents

The patient records of the biological index mothers were obtained and photocopied. In the data reported here, the hospital diagnosis of schizophrenia or paranoid psychosis has been used as a presumptive measure of genetic vulnerability in the adopted-away index offspring. These hospital diagnoses are being checked by several psychiatrists independently of each other. Also, two other raters (psychiatric residents) have applied the Research Diagnostic Criteria (RDC) to the hospital records of the biologic mothers (16, 17). Research interviews with the biologic index mothers are in progress; to date, 85 index mothers have been interviewed and tested. In addition, biologic control mothers, and biologic index and control fathers will be interviewed when possible. These psychiatric interviews include a modified Present State Examination (PSE), with added items that facilitate making DSM-III and RDC diagnoses, plus information about the biologic family psychiatric history, the ten-card Rorschach, and the MMPI. In as much detail as possible, data also are obtained on psychiatric hospitalizations and symptoms, if any, and personal characteristics of the biologic relatives of the biologic index and control parents, including formal diagnoses, personal eccentricities, patterns of adjustment, and major somatic illnesses.

The individual Rorschachs of the various family members, both biologic and adoptive parents, both index and controls, as well as the adoptive offspring, are being blindly evaluated with a variety of scoring systems, including traditional Rorschach scores, psychodiagnostic ratings, and measures of thought disorder and communication deviance. The MMPIs from the adoptees are being used for independent assessments to be compared with clinical evaluations.

Follow-Up Assessments

No face-to-face follow-up assessments of adoptive families have been carried out so far, but telephone interviews have been conducted 5 to 7 years after the initial assessment with 92 of the adoptive families. One newly schizophrenic offspring and one suicide have been found so far as a result of the telephone follow-ups. We also plan to invite all the offspring to a personal assessment that will include standardized tests and interviews (possibly videotaped).

Preliminary Results with Clinical Mental Health Ratings

By September, 1985, about 270 families, index and controls combined, had been contacted for field study, with data from 252 partially scored. We must point out that all results at this time are still preliminary because all the families have not yet been interviewed.

Health Ratings of Adoptive Offspring

The four psychiatrists who have carried out the fieldwork with the adoptive families have so far made global clinical ratings of 252 of the adoptees. The psychiatrists have been blind with respect to the schizophrenic and index versus control status of the biologic mothers of the adoptees. A six-point scale of severity of disturbance has been used. Ratings 1 and 2 mean "healthy in a clinical sense" and 3 to 6 refer to "clinical cases." Nine have been given diagnoses at level 6 (psychosis); 17 were at level 5 ("borderline"); and 29 at level 4 ("character disorder"). We do not use here the DSM-III definition of borderline; our definition is broader, in the sense of marginally psychotic symptoms. The term "character disorders" is used to refer to nonpsychotic but still severe personality disorders, such as schizoid personality disorder.

Many of the offspring interviewed so far are relatively young; one-third of them were less than 20 years old and may not have passed through the age of risk for schizophrenia. One might expect that the longer the delay in being transferred from a schizophrenic mother to an adopting family, the worse the global ratings of the offspring would be. This does not seem to be the case (18).

TABLE 1

Mental Health Ratings of Offspring
(Matched Pairs, as of 9/85)

Clinical Ratings of Offspring	Biologic Mothers Hospital Diagnosis of Schizophrenia Index	 Controls
Healthy	1	9
Mild disturbance	45	45
Neurotic	27	34
Character disorder	15	11
"Borderline"	10	5
Psychotic	7	1
Totals	105*	105

*one-tailed sign test = .0114

Table 1 shows the mental health ratings of the index and control group for the 105 pairs in which both the index and matched control were examined. Of 8 psychotic cases, 7 are offspring of schizophrenics, and only 1 is a control offspring. (In the total sample, which includes cases in which only one of a matched pair has thus far been studied, additional psychoses are found.) One of the psychotic index cases received the diagnosis of manic-depressive psychosis (confirmed by a separate rater), 5 of schizophrenia, and 1 of paranoid psychosis. The percentage of severe diagnoses (levels 4 to 6) is 30.5% in the index group and 16.2% in the control group. In a general way, these figures are similar to the Rosenthal et al.(12) findings.

Family Mental Health Ratings

The total interview material from the two-day home visits by the four psychiatrists also has been used for their global ratings of the mental health of the families. Assessed through interviews with whole families and with parental couples, five categories of family mental health have been differentiated.

1. **Healthy** denotes families in which anxiety is low and the boundaries between individuals and generations (and to the outside world) are clearly defined. Primitive transactional defenses are not used, and interaction is unambiguous and mutual. There is no overt, chronic transactional conflict

in the family. Acknowledgment and empathy of family members with one another are consistently present.

2. **Mildly disturbed** denotes families in which there may be transient transactional conflicts and observable mild anxiety or depressive moods. Primitive transactional defenses are seldom used. The boundaries between generations and between the family and the outside world are clear. The reality testing is good. (Categories 1 and 2 are both within the range of "normal" family functioning and, for most purposes, should be grouped together.)

3. **Neurotic** denotes those families in which there exists an unresolved transactional conflict of mild or moderate severity. The interpersonal patterns in the family are clear, but they also are to some extent restricted and repetitive. The boundaries between the generations and between the family and the outside world are clear. Reality testing by the family is good.

4. **Rigid, syntonic**, analogously to ego-syntonic, individual functioning, describes those families that believe their functioning is adequate, but others see them as maladaptive or dysfunctional in the presence of major life-event and life-cycle transitions. Major family conflicts are unresolved and unacknowledged. Overt anxiety is usually low. Family members draw a sharp, inflexible boundary between experience within the family and outside the family. Boundaries within the family (between generations and between individuals) are blurred. Family patterns do not change (or change only after convulsive eruptions) despite major life events and role changes (rigid homeostasis).

5. **Severely disturbed** characterizes those families in which conflict is open and often chaotic. Anxiety level is high and basic trust low. All boundaries are unstable and unclear between individuals, between generations, and between the family and the outside world. Agreement on reality (reality testing) is low. Primitive transactional defenses (such as projective identification and splitting) are common. Family patterns are seldom in stable equilibrium. (Group 5 families show more *overt* disturbance than group 4, but the impact of these differing patterns on the family members may be equally marked in these two groups. For most purposes, they should be grouped together at present.)

These descriptions of the adoptive families are an attempt to identify the most common characteristics of the families in the different categories. We emphasize the following features in making these ratings: anxiety levels; boundary functions between individual members, between generations, and between the family and the outside world; quality of parental coalition and interaction; communicational clarity and deviance; balance of flexibility and stability under changing conditions; well-functioning or dysfunctional conflicts; empathy; power relations; reality testing; and basic trust.

The four interviewers have been conducting interrater reliability studies from audiotapes and have evolved a multidimensional family rating scale that will specify details of the initial, more global ratings of the adoptive families, from which data are reported here. Case vignettes of two adoptive families in the "rigid, syntonic" and "severely disturbed" groups will help clarify the characteristics of these seriously dysfunctional families.

Case Example of a Rigid, Syntonic Family

K is an 18-year-old girl, the only child of her adoptive parents. The parents were nearly 50 years old when, after a short period of deliberation, they decided to adopt a child. In their marital relationship, their activities were sharply divided into nonoverlapping, complementary roles. Their emotional life took place in parallel; they expressed few feelings, positive or negative, to each other, and K was expected to show similar restraint. The parents were also highly religious, with strict moral standards. They have never quarreled, although they have had many differences of opinion. The disagreements have been blurred, and the atmosphere of the family could be described as pseudomutual (26).

While K was a child, things went well although upbringing varied from extreme strictness to difficulty in setting limits. The family's religious attitude separated them from their neighbors, and the parents took K's relations with her peers as a breach of loyalty, though they also worried about K being alone so much. As the parents became sickly, it was difficult for them to continue running their small farm. Although it would have been economically possible for them to move, they felt duty-bound to remain. At the same time, they expected K to work on the farm. When she was not motivated to do so, they accused her of causing their somatic symptoms. When K reached puberty, the parents felt her sexuality was "sinful" and they were sure she would become a "bad woman" unless they strictly controlled her activities. This further served to isolate the family from their environment, in which they saw evil everywhere. Although the adoptive parents had no knowledge about the biologic parents of K, they openly blamed her "badness" on her heredity, in addition to blaming the irreligious community in which they lived.

At age 15, K's schoolwork deteriorated and she was sent to a child guidance clinic. However, the parents rejected the clinic because of fears that the girl would be somehow encouraged to have too much sexual freedom. K nevertheless continued to have contact with the clinic social worker, who supported K when she abruptly announced that she did not wish to return home. She obtained residence and a job as an aide in a home for the aged, and, thereafter, both parents and daughter refused to see each other.

In joint interviews with the parents, their communication was stiff and constricted, although unambiguous and highly rational. They exhibited no overt anxiety. All three family members have had numerous psychosomatic symptoms. There seemed to be little empathy between the parents and K and, in a sense, they have emotionally abandoned each other.

Case Example of a Severely Disturbed Family

The adoptive father of P, a girl of 19, was a primary school teacher; the mother was a kindergarten teacher. They had been married during the war in 1943 after hardly any contact except by correspondence. The father had threatened to commit suicide unless the mother married him. The parents have been emotionally distant from each other throughout their marriage, devoting themselves to P and four older, biologic children. Before P's adoption, the youngest biologic child had started school, and the marriage seemed about to break down. The adoption of P was a conscious effort to save the marriage. Ever since her infancy, P has been the bond between her adoptive parents, understanding both of them and solving their conflicts, while both parents have leaned upon and parentified her. At the same time, however, both parents attributed to P's biologic background some of the potential madness they explicitly feared in themselves. They spoke of their strenuous efforts to protect her from becoming crazy, and their relief that they had been able to preserve her sanity for so long.

The relationships between the parents and their biologic children have always been conflictual, but P has tried to be loyal to both her siblings and parents. When the parents were temporarily separated at the time of P's puberty, she first stayed with her father but then, after a couple of years, moved to her mother in order to help her—simultaneously "making way" for the father's return. The parents were subsequently reunited, but they now live in different, nearby buildings. Alternately, they first quarrel violently and then speak of their complete harmony. The communication between the spouses is ambiguous and unclear, and their conversation is difficult to follow because it is highly abstract and lacks any clearly shared focus. The loyalty bonds between the child and the parents are strong despite the many family conflicts. None of the biologic children have been able to become fully independent; the older biologic offspring are presently having marital difficulties because of their emotional ties to the parents.

Both parents openly compete for P's favor. P finds it difficult to express her ambivalent feelings toward her parents. When in their company, her behavior is more infantile than it is outside of the home (at school or with friends), where she gets along well. Even so, both parents consider that there is a special need to protect her because "she is so puny."

The family boundaries with the surrounding community are confused. The parents believe that some neighbors are dangerous communists and that others are ideal and perfect families. Anxiety in the family is highly variable. Some matters arouse intense anxiety but other issues, even problems that ordinarily are perceived as inherently complex and difficult, give rise to hardly any concern. The family members suffer from relatively frequent somatic symptoms.

Relationship of Adoptive Family and Adoptee Ratings

If one looks at the relation of dysfunction in adoptive families to the mental health ratings of the offspring in the total index and control sample, of the nine psychotic cases (where the family also has been rated), two have grown up in "neurotic" families, three in rigid, syntonic families, and four in severely disturbed adoptive families (see Table 2). All adoptees with a borderline syndrome, except one, have grown up in seriously dysfunctional families. Note that there are no borderline or psychotic offspring who were reared in healthy or mildly disturbed families.

Note that in less than one-third of the cases, the biologic index mother

TABLE 2
Clinical Ratings of Index and Control Offspring and Their Adoptive Families (Cases Studied as of 9/85)

Clinical Ratings of Offspring	**Clinical Ratings of Adoptive Families**					
	Healthy	**Mild Disturbance**	**Neurotic**	**Rigid, Syntonic**	**Severe Disturbance**	**Total**
	1	**2**	**3**	**4**	**5**	
Healthy	6	2	4	0	0	12
Mild disturbance	8	58	30	15	1	112
Neurotic	1	16	23	19	12	71
Character disorders	0	3	7	13	6	29
"Borderline syndrome"	0	0	1	7	9	17
Psychotic	0	0	2	3	4	9
Total	15	79	67	57	32	250

had her psychosis before adoption. In most cases the psychotic symptoms of the biologic index mothers did not become manifest until later. Hence, it is not likely that information about psychosis could have influenced the placement. One can, of course, ask whether the vulnerable child might have had an impact upon his or her adoptive parents.

In both the index and control groups, the mean ratings of the offspring were more disturbed when the dysfunction in the adoptive family was more severe. However, a difference between the offspring of schizophrenics and the offspring of controls comes into view when the adoptive family has been considered rigid, syntonic, or severely disturbed.

Adoptees Reared in Seriously Dysfunctional Adoptive Families

In our earlier report (20) on 88 matched pairs, we specifically compared index versus control adoptees reared in seriously dysfunctional adoptive families (groups 4 and 5). Only 8% of these index adoptees have been rated healthy, but 63% have had a severe disturbance (character disorder or worse). In contrast, of the control cases reared in seriously disturbed adoptive families, 23% of the offspring remained healthy and only 37% severely disturbed. The combination of a schizophrenic biologic mother and seriously disturbed adoptive family was associated in the adoptee with a much higher likelihood of severe disturbance and a lower likelihood of health.

Severely Disturbed Index Adoptees

The trend showing interaction of presumptive genetic vulnerability and a seriously dysfunctional rearing family also can be examined by starting with the severely disturbed adoptees and a seriously dysfunctional rearing family (see Table 3). Of 115 index adoptees, 6.9% have been diagnosed as psychotic; 15.5% as either psychotic or borderline; and 29.3% have been given a severe diagnosis, including character disorder. However, in the subsample (43 offspring) that has been reared in seriously disturbed adoptive families, the same figures are doubled: 14% as psychotic; 34.9% as psychotic *and* borderline; and 60.5% were given a severe diagnosis. In the subsample (24 offspring) with a neurotic rearing environment, 8.3% were psychotic, 12.5% psychotic or borderline, and 25% were given a severe diagnosis. In striking contrast, there are no psychotic, no borderline, and only three character disorder offspring reared in 48 healthy or mildly disturbed adoptive families. This again supports the hypothesis of interaction between heredity and family environment; however, these data cannot resolve the question of direction of effects.

TABLE 3

Adoptive Family Ratings of Disturbed Index Adoptees

Disturbed Index Adoptees (n = 60)			**Global Clinical Ratings of Adoptive Families**					
		%	**Seriously Dysfunctional* (n = 43)**	%	**Neurotic (n = 24)**	%	**Healthy** (n = 48)**	%
Psychotic	(8/115)	6.9	(6/43)	14	(2/24)	8.3	(0/48)	0
Psychotic + "Borderline"	(18/115)	15.5	(15/43)	34.9	(3/24)	12.5	(0/48)	0
Psychotic + "Borderline" + Character Disorder	(34/115)	29.3	(26/43)	60.5	(6/24)	25	(2/48)	4.2

Note: Total n of all index adoptees = 115.
*groups 4 and 5 in family ratings
**groups 1 and 2 in family ratings

Individual Parental Mental Health Ratings

The mental health ratings of the adoptive mothers and fathers corresponded to each other significantly. Of the 35 adoptive mothers with severe diagnoses, 24 had spouses who also had a severe diagnosis. At the same time, of the 92 "healthy" adoptive mothers, 59 had "healthy" spouses (18).

One might ask whether the mental health ratings of the adoptive fathers and mothers as individuals also are related to the ratings of the offspring. For the whole sample (indexes and controls), there is a significant difference between the mental health ratings of the offspring of healthy versus disturbed adoptive parents, considered separately. When we combined the ratings of the adoptive parents, we found that when one of the adoptive parents had been considered healthy and the other disturbed, the offspring had significantly more healthy ratings compared with offspring of both parents rated as disturbed. It seems that when one parent is disturbed, the healthy one can compensate for the family situation (18). Wynne et al.'s (28, 30) results also were most striking for the parents as pairs.

Preliminary Results with Test Ratings

The global clinical ratings about the adoptive families can be regarded as contaminated by the procedure in which the same psychiatrist interviewed and tested both the families as units and the individual family members. In order to obtain permission to see these families, the condition was that we were not to have more than one person see each family. The individual and family clinical ratings correlated with each other significantly (20). There fore, the question can be raised whether the family interviews and ratings, which were done first, may have influenced the later ratings of the offspring. Several alternative procedures with test data are being used to evaluate the possibility of a kind of halo effect that may have biased the clinical ratings of the offspring and adoptive families.

MMPI Ratings of Adoptees

One of the methodologic checks has been carried out using the MMPIs obtained from the adoptive offspring. The MMPI ratings were assessed blindly by a psychologist who was not aware of clinical data from the families or of the mental health ratings made for the offspring themselves. The offspring, who were individually classified as severely disturbed in their MMPIs, had been reared significantly more often in disturbed adoptive families. The MMPI ratings of the offspring varied according to the independent clinical ratings of the adoptive families. The MMPI ratings of the offspring corresponded to the clinical ratings independently made of them. The results were highly significant (20). Of the MMPI scales, the psychopathy and schizophrenia scales correlated significantly with the clinical ratings of the offspring, and the depression scale and the paranoia scale correlated at the level of a trend. Further assessments along these lines will be carried out using other MMPI scoring procedures as well as individual Rorschach assessments of communication deviance and of thought disorder in order to assess the individual characteristics of adopted-away offspring separately, insofar as possible, from the family system evaluation.

Adoptive Family Ratings with the Beavers-Timberlawn Scales

As another check through which independent ratings were obtained, we used the Beavers-Timberlawn Family Rating Scales (6) on Spouse Rorschach audiotapes (and separately for Family Rorschach audiotapes). These are five-point rating scales:

1. **Overt power** is concerned with issues of leadership, authority, con-

trol, and interpersonal influence. The scale ranges from chaos to degrees of dominance, to a leadership pattern, and to shared leadership.

2. The **parental coalition scale** assesses the apparent strength or weakness of that coalition. It involves both the instrumental and affective components of the relationship.

3. The **closeness scale** combines the appraisal of two variables: (a) separateness of individual boundaries and (b) interpersonal distance. The scale ranges from those families with distinct boundaries and high level of closeness to those with distinct boundaries and great interpersonal distance, and to those families with vague and indistinct boundaries among members.

4. **Family mythology** assesses the congruence between a family member's family image and the rater's appraisal of the family.

5. **Goal-directed negotiation** refers to ways in which the family solves problems. Efficient negotiation involves the exploration of each member's opinions and feelings, the search for a consensus, or the ability to compromise.

6. **Clarity of expression** ranges from communications that are very clear to those in which hardly anyone is ever clear.

7. **Responsibility** involves the degree to which the family system encourages members to accept responsibility for individual actions, feelings, and thoughts.

8. **Invasiveness** involves rating the family on the number of intrusive statements. Intrusions, invasions, or "mind reading" involve one person's telling (not asking) another family member what that other member thinks or feels.

9. **Permeability** involves the degree to which the family acknowledges messages from all family members. Such acknowledgements may be verbal or nonverbal.

10. **Range of feelings** rates aspects of the breadth of a family's affective system. It measures the degree to which the family encourages or tolerates the expression of feelings of all kinds.

11. The **mood and tone scale** measures the quality of what can be called the family's basic mood. This may range from warm, affectionate, optimistic, polite, to hostile, depressed, pessimistic, or hopeless.

12. The **unresolvable conflict scale** reflects the impact of conflict on the problem-solving capacity of the family (observer's judgment).

13. The **empathy scale** measures the degree to which the family responds to family members' feelings with understanding.

14. The **global health-pathology scale** measures the family's overall level of competence.

A psychiatrist who had no clinical contact with the families made these ratings of functioning by listening only to the audiotaped discussion of the adoptive parents while they were trying to reach agreement on Rorschach percepts. Her global ratings corresponded to the clinical ratings made by the psychiatrists who had interviewed the families. Note that the offspring is not present in the Couple Rorschach, so his or her behavior does not bias this Consensus Rorschach rating. However, some of the Couple Rorschach interactions are quite brief and are not highly useful for making valid and reliable ratings of the couple. Usually, the Family Rorschach provides more material for rating purposes. The psychiatrist made predictions of the degree of disturbance of the offspring from the Couple Rorschach and later from the Family Rorschach.

In Table 4, we can see how the Beavers-Timberlawn ratings from the Couple Rorschach correspond to the clinical ratings made independently. Invasiveness, closeness, responsibility, permeability, and empathy of the couples are significantly correlated with the mental health ratings of the adoptive *families*, made from the more comprehensive clinical interviews. All these ratings were made from Spouse Rorschach audiotapes without offspring being present. In spite of this, the closeness, empathy, overt power, and parental coalition scales correlate significantly with the mental health ratings of the *offspring*.

In Table 5, we can see the same ratings from Family Rorschach audiotapes where the offspring was present; 12 out of 14 scales were significantly correlated (better than $p<.05$) with the clinical ratings of the adoptive *families*, based on clinical interviews. Correlations with the mental health ratings of the *offspring* also were surprisingly high. Global evaluation, goal-directed negotiation, mood and tone, invasiveness, clarity of expression, closeness, family mythology, permeability, and responsibility were correlated significantly with adoptees' clinical ratings. Only 3 out of 14 scales did not show a trend of correlation between the blind ratings of family interaction in the Family Rorschach test and the clinical ratings of the adoptees' mental health.

Discussion

Given an opportunity to replicate the study, we would change the sampling to include all biologic mothers having a hospital diagnosis of functional psychosis. Concepts of psychiatric diagnoses have changed since 1967–1968 when this study was planned. It would have been useful to include affective psychoses in order to check more specifically the possible genetic risk for schizophrenia versus affective psychoses, as well as possible differences in family rearing patterns.

Practical considerations made it necessary for us to investigate the

TABLE 4*

Couple Interaction Versus Clinical Ratings of Adoptive Families and Adoptees

Beavers-Timberlawn Scales Clinical Ratings of for Rating Interaction in Couple Consensus	Adoptive Families (n = 100)	Adoptee Mental Health Ratings
Overt Power	.1347	**.0352**
Parental Coalition	.1343	**.0454**
Closeness	**.0076**	**.0007**
Mythology	.0607	.0957
Goal-Directed Negotiation	.2945	.5427
Clarity of Expression	.5861	.6325
Responsibility	**.0116**	.0993
Invasiveness	**.0010**	.0540
Permeability	**.0236**	.0548
Range of Feelings	.1427	.0653
Mood and Tone	.1170	.3297
Unresolvable Conflict	.0934	.2454
Empathy	**.0248**	**.0035**
Global	.0891	.1503

TABLE 5*

Family Interaction Versus Clinical Ratings of Adoptive Families and Adoptees

Beavers-Timberlawn Scales for Rating Interaction in Family Consensus Rorschach (Including Offspring)	Clinical Ratings of Adoptive Families (n = 113)	Adoptee Mental Health Ratings
Overt Power	**.0070**	.0776
Parental Coalition	.0588	.2433
Closeness	**.0126**	**.0475**
Mythology	**.0182**	**.0000**
Goal-Directed Negotiation	.2365	**.0000**
Clarity of Expression	**.0089**	**.0064**
Responsibility	**.0005**	**.0000**
Invasiveness	**.0499**	**.0338**
Permeability	**.0012**	**.0000**
Range of Feelings	**.0272**	.1150
Mood and Tone	**.0230**	**.0449**
Unresolvable Conflict	**.0156**	.1897
Empathy	**.0005**	.0880
Global	**.0168**	**.0000**

*Columns two and three are p values derived from chi-square for five levels on each Beavers-Timberlawn Scale versus five levels in the clinical ratings of the adoptive families and six levels of adoptee mental health ratings. Boldface figures are significant at $p < .05$.

families and their members in their homes. The danger of bias was of special concern because an administrative requirement for carrying out the research was that no more than one investigator be allowed to visit each family. Thus, the interviewer had to conduct all of the interviews and tests with individual family members, the parents, and the family as a whole. It was not realistic to invite these nonpatient families to the laboratory or hospital. The number of refusals probably would have been high and, hence, would have produced a sample bias because families with more psychopathology would be more likely to refuse. Also, as we expected, much valuable information on verbal and nonverbal behavior of family members has been obtained during these home visits, and the home visit also improved the quality of our contact with the families. On the other hand, the same interviewer had to meet and rate both the parents and the adoptee. As a partial corrective to the possible bias of a "halo effect," we believed that it was important to collect tape-recorded interview and test data that can be rated independently by other investigators. We also have believed that multiple measures obtained from different procedures are superior to single measures in minimizing bias. Nevertheless, because of the danger that the experimental procedures would be skewed in the home setting, we sought additional, independent test measures, such as the MMPI, to check whether family and individual evaluations may have been selectively skewed.

Interaction of genetic and family environmental factors can be interpreted in several ways. There is a possibility that genetic factors are specific and necessary and may interact with nonspecific environmental factors. Another possibility is that genetic factors are nonspecific and contribute to vulnerability not only to schizophrenia but also to a broader class of psychopathology. Genetically transmitted vulnerability (expectable in only a portion of those at risk) may be a necessary precondition for schizophrenia, but a disturbing rearing environment may also be necessary to transform the vulnerability into clinically overt schizophrenia. Healthy family rearing also can be a protective factor for a child at risk. There is a possibility that the genetic vulnerability of the offspring manifests itself in a way that is disturbing to the adoptive family. The direction of effects, that is, whether greater weight should be attributed to genetic risk versus family disturbance, will need to be examined more definitively through the longitudinal combination of the adoptive family strategy and the risk research strategy for studying families prospectively, beginning prior to the onset of illness in the offspring. At present, genetic-environmental interaction effects are evident; there is no attribution of direction of effects or causality in the concept of interaction.

Kendler et al. (3) presented three major models for the joint effects of genes and environment on liability to psychiatric illness: additive effects of genotype and environment, genetic control of sensitivity to the environment, and genetic control of exposure to the environment. If the longitudinal findings confirm our present data, our results will best fit the second model: genetic control of sensitivity to the environment. The children at risk (offspring of schizophrenic mothers) seem to be more sensitive to and to become more disturbed when in interaction with a disordered rearing family environment.

REFERENCES

1. Gottesman, I. I., & Shields, J. *Schizophrenia: The epigenetic puzzle*. Cambridge: Cambridge University Press, 1982.

2. Heston, L. L. Psychiatric disorders in foster home reared children of schizophrenic mothers. *British Journal of Psychiatry 112*: 819–825, 1966.

3. Kendler, K. S., & Eaves, L. J. Models for joint effect of genotype and environment on liability to psychiatric illness. *American Journal of Psychiatry 143*: 279–289, 1986.

4. Kety, S. S., Rosenthal, D., Wender, P., Schulsinger, F., & Jacobsen, B. The biologic and adoptive families of adopted individuals who became schizophrenic: Prevalence of mental illness and other characteristics. In L. C. Wynne, R. Cromwell, & S. Matthysse (eds.), *The nature of schizophrenia: New approaches to research and treatment*. New York: John Wiley & Sons, 1978.

5. Laing, R. D., Phillipson, H., & Lee, A. R. *Interpersonal perception: A theory and a method of research*. London: Tavistock Publications, 1966.

6. Lewis, J. M., Beavers, W. R., Gosset, J. T., & Phillips, V. A. *No single thread: Psychological health in family systems*. New York: Brunner/Mazel, 1976.

7. Liem, J. H. Family studies of schizophrenia: An update and commentary. *Schizophrenia Bulletin 6*: 429–455, 1980.

8. Loveland, N. T. The relation Rorschach: A technique for studying interaction. *Journal of Nervous and Mental Disease 142*: 93–105, 1967.

9. ______, Wynne, L. C., & Singer, M. T. The Family Rorschach: A new method for studying family interaction. *Family Process 2*: 187–215, 1963.

10. Reiss, D. The family and schizophrenia. *American Journal of Psychiatry 133*: 181–185, 1976.

11. Rosenthal, D., Wender, P. H., Kety, S. S., Schulsinger, F., Welner, J., & Reider, R. O. Parent-child relationships and psychopathological disorder in the child. *Archives of General Psychiatry 32*: 466–476, 1975.

12. ______, Wender, P. H., Kety, S. S., Welner, J., & Schulsinger, F. The adopted-away offspring of schizophrenics. *American Journal of Psychiatry 128*: 307–311, 1971.

13. Tienari, P. Psychiatric illnesses in identical twins. *Acta Psychiatrica Scandinavica (Suppl.) 171*: 1–195, 1963.

14. ______. Intrapair differences in male twins with special references to dominance-submissiveness. *Acta Psychiatrica Scandinavica (Suppl.) 188*: 1–166, 1966.

15. ______. Schizophrenia in Finnish male twins. In H. Lader (ed.), Studies of schizophrenia. Special publication of the *British Journal of Psychiatry 10*: 29–35, 1975.

16. ______, Lahti, I., Naarala, M., Sorri, A., Pohjola, J., Kaleva, M., & Wahlberg, K.-E. Biologic mothers in the Finnish adoptive family study: Alternative definitions of schizophrenia. In P. Pichot, P. Berner, R. Wolf, & K. Thau (eds.), *Psychiatry. Vol. 1*. New York: Plenum Press, 1985.

17. ______, Sorri, A., Lahti, I., Naarala, M., Wahlberg, K.-E., Moring, J., Pohjola, J., & Wynne, L. C. Interaction of genetic and psychosocial factors in schizophrenia. The Finnish adoptive family study: A longitudinal combination of the adoptive family strategy and the risk research strategy. *Schizophrenia Bulletin*, in press.

18. ______, Sorri, A., Lahti, I., Naarala, M., Wahlberg, K.-E., Pohjola, J., & Moring, J. Interaction of genetic and psychosocial factors in schizophrenia. *Acta Psychiatrica Scandinavica 71* (Suppl. 319): 19–30, 1985.

19. ______, Sorri, A., Lahti, I., Naarala, M., Wahlberg, K.-E., Rönkkö, T., Moring, J., & Pohjola, J. Family environment and the etiology of schizophrenia: Implications from the Finnish adoptive family study of schizophrenia. In H. Stierlin, F. B. Simon, & G. Schmidt (eds.), *Familiar realities: The Heidelberg Conference*. New York: Brunner/Mazel, 1987.

20. ______, Sorri, A., Lahti, I., Naarala, M., Wahlberg, K.-E., Rönkkö, T., Pohjola, J., & Moring, J. The Finnish adoptive family study of schizophrenia. *Yale Journal of Biology and Medicine 58*: 227–237, 1985.

21. ______, Sorri, A., Naarala, M., Lahti, I., Bostrom, C., & Wahlberg, K.-E. The Finnish adoptive family study. Family-dynamic approach on psychosomatics: A preliminary report. *Psychiatry and Social Science 1*: 107–115, 1981.

22. ______, Sorri, A., Naarala, M., Lahti, I., Pohjola, J., Bostrom, C., & Wahlberg, K.-E. The Finnish adoptive family study: Adopted-away offspring of schizophrenic mothers. In H. Stierlin, L. C. Wynne, & M. Wirsching (eds.), *Psychosocial intervention in schizophrenia: An international view*. Berlin: Springer-Verlag, 1983.

23. Wahl, O. F. Monozygotic twins discordant for schizophrenia: A review. *Psychological Bulletin 83*: 91–106, 1976.

24. Watt, N. F., Anthony, E. J., Wynne, L. C., & Rolf, J. E. (eds.). *Children at risk for schizophrenia: A longitudinal perspective*. Cambridge: Cambridge University Press, 1984.

25. Wender, P. H., Rosenthal, D., & Kety, S. S. A psychiatric assessment of the adoptive parents of schizophrenics. In D. Rosenthal & S. S. Kety (eds.), *The transmission of schizophrenia*. Oxford: Pergamon Press, 1968.

26. Wynne, L. C., Ryckoff, I. M., Day, J., & Hirsch, S. I. Pseudo-mutuality in the family relations of schizophrenics. *Psychiatry 21*: 205–220, 1958.

27. ______, Cromwell, R., & Matthysse, S. (eds.). *The nature of schizophrenia: New approaches to research and treatment*. New York: John Wiley & Sons, 1978.

28. ______, Singer, M. T., Bartko, J. J., & Toohey, M. L. Schizophrenics and their families: Research on parental communication. In J. M. Tanner (ed.), *Developments in psychiatric research*. London: Hodder & Stoughton, 1977.

29. ______, Singer, M. T., & Toohey, M. L. Communication of the adoptive parents of schizophrenics. In J. Jørstad & E. Ugelstad (eds.), *Schizophrenia 75: Psychotherapy, family studies, research*. Oslo: Universitetsforlaget, 1976.

30. ______, Toohey, M. L., & Doane, J. A. Family studies. In L. Bellak (ed.), *Disorders of the schizophrenic syndrome*. New York: Basic Books, 1979.

3

PARENTAL PSYCHOPATHOLOGY AND FAMILY SYSTEM VARIABLES AS PREDICTORS OF CHILD COMPETENCE

LYMAN C. WYNNE
University of Rochester
Rochester, New York

THE University of Rochester Child and Family Study (URCAFS), initiated in 1972, is a risk research program concerned with cross-sectional and developmental relationships between three areas: (a) parental health and psychopathology, (b) family system functioning and dysfunctioning, and (c) child health and psychopathology. The central goal of this report is to identify the parental and family variables in this study that differentiate among healthy and dysfunctional children, all of whom are presumptively at genetic risk for serious psychopathology in the future. Which aspects of parental psychopathology and family relationships account for variance in child competence and dysfunction? Findings that relate to this question may be useful for the selection of variables in continuing prospective, longitudinal research on this and other samples, and in planning strategies of preventive interventions.

For purposes of sample selection in URCAFS, risk of later mental illness for children, ages 4 to 10, was initially defined by parental hospitalization for a "functional" mental illness, including schizophrenia. We also wished to define risk status in terms of dysfunctional family communication and relationship patterns (21, 22); however, to select and recruit families by family relationship criteria was regarded as cumbersome and impractical. Therefore, family dysfunction became a secondary criterion of risk status determined after initial research evaluation. Although we were particularly interested in schizophrenia and its developmental precursors, we believed that a focus on children at risk only for narrowly defined schizophrenia that would not be diagnosable for 10 to 30 years would be wasteful of the opportunity to use the risk research framework for broader studies of developmental psychology and psychopathology. We planned a long-term prospective study of developmental factors that hypothetically are precursors of clinical schizophrenia and other serious psychiatric disorders or, alternatively, may protect against disorder despite the presence of risk factors.

In the Rochester risk research program, 145 families were initially assessed from 1972 to 1976. The criteria for sample selection were: (a) a Caucasian, middle-class parent hospitalized for a functional psychiatric disorder and (b) an index son, in one of three age groups (4, 7, or 10), who was being reared in the household of both biologic parents, and who was not initially in psychiatric care.

The predictor variables evaluated in URCAFS were organized into three areas: child, parent, and family. Each area was mapped into several domains. Wynne (23) has presented a full list of the variables. Detailed descriptions of methods of data collection and early studies of their relationships with one another are presented in various publications from the research group (see especially 2, 7, 24).

Child Variables

The assessment of children was carried out using three sources: (a) peer and teacher ratings in the school; (b) ratings by the parents, using the Rochester Adaptive Behavior Interview (RABI; 8); and (c) evaluations by health professionals (27). The latter took place with five kinds of data: obstetrical, neurological, psychophysiological, psychological test, and clinical psychiatric assessments. The clinical psychiatric studies included standardized diagnostic typologies, evaluation of global competence, and an evaluation using a Q-sort technique devised in this program (15).

Full-scale reassessment of offspring and families was carried out three years after initial evaluation, with the intention that a convergence design for the accelerated study of longitudinal processes would be fulfilled (3). Thus, at three-year follow-up the index children were age 7, 10, or 13. Further follow-up focusing on the offspring has been carried out periodically. At present, the offspring are mostly in late adolescence, only now starting to enter the age period of highest risk for major mental disorders.

Both initially and at three-year follow-up, assessment of the children was most satisfactory in the school setting, as carried out in a comprehensive manner by Fisher (7). A special advantage of the school ratings was that they were totally independent of other data about the children, with all same-sexed classmates as controls within each classroom. Although the children showed considerable behavioral and emotional variation, only a small portion fit into standard psychiatric categories, such as those in DSM-III. The peer and teacher ratings provided a wide range of functional differentiation among the children long before the major psychiatric disorders of adolescence or adulthood ordinarily become diagnosable. We were encouraged in the use of peer ratings by the earlier finding of Cowen and his colleagues (4) that, when 10-year-old children were assessed by clinicians, parents, teachers, and peers, only the peer ratings predicted significantly to psychiatric disability 15 years later.

Parental Variables

Data from and about individual parents in the study have been discussed by Kokes and his co-workers (see 11, 12). The narrative accounts of index parent histories that were reviewed in hospital charts at the time of initial research assessments (1972–1976) were often quite detailed. However, because of the lack of criteria in DSM-II, which was in use at that time, the investigators distrusted the adequacy and consistency of the hospital diagnoses. Therefore, research diagnoses were obtained by two teams, one of whom used the Present State Examination (PSE) and modifications of the WHO interview. As DSM-III criteria became formulated during the course of the study, the data were reviewed until diagnoses were stabilized with the publication of DSM-III in 1980. In addition to these typological DSM-III diagnoses, dimensionalized assessments of parental psychopathology, especially chronicity and severity, and a rating of social and work functioning were obtained. Tables 1 through 5 summarize the groupings of the parents according to these diagnoses and dimensions.

Family Interaction and Communication Variables

The Rochester study includes six family interaction and communication procedures. Data from two procedures, the Consensus Rorschach (13) and the Family Free Play (2) are reported here. The entire family, excluding children younger than age 4, participated in the *Consensus Rorschach*. In this procedure, the family members are asked to reach as many agreements as they can about what a Rorschach inkblot looks like to them. Instructions are first given to the parents and they carry out this task without the presence of the children *Couples Rorschach*). They then are asked to explain the task to the children and to reach consensus as a family (*Family Rorschach*). Except for necessary task instructions, no investigators are present when the

TABLE 1*

DSM-III Diagnoses of Index Parent
(Total n = 145)

URCAFS Diagnostic Groups	DSM-III	Number: Male	Female	Total	Total per Group
1. Schizophrenic disorders:					
1.1 Schizophrenia	All 295 except 295.40 + 295.70	10	8	18	20
1.2 Schizophreniform	295.40	2	0	2	
2. Psychotic affective disorders:					
2.1 Major depression with psychotic features	296.24 + 296.34	3	8	11	38
2.2 Bipolar psychosis	296.44, 296.54, 296.64	7	20	27	
3. Psychoses not elsewhere classified:					
3.1 Schizoaffective disorder	295.70	0	9	9	10
3.2 Atypical psychosis	298.90	0	1	1	
4. Personality disorders:					
4.1 Severe: Schizotypal, schizoid, paranoid, borderline	301.00, 301.20, 301.22, 301.83	5	6	11	30
4.2 Moderate: Histrionic, dependent, compulsive, and passive-aggressive	301.50, 301.60, 301.40, 301.84	1	18	19	
5. Nonpsychotic affective disorders:					
5.1 Major depression with melancholia	296.23, 296.33	1	8	9	
5.2 Depressive disorder without melancholia	296.22, 296.32, 300.40, 309.00, 309.28, 296.82	4	18	22	39
5.3 Bipolar disorder without psychosis	296.62, 296.52, 296.42, 301.13	1	7	8	
6. Nonpsychotic nonaffective disorders:					
Anxiety disorders	300.02	5	3	8	

*Tables 1–5 are from chapter III by Kokes, Perkins, Harder, and Strauss, in Baldwin, Cole, and Baldwin (see 2).

TABLE 2

Four-Category Classification of the Diagnosis of Index Parents

	Number		
	Fathers	**Mothers**	**Total**
1. Schizophrenic-like nonaffective disorders (1.1 + 4.1)	15	14	29
2. Affective psychoses (2.1 + 2.2 + 3.1)	10	37	47
3. Nonpsychotic nonaffective (4.2 + 6.0)	6	21	27
4. Nonpsychotic affective (5.1 + 5.2 + 5.3)	6	33	39
Subtotal	37	105	142
1.2 + 3.2 omitted	2	1	3
Total	39	106	145

tasks are carried out. The entire procedure is videotaped to facilitate later scoring on a number of family interaction scales.

Several elements of the task should be noted: (a) There is a specific task—to reach agreement on percepts; (b) an achievement standard is implied—to reach as many agreements as possible; (c) limits are imposed—all must sit at a table and participate; (d) responsibility is given to the group for task closure—the family is told to ring the bell when they are done; and (e) certain work is assigned to the parents—they are to instruct the children about the task.

In the *Family Free Play*, only the mother, father, and index son participate. No specific task is given; few limits are set; the only request is that the family play as they might at home. A standard set of age-appropriate toys are provided. They are sufficiently complicated and difficult so that children may need parental help and the parents may be prompted to help. The toys are also interesting to the parents and many parents play with them alone. The parents are not required to play with their children, but no adult pastimes (for example, magazines or books) are provided.

For purposes of this program, the family variables were divided into three domains: communication/attention; affect/relationship; and family structure.

Communication

Our interest in scoring communication deviance originates with the work of Singer and Wynne (17, 19) in the area of communication deviance (CD). We have measures of parental CD from the conjoint family interaction tasks (5) as well as from individual Rorschach sessions (18), and measures of healthy, constructive communication from both procedures (1, 16). Measures of healthy communication are related to but not simply the inverse of CD.

TABLE 3

Hospitalizations and Chronicity by Diagnostic Category

Diagnostic Category	Number of Hospital-izations	Total Weeks of Hospital-izations	Course			% Chronic	Too Recent to be Classified
			Single Episode	Episodic	Chronic		
Schizophrenic-like (psychotic nonaffective), n = 29	2.65	14.79	5	1	17	77	7
Affective psychotic, n = 47	3.58	41.38[a]	7	14	20	49	6
Nonaffective nonpsychotic, n = 27	1.59	3.39	3	0	12	80	12
Affective nonpsychotic, n = 39	2.05	7.38	7	7	15	52	10
Total sample	2.58	19.50	21	22	64	60	35
SIGNIFICANCE*							
Affectivity	$p < .05$	N.S.	–	–	–	$p < .001$	–
Psychosis	$p < .001$	$p < .01$	–	–	–	N.S.	–
Affectivity × psychosis	N.S.	N.S.	–	–	–	N.S.	–
Four diagnostic categories	–	–	$\chi^2 = 18.72$, $p < .01$			–	–

[a]This group includes four people with hospitalization in excess of 150 weeks.

*Four-way ANOVA (affectivity × psychoticism × age of child × sex of index parent) using BMDQ4V program, repeated for weighted and unweighted means to check for discrepancies.

TABLE 4

Average Global Assessment Scores by Diagnostic Category

Diagnostic Category	GAS at Hospitalization	GAS at URCAFS	Improvement	Spouse GAS at URCAFS
Schizophrenic-like (psychotic nonaffective), n = 29	31.00	53.07	22.07	66.62
Affective psychoses, n = 47	30.85	61.33	30.52	67.43
Nonaffective, nonpsychotic disorder, n = 27	40.96	61.89	20.93	71.37
Affective nonpsychotic disorder, n = 39	39.33	64.82	25.49	67.08
Total sample	35.13	60.70	25.57	67.92
SIGNIFICANCE				
Affectivity	N.S.	$p<.01$	$p<.001$	N.S.
Psychosis	$p<.001$	$p<.01$	N.S.	N.S.
Affectivity × psychosis	N.S.	$p<.01$	N.S.	N.S.

TABLE 5

Average Social and Work Function Scores by Diagnostic Category

	Index Parent		Spouse	
Diagnostic Category	Social Function	Work Function	Social Function	Work Function
Schizophrenia-like (psychotic nonaffective)	2.50	2.86	3.15	3.55
Affective psychoses	3.06	3.48	3.10	3.77
Nonaffective nonpsychotic	3.20	3.50	3.20	3.59
Affective nonpsychotic	3.37	3.63	3.01	3.72
Total sample	3.06	3.40	3.10	3.68
SIGNIFICANCE				
Affectivity	$p<.05$	$p<.01$	N.S.	$p<.05$
Psychosis	$p<.01$	$p<.01$	N.S.	N.S.
Affectivity × psychosis	N.S.	$p<.05$	N.S.	N.S.

Affect

The British work on attitudinal expressed emotion (20) and the work of Doane, Goldstein, and Rodnick (6) on interactional affective style have demonstrated the longitudinal predictive power of measures of family affect. The generalizability of these findings is being intensively studied in research centers throughout the world. In our risk research, we use measures of positive and negative affect in the Consensus Rorschach and a measure of positive affect in the Free Play.

Family Structure

This includes measures of the relative activity and involvement of each of the family members in each task. In both the Consensus Rorschach and the Free Play, there are obvious and striking differences between families in the rate and total amount of interaction among family members, that is, in who initiates the interaction and to whom the interactions are directed. A balance of parent and child initiations in the tasks suggest their mutual engagement, and this relates directly to the children's cognitive and psychosocial development.

Preliminary Findings

Parental Psychopathology and Child Dysfunction

In predicting cross-sectionally from parental psychopathology to child school competence (independently rated at initial assessment by peers and teachers), DSM-III category differences, including schizophrenics versus other diagnostic groups, were not associated with child differences. Also, clustering parental diagnoses of psychoses plus severe personality disorders versus nonpsychotic diagnoses failed to predict child competence significantly. Indeed, there was a trend for the parents with *non*psychotic chronic depression and moderate personality disorders to have children rated as more incompetent by teachers (see Table 6).

In contrast to these findings, parental diagnoses clustered into affective versus nonaffective groups were highly correlated with initial child functioning. Ratings of the illnesses of the index parents on a dimension of chronic versus episodic were also correlated with school ratings of their children (see Table 6). That is, children whose parents have affective and/or episodic illnesses were rated to be performing much better than were children whose parents have chronic or nonaffective illnesses. These two effects were independent and additive and together account for 19% of the variance in the overall teacher rating and for 16% of the variance in the overall peer rating.

Breakdowns and Dysfunction to Date: Because the offspring have only begun to enter the age range of high risk for major psychiatric disorders, data on their status must be regarded as preliminary; intermediate (not final) outcomes can be reviewed.

Table 7 shows 1982 data for intermediate outcomes 6 to 9 years after the initial study in relation to diagnosis of index parent. One index son and

TABLE 6

The Relationship Between Parental Illness and Children's School Functioning

Illness Variable	Overall Teacher Rating[a]	Overall Peer Rating[a]
Nonaffective (n = 32)	46.1	46.7
Affective (n = 66)	52.1	53.2
	$t = -3.23$	$t = -3.39$
	$p < 0.002$	$p < 0.001$
Psychotic (n = 51)	51.6	52.2
Nonpsychotic (n = 47)	48.3	49.6
	$t = 1.69$	$t = 1.33$
	$p < 0.09$	$p < 0.19$
Chronic (n = 47)	46.5	47.5
Episodic (n = 51)	53.4	54.2
	$t = 4.07$	$t = 3.68$
	$p < 0.001$	$p < 0.001$

[a]Teacher and Peer Ratings are constructed so that each child's classroom mean is 50, with a standard deviation of 10. Higher scores reflect better adjustment.

siblings in six other families were hospitalized for psychiatric problems during this period. Their symptomatic conditions were as follows:

- mixed personality disorder, including schizotypal features, with abuse of multiple drugs and a brief psychotic episode precipitated by drug abuse
- schizophreniform disorder, responding rapidly to neuroleptic medication
- hospitalization for slashing wrist; impulsive or depressive features
- serious problems with drugs and alcohol
- unsocialized, aggressive reaction of adolescence
- suicidal gesture and behavioral problems necessitating placement in a residential treatment home
- borderline personality disorder (secondary diagnosis, atypical psychosis), but hospitalized for treatment of severe conduct disorder.

From the standpoint of parental risk factors, these 7 offspring were found in families with parents having six different categories of diagnoses, including one parent with schizophrenia, one with a schizophrenia-spectrum

TABLE 7*

1982 URCAFS Follow-Up

Diagnosis of Index Parent	n	Hospitalized Offspring	Families with a Disturbed Offspring n	Families with a Disturbed Offspring %	Families with Disturbed Index Offspring	No. of Disturbed Sibs of Index Offspring
Schizophrenia	18	Sib	11	61	7	11
Schizophreniform	2		0	0	0	0
Psychotic Depr.	11		4	36	2	3
Psychotic Bipolar	27	2 Sibs	13	48	5	11
Schizoaffective	9	Sib	4	44	3	6
Atypical psychosis	1		1	100	0	1
"Severe" Personality Disorder	11	Sib	8	73	6	9
"Mod." Pers. Dis.	19	Sib	11	58	8	7
Melancholia	9		2	22	2	1
Other nonpsychotic	22		11	50	5	9
Nonpsychotic bipolar	8		6	75	5	7
Anxiety Disorder	8	Index	4	50	3	4
	145	7	75	52	46	69

*Prepared from data assembled by Dr. Patricia Perkins.

personality disorder, two with bipolar psychoses, one with schizoaffective psychosis, and one with histrionic personality disorder.

Although only a small number of offspring in these families have so far been hospitalized, there is a high proportion showing ominous disturbances by late adolescence. In 75 (52%) of the URCAFS families, one or more offspring had either been in treatment or a mental health professional had recommended treatment. Examining the outcome data of Table 7 in special groupings, it is interesting to note the following percentage of families with disturbed offspring: parents with a schizophrenia-spectrum diagnosis (schizophrenia plus severe personality disorder)—66%; episodic psychoses (schizophreniform, bipolar, and schizoaffective)—45%; chronic, nonpsychotic personality disorders (depression and anxiety disorders)—55%. It is also interesting that the offspring of schizophrenics and the parents with personality disorders have an equal frequency (66%) of disturbed offspring. (Here I am adding to DSM-III personality disorders the category of nonpsychotic bipolar disorders, which could better be labeled as cyclothymic personality disorder.)

Family System Variables and Child Competence in School

Composite Cross Situational Measures of Parental Communication

Within the domain of communication in the family area, J. E. Jones, Wynne, Al-Khayyal, et al. (8) scored and analyzed communication deviance from three different procedures: individual Rorschach, individual TAT, and Family Rorschach. For the Family Rorschach, healthy communication (HC) was also scored. A combined parental communication measure was produced by tabulating the number of times parents were high on the three CD measures and showed poor functioning on the HC measure, and then subtracting the number of times that parents were low on CD and had a healthy profile on HC. This produced a composite variable with 9 points (from +4 to −4). In order to do an analysis of variance, this measure was trichotomized (+4 to +1; 0; −1 to −4) into low, intermediate, and high levels of deviance.

Table 8 shows that for the 10-year-old group in URCAFS, all associations between the parental composite CD variable and child competence in the school setting were highly significant. These findings are especially remarkable because the school ratings of the index children by teachers and peers were obtained entirely independently of the family assessments done within the hospital research setting. Across all the areas of child functioning (cognitive/academic, social/emotional, and rule-following/compliance) and for ratings by both teachers and peers, the children of parents with a high level of CD were rated consistently as less competent. Furthermore, a consistent linear relationship across the three levels of parental communication was maintained with respect to each child measured. In addition, it can be noted that parental CD was not related to social class within this sample.

These findings strongly support the hypothesis that deviant parental communication patterns are reflected in the incompetent school functioning of their 10-year-old sons. For those children doing poorly, the parents tend to have high CD across situations. Conversely, children doing well tend to have parents who are consistently free of CD across procedures. For these two extreme groups, CD appears to be a consistent cross-situational style. However, for intermediate cases and the sample as a whole, Doane (5) found little correlation between CD measures across situations. The relative independence of the measure across situations suggested the potential value of a

TABLE 8

Average Level of Child Functioning: 10-Year-Olds Rated by Teachers and Peers for Three Levels of Parental Communication Deviance

		Child Variable					
Composite Parental Communication Deviance	**n**	**Cognitive Academic**	**Social Emotional**	**Rule Following Compliance**	**Mean Peer**	**Mean Teacher**	**Overall Competence**
Low	27	2.96	2.04	2.85	54.9	55.8	6.74
Intermediate	9	2.67	1.44	2.11	52.5	52.3	5.67
High	19	1.21	1.05	1.63	44.7	43.4	3.58
F (2, 52) Linear Test		17.79	11.68	9.31	11.75	29.14	23.58
p (one-tailed)		$<.0001$	$<.0006$	$<.0018$	$<.0006$	$<.0001$	$<.0001$

composite variable in which different communication measures contribute together to predict criterion variance in the child. Hence, Jones et al. (9) advised anyone wanting to measure communication variables to do so with multiple, short procedures rather than rely on a single, long procedure, such as using only a 10-card Rorschach or only a set of TAT cards. A strategy of multiple methods that combined the separate communication measures yielded enhanced predictive power.

Cross-Domain Family Assessment

The Family Consensus Rorschach and the Family Free Play each tap variables across all three of the domains of communication, affect, and family structure. Family variables from each of these tasks were related to child functioning. Table 9 illustrates some of the data that have been obtained.

In the domain of communication, both CD and HC measures of the mother in the Consensus Family Rorschach were highly related to the children's school functioning. In the domain of affect, the mother's negative

TABLE 9

The Relationship Between Family Interaction and Children's School Functioning[a]

	Overall Teacher Rating (n = 98)	**Overall Peer Rating (n = 100)**
Communication		
Mother's healthy communication	0.24	0.21
in Family Rorschach	$p<0.01$	$p<0.03$
Mother's communication deviance	−0.24	−0.15
in Family Rorschach	$p<0.01$	$p<0.07$
Affect		
Mother's negative affect	−0.26	−0.19
in Family Rorschach	$p<0.01$	$p<0.03$
Father's positive affect	0.24	0.27
in Free Play	$p<0.01$	$p<0.01$
Family Structure		
Parent-child activity/balance	0.23	0.18
in Free Play	$p<0.01$	$p<0.04$
Father-child activity/balance	0.26	0.31
in Family Rorschach	$p<0.01$	$p<0.001$

[a]Pearson product-moments correlations; *p* values are for one-tailed tests.

affect in the Family Rorschach and the father's positive affect in the Family Free Play procedure were related to the children's school rating. A family structure variable, the amount and proportion of parent-child interaction initiated by the parents and the children in the Family Rorschach and by the father in the Family Free Play was also significantly related to the children's school functioning. In the "balance" measure, relatively equal but age-related proportions of parent-initiated and child-initiated interaction predicted to better functioning of the child in contrast to poor child functioning in school if either the child or the parents participated very frequently or infrequently.

Using a stepwise multiple regression to select the most efficient combination of family variables, Wynne and Cole (24) have shown that variables from each of the domains of communication, affect, and family structure make independent, highly significant contributions to the prediction of school ratings for the children. For both kinds of ratings (see Table 10), composite family measures explain 27% of the variance ($p<.0001$). The percentage of variance explained is higher for the 10-year-old sample than for the 7-year-old sample, suggesting that the family influence has heightened during this 3-year period.

Combination and Interaction of Parental Psychopathology and Family Variables

An important question was whether parental illness risk variables and family interaction risk variables *each* contributed separately to prediction of the children's school functioning or whether knowledge of either one was sufficient? Our hypothesis is that *both* are important. To test this hypothesis, we used six variables for the teacher ratings and five for the peer ratings. For assessing parental psychopathology, we used chronic versus episodic course as one variable, and affectivity versus nonaffectivity as the other variable, both of which had been shown to be predictive of child functioning. Among the family interaction variables in the domain of family structure, we used activity/balance in the father-son interaction in the Free Play procedure. In the affective domain, we used the father-to-son warmth measure from the Free Play and the mother's negative affect statements from the Consensus Rorschach; the latter measure was omitted for the peer ratings because it did not contribute additional variance to the peer-rating prediction. In the communication domain, we used the mother's healthy communication in the Consensus Rorschach.

When the parental and family sets of variables are combined in a stepwise multiple regression, adding the family interaction ratings to the parental psychopathology variables increased the explained variance (R^2) in the teacher ratings of the children from 19% to 34%(F [6, 87]$=7.42$;

TABLE 10

Composite Family Measure Predicting Children's School Functioning

Composite Measure	Teacher Ratings	Peer Ratings
Communication		
Family Rorschach Mother's healthy communication		
Family Rorschach Mother's communication deviance	$R=.52$	$R=.52$
Affect	$R^2=.27$	$R^2=.27$
Free Play Father's positive affect	$F(4,90)=8.30$	$F(3,94)=11.88$
Family Rorschach Mother's negative affect	$p \leq .0001$	$p \leq .0001$
Structure		
Free Play Father-child activity/balance		
Family Rorschach Parent-child activity/balance		

$p<.0001$). In the peer ratings, the explained variance is increased from 16% to 34% (F [5, 91] = 9.18; $p<.0001$). The increase in the explained variance for each set of ratings is significant at $p<.01$. Reversing the procedure and adding the parental psychopathology variables to the family interaction variables increases the explained variance both in the teacher and the peer ratings from 27% to 34%. These increases are significant at $p<.02$ (24).

Thus, dimensionalized parental illness and family interaction variables *each* contribute significantly and independently to variance in ratings carried out entirely separately in the school by teachers and peers of the index sons in these families.

Discussion and Summary

1. Tentatively, we are learning that parental psychopathology appears to be related to child functioning outside the family in the school setting. Chronicity and a narrow range of affective expression seem to be associated with poor child functioning. Children are more competent if the parents have been ill only episodically and if they have a wide range of available

affect. In contrast, no association could be found between traditional diagnostic categories, such as schizophrenia, and either child school functioning or adolescent psychiatric breakdowns. That is, *dimensions* of parental psychopathology, but not *typologic* diagnostic categories of parental psychopathology, differentiate competent and incompetent children who have not, it is true, yet passed through the age of risk for adult mental illness.

The advantages of studying an array of parental diagnoses beyond schizophrenia become apparent in this aspect of the study. However, if schizophrenic disorders are genetically heterogeneous, some genetically important subgroups of the most severely ill schizophrenics may not be represented in this sample of parents. On the other hand, those schizophrenics who are most impaired are less likely to have produced offspring. Hence, one can argue that those kinds of schizophrenics who have contributed to the genetic pool are most likely to be represented in this sample.

2. Family relationship variables—the presence of healthy communication with a low degree of communication deviance, positive affective relationships, and an age-appropriate balance in interaction between parents and children, with each taking the initiative—are associated with favorable or even superior functioning of the children in this sample, *despite* the risk factor of a parental psychiatric hospitalization. Thus, perhaps the most interesting and important finding to date is the elucidation of family relationship variables that promote health in these families despite the expectably adverse effects of serious parental disorders. The diversity, both positive and negative, in the levels of social and cognitive competence of the children at ages 4, 7, and 10 is striking. This preliminary impression will need to be reexamined in the light of later development of these families and children. It is quite possible that the impact of affectively labile parents on these children may not be manifest until later in adolescence or adulthood, but such an impact is not apparent in the data reported here.

3. Further study of the additive effects and nonadditive joint effects of parental psychopathology and family relationship variables clearly is indicated. Preferably, such work should include measures from direct observation of family interaction. Parental psychopathology is often loosely regarded as predominantly environmental. Such a simplistic distinction is inadequate and misleading. The comparative power of alternative experimental designs in resolving questions of joint effects needs exploration in detailed conceptualizations and model building (10).

4. Risk research should be combined with pedigree studies in which careful assessment of the family history is pursued. A stumbling block has been changing diagnostic criteria over the years, which has made it difficult to give weight to reports from the past. Further efforts to obtain case records

and make rediagnoses whenever possible are needed. In some instances, pedigrees that will be useful to study with gene-marker techniques will no doubt be identified.

5. Further methodologic studies of family interaction measures that are relevant to psychopathology are needed. Data analysis using aggregate scores will be on a much more firm conceptual basis when combined with study of temporal patterns. In our preliminary explorations, lag sequential analysis has appeared to be especially promising. In addition, at the level of data collection, our experience strongly supports the concept of using multiple family interaction measures, each of which can be carried out quickly, for example, in 5 to 15 minutes, versus single measures that may take an hour or more but tap only a narrow range of variables (9, 25, 26). This point is applicable to measures of family communication that can be looked at across tasks and situations, but it also applies to measures of social and occupational functioning, and to measures of expressed emotion and affective style.

6. Conceptual and empirical reconciliation is needed between (a) the belief that it is important to include all members of a family as a system in family interaction studies, and (b) the practical requirements of standardizing and simplifying data collection and analysis in which an "artificial" triad of father, mother, and one index child, for example, may be studied, but siblings, grandparents, and others who may be significant in family interaction patterns, are left out.

Current risk studies with family interaction measures usually have begun with intact, two-parent families. This design not only is susceptible to Berkson's fallacy, as Mednick (14) has pointed out, but also the size of samples that can readily be generated is greatly reduced by this restriction. It is possible to conduct family interaction studies with whoever is living together, and then to see empirically whether the type of family structure makes a difference; but larger samples and collaboration in research consortiums may then be required.

7. Finally, risk research should be designed so as to help clarify the most appropriate nosological boundaries and criteria for a genetically relevant schizophrenia spectrum. DSM-III and its successors should be regarded as working hypotheses, not as a clinical or research framework molded in concrete. Validation of family research ideas should not rely exclusively or even primarily upon diagnostic categories applied to individuals, nor upon single measures of family interaction or communication. Dimensionalized approaches to the study of individual psychopathology and family can and should be explored. Testing of crisp hypotheses about interaction between these realms is timely and almost certain to be illuminating.

REFERENCES

1. Al-Khayyal, M. Healthy parental communication as a predictor of child competence in families with a schizophrenic and psychiatrically disturbed nonschizophrenic parent. Unpublished doctoral dissertation, University of Rochester, 1980.

2. Baldwin, A. L., Cole, R. E., & Baldwin, C. P. (eds.). Parental pathology, family interaction, and the competence of the child in school. *Monographs of the Society for Research in Child Development* (Serial No. 197) *7*: 1–84, 1982.

3. Bell, R. Q. Convergence: An accelerated longitudinal approach. *Child Development 24*: 145–152, 1953.

4. Cowen, E. L., Pederson, A., Babigian, H., Izzo, L. D., & Trost, M. A. Long-term follow-up of early detected vulnerable children. *Journal of Consulting and Clinical Psychology 41*: 438–446, 1973.

5. Doane, J. A. Parental communication deviance as a predictor of child competence in families with a schizophrenic and nonschizophrenic parent. Unpublished doctoral dissertation, University of Rochester, 1977.

6. ———, Goldstein, J. J., & Rodnick, E. H. Parental patterns of affective style and the development of schizophrenia spectrum disorders. *Family Process 20*: 337–349, 1981.

7. Fisher, L. et al. Child competence and psychiatric risk. *Journal of Nervous and Mental Disease 168* (6 articles), 1980.

8. Jones, F. H. The Rochester Adaptive Behavior Inventory: A parallel series of instruments for assessing social competence during early and middle childhood and adolescence. In J. Strauss, H. Babigian, & M. Rolf (eds.), *The origins and course of psychopathology: Methods of longitudinal research*. New York: Plenum Press, 1977.

9. Jones, J. E., Wynne, L. C., Al-Khayyal, M., Doane, J. A., Ritzler, B., Singer, M. T., & Fisher, L. Predicting current school competence of high-risk children with composite cross-situational measure of parental communication. In N. F. Watt, E. J. Anthony, L. C. Wynne, & J. E. Rolf (eds.), *Children at risk for schizophrenia: A longitudinal perspective*. New York: Cambridge University Press, 1984.

10. Kendler, K. S., & Eaves, L. J. Models for the joint effect of genotype and environment on liability to psychiatric illness. *American Journal of Psychiatry 143*: 279–289, 1986.

11. Kokes, R. F., Harder, D., Perkins, P., & Strauss, J. S. Diagnostic, symptomatic, and descriptive characteristics of parents in the University of Rochester Child and Family Study. In N. F. Watt, E. J. Anthony, L. C. Wynne, & J. E. Rolf (eds.), *Children at risk for schizophrenia: A longitudinal perspective*. New York: Cambridge University Press, 1984.

12. ———, Perkins, P., Harder, D., & Strauss, J. S. Diagnostic, symptomatic, and descriptive characteristics of parents in the University of Rochester Child and Family Study. In A. L. Baldwin, R. E. Cole, & C. P. Baldwin (eds.), Parental pathology, family interaction, and the competence of the child in school. *Monographs of the Society for Research in Child Development* (Serial No. 197) *7*, 1982.

13. Loveland, N. T., Wynne, L. C., & Singer, M. T. The Family Rorschach: A new method for studying family interaction. *Family Process 2:* 187–215, 1963.

14. Mednick, S. A. Berkson's fallacy and high-risk research. In L. C. Wynne, R. L.

Cromwell, & S. Matthysse (eds.), *The nature of schizophrenia: New approaches to research and treatment*. New York: John Wiley & Sons, 1978.

15. Munson, S., Baldwin, A. L., Yu, P., Baldwin, C. P., & Greenwald D. A clinical research approach to the assessment of adaptive function in children at risk. In N. R. Watt, E. J. Anthony, L. C. Wynne, & J. E. Rolf (eds.), *Children at risk for schizophrenia: A longitudinal perspective*. New York: Cambridge University Press, 1984.

16. Schuldberg, D. Healthy features in the individual Rorschach transactions of parents of children at risk for severe mental disorders. Unpublished doctoral dissertation, University of California, Berkeley, 1981.

17. Singer, M. T., & Wynne, L. C. Thought disorder and family relations of schizophrenics: IV. Results and implications. *Archives of General Psychiatry 12*: 201–212, 1965.

18. ______, & Wynne, L. C. Principles for scoring communication defects and deviances in parents of schizophrenics: Rorschach and TAT scoring manuals. *Psychiatry 29*: 260–288, 1966.

19. ______, Wynne, L. C., & Toohey, M. L. Communication disorders and the families of schizophrenics. In L. C. Wynne, R. L. Cromwell, & S. Matthysse (eds.), *The nature of schizophrenia: New approaches to research and treatment*. New York: John Wiley & Sons, 1978.

20. Vaughn, C. E., & Leff, J. P. The influence of family and social factors on the course of psychiatric illness: A comparison of schizophrenic and depressed neurotic parents. *British Journal of Psychiatry 129*: 125–137, 1976.

21. Wynne, L. C. Family research on the pathogenesis of schizophrenia: Intermediate variables in the study of families at high risk. In P. Doucet & C. Laurin (eds.), *Problems of psychosis*. Amsterdam: Excerpta Medica, 1969.

22. ______. Family interaction: An alternative starting point for evaluating risk of psychosis. In E. J. Anthony, C. Koupernik, & C. Chiland (eds.), *The child and his family: Vulnerable children*. New York: John Wiley & Sons, 1978.

23. ______. The University of Rochester Child and Family Study: Overview of research plan. In N. F. Watt, E. J. Anthony, L. C. Wynne, & J. E. Rolf (eds.), *Children at risk for schizophrenia: A longitudinal perspective*. New York: Cambridge University Press, 1984.

24. ______, & Cole, R. E. The Rochester risk research program: A new look at parental diagnoses and family relationships. In H. Stierlin, L. C. Wynne, & M. Wirsching (eds.), *Psychosocial intervention in schizophrenia: An international view*. Berlin: Springer-Verlag, 1983.

25. ______, Jones, J. E., & Al-Khayyal, M. Healthy family communication patterns: Observations in families "at risk" for psychopathology. In F. Walsh (ed.), *Normal family processes*. New York: Guilford Press, 1982.

26. ______, Jones, J. E., Al-Khayyal, M., Cole, R.E., & Fisher, L. Familial risk factors in psychopathology. In M. Goldstein (ed.), *Preventive intervention in schizophrenia: Are we ready*? Washington DC: United States Department of Health & Human Services, 1982.

27. Yu, P., Prentky, R., Fisher, L., Baldwin, A. L., Greenwald, D., Munson, S., & Baldwin, C. P. Child competence as assessed by clinicians, parents, teachers, and peers. In N. F. Watt, E. J. Anthony, L. C. Wynne, & J. E. Rolf (eds.), *Children at risk for schizophrenia: A longitudinal perspective*. New York: Cambridge University Press, 1984.

4

CHRONIC VERSUS EPISODIC STRESS AND THE ADJUSTMENT OF HIGH-RISK OFFSPRING*

JOHN E. RICHTERS
National Institute of Mental Health
Bethesda, Maryland

THE CONCEPT of high risk has gained considerable currency during the past few decades among researchers interested in the etiology of schizophrenia and related disorders. For children with one schizophrenic parent, the risk of being diagnosed schizophrenic is 10 to 15 times greater than the population base rate of 1 percent (3, 10, 25, 26). This risk rate climbs to 44% for children with both parents diagnosed as schizophrenic (7). In addition to elevated risk for schizophrenia, between 35 and 50 percent of all children with a schizophrenic parent are likely to manifest some form of serious maladjustment as adults (11, 20, 25). Similar patterns of risk for maladjustment and psychopathology have been documented more recently for children of affectively disordered parents as well (2, 5, 35).

A question of considerable import for those interested in etiology is the extent to which these risk rates are influenced by genetic and environmental factors. It is true that there is clear evidence for a genetic component in at least some forms and/or instances of schizophrenia (10) and other types of psychopathology (27). It should be emphasized, however, that this evidence provides no basis for assuming that the majority of those diagnosed suffer from a genetic diathesis. And it provides even less of a basis for assuming that the majority of their offspring inherit such a diathesis. Certainly, an as-

*The research reported in this paper was supported by National Institute of Mental Health grant MH21145, Sheldon Weintraub, Principal Investigator. The author gratefully acknowledges the thoughtful contributions of Jill M. Hooley to an earlier version of this paper.

yet unknown percentage of high-risk offspring may possess an as-yet undemonstrated genetic diathesis for as-yet unspecified forms of malfunctioning. But to assume a priori that this is the case is to risk constraining and/or bringing premature closure to potentially important environmental lines of inquiry.

Beginning most notably with the seminal work of Mednick and Schulsinger (14), the offspring of psychiatrically ill parents have been the focus of a growing number of prospective, longitudinal studies. These efforts share in common the goal of identifying personal and environmental characteristics that discriminate those who are eventually diagnosed as having a major psychiatric disorder—or suffer other forms of maladjustment—from those who are not. It has been estimated that approximately 15 of these so-called high-risk projects have spent in excess of $11.5 million during the past two decades through their efforts to document ongoing patterns of development among high-risk offspring (31).

The first two decades of high-risk research have yielded a wealth of descriptive information about the characteristics of children with disordered parents across a wide range of variables, including measures of cognitive (12, 18, 26), attentional (8, 17), academic (23, 24), social (33, 34), and neurological functioning (9). In addition, much has been learned about patterns of family interaction within the families of disturbed parents (35, 36) and disturbed children (22). In general, these studies have consistently confirmed the initial expectations of researchers. Among the high risk for schizophrenia projects, for example, children of schizophrenic parents have been found to fare less well than the children of normal-control families in many domains of functioning. When appropriate control groups have been employed, however, similar patterns of deviance have been found among the offspring of affectively disordered parents on many of these same measures (13). Thus, most of the deviance documented thus far among children of disturbed parents appears *not* to be specific to any particular diagnostic category. Instead, it is more appropriately attributable at this stage to as-yet unknown factors associated with having a psychiatrically ill parent.

Cross-sectional comparisons of high-risk and control samples that characterize much of the high-risk literature to date have been essential in highlighting characteristic differences across sample groups on a wide range of outcome variables. Group comparisons are nonetheless inherently limited in their ability to address and pursue the very questions they raise concerning paths of influence among variables that might predict and explain differences in adjustment among high-risk offspring. Thus, the high-risk studies *have* been successful in yielding descriptive portraits of the functioning deficits, adjustment levels, and family characteristics of children at risk; but they have been considerably less successful in gaining theoretical distance from the world view that bad things tend to go together. It is clear, however, that this state of affairs reflects less on the quality of data generated by the high-risk studies than it does on the kinds of questions asked of the available data.

The challenge that lies ahead for high-risk researchers—and more generally for researchers interested in the relationship between family factors and psychopathology—is one of proceeding from the level of diagnostic group differences in children's adjustment to analyses of individual differences within and across groups that may account for the striking degree of heterogeneity often found. This will require *inter alia* the adoption of conceptual frameworks that can facilitate the formulation of hypotheses and provide guidance in the interpretation of research findings.

The Diathesis-Stress Model

Despite the diversity of theoretical orientations represented among the high-risk projects, most researchers characterize themselves as working within a common diathesis-stress framework that acknowledges, in principle, the roles of both heredity and environment in the development of psychopathology. This diathesis-stress (15, 25) or vulnerability (37) model holds that individuals may inherit and/or acquire trait-like deviations or vulnerabilities that mediate their risk for eventual onset of psychopathology. These vulnerabilities constitute an individual's diathesis, and are conceptualized broadly as characteristics of functioning that lower his or her threshold of susceptibility to environmental stressors that may subsequently trigger the onset of maladjustment and/or psychopathology.

Thus, the vulnerability model assigns a dual role to stress. Certain environmental stressors may have a *formative* influence on individuals by increasing their vulnerability to a disorder. Others may have a *precipitating* influence by triggering the actual onset of an episode. As Spring and Coons (30) recently pointed out in a discussion of schizophrenia, it is possible for individuals either to inherit or acquire certain vulnerabilities to psychopathology, yet still not succumb to an episode if they are not subjected to the eliciting stressors. Other individuals, according to the general model, may possess no known vulnerability to a disorder and yet may still succumb to an episode if the eliciting stressors are of sufficient magnitude.

Beyond these general postulates, the diathesis-stress model of psychopathology—and more generally, of maladjustment—leaves open a host of more specific questions concerning 1) the domains of functioning in which vulnerabilities to particular disorders may be manifest, 2) the types of stressors that might mutually or differentially influence one's vulnerability to and eventual onset of disorder(s), 3) whether vulnerabilities should be conceptualized as dichotomous or continuous variables, 4) how distal environmental events might influence or translate into an increase in one's vulnerability, and 5) the specific processes through which vulnerabilities might interact with subsequent stressors to influence the onset of a disorder. In short, the diathesis-stress model itself yields no conclusions about the development of maladjustment and psychopathology. Instead, it provides an important framework for the formulation of research questions, and at the same time provides a conceptual structure within which the meaning and significance of research findings can be evaluated.

Assessing Patient-Related Stress

Formal psychiatric diagnoses such as schizophrenia, major depression, and bipolar disorder by themselves convey only limited information about the salient characteristics of a patient's disorder (for example, history, approximate age of onset, duration and severity of episodes, and quality of inter-episodic adjustment). From an environmental perspective, however, each of these factors is of potential relevance to assessments of the degree of patient-related stress created within the family. Disturbed parents—even within a given diagnostic category—may show considerable variation in the nature and severity of their symptoms during episodes, creating different levels of family disruption and discord prior to and in the wake of psychiatric hospitalization. Disturbed parents also differ in the chronicity of their illnesses, as assessed by the extent to which their trajectories are characterized by improvement, deterioration, and/or turbulence over time. For some, an illness may result in a single hospitalization of short duration with more or less full recovery. For others, there may be extended periods of normal or near-normal functioning, with perhaps two or three hospitalizations across a lifetime. Still others may suffer frequent and lengthy hospitalizations, and show poor levels of inter-episodic adjustment. A focus on the chronic and episodic characteristics of psychiatric disorders may thus be of central importance to any analysis of the stressors to which high-risk children are exposed. In addition, such a focus holds considerable potential for addressing important questions of individual differences in children's adjustment levels.

The present study is one component in a series of analyses designed to examine the heuristic value of distinguishing between chronic versus episodic sources of patient-related stress in the lives of high-risk children. In particular, this study seeks to determine whether it is a patient's hospitalization history and its concurrent correlates (for example, symptoms, episodic role functioning impairment), or baseline levels of functioning between episodes—or both—that exact a toll on families and offspring. The analysis first examines the relation between these sources of stress and both the childhood and young-adulthood adjustment levels of high-risk offspring. Following this, the contributions of these sources of patient-related stress to descriptions of early family life provided by the offspring and their non-diagnosed parents are examined.

Method

Subjects

Families in the present study are participants in the Stony Brook High-Risk Project (16), a prospective, longitudinal study of children at risk for schizophrenia and related disorders. All patients with school-aged children who had been recently admitted to one of four psychiatric hospitals in Suffolk County, Long Island, and whose primary diagnosis was not one of alcoholism, drug abuse, or central nervous system impairment were considered eligible to participate. Diagnosis was based on interview data obtained from the Current and Past Psychopathology Scales (CAPPS; 6); an abbreviated version of the MMPI (12); structured interviews with both patient and spouse; and a review of available hospital case-history records. Each case was independently evaluated by two of three experienced diagnosticians, and diagnoses were assigned on the basis of criteria that closely approximate the Research Diagnostic Criteria (RDC; 28) and those of DSM-III (1). Diagnostic agreement was high, with kappas ranging from .92 (unipolar depression, bipolar disorder) to .94 (schizophrenia). The present analyses focus on data collected from 274 (75%) of 365 target offspring from the original sample who have reached their eighteenth birthdays. The remaining 91 offspring who are at least age eighteen and who have not yet been assessed include 44 subjects (13%) who are currently in the process of being assessed, 21 subjects (6%) who refused to participate further, and 21 subjects (6%) whose whereabouts could not be determined. An additional 11 subjects were dropped from the present analyses because complete information on the hospitalization histories of their patient-parents was not available. The 263 target offspring for whom complete assessments are available include 148 females (66%) and 115 males (44%) from 107 families. Table 1 presents a breakdown of these offspring by their sex and the diagnostic status of their ill parent.

TABLE 1

Target Offspring (Young-Adults) by Sex and Diagnosis of Patient-Parent

	Diagnosis of Patient-Parent[a]				
Sex of Offspring	**Schizophrenic**	**Unipolar[b]**	**Bipolar[c]**	**Other**	
Male	31	43	34	7	115
	(53)	(43)	(45)	(25)	(44)
Female	27	58	42	21	148
	(47)	(57)	(55)	(75)	(56)
Totals	58	101	76	28	263

[a]Number in parentheses denote column percentages.

[b]Five offspring were excluded from the main analyses because hospitalization information for their patient-parents was not obtainable.

[c]Six offspring were excluded from the main analyses because hospitalization information for their patient-parents was not obtainable.

Measures

Childhood Adjustment

Measures of peer- and teacher-rated adjustment levels in the high-risk offspring were assessed at the outset of the project. At this time, the majority of the children were in elementary school. To protect the confidentiality of target children and families, identities of specific children chosen for assessment were concealed from teachers, school personnel, and classmates. As a further safeguard, testing was conducted as a class activity; all of the same-sex classmates of each target child were assessed both by teachers and classmates.

Teacher Ratings: Teacher ratings were obtained from administration of the Devereux Elementary School Behavior Rating Scale (DESB; 29). The DESB consists of 47 behavior items that are rated by the teacher using a 5- or 7-point rating scale. The DESB has been demonstrated to have impressive test-retest reliability and high levels of interrater agreement between teachers and teacher-aides. In addition, the DESB has been shown to discriminate well among groups of problem children. In an effort to reduce the standard DESB scales to a manageable and interpretable set of variables, we conducted a series of cluster analyses. These analyses yielded four scales: aggression-disruptiveness, cognitive competence, social competence, and achievement anxiety (for complete details, see 33).

Peer Ratings: The Pupil Evaluation Inventory (PEI; 19), was used to obtain peer ratings of the children. This inventory consists of an item-by-peer matrix in which descriptions appear as rows and the names of children in the class appear as columns. The protocol requires each child in a class to check the name of each other child that he or she believes to be described by each item. The PEI consists of 34 items that assess the dimensions of: aggression and/or disruptiveness, unhappiness and/or withdrawal, and likability and social competence. The PEI has satisfactory (split-half) internal consistency. Acceptable levels of interrater agreement between males and females have also been demonstrated (33).

Young-Adulthood Adjustment

Efforts were made to contact all target offspring from the original sample for extensive clinical interviews after they had reached age eighteen (approximately 11 years following the elementary school assessments). The present analyses are based on a subset of data available from this assessment battery, including indices of social and occupational functioning as well as personality profiles of the offspring.

Social and Occupational Functioning: All assessments began with a semistructured interview of current functioning. On the basis of information obtained from this interview, all subjects were then assigned scores ranging from 1 (high) to 5 (low) on the following eight scales: occupational performance, occupational stability, goal orientation and aspirations, goal-directed behaviors, academic high school/college performance, nonacademic high school/college performance, friendship pattern, and sexual adjustment.

Summary scores for each domain of functioning were then analyzed in the service of generating a single, continuous measure of current young-adulthood adjustment. When assessed as a single scale, these eight summary scores yielded an alpha reliability of .80, with a mean (corrected) item-to-scale correlation of .52. Interrater agreement for each summary score was assessed through comparisons of the interviewers' ratings with those of independent raters who had access to interview summary-transcripts. An analysis of agreement between the original and independent raters yielded an average agreement coefficient of .81 across the scale's eight items.

Retrospective Descriptions of Early Family Life: During the assessment interview, all subjects also completed a 92-item Q-sort describing their home environments in early childhood. This environmental Q-sort (EQ), developed by Block (4), includes descriptions of the subject's mother, father, and family environment with respect to characteristic values, attitudes, and behaviors. Items are printed on separate cards; the subject arranges the cards in order of saliency for his or her recollection of early home life. Descriptions that are considered most characteristic are assigned low scores; those considered least characteristic are assigned high scores. For present purposes, the EQ items for each subject were clustered on the basis of rational and empirical considerations to yield the following nine scales: stability of early home life, warmth of early family environment, socialization orientation of family practices, and separate scales for mother and father describing emotional warmth, role-modeling orientation, psychopathology, and restrictiveness. Alpha reliabilities for the scales ranged from .60 to .80.

Independent Measures

Patient Premorbid Functioning

Premorbid functioning of patient-parents was assessed by compositing the following ratings from the past history section of the CAPPS: adolescent friendship pattern, highest school grade, highest occupational level achieved, sexual adjustment, highest level of sexual adjustment, adult friendship pattern, and I. Q. estimate. These items, which collectively yield a summary assessment of the patient-parents' levels of functioning prior to first diagnosis, were analyzed to create a single summary measure of the patient's level of premorbid functioning. Reliability analysis yielded a coefficient alpha of .63.

Table 2 presents the mean levels of premorbid functioning according to diagnosis of patient-parent. As indicated, a one-way analysis of variance yielded a significant overall effect for diagnosis ($F\,[3,150]=8.24$, $p<.01$);

TABLE 2

Patient-Parent Illness Characteristics by Diagnosis

	Patient-Parent Diagnosis				
Illness Characteristics	**Schizophrenic**	**Unipolar**	**Bipolar**	**Other**	
Premorbid functioning[a]	3.83 (.71)	3.51 (.70)	3.14 (.74)	3.66 (.59)	n = 87
Total days in hospital[b]	210 (282)	149 (213)	187 (202)	98 (84)	n = 107
Number of hospitalizations[c]	4.00 (4.24)	2.56 (2.07)	3.79 (2.33)	2.33 (1.22)	n = 107

[a] $F\,[3,84]$, $p>.05$; subsequent Scheffe tests revealed that bipolar patient-parents had significantly higher levels of premorbid functioning than schizophrenics ($p<.05$).

[b] $F\,[3,104]=.51$, $p>.1$

[c] $F\,[3,104]=2.26$, $p=.08$

bipolar patients showed significantly higher levels of premorbid functioning than schizophrenics ($p < .05$).

In the analyses that follow, this composite measure of premorbid functioning is employed as an indirect index of the patients' likely levels of baseline functioning between episodes of hospitalization.

Patient Hospitalization History

Patients' hospitalization histories are represented in the present analyses by two related variables that reflect the total number of days spent in hospital across the patients' lifetimes, and the total number of hospitalizations. Table 2 presents a breakdown of number of days in hospital and total number of hospitalizations by diagnosis of the patient-parent. As indicated, there were no overall differences across these groups for either total number of hospitalizations or total days in hospital.

Spouse Ratings of Patient and Family

Upon entry into the project, patients and their spouses were interviewed separately using the family evaluation form (FEF; 32). The FEF elicits the interviewee's assessments of his or her spouse as well as characteristics of the family as a whole. Seven scales based on the FEF are used in the present analyses: marital disruption, lack of family cohesiveness, patient-related family disruption, patient-related child disruption, patient-homemaker role disruption, patient's overall role impairment, and burden of patient on family.

Results

Patient-Related Stress and Offspring Adjustment

Childhood

A primary focus of the present study concerns the extent to which chronic and episodic sources of stress created by the patient-parent are related to measures of the children's adjustment. Because the peer and teacher ratings are correlated between and among themselves, a multivariate multiple regression analysis was first conducted to establish the presence of a significant overall relationship between sets of independent and dependent variables. Previous analyses have demonstrated age effects for several of these childhood adjustment measures; age at time of assessment was therefore entered as a first block in each analysis, followed by the two patient-parent hospitalization history variables and the composite measure of patient premorbid functioning. The results of each analysis are presented in Table 3.

TABLE 3

Patient-Related Stress and Childhood Adjustment
(F-Values for Partial Regression Coefficients)

	Sources of Patient-Related Stress		
	Step 1 Age at Assessment	**Step 2 Premorbid Functioning**	**Step 3 Hospitalization History**
Childhood Adjustment			
Peer ratings (n = 172)			
Aggression	.38	5.77**	3.13*
Withdrawal	2.97	.96	.11
Social competence	4.04*	5.25*	.14
Teacher ratings (n = 248)			
Aggression	.79	1.59	1.38
Cognitive Competence	1.40	5.82**	.86
Social competence	21.86**	16.67**	1.34
Young Adulthood Adjustment (n = 217)			
Social/occupational		5.13**	1.31

*$p < .05$
**$p < .01$

As indicated, the analyses yielded a significant main effect for premorbid functioning on two of the three peer-rated adjustment measures and on two of the three teacher-rated adjustment measures. In particular, patient-parent levels of premorbid functioning were significantly related to peer-rated aggression, peer-rated social competence, teacher-rated cognitive competence, and teacher-rated social competence. Patient-parent premorbid functioning was not, however, related to either peer-rated withdrawal or teacher-rated aggression.

Variables representing number of days in hospital and number of hospitalizations were significantly associated with only one of the six children's adjustment measures: specifically, peer-rated aggression. The hospitalization variables were not related to peer-rated social competence, or to teacher-rated aggression, social competence, or cognitive competence. Parallel sets of regression analyses undertaken separately for males and females indicated no significant differences among the variables of interest according to sex of child.

Young-Adulthood

The previous analysis demonstrated a relatively consistent relationship between patients' levels of premorbid functioning and their children's early adjustment. Hospitalization history variables, on the other hand, contributed significantly to only peer-rated aggression. Nonetheless, the possibility remained that the effects of a parent's hospitalization pattern are cumulative, and emerge as a significant factor only later in the child's development. To test this possibility, the adjustment scores of the young-adult sample were regressed on the same variables representing patient premorbid functioning and hospitalization history. As the results presented in Table 3 indicate, patient-parent premorbid functioning was again significantly related to offspring young-adulthood adjustment. The variables representing total days in hospital and number of hospitalizations, however, were not significantly related to young-adulthood adjustment.

Patient-Related Stress and Family Environment

The analyses summarized above indicate a consistent relationship between patients' premorbid functioning and the social adjustment of their offspring in both early childhood and young adulthood. The analyses also revealed that patient hospitalization histories are relatively weakly related to childhood adjustment, and that the association disappears by young adulthood. This raises an interesting question about whether the stressors associated with patients' episodic illnesses and hospitalizations have a measurable impact on their families. To examine this question, the retrospective descriptions of early home life (EQ scales) provided by the offspring were entered into a series of hierarchical regression equations, again using patient premorbid functioning and hospitalization history as predictors. Because the EQ scales are themselves intercorrelated, these analyses were preceded by a multivariate multiple regression analysis; the analysis confirmed an overall significant relationship between the sets of independent and dependent variables.

For descriptive purposes, separate regression analyses were next conducted for each of the three composite scales, representing items concerning mother, father, and home. As in earlier analyses, each composite scale was regressed on the summary measures of patient premorbid functioning and hospitalization history.

The results presented in Table 4 indicate that both sources of patient

TABLE 4

Patient-Related Stress and Family Environment as Rated by Offspring (F Values for Partial Regression Coefficients)

	Step 1 Premorbid Functioning	Step 2 Hospitalization History
EQ Composite Scales (n = 150)		
Mother	15.85**	7.07**
Father	5.56*	5.50**
Home	11.70**	5.26*

*$p < .05$
**$p < .01$

stress were significantly and independently related to offspring descriptions of early home life. In particular, patient-parent levels of premorbid functioning were significantly related to their offsprings' composite descriptions of mother, father, and home. Similarly, patient-parent hospitalization histories were significantly and *independently* related to assessments of mother, father, and home, while controlling for the effects of premorbid functioning.

In summary, the offspring of patient-parents with relatively poor levels of premorbid functioning and/or with more chronic patterns of hospitalization described their mothers, fathers, and early home lives more negatively than offspring of patients with higher levels of premorbid functioning and/or with less chronic hospitalization histories.

Retrospective Bias

Because the offspring EQ ratings of early home life are retrospective accounts, the possibility that their ratings were influenced by current levels of adjustment was considered. The details of these analyses are reported elsewhere (21). In a series of extreme-group *t*-tests undertaken to address the retrospective bias question, offspring with the 20% highest and 20% lowest levels of current adjustment were compared on each of the EQ scales. Not only were there no significant differences between the groups on any of the eleven EQ scales, but inspection of the group means revealed no consistent trend for the more poorly adjusted offspring to rate their parents or early home lives more negatively than offspring who were relatively well adjusted ($p > .1$ for all comparisons).

For comparison purposes, target offspring were re-grouped according to the diagnoses of their patient-parents, and a one-way analysis of variance was conducted on each EQ scale. No significant differences were found for any of the eleven EQ scales according to diagnosis of patient-parent. Moreover, an inspection of group means across the scales revealed no overall trend for the offspring of any diagnostic group to rate their parents and/or early home lives consistently more positively or negatively than the offspring of any other diagnostic group.

In a final effort to address the question of retrospective bias, the EQ ratings of the offspring were compared with analogous ratings of family provided by their nondiagnosed parents when they entered the study approximately eleven years earlier. Most of the resulting correlations were of modest magnitude (.22 to .53)—nonetheless, an impressive range given that these relationships are based on reports of different aspects of patient and family functioning, from different sources (that is, parent and offspring), with understandably different perspectives, and over a period averaging eleven years. Particularly noteworthy were the significant correlations between spouse ratings of patients' burden on the family and offspring ratings of home stability, $r\ (69) = .39$, $p > .01$; patient warmth, $r\ (69) = -.23$, $p < .05$; role functioning, $r\ (69) = .33$, $p < .01$; and restrictiveness, $r\ (69) = .33$, $p < .01$.

Discussion

The present study provides support for the heuristic value of distinguishing between chronic and episodic patient-related stress in the lives of high-risk offspring. Patient-parent levels of premorbid functioning were significantly related to the peer- and teacher-rated adjustment of their offspring in early childhood, as well as their social and occupational adjustment in young-adulthood. Patient-parents' hospitalization histories, in contrast, were relatively weakly related to the early childhood adjustment measures, and were unrelated to young-adulthood adjustment.

When evaluated in isolation, these data suggest that the episodic stresses associated with parental bouts of psychiatric illness and hospitalization have only a weak and transient influence on the adjustment of their children. When these data are interpreted in the context of the retrospective descriptions of early home life provided by the offspring, however, a somewhat different picture emerges. Both the patients' levels of premorbid functioning and their hospitalization histories were significantly and independently related to the early home life descriptions of their offspring. Thus, it appears that episodic stress associated with multiple hospitalizations may have an *indirect* effect on the adjustment of high-risk offspring through its influence on various aspects of family life. Whether this influence can be isolated and/or traced from early childhood through young adulthood is an important issue currently being addressed in a related study on the same sample.

It is worthy of note that the adjustment of offspring did not differ significantly according to the diagnostic categories of their patient-parents on any of the retrospective EQ descriptions of mother, father, or early home life. These results are consistent with the general failure of researchers to find reliable differences in the adjustment levels of high-risk offspring according to diagnosis of patient-parent. Rather, the early home-life ratings provided by the offspring seemed to be influenced by two factors that cut across formal DSM-III diagnosis, namely, episodic stress associated with multiple hospitalizations, and the more chronic stress of living with a patient-parent with poorer levels of functioning *between* episodes of hospitalization.

Despite the encouraging results of this study, a few notes of caution are in order. First, the present analyses employed an indirect measure of the patients' levels of functioning between episodes. These analyses were designed primarily to examine the heuristic value of discriminating between chronic and episodic sources of patient-related stress; it was therefore necessary to employ a measure of inter-episodic functioning that was independent of the patients' levels of functioning when they entered the project during an episode. Future analyses will triangulate these results with more detailed and direct measures of inter-episodic functioning assessed during subsequent phases of the study. Similarly, episodic stress was indexed by frequency and duration of hospitalizations. An obvious question that remains unanswered by these data concerns exactly what it is about patient hospitalization history that accounts for its significant association with spouse and offspring ratings of family environment. Again, subsequent analyses will focus on patient symptom profiles surrounding hospitalizations in an effort to determine whether it is hospitalizations *per se* and the disruptions they cause within the family, or the specific symptom patterns surrounding hospitalizations that account for this association. In a related vein, we are currently taking advantage of the tremendous within-family variability among children in our sample by examining the timing and overall levels of their exposure to patient-parent hospitalization history. Within many of our target families there are children who have been exposed to multiple patient-parent hospitalizations since birth, whereas younger siblings have been largely spared this exposure. Comparisons of offspring within the same family on age-corrected measures of adjustment and EQ ratings hold considerable potential for isolating specific influences associated with exposure to multiple patient-parent hospitalizations.

Despite the limitations of this study, we are nonetheless encouraged in our efforts to document specific types of stressors associated with having a psychiatrically ill parent. Ultimately, analyses such as these may allow us to exploit the concept of environmental stress at increasingly more specific levels of analysis that can both contribute to and benefit from direct studies of family interaction.

REFERENCES

1. American Psychiatric Association. *Diagnostic and statistical manual of mental disorders* (3rd ed.). Washington DC: American Psychiatric Association, 1980.

2. Billings, A. G., & Moos, R. H. Comparisons of depressed and nondepressed parents: A social and environmental perspective. *Journal of Abnormal Psychology 11*: 463–485, 1983.

3. Bleuler, M. *The schizophrenic disorders: Long-term patients and family studies* (translated by S. M. Clemens). New Haven: Yale University Press, 1978.

4. Block, J. H. *The Q-Sort method in personality assessment and psychiatric research.* Springfield IL: Charles C. Thomas, 1961.

5. Cytryn, L., McKnew, D. H., Bartko, J. J., Lamour, M., & Hamovit, J. *Journal of the American Academy of Child Psychiatry 21*: 389–391, 1982.

6. Endicott, J., & Spitzer, R. L. Current and past psychopathology scales (CAPPS): Rationale, reliability, and validity. *Archives of General Psychiatry 27*: 678–687, 1972.

7. Erlenmeyer-Kimling, L. Studies on the offspring of two schizophrenic parents. In D. Rosenthal & S. S. Kety (eds.), *The transmission of schizophrenia.* Oxford: Pergamon Press, 1968.

8. ______, & Cornblatt, B. Attentional measures in a study of children at high-risk for schizophrenia. In L. C. Wynne, R. L. Cromwell, & S. Matthysse (eds.), *The nature of schizophrenia: New approaches to research and treatment.* New York: John Wiley & Sons, 1978.

9. Friedman, D., Erlenmeyer-Kimling, L., & Vaughn, H. G. Event-related potential (ERP) methodology in high-risk research. In N. F. Watt, E. J. Anthony, L. C. Wynne, & J. E. Rolf (eds.), *Children at risk for schizophrenia: A longitudinal perspective.* Cambridge: Cambridge University Press, 1984.

10. Gottesman, I. I., & Shields, J. *Schizophrenia and genetics: A twin study vantage point.* New York: Academic Press, 1972.

11. Heston, L. L. Psychiatric disorders in foster-home reared children of schizophrenic mothers. *British Journal of Psychiatry 112*: 819–825, 1966.

12. Kincannon, J. C. Prediction of the standard MMPI scale scores from 71 items: The Mini-Mult. *Journal of Consulting and Clinical Psychology 32*: 319–325, 1968.

13. Lewine, R. R. J. Stalking the schizophrenia marker: Evidence for a general vulnerability model of psychopathology. In N. F. Watt, E. J. Anthony, L. C. Wynne, & J. E. Rolf (eds.), *Children at risk for schizophrenia: A longitudinal perspective.* Cambridge: Cambridge University Press, 1984.

14. Mednick, S. A., & Schulsinger, F. Some premorbid characteristics related to break-

down in children with schizophrenic mothers. *Journal of Psychiatric Research 6* (Suppl. 1): 354–362, 1968. Reprinted in D. Rosenthal and S. Kety (eds.), *The transmission of schizophrenia*. Oxford: Pergamon Press, 1968.

15. Meehl, P. E. Schizotaxia, schizotypy, schizophrenia. *American Psychologist 17*: 827–838, 1962.

16. Neale, J. M., & Weintraub, S. Children vulnerable to psychopathology: The Stony Brook High-Risk Project. *Journal of Abnormal Child Psychology 3*: 95–113, 1975.

17. ______, Winters, K. C., & Weintraub, S. Information processing deficits in children at high risk for schizophrenia. In N. F. Watt, E. J. Anthony, L. C. Wynne, & J. E. Rolf (eds.), *Children at risk for schizophrenia: A longitudinal perspective* Cambridge: Cambridge University Press, 1984.

18. Oltmanns, T. F., Weintraub, S., Stone, A. A., & Neale, J. M. Cognitive slippage in children vulnerable to schizophrenia. *Journal of Abnormal Child Psychology 6*: 237–245, 1978.

19. Pekarik, E., Prinz, R., Liebert, D., Weintraub, S., & Neale, J. M. The pupil evaluation inventory. *Journal of Abnormal Child Psychology 4*: 83–97, 1976.

20. Reisby, N. Psychosis in children of schizophrenic mothers. *Acta Psychiatrica Scandanavica 43*: 8–20, 1967.

21. Richters, J. E., & Hooley, J. M. Psychopathology and family life: A prospective look at retrospective accounts, manuscript in preparation.

22. Rodnick, E. H., Goldstein, M. J., Lewis, J. M., & Doane, J. A. Parental communication style, affect, and role as precursors of offspring schizophrenia-spectrum disorders. In N. F. Watt, E. J. Anthony, L. C. Wynne, & J. E. Rolf (eds.), *Children at risk for schizophrenia: A longitudinal perspective*. Cambridge: Cambridge University Press, 1984.

23. Rolf, J. E. The social and academic competence of children vulnerable to schizophrenia and other behavior pathologies. *Journal of Psychology 80*: 225–243, 1972.

24. ______, & Garmezy, N. The school performance of children vulnerable to behavior pathology. In D. F. Ricks, A. Thomas, & M. Roff (eds.), *Life history research in psychopathology* (Vol. 3). Minneapolis: University of Minnesota Press, 1974.

25. Rosenthal, D. *Genetic theory and abnormal behavior*. New York: McGraw-Hill, 1970.

26. Sameroff, A. J., & Zax, M. In search of schizophrenia: Young offspring of schizophrenic women. In L. C. Wynne, R. L. Cromwell, & S. Matthysse (eds.), *The nature of schizophrenia: New approaches to research and treatment*. New York: John Wiley & Sons, 1978.

27. Slater, E., & Cowie, V. *The genetics of mental disorders*. London: Oxford University Press, 1971.

28. Spitzer, R. L., Endicott, J., & Robins, E. Research diagnostic criteria: Rationale and reliability. *Archives of General Psychiatry 35*: 773–782, 1978.

29. Spivack, G. S., & Swift, M. *The Devereux Elementary School Behavior Rating Scale Manual*. Devon PA: Devereux Foundation, 1967.

30. Spring, B., & Coons, H. Stress as a precursor of schizophrenia. In R. W. J. Neufeld (ed.), *Psychological stress and psychopathology*. New York: McGraw-Hill, 1982.

31. Watt, N. F. In a nutshell: The first two decades of high-risk research in schizophrenia. In N. F. Watt, E. J. Anthony, L. C. Wynne, & J. E. Rolf (eds.), *Children at risk for schizophrenia: A longitudinal perspective*. Cambridge: Cambridge University Press, 1984.

32. Weintraub, S., & Neale, J. M. The Stony Brook High-Risk Project. In B. Feingold & C. Bank (eds.), *Developmental disabilities of early childhood*. Springfield IL: Charles C. Thomas, 1978.

33. ______, & Neale, J. M. The Stony Brook High-Risk Project. In N. F. Watt, E. J. Anthony, L. C. Wynne, & J. E. Rolf (eds.), *Children at risk for schizophrenia: A longitudinal perspective*. Cambridge: Cambridge University Press, 1984.

34. ______, Prinz, R., & Neale, J. M. Peer evaluations of the competence of children vulnerable to psychopathology. *Journal of Abnormal Child Psychology 4*: 461–473, 1978.

35. Weissman, M. M., Prusoff, B. A., Gammon, G. D., Merikangas, K. R., Leckman, J. F., & Kidd, K. K. Psychopathology in the children (ages 6–18) of depressed and normal parents. *Journal of the Academy of Child Psychiatry 23*: 79–84, 1984.

36. Wynne, L. C., Singer, M. T., Bartko, J. J., & Toohey, M. L. Schizophrenics and their families: Research on parental communication. In J. M. Tanner (ed.), *Developments in psychiatric research*. London: Hodder & Stoughton, 1977.

37. Zubin, J., & Spring, B. Vulnerability—A new view of schizophrenia. *Journal of Abnormal Psychology 86*: 103–126, 1978.

5

THE INTERACTION BETWEEN FAMILY TRANSACTIONS AND INDIVIDUAL DIFFERENCES IN THE ATTENTIONAL PROCESSES OF SCHIZOPHRENIC PATIENTS

ROBERT F. ASARNOW
University of California, Los Angeles

THE participants at this conference have described how family transactions influence the development and course of psychiatric disorders. Quite naturally, the robustness and generality of the effects of particular family transaction variables have been emphasized. In my discussion, however, I raise the possibility that the effects of certain family transaction variables on the development and course of schizophrenic disorders can be moderated by a special class of individual difference traits. These traits are individual differences in controlled attentional processes, which appear to index a predisposition toward schizophrenic disorder.

The concept that people vary in their response to the same environmental variable has been discussed under the rubric of "person by situation interactions" in personality psychology (see 29 for a review) and "transactional models of development" in developmental psychology (see 33 for a review). In the field of psychopathology, this concept is central to epigenetic models of the development of psychopathology. Epigenesis has been defined by Singer and Wynne (35) as "interchanges or transactions at each developmental phase [that] build upon the outcome of earlier transactions. This means that constitutional and experiential influences recombine in each developmental phase to create new biologic and behavioral potentialities which then help determine the next phase" (p. 208). The epigenetic point of view "implies feedback loops in which the individual modifies the same environment that continues to be formative of his personal qualities over time" (45, p. 704).

While there appears to be a general sympathy for models of schizophrenic disorder that emphasize the interaction of organismic and environmental variables, this sympathy has rarely been translated into rigorous examination of how organismic and environmental variables interact to determine the onset and course of schizophrenic disorders. Much current psychiatric research appears to be characterized by a search for immutable, toxic biological or environmental factors that can, in isolation from each other, account for the development and/or course of schizophrenia. One reason for this state of affairs is that only recently have traits in schizophrenic individuals been identified which fit the definition of individual difference traits. Since the astronomer Bessel first measured the "personal equation" in 1816, individual difference traits have been defined as stable characteristics that predict important differences between individuals. During the last fifteen years, evidence has accumulated that impairments in controlled attentional processes may be an important individual difference trait in schizophrenic individuals. As will be detailed below, these impairments appear to index a vulnerability or predisposition to develop a schizophrenic disorder. These impairments lie at the interface between the biological vulnerability to schizophrenic disorder and the characteristic pattern of social interactions associated with the disorder. As a consequence, impairments in controlled attentional processes seem particularly likely to moderate the effect of social transactions on some schizophrenic individuals.

In the next section I briefly review the evidence indicating that one measure of controlled attentional processes, a partial report span of apprehension task, may measure an important individual difference trait in schizophrenic individuals. I then summarize the results of a recently completed study that suggests important links between the controlled attentional processes tapped by partial report span of apprehension tasks and certain family transaction variables that have been shown by participants at this conference to affect the course of schizophrenic disorder.

The Span of Apprehension Task as an Index of Vulnerability to Schizophrenic Disorder

Over the past fifteen years there has been a vigorous search for measures of attention that show sensitivity to schizophrenic impairment over wide variations in the clinical state we now know is characteristic of this disorder (12, 47,48). This search was impelled by the belief (see 3, 13, 48) that measures which detect stable impairments in individuals who share the trait of vulnerability to schizophrenic disorder, but who are in different clinical states at the time of testing, are not merely reflecting a clinical state but may be tapping the trait of vulnerability to schizophrenic disorder. Measures of attention have been widely used because of the prominence of attentional problems in the phenomenology of schizophrenia (see 11, 17, 21) and the sensitivity of psychological laboratory attentional measures to schizophrenic impairment (see 18, 23, 42 for reviews). A number of attention-demanding tasks, including, for example, continuous performance tests (26, 31, 32, 44), a digit span distractibility task (28), dichotic listening tasks (38), and both simple (30, 39) and cross-modal (41) reaction-time tasks have been shown to detect dysfunction in schizophrenic patients and in nonpsychotic individuals who are statistically at risk for developing a schizophrenic disorder, such as the children of schizophrenic parents (see 1, 2, 25, 27 for reviews). I shall illustrate this line of research by reviewing a series of studies conducted to determine if a partial report span of apprehension task detects dysfunction in schizophrenic patients across wide variations in clinical state and in individuals thought to be at risk for schizophrenic disorder.

The forced choice, partial report span of apprehension task we used in the studies below was originally developed (15, 36) to measure the amount of information people can extract from briefly presented (50 milliseconds) visual displays. This task provides an index of the efficiency of visual attentional processes. This task requires subjects to indicate which of two predesignated target letters are present in arrays of tachistoscopically presented letters. In a seminal series of studies, Neale and his colleagues (24) showed that schizophrenic patients had a smaller span of apprehension than did normal controls and nonpsychotic psychiatric patients (22).

To determine whether the partial report span of apprehension task taps vulnerability to schizophrenic disorder, we turned to the study of children at risk for schizophrenia. The high-risk group were foster children whose biological mothers were schizophrenic, but whose foster parents had no history of severe psychiatric disorder. These children had never been psychotic and were, therefore, free of the effects of "stigmatization," medication, and institutionalization found in hospitalized schizophrenic patients. The high-risk group (see 8–10, 40) obtained significantly lower scores than did foster children without a family history of schizophrenic disorder and a community control group on a partial report span of apprehension task as well as on the Spokes test from the Halstead-Reitan battery and a concept formation task. A cluster analysis of scores on the battery of attention tasks indicated that only a subset of the high-risk children had impaired attentional performance. The high-risk children with impaired performance on the above task showed certain behavioral characteristics, including social isolation, difficulties with the student role, and difficulty in modulating aggression, which had been found in retrospective studies to represent the premorbid state of schizophrenia (19). They also obtained elevated scores on the schizophrenia scale of the MMPI.

If the partial report span of apprehension task is tapping vulnerability to schizophrenic disorder, it should detect dysfunction, not only in actively disturbed, schizophrenic patients and children at risk for schizophrenia, but also in schizophrenic patients during the post-psychotic stages of the disorder when there has been substantial abatement of acute schizophrenic symptomology. In an initial study (3), we found that hospitalized, acutely disturbed schizophrenics and schizophrenic outpatients in the partial recovery phase of the disorder detected significantly fewer target stimuli in the 10-letter condition of this task than did normal controls. The acute and partially recovered schizophrenics did not differ from each other. In addition, as can be seen in Figure 1A, the acute and remitted schizophrenics showed the same level and pattern of performance as the subset of children in our high-risk study. If acutely and partially recovered schizophrenic patients as well as

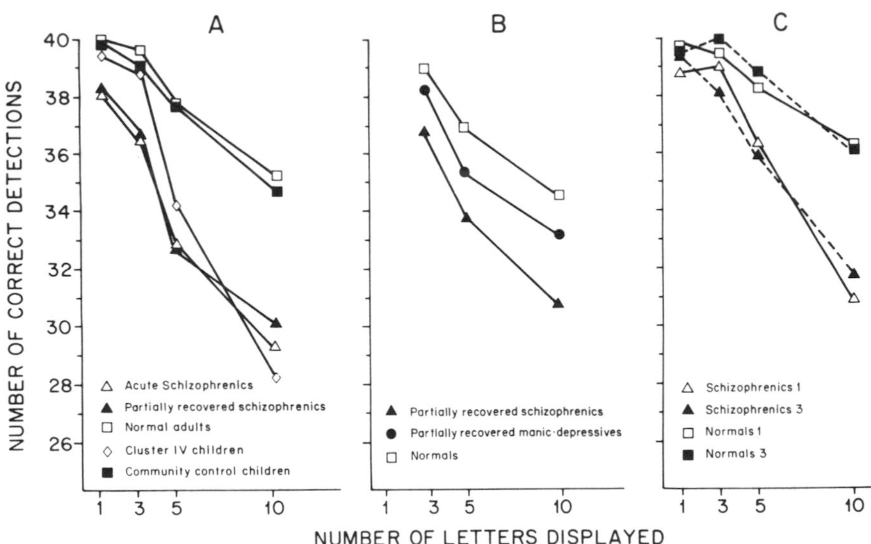

Fig. 1. Mean number of correct detections of the target stimulus as a function of the number of letters displayed for 1A: acute schizophrenics, partially recovered schizophrenics, and normal adult controls (see 3), and cluster IV (4 high-risk and 1 foster-control child) and clusters I and II combined (see 8); 1B: partially recovered schizophrenic and manic-depressive patients and normal controls (see 4); 1C: schizophrenic patients tested while acutely disturbed (session 1) and partially recovered (session 2), and normal subjects tested over the same intervals (see 5).

children at risk for schizophrenia all show deficits on the span of apprehension task (relative to normal controls) then these impairments cannot be merely reflecting a general state of disorganization, the presence of acute psychotic symptoms, or the consequences of institutionalization.

A subsequent study (4) replicated and extended these findings. A new sample of schizophrenic outpatients made significantly fewer correct detections (see Figure 1B) of the target stimuli than did a group of manic-depressive patients and normal controls on the five and ten-letter arrays of the span of apprehension task. The fact that schizophrenic patients, at least during the partial recovery phase of the disorder, could be differentiated from similarly stabilized manic-depressive patients suggests that there is some degree of diagnostic specificity for impairments on the span of apprehension task.

The preceding studies of acutely disturbed and partially recovered schizophrenic patients were cross-sectional. As a consequence, it is possible that the cohort of partially recovered, outpatient schizophrenics available for testing could have represented a subset of patients who had made the least adequate post-hospitalization adjustment and were thus available for retesting. To determine if the residual impairment found in this group might simply be a reflection of their minimal clinical recovery, we (5) conducted a longitudinal study of schizophrenic patients. Patients were tested on the span of apprehension test during inpatient hospitalization when they were acutely disturbed, and three months later as outpatients. Normal control subjects were tested over a comparable 12-week interval. Schizophrenic patients continued to show impaired performance on the span of apprehension task relative to normal controls (see Figure 1C), even though there was significant improvement in both overall clinical condition and specific aspects of thought disorder over the 12-week interval. These findings corroborated the results of the previous cross-sectional studies, indicating that the span of apprehension task is sensitive to schizophrenic dysfunction across wide variations in clinical state and, therefore, may be a marker of schizophrenia.

Another test of whether the span of apprehension task is tapping a trait associated with vulnerability to schizophrenic disorder is to determine if the task shows the temporal stability required of a measure tapping a trait. To determine if a task measures a trait, it is necessary to determine not only that the performance of a group of subjects on this task does not change over time, as we had found in the previous longitudinal study, but also that there is significant stability of individual performance over time. We observed a highly significant correlation ($r = .72$) in the span of apprehension performance of the schizophrenic patients over the 12-week period studied (5). These findings have been corroborated (6) in a recent longitudinal study of

36 chronic schizophrenic patients, in which we found significant correlations on the 10-letter array of the span of apprehension over 12-week ($r = .79$) and six-month intervals ($r = .68$).

If the span of apprehension task taps vulnerability to schizophrenia, individuals with no personal history of psychiatric disorder who show impairments on this task might be expected to manifest some of the clinical and personality traits characteristic of the schizotypal or psychosis-prone individual. This hypothesis was tested (7) by selecting subjects (from temporary employment agencies) who reported no history of psychiatric disorder and dividing them into groups with good and poor performance on the span of apprehension task. Subjects who had performed poorly on the span of apprehension task scored significantly higher on the schizophrenia scale of the MMPI, two indices of schizotypy (the schizodia and schizophrenism scales) and an index of subclinical schizophrenic thinking (the magic ideation scale; 14) than did the balance of the subjects. The poor-span group did not show generalized elevation on the MMPI, suggesting some degree of specificity for the relationship between span of apprehension performance and scores on indices of schizotypy and psychotic-like experiences. The finding that individuals without a personal history of psychiatric disorder who show impaired performance on the span of apprehension task have personality and clinical traits characteristic of schizotypy or psychosis-prone individuals provides additional support for the hypothesis that impairment on this test may tap a trait associated with vulnerability to schizophrenic disorder.

Correlates of Individual Differences on the Partial Report Span of Apprehension Task

Examination of the frequency distribution of the scores of schizophrenic patients on the 10-letter condition of the partial report span of apprehension task reveals that only a subgroup of schizophrenics are impaired on this task (5). If this task taps an important individual difference trait in schizophrenia, schizophrenic patients who show impaired performance on this task should differ in important ways from schizophrenic patients who do not show impaired performance.There are no obvious demographic or phenomenological differences between schizophrenic patients with good and poor performance on this task (4).

The results from two recent studies, however, indicate that schizophrenic patients with good and poor performance on this task differ in their response to neuroleptic treatment. The schizophrenic patients who showed the least initial change in span of apprehension performance in response to neuroleptic treatment showed the least reduction in schizophrenic thought disorder in response to *short*-term, low-dose neuroleptic treatment (20). This finding is consistent with the hypothesis (37) that neuroleptic drugs may reduce schizophrenic symptoms in some patients by enhancing certain aspects of information processing. Another recently completed study (6) provided dramatic evidence of how individual differences in performance on the partial report span of apprehension task in predicting which schizophrenic patients will benefit from *long*-term neuroleptic treatment. Schizophrenic patients with poor-span performance had a significantly lower rate of exacerbations and relapses over a two-year period when placed on 25 mg/day of Fluphenazine decanoate than schizophrenic patients with good-span performance who received the same dose of Fluphenazine. The schizophrenic patients with good-span performance receiving 25 mg/day of Fluphenazine decanoate have a greater rate of exacerbations and relapses than schizophrenic patients with good-span performance who receive 5 mg/day of Fluphenazine decanoate. It is possible that a higher dosage of neuroleptics may have a toxic effect on schizophrenic patients who do not have an information processing impairment. In contrast, when the same high dosage is given to patients with poor-span performance, it has a protective effect in forestalling relapse, particularly during the second year of treatment when most patients in the low-dose group begin to exacerbate and relapse.

Impaired performance on the partial report span of apprehension task appears to be a characteristic of schizophrenic or individuals vulnerable to schizophrenic disorder that can be detected across wide variations in clinical state. The significant correlations over intervals as long as six months indicate that individual differences on this task are stable over time. The study cited above suggests that individual differences on the span of apprehension task are associated with clinically significant differences in response to high and low doses of neuroleptic treatment. Could individual differences on this task predispose patients to respond differently to family interaction patterns?

Relation Between Individual Measures of Impaired Attention and Family Communication Deviance

A recently completed study (43) provides a critical link between studies of the attentional competence of schizophrenic patients and family transactional patterns. The same partial report span of apprehension task that was used in the studies cited above was administered to a group of young male schizophrenics and their mothers. The mothers were also administered the procedure for assessing communication deviance developed by Goldstein and his colleagues at UCLA (see Chapter 1). A statistically significant correlation was observed ($r = .55$) between the span of apprehension performance of the young male adult schizphrenics and that of their mothers. None of these mothers had a history of schizophrenic disorder. While this correlation, of course, does not tell us that there is a genetic basis for the association between the performance of the schizophrenic patient and his mother, it does suggest a familial transmission of impaired attention.

In addition, those mothers with impaired performance on the span of apprehension task had elevated scores on communication deviance (CD) factors 2 and 6. Factor 2 measures "rather serious perceptual distortions" (16), while factor 6 measures problems in integrating elements of a story. Individuals with high scores on factor 6 typically simplify complex realities by ignoring part of it (16). It is noteworthy that CD factors 2 and 6 have been used in previous research (16) to classify families as high, intermediate, or low in CD. The singular importance of factors 2 and 6 derives from their sensitivity to the subtle distortions of reality that leave the listener puzzling over whether he or she is attending to the same reality as the speaker (16). The fact that schizophrenic patients with the most impaired performance on the span of apprehension task tend to have mothers with impaired span performance and elevated scores on CD factors 2 and 6 suggest that CD factors 2 and 6 and the span of apprehension task may tap a common attentional impairment.

These data suggest that there may be two, not mutually exclusive mechanisms by which individual vulnerability measures and aspects of the family environment may interact to co-determine whether an individual develops schizophrenic disorder, and the course of the disorder once it emerges. The first mechanism is the different risks of exposure to stressful family transactions for schizophrenic patients with and without impairments in controlled attentional processes. Almost all of the schizophrenic patients with poor performance on the span of apprehension task had mothers with elevated scores on CD factors 2 and 6. Conversely, relatively few of the schizophrenic patients with good performance on the span of apprehension task had elevated scores on these two CD factors. The stressful effect on schizophrenic patients of exposure to family transactions with high loadings of CD has been emphasized in a number of presentations at this conference. It appears that patients with poor span of apprehension performance have a much greater risk of being exposed to stressful family interaction, such as communication deviance, than do patients who do not have poor-span performance. The link between the schizophrenic patient's attentional impairment and the mother's elevated scores on CD factors 2 and 6 may be that the mother's CD is an interactional manifestation of her own attentional impairments.

A second way that individual differences in the efficiency of controlled attentional processes might predispose schizophrenic individuals to respond differentially to certain family transaction patterns is that the effects of the same family transaction pattern are experienced differently by patients depending upon the integrity of their attentional processes. There is some evidence that certain skills important for the development and maintenance of social relationships make extensive demands on an individual's ability to monitor and switch between multiple sources of information. For example, studies of children's friendship formation indicate the importance of empathy, the reading of internal cues, and sensitivity to the affective reactions of others for developing successful friendships (46). Those schizophrenic patients with impaired attentional processes may be uniquely unable to respond to this variety of cues presented in real time (34).

It may be precisely those schizophrenic patients who, because of their own attentional impairments, are the most vulnerable to the effects of confusing, ambiguous, and affectively laden family transactions, are the individuals most likely to be exposed to such transactions. Exposure to these transactional stresses may further impair the patient's attentional functioning and reduce the patient's ability to cope with these stressful transactions. This process, at least in those forms of schizophrenia characterized by the presence of attentional impairments in schizophrenic patients and their mothers, is consistent with epigenetic models of schizophrenia.

The intriguing findings from the study of Wagener and her colleagues (43) underscores the importance of conducting process-oriented studies to elucidate rigorously the ways in which individual difference traits in schizophrenic individuals, such as measures of attention processes, interact with specific patterns of family transactions in real time to influence the development and course of schizophrenic disorders.

REFERENCES

1. Asarnow, J. R., & Goldstein, M. J. Schizophrenia during adolescence and early adulthood: A developmental perspective on risk research. *Clinical Psychology Review 6*: 211–235, 1986.

2. Asarnow, R. F. The search for the psychobiological substrate of schizophrenia: A perspective from studies of children at risk for schizophrenia. In R. Tarter (ed.), *The child at risk*. New York: Oxford University Press, 1983.

3. ______, & MacCrimmon, D. J. Residual performance deficit in clinically remitted schizophrenics: A marker of schizophrenia? *Journal of Abnormal Psychology 87*: 597–608, 1978.

4. ______, & MacCrimmon, D. J. Span of apprehension deficits during the postpsychotic stages of schizophrenia: A replication and extension. *Archives of General Psychiatry 38*: 1006–1011, 1981.

5. ______, & MacCrimmon, D. J. Attention/information processing, neuropsychological functioning and thought disorder during the acute and partial recovery phases of schizophrenia: A longitudinal study. *Psychiatry Research 7*: 309–319, 1982.

6. ______, Marder, S. R., Mintz, J., Van Putten, T., & Zimmerman, K. E. The differential effect of low and conventional doses of fluphenazine decanoate on schizophrenic outpatients with good or poor information processing abilities, submitted for publication.

7. ______, Nuechterlein, K. H., & Marder, S. R. Span of apprehension performance, neuropsychological functioning, and indices of psychosis-proneness. *Journal of Nervous and Mental Disease 171*: 662–669, 1983.

8. ______, Steffy, R. A., MacCrimmon, D. J., & Cleghorn, J. M. An attentional assessment of foster children at risk for schizophrenia. *Journal of Abnormal Psychology 86*: 267–275, 1977.

9. ______, Steffy, R. A., MacCrimmon, D. J., & Cleghorn, J. M. An attentional assessment of foster children at risk for schizophrenia. In L. C. Wynne, R. L. Cromwell, S. Matthysse (eds.), *The nature of schizophrenia: New approaches to research and treatment*. New York: John Wiley & Sons, 1978.

10. ______, Steffy, R. A. MacCrimmon, D. J., & Cleghorn, J. M. The McMaster-Waterloo Project: Ten years later. *Schizophrenia Bullentin*, in press.

11. Bleuler, E. *Dementia praecox or the group of schizophrenias* (translated by J. Zinkin). New York: International Universities Press, 1950.

12. ______. The long-term course of schizophrenic psychoses. In L. C. Wynne, R. L. Cromwell, & S. Matthysse (eds.), *The nature of schizophenia: New approaches to research and treatment*. New York: John Wiley & Sons, 1978.

13. Cromwell, R., & Spaulding, W. How schizophrenics handle information. In W. E. Fann, I. Karacan, A. D. Pokorny, & R. L. Williams (eds.), *The phenomenology and treatment of schizophrenia*. New York: Spectrum Press, 1978.

14. Eckblad, M., & Chapman, L. J. Magical ideation as an indication of schizotypy. *Journal of Consulting and Clinical Psychology 51*: 215–225, 1983.

15. Estes, W. K., & Taylor, H. A. A detection method and probabilistic models for assessing information processing from brief visual displays. *Proceedings of the National Academy of Science 52*: 446–454, 1964.

16. Jones, J. E. Patterns of transactional style deviance in the TAT's of parents of schizophrenics. *Family Process 16*: 327–337, 1977.

17. Kraepelin, E. *Dementia praecox and paraphrenia* (translated by R. M. Barclay). Edinburgh: E. & S. Livingstone, 1919.

18. Lang, P. H., & Buss, A. H. Psychological deficit in schizophrenia: II. Interference and activation. *Journal of Abnormal Psychology 70*: 77–106, 1965.

19. MacCrimmon, D. J., Cleghorn, J. M., Asarnow, R. F., & Steffy, R. A. Children at risk for schizophrenia: Clinical and attentional characteristics. *Archives of General Psychiatry 37*: 671–674, 1980.

20. Marder, S. R., Asarnow, R. F., & Van Putten, T. Information processing and neuroleptic response in acute and stabilized schizophrenic patients. *Psychiatry Research 13*: 41–49, 1984.

21. McGhie, A., & Chapman, J. Disorders of attention and perception in early schizophrenia. *British Journal of Medical Psychology 34*: 103–116, 1961.

22. Neale, J. M. Perceptual span in schizophrenia. *Journal of Abnormal Psychology 77*: 196–204, 1971.

23. ______, & Cromwell, R. L. Attention and schizophrenia. In B. A. Maher (ed.), *Progress in experimental personality research* (Vol. 5). New York: Academic Press, 1970.

24. ______, McIntyre, C. W., Fox, R., & Cromwell, R. L. Span of apprehension in acute schizophrenics. *Journal of Abnormal Psychology 74*: 593–596, 1969.

25. ______, & Oltmanns, T. F. *Schizophrenia*. New York: John Wiley & Sons, 1980.

26. Nuechterlein, K. H. Signal detection in vigilance tasks and behavioral attributes among offspring of schizophrenic mothers and among hyperactive children. *Journal of Abnormal Psychology 92*: 4–28, 1983.

27. ______, & Dawson, M. E. Information processing and attentional functioning in the developmental course of schizophrenic orders. *Schizophrenia Bulletin 10*: 160–203, 1984.

28. Oltmanns, T. F. Selective attention in schizophrenic and manic psychosis: The effect of distraction on information processing. *Journal of Abnormal Psychology 87*: 21–225, 1978.

29. Pervin, L. A. Personality: Current controversies, issues and directions. In M. R. Rosenzweig & L. W. Porter (eds.), *Annual review of psychology 36*: 83–114, 1985.

30. Rodnick, E. H., & Shakow, D. Set in the schizophrenic as measured by a composite reaction time index. *American Journal of Psychiatry 97*: 214–225, 1940.

31. Rutschmann, J., Cornblatt, B., & Erlenmeyer-Kimling, L. Sustained attention in children at risk for schizophrenia. *Archives of General Psychiatry 34*: 571–575, 1977.

32. ______, Cornblatt, B., & Erlenmeyer-Kimling, L. Sustained attention in children at risk for schizophenia: Finding with two visual continuous performance tests in a new sample. *Journal of Abnormal Child Psychology 14*: 365–385, 1977.

33. Sameroff, A. Development and the dialectic: The need for a systems approach. In W. A. Collins (ed.), *The concept of development: Minnesota Symposium on Child Psychology* (Vol. 15). Hillsdale NJ: Lawrence Erlbaum, 1982.

34. Sherman, T., & Asarnow, R. F. The cognitive disabilities of the schizophrenic child. In M. Sigman (ed.), *Children with emotional disorders and developmental disabilites: Assessment and treatment*. Orlando: Grune & Stratton, 1985.

35. Singer, M. T., & Wynne, L. C. Thought disorder and the family relations of schizophrenics: IV. Results and implications. *Archives of General Psychiatry 12*: 201–212, 1965.

36. Sperling, G. The information available in brief visual presentations. *Psychological Monographs 74*: Whole No. 498, 1960.

37. Spohn, H. E., LaCoursiere, R. B., Thompson, K., & Coyne, L. Phenothiazine effects on psychological and psychophysiological dysfunction in chronic schizophrenics. *Archives of General Psychiatry 34*: 633–644, 1977.

38. Spring, B. J., Levitt, M., Briggs, D., & Benet, M. Distractibility in relatives of schizophrenics. Paper presented at the 91st convention of the American Psychological Association, Anaheim CA, August, 1983.

39. Steffy, R. A. An early cue sometimes impairs process schizophrenic performance. In L. C. Wynne, R. L. Cromwell, & S. Matthysse (eds.), *The nature of schizophrenia: New approaches to treatment and research*. New York: John Wiley & Sons, 1978.

40. ______, Asarnow, R. F., Asarnow, J. R., MacCrimmon, D. J., & Cleghorn, J. M. The McMaster-Waterloo High-Risk Project: Multifaceted strategy for high-risk research. In N. F. Watt, E. J. Anthony, L. C. Wynne, & J. E. Rolf (eds.), *Children at risk for schizophrenia: A longitudinal perspective*. Cambridge: Cambridge University Press, 1984.

41. Sutton, S., Spring, B. J., & Tueting, P. Modality shift at the crossroads. In L. C. Wynne, R. L. Cromwell, & S. Matthysse (eds.), *The nature of schizophrenia: New approaches to treatment and research*. New York: John Wiley & Sons, 1978.

42. Venables, P. H. Input dysfunction and schizophrenia. In B. A. Maher (ed.), *Progress in experimental personality research* (Vol. 1). New York: Academic Press, 1964.

43. Wagener, D. K., Hogarty, G. E., Goldstein, M. J., Asarnow, R. F., & Browne, A. Information processing and communication deviance in schizophrenic patients and their mothers. *Psychiatry Research 18*: 365–377, 1986.

44. Wohlberg, G. W., & Kornetsky, C. Sustained attention in remitted schizophrenics. *Archives of General Psychiatry 28*: 533–537, 1973.

45. Wynne, L. C. From symptoms to vulnerability and beyond: An overview. In L. C. Wynne, R. L. Cromwell, & S. Mattyhsse (eds.), *The nature of schizophrenia: New approaches to research and treatment*. New York: John Wiley & Sons, 1978.

46. Zahn-Waxler, C., Iannotti, R., & Chapman, M. Peers and prosocial development. In K. Rubin & H. Ross (eds.), *Peer relationships and social skills in childhood*. New York: Springer-Verlag, 1982.

47. Zubin, J., Magaziner, J., & Steinhauer, S. R. The metamorphosis of schizophrenia: From chronicity to vulnerability. *Psychological Medicine 13*: 551–571, 1983.

48. ______, & Spring, B. Vulnerability—A new view of schizophrenia. *Journal of Abnormal Psychology 86*: 103–126, 1977.

6

COMMUNICATION PATTERNS OF MOTHERS WITH AFFECTIVE DISORDERS AND THEIR RELATIONSHIP TO CHILDREN'S STATUS AND SOCIAL FUNCTIONING*

CONSTANCE HAMMEN, DAVID GORDON, DORLI BURGE, CHERI ADRIAN, CAROL JAENICKE
University of California, Los Angeles

DONALD HIROTO
Veterans Administration Medical Center
Brentwood, California

A SEARCH for new methods to explore the antecedents of psychopathology has created enormous interest in high-risk studies. There has been a particularly noteworthy increase in studies of children of parents with affective disorders (see 4, 29 for reviews). Not surprisingly, support is accumulating for the hypothesis that these children are at high risk for psychopathology, particularly for depression.

As Beardslee et al. (4) and others have noted, however, the conclusions

*The research was funded in part by a Veterans Administration research grant to Dr. Hiroto and Dr. Hammen, and in part by a research award from the William T. Grant Foundation to Dr. Hammen. We are grateful for the cooperation of the families, and to the many agencies, professionals, and volunteer staff members who assisted us but are too numerous to mention individually. The continuing help of Brian Zupan, Kelly Ellis, and Jean Kaufman deserves special thanks.

that can be drawn from most of these studies are limited because of methodological problems. For instance, many studies have failed to separate children of unipolar and bipolar parents, despite the possibility that there are different types and mechanisms of risk. There has been inadequate attention to the severity and chronicity of disorder in the parents. Outcome measures of children's functioning have rarely been direct and comprehensive, despite considerable research indicating the importance of structured interviews with parents and children and the use of standard, operational diagnostic criteria (9, 14, 23, 30, 34). Additionally, a major shortcoming in most studies is the absence of appropriate control groups with which to examine the nonspecific effects of stress and disruption so evident in the lives of families with a psychiatrically ill parent. Finally, the great majority of existing studies are cross-sectional, which limits the reliability of diagnostic conclusions; as Rutter (35) has stated, longitudinal data are also critical for examining mechanisms of risk.

Another common shortcoming in the proliferation of risk studies of offspring of parents with affective disorders is the paucity of theory-guided investigations. In addition to the genetic hypothesis of risk, which is typically implicit in offspring studies, a number of potential psychosocial mediators of risk are readily derivable from contemporary theories of depression but rarely have been tested explicitly in studies of children of depressed parents. Three types of mechanisms are of interest in contemporary theory: stress and coping variables, which have frequently been linked with adult depression (see 7, 37) and with children's psychopathology (see 18); cognitive social-learning variables, principally studied with depressed adults but which also have significant implications for vulnerability in children (see 2, 5, 20, 22); and family interaction variables that may mediate vulnerability. The UCLA Family Stress Project is exploring how all of these factors and their mechanisms of interaction produce psychopathology in children. This chapter will discuss our findings with respect to family interaction variables hypothesized to be one mediator of children's risk.

Theorists and therapists with widely divergent approaches to depression agree on the importance of the mother-child bond in the development of a child's competence and self-esteem (see 5, 24). The critical, rejecting parent, for example, has been linked to depression in offspring by psychoanalytic theorists such as Abraham (1), while cognitive formulations of depression acknowledge the likely role of critical or unloving parents in the development of negative self-schemas that create depressive vulnerability (see 5, 19). Because many of the symptoms of the syndrome of depression such as anhedonia, irritability, withdrawal, and negativism may disturb parenting behavior, it is easy to speculate about the ways in which depression in a mother may be linked to depression in her children. To date, although the studies are limited in scope and quality, there are several empirical grounds for further exploring this link: retrospective reports of the childhoods of depressed adults (10, 12, 26, 31); clinical reports of impaired parental functioning in depressed women (8, 38); and clinical studies of the families of depressed children (27, 33).

Overall, the studies point to impaired parent-child relations in families with depressed parents or depressed children. Such studies provide the impetus for further research but are themselves sometimes marred by methodological inadequacies. Foremost among the shortcomings is a reliance on parental self-report or data obtained from interviews or records that may be limited in accuracy and completeness. Direct observations are notably absent, and the need for investigations with clear, overt operational definitions of key constructs, such as criticism or poor communication, is apparent.

The work to be reported describes preliminary results of a project designed to overcome the major methodological shortcomings of previous offspring risk research in depression. The design is longitudinal, and contrasts both unipolar and bipolar mothers with comparison groups of normal and medically ill mothers. The affective disorder groups have severe and chronic disorders. Children's functioning is assessed directly in various ways, including interviews; and mother-child interactions on two different tasks are observed and recorded. The analyses focus on the nature of observed maternal interaction behaviors and their relation to maternal diagnoses and other maternal characteristics, and the associations between maternal interactions and children's diagnoses and psychosocial functioning.

Methods

Participants

Families were eligible for the study if the mother had a treated chronic or recurrent unipolar depressive disorder, bipolar disorder, a chronic medical disorder (early onset, insulin-dependent diabetes or early severe arthritis), or had no history of major psychopathology or treatment. Mothers and children between ages 8 and 16 were included, and if the family had more than two children in that age range, only the youngest and oldest were included. The sample consisted of 13 unipolar mothers with 19 children, 9 bipolar mothers with 12 children, 14 women with medical disorders and 18 children, and 22 normal mothers and their 35 children. The normal group was subdivided on a dimension of chronic stress, described below; there were 8 "high-stress" and 14 "low-stress" normal families.

The unipolar mothers had a mean age for onset of depression of 18.6

years (SD = 8.2), and reported an average of 15.5 (SD = 12.6) lifetime episodes of major depression, excluding 3 persons who said they had had "too many to count" of discrete episodes; they had experienced a mean of 2.1 hospitalizations for depression (SD = 2.3). The bipolar women had a mean age of onset of 22.0 (SD = 10.5), and a mean of 5.9 episodes of major depression (SD = 3.3), along with their manic or hypomanic episodes. They had been hospitalized for psychiatric treatment an average of 2.3 times (SD = 2.2). The medical group had a mean onset of illness of 17.4 years (SD = 11.1), and they had experienced a mean of 5.5 (SD = 8.8) hospitalizations for treatment of their disorders.

Overall, there were equal numbers of boys and girls in the sample, and their mean ages did not differ significantly across groups; racially the majority of children were white (87%), with black and Hispanic families divided equally across groups (except that there were no nonwhite families in the medical sample). Marital status of the mother indicated significant differences in the distribution of currently married women, χ^2 (4) = 16.1, $p < .002$; while only 36% of the women were married and living with the original spouse, the affective disorders groups in particular contained fewer currently married women. Finally, despite efforts to recruit normal families from the same or demographically similar schools as families in the other groups, the Hollingshead Two-Factor index of socioeconomic status suggested that the high-stress normal group contained fewer high-SES families than the other groups, although an analysis of variance on raw classification scores indicated no overall significant differences between groups.

Procedures

Data were collected at three points: an initial session with the mother alone, a family session with the mother and children about 2–4 weeks later, and regular 6-month follow-up contacts with the mother and children. To date, families have been followed for periods varying from 6 months to 3 years.

Information about the Mother

Information about current and past psychiatric functioning was obtained with the Schedule for Affective Disorders and Schizophrenia-Lifetime version (SADS-L) (17); The Beck Depression Inventory (BDI) (6); and a short form of the MMPI used principally to confirm the status of the normal comparison women.

The diagnostic interviews revealed the presence of depressive experiences in a few of the medically ill women (no attempt had been made to exclude such women from the study); even some women with nondiagnosable depressions reported periods of mood depressions of varying lengths. Because of our focus on maternal lifetime depression as related to the children's outcomes, it seemed valuable to assess all the mothers' depressive experiences on a comparable scale. A 7-point scale was devised that consisted of objectively defined points based on quantifiable factors such as number of hospitalizations or treatment, and number of episodes of major or minor depression. In addition, episodic and chronic life stress was assessed by the Life Stress Inventory of the PERI (16), and by semi-structured life-stress interviews conducted at follow-ups. In order to scale the measurement of ongoing stress, 7 content areas (for example, marital/social, economic) were rated on 5-point scales, with specific behavioral descriptors defining each point. Using all available information about the mother and her circumstances, two teams of raters made independent life-stress judgments on a subsample of families, with interrater reliabilities ranging between .93 and .99 across contents—all highly significant.

Information about the Children

Current and past diagnostic information about children was obtained from the Kiddie-SADS (K-SADS) (28). The child and mother were interviewed separately, and information was combined by the research team for final diagnoses. Current mood and self-esteem were assessed with the self-report Children's Depression Inventory (CDI) (25) and Self-Concept Scale (32), respectively. General behavioral symptoms and social competence were assessed with the mother-completed Child Behavior Check List (CBCL) (3). School behaviors were assessed on the basis of reports from children, mothers, and teachers. Because of variations in grading systems and sanctions across schools, overall ratings were made on the basis of all available data; two 5-point scales were devised, one for academic performance and one for behavioral functioning. In addition, a teacher identified as the instructor most in contact with the child was asked to complete the Conners' Teacher Rating Scale of symptoms of behavior disorders observed in school (11).

Maternal Interactions with the Child

Two tasks representing different stimulus situations were used to obtain ratings of mother-child interactions. The first was a game intended to elicit achievement motives and behaviors, based on the "Mr. Blockhead" task developed and used by Henker and Whalen (39). The child performs while blindfolded. The mother is given a photograph of colored blocks assembled in a definite configuration, and the child's task is to build the same pattern following verbal instructions from the mother. The experimenter induces an achievement set by informing the pair that most children stack 8 of the 10 blocks in five minutes; in reality the difficulty level increases with each block so that such success is rarely possible (participants were fully debriefed after the task). The second task was designed to observe verbal conflict and problem solving. Using a modified revealed differences format, the pair is asked to discuss a common topic of disagreement, selected from items they had previously listed as areas of conflict, with the goal of working toward some resolution. In both tasks the experimenter left the room, but the interactions were videorecorded for five minutes each.

Scoring the Interaction Tasks

Each utterance occurring during the first, middle, and fifth minutes was transcribed and coded into 20 mutually exclusive content categories adapted from the Peer Interaction Rating System (39), with certain categories of theoretical interest added. Raters were trained to high levels of reliability, and were blind to mother and child diagnostic status. The original 20 categories were subsequently reduced by combining highly correlated and theoretically similar or rarely observed items. The results to be presented focus only on maternal behaviors; seven scores were computed, representing major affective and task-relevant responses:

1. *Negative task and personal feedback*: This includes negatively valenced evaluative comments on performance or personal attributes and signs of displeasure, impatience, annoyance, and the like.

2. *Task discomfirmation*: These are negative feedback remarks about performance, but are intended to redirect performance without reflecting annoyance.

3. *Task confirmation*: These are positive feedback statements about task performance. They are informational and intended to reinforce and maintain the child's behavior, but they are generally neutral in tone.

4. *Positive feedback*: These are stronger and more evaluative statements than the previous category and refer to both task-specific performance and personal attributes of the child.

5. *Negative self-feedback*: These are self-critical remarks referring either to the task or to personal characteristics.

6. *Task-productive comments*: These are declarative statements providing instructions, directions, suggestions, commands, factual information, or opinions.

7. *Off-task commentary*: These are nonfunctional comments about the task or about unrelated matters.

The seven categories were scored for the Achievement Task (AT). The Conflict Task (CT) was similar but with one modification: items 3 and 4 were combined because of their high intercorrelations and relatively low frequencies, which resulted in 6 scoring categories.

Results

Children's Outcomes by Group

The first question was the extent to which children's diagnostic, behavioral, and school functioning vary by maternal condition. Table 1 summarizes outcomes on the major variables (see 21 for complete details). The groups differed significantly in presence/absence of any disorder (current including 6-month follow-up if available—and lifetime combined), χ^2 (4) = 27.89, $p < .001$, with the two affective disorders groups reporting very high rates, and moderate rates for the medical and high-stress groups as compared with the low-stress normal group. A similar pattern was observed for depressive disorders specifically, χ^2 (4) = 4.45, $p < .05$; when only rates of major depression are counted, the unipolar group exceeded all others, including the bipolar group. It is notable that 8 of 10 children who required

TABLE 1

Group Means on Children's Psychological Functioning Variables

	Mother's Group				
Variables	**Unipolar**	**Bipolar**	**Medical**	**High Stress**	**Low Stress**
Current or Lifetime Diagnosis					
% any diagnosis	74.0	92.0	50.0	62.0	9.0
% any affective disorder	74.0	67.0	44.0	38.0	4.0
% major depression	42.0	25.0	17.0	23.0	0.0
Children's Depression Inventory	7.3[b]	7.0[ab]	4.3[ab]	6.9[ab]	2.6[a]
	(5.0)	(6.8)	(5.5)	(5.8)	(2.7)
Social Competence (CBCL)	36.8[a]	43.8[ab]	48.2[b]	46.9[b]	48.0[b]
	(12.3)	(16.0)	(10.6)	(7.6)	(11.3)
Behavior Problems (CBCL)	66.8[c]	54.9[ab]	54.9[ab]	60.0[bc]	49.1[a]
	(12.0)	(8.5)	(11.8)	(8.5)	(10.1)
Conners Teacher Ratings	26.2[a]	14.0[a]	21.2[a]	14.0[a]	13.4[a]
	(16.2)	(8.2)	(15.3)	(10.7)	(8.1)
Academic Performance Rating	2.8[a]	3.0[a]	3.6[ab]	3.7[ab]	4.2[b]
	(1.4)	(1.1)	(1.1)	(0.6)	(0.7)
School Behavior Rating	2.7[a]	3.8[b]	3.8[b]	3.9[b]	4.1[b]
	(1.2)	(1.1)	(0.9)	(0.6)	(0.5)

Note: Figures in parentheses are standard deviations. Means sharing the same superscripts within each variable do not differ significantly. More negative outcomes are indicated by higher scores, except CBCL Social Competence where higher scores indicate more competence, and the two school ratings where higher scores indicate more positive performance.

psychiatric hospitalization (mostly for depression) had mothers with unipolar depression. There were no gender or age differences in diagnoses.

Measures of psychological functioning indicated that the children of unipolar mothers differed significantly from the low-stress children on self-reported mood and mother-reported social competence and behavior problems. Bipolar children did not differ from low-stress children. However, as Table 1 indicates, the unipolar offspring did not reliably differ from the other groups at risk. Similarly, while school behavior measures indicated poorest academic performances and school behavior in children of unipolar mothers, patterns of significant differences varied by which groups were compared.

Thus, across measures, the unipolar children showed the highest levels of impairment, and the low-stress children the least, with the other groups often midway between these extremes. Depending on the variable, the bipolar offspring sometimes resembled the unipolar but more commonly were similar to the other groups. This suggests the necessity of keeping children of unipolar and bipolar parents separate in comparisons of offspring.

Maternal Predictors of Children's Outcomes

The comparisons by group established that while children of unipolar mothers had high rates of diagnoses of all kinds and impairment on various measures, these effects were not specific to unipolar offspring, occurring at least to a moderate extent in children whose mothers experienced other problems such as chronic medical illness or stressful circumstances. The next step was to pursue the characteristics of the mothers that were predictive of children's outcomes, and specifically to investigate the relative contributions of three variables: extent of lifetime depressive experiences (lifetime depression scale scores), current depressive symptomatology (BDI score), and chronic stressful conditions (average ongoing stress-scale score across content areas).

The three independent variables were entered stepwise in multiple regressions to predict each of the major outcomes for children. The three variables in combination yielded significant multiple regressions for all variables except two (CDI and Conners' Teacher Ratings), where only a single predictor was significant; however, in each equation only one or two of the variables made a unique significant contribution, and these are reported. For prediction of diagnoses, both ongoing stress and lifetime depressive experiences were significant; the overall R^2 was .25 for any diagnoses, contributed mostly by ongoing stress ($R^2 = .18$); and for diagnoses of depression, overall $R^2 = .30$, contributed mostly by maternal depressive experiences ($R^2 = .20$).

Maternal lifetime depression contributed significantly only to one other variable, CDI, with a modest R^2 of .08. Ongoing stress contributed significantly to one other outcome, CBCL behavior problems, in an equation with $R^2 = .33$, which was contributed mostly ($R^2 = .23$) by the mother's current mood. The mother's current mood, in fact, emerged as the major predictor of 4 additional outcomes besides CBCL behavior problems: CBCL social competence, ratings of academic problems, school behavior problems, and Conners' teacher ratings. Overall R^2 values on these equations were modest although significant, ranging between .09 and .33.

Across outcome variables, maternal characteristics were most strongly predictive of children's diagnoses, CBCL behavior problems, and academic performance. Most importantly, children's functioning was differentially associated with different maternal characteristics, such that current depressed mood (which is not unique to affective disorder mothers) was a significant predictor of many of the variables indicating children's current functioning, while severe and chronic depression (lifetime depressive experience) was the major predictor, with stress, of depressive diagnoses in the children. The occurrence of any diagnoses, affective and nonaffective, was most strongly related to ongoing maternal stress.[1]

Maternal Interactions by Group

The next question was whether the different groups of mothers display different styles of interaction with their children. Table 2 presents the means for each of the major interaction variables. In the interest of brevity of presentation, the analyses were conducted for the two tasks combined, although the tasks are different and had somewhat different requirements for appropriate behavior.

Theoretically most salient was the comparison between unipolar mothers and those in each other group. Planned comparisons indicated that on all but a single variable, the unipolar and low-stress normal mothers differed significantly, but few significant differences emerged between the unipolar and remaining groups (although the unipolar mothers gave more negative feedback than the medical and high-stress mothers). Thus, while the unipolar mothers tended to be more negative and less task productive, their behaviors were not particularly unique.

In order to pursue this issue and to determine the relative contribution

[1]It should be noted that because some families contributed two children to the analyses, the statistical criteria of independence of observations may not be strictly met. However, analyses based on only one child per family were not different from those from the total sample and, therefore, results from the larger sample are reported.

TABLE 2
Means for Maternal Interaction Behaviors (Combined Tasks)

Variables	Unipolar (1)	Biopolar (2)	Medical (3)	High Stress (4)	Low Stress (5)	Significant Contrast[a]
	Groups					
Negative feedback[b]	6.36	4.60	2.00	2.92	1.15	1 vs. 3; 1 vs. 4; 1 vs. 5
	(5.70)	(3.00)	(2.40)	(3.20)	(2.50)	
Disconfirmation	20.43	16.30	18.70	16.17	14.30	1 vs. 5
	(11.40)	(7.50)	(9.50)	(5.20)	(8.40)	
Confirmation[b]	20.07	19.20	22.43	19.83	22.95	–
	(8.40)	(6.00)	(6.80)	(7.20)	(7.50)	
Negative self-feedback	.86	1.10	.71	.08	.25	1 vs. 4
	(1.40)	(1.20)	(1.10)	(0.30)	(0.60)	
Task productive comments	53.93	61.80	56.14	58.33	67.85	1 vs. 5
	(10.10)	(10.10)	(10.70)	(16.00)	(16.70)	
Offtask comments	8.50	6.7	5.0	6.58	3.90	1 vs. 5
	(5.80)	(5.00)	(3.60)	(10.90)	(3.30)	

[a]The unipolar group was compared with each other group. Only significant contrasts are noted, (p at least $<.05$).

[b]In separate analyses, SES was entered as a covariate because it was significantly related to the Negative Feedback and Confirmation variables. The results were similar to those reported with one exception: for Confirmation statements, there was a significant difference between Unipolar and Bipolar groups, with the latter producing fewer positive remarks.

of the mother's lifetime depression status, current mood, and chronic stress to each interaction behavior, stepwise multiple regression analyses were conducted. Of the six interaction scores, the four affective items were significantly predicted by the combination of the three variables, but not the two task-relevant items. Severity of lifetime depressive experiences was a unique predictor only of negative self-feedback, while chronic stress was a significant unique contributor to confirmation (overall $R^2 = .22$), disconfirmation (overall $R^2 = .14$), and negative feedback (overall $R^2 = .41$). In the latter equation, current mood (BDI score) was also a significant unique predictor. These analyses implicate stress in the negative affective tone of the interactions, with lifetime depressive status contributing less unique variance. Similar analyses using SES instead of stress yielded nearly identical results, probably owing to their high correlation with each other ($r = .63$).

Prediction of Children's Outcomes by Maternal Interaction

The next set of analyses examined the relationship between maternal interactions and children's outcomes. Specifically, we predicted that presence of negative behaviors and absence of positive behaviors would be associated with higher levels of diagnoses and impaired psychosocial functioning. Stepwise regression analyses were conducted for each child outcome variable, allowing the positive and negative scores to enter in the order of their contributions. In addition, the child's age was entered in the stepwise phase, and an interaction term capturing the combination effects of positive and negative maternal remarks was entered last. Using the combined task variables, there was one positive score (combining both confirmation and positive feedback) and two negative scores (negative feedback and disconfirmation).

Table 3 presents the results of the regression analyses. All of the children's outcome scores were significantly predicted by maternal behaviors. In nearly every outcome, maternal negative feedback was the strongest predictor of dysfunctional outcome, and in four equations such critical remarks were a significant predictor independent of the other variables. Positive comments to the child were less often significantly associated with outcomes, but appeared to be a significant protective factor associated with fewer diagnoses of any kind and better academic performance. The interaction of criticism and positive remarks was not significantly associated with outcomes. Together, the results lend support to the hypothesis that negative and critical behaviors by the mother toward the child are associated with less favorable outcomes. Although less strongly and independently related, it also appears that presence of positive behaviors is associated with more favorable outcomes.

Discussion

The preliminary results of this longitudinal investigation of children of mothers with affective disorders and of potential risk mediators point to several conclusions. First, it appears that children of depressed mothers, especially unipolar mothers, have high rates of depressive diagnoses as well as other diagnoses, and are seen by themselves, their mothers, and their teachers as more impaired on various psychosocial measures. However, a second point is that such impairments are not unique to children of mothers with affective disorders, and are associated across diagnostic groups with increased levels of maternal chronic stress and nonspecific depressed mood.

TABLE 3
Multiple Regressions to Predict Children's Outcomes from Maternal Interaction Behaviors[a]

Variable	Change in R^2	Significance	Simple R
Any diagnoses (current and lifetime)			
Negative feedback	.11	–	.33
Age	.07	$p<.025$	.33
Confirmation	.06	$p<.05$	–.33
Disconfirmation	.00	–	.15
Positive × negative	.00	–	.28
Overall $R^2=.25$; F [5,64] = 4.16, $p<.005$.			
Diagnosis of depression (current and lifetime)			
Negative feedback	.09	$p<.05$	.31
Disconfirmation	.04	–	.28
Overall $R^2=.14$; F [2,67] = 5.38, $p<.01$.			
CDI			
Age	.07	$p<.05$	.26
Confirmation	.03	–	–.17
Overall $R^2=.10$; F [2,66] = 3.49, $p<.05$.			
CBCL Social Competence			
Negative feedback	.21	$p<.01$	–.46
Age	.02	–	–.23
Disconfirmation	.02	–	–.23
Confirmation	.01	–	.25
Overall $R^2=.26$; F [4,65] = 5.62, $p<.001$.			
CBCL Behavior Problems			
Negative feedback	.15	$p<.01$	.39
Disconfirmation	.03	–	.27
Confirmation	.01	–	–.08
Age	.01	–	.15
Positive × negative	.00	–	.34
Overall $R^2=.20$; F [4,65] = 4.10, $p<.01$.			

Third, the groups of mothers differed on a number of behaviors observed in brief interaction tasks with their children; unipolar mothers were especially likely to display more negative, critical interactions, and fewer positive as well as fewer task-productive and more off-task remarks. Such patterns were more associated with maternal chronic stress than with lifetime diagnostic condition. Finally, children's diagnoses and maladaptive functioning were especially strongly associated with the extent of mothers' negative feedback and disconfirmation as observed in the interaction tasks.

The high rate of psychopathology in children of depressed mothers is consistent with recent findings, especially the most recent investigations that also included bipolar families (13, 15). Features of the present study that

TABLE 3
Continued

Variable	Change in R^2	Significance	Simple R
Academic Performance			
Negative feedback	.15	–	–.39
Age	.04	–	–.27
Confirmation	.04	$p < .05$	.29
Positive × negative	.01	–	–.36
Overall $R^2 = .23$; F [4,65] = 4.97, $p < .005$.			
School Behaviors			
Negative feedback	.12	–	–.35
Age	.07	$p < .025$	–.33
Confirmation	.04	–	.29
Disconfirmation	.00	–	–.16
Positive × negative	.00	–	–.29
Overall $R^2 = .23$; F [5,64] = 3.91, $p < .005$.			
Conners Teacher Ratings			
Negative feedback	.22	$p < .01$	.47
Age	.03	–	.25
Confirmation	.01	–	–.23
Disconfirmation	.00	–	.10
Overall $R^2 = .25$; F [4,40] = 3.41, $p < .05$.			

[a]Combined scores across the two interaction tasks. Only variables contributing to a significant overall R^2 are reported; F values are for the overall equation in which at least one variable attained individual unique significance. For children's outcome variables more negative outcomes are indicated by higher scores, except CBCL Social Competence where higher scores indicate more competence, and the two school ratings where higher scores indicate more positive performance.

probably contributed to the finding of extremely high rates of diagnoses were the direct evaluation of the children, inclusion of women with chronic and recurrent depression rather than single episodes, and use of only mothers as the parent-patients as well as the primary caretakers.

Although the high rates of disorder in the children of women with affective disorders present no surprise, the extent of disorder in the comparison children of medically ill and highly stressed women raises significant conceptual issues. Analyses of the contributions of chronic stress and mood depression, apart from diagnostic history, clearly implicate the potential concomitants of depressive status, and not merely the diagnostic condition itself, as a factor in children's outcomes. Stressful conditions may be a result of psychiatric impairment, or even a cause of it. The data suggest that in contrast to a strictly genetic interpretation, which is often given to offspring outcomes, it is necessary to consider the psychosocial context in which children of depressed parents are raised. Thus, depressed mothers may not only inflict the symptoms of the illness on their children in the way they interact with them, but may also experience high levels of concomitant chronic stress, which will affect the way they interact with the children. The data suggest that highly stressed women, whether stressed by medical illness, aspects of their psychiatric condition, or environmental conditions not associated with psychiatric disturbance, interact with their children in relatively critical and negative ways, with less positive feedback and confirmation. These negative interactions in turn were seen to be associated with more impaired functioning on the various diagnostic and psychosocial measures for the children. The results of the present study are consistent with the conclusions of Sameroff, Barocas, and Seifer (36) in a study of preschoolers of psychiatrically ill, high-SES, and low-SES mothers: "caretaking environments in which high levels of stress exist, whether through economic or emotional instability, produce young children with high levels of incompetent behavior" (p. 514).

Although an important aspect of the present research is the demonstration of a link between maternal interactions and children's dysfunction, the correlational nature of the data needs to be emphasized. While we have chosen to interpret the relationship as maternal behaviors affecting children and ultimately eventuating in impairment, the effect of maladaptive child behavior on the mother cannot be overlooked. It is possible that critical and negative interactions may result in part from problematic behavior of the child. Whatever the initial impetus for maternal negativism is, the child's continuing problematic behaviors must certainly have an impact on the mother over time. The effect of the child on maternal behavior is suggested by the finding that children's age was significantly associated with maternal behavior. The status of the child may also indirectly affect interaction because of different expectations the mother may hold for the child at different ages, based as well on her previous positive or negative experiences with the child.

Further analyses are underway that will attempt to determine more precisely the potential impact of maternal behavior on children. One clear need is for the analyses of sequences of interactions, studying both children's and mothers' responses to each other during the tasks. The tasks represent only limited samples of behavior, somewhat constrained by the laboratory environment, and our analyses assumed that the mothers' current behavior was relatively representative of typical, past behavior. Nevertheless, they may yield data useful to the study of the immediate impact of the mother and child on each other.

The present investigation is limited by the absence of a nonaffective psychiatric comparison group that would help sort out the unique contributions of affective disorder to children's risk. Although the original design called for such a group, finding mothers with comparably severe and chronic disorders but without significant affective symptoms proved to be impractical. It also remains for further research to indicate more clearly the conditions under which children's reactions to maternal criticism and negative interactions will take the form of depressive disorders or some other type of psychopathology. In this regard, while the present research has emphasized psychosocial factors associated with children's outcomes, we do not discount the effects of genetic factors that might contribute to vulnerability and/or symptoms specificity. The ultimate goal of the research is to explicate more clearly the interaction of biological, behavioral, and social sources of risk to children as a basis for effective prevention and treatment.

REFERENCES

1. Abraham, K. A short story of the development of the libido, viewed in the light of mental disorders. In E. Jones (ed.), *Selected papers of Karl Abraham, M.D.* (translated by D. Bryan & A. Strachey). London: Hogarth Press, 1949.

2. Abramson, L. Y., Seligman, M. E. P., & Teasdale, J. D. Learned helplessness in humans: Critique and reformation. *Journal of Abnormal Psychology 87*: 49–74, 1978.

3. Achenbach, T. M. The child behavior profile: I. Boys 6–11. *Journal of Consulting and Clinical Psychology 46*, 478–488, 1978.

4. Beardslee, W. R., Bemporad, J., Keller, M. B., & Klerman, G. L. Children of parents with major affective disorder: A review. *The American Journal of Psychiatry 140*: 825–832, 1983.

5. Beck, A. T., Rush, A. J., Shaw, B., & Emery, G. *Cognitive therapy of depression*. New York: Guilford Press, 1979.

6. ______, Ward, C. H., Mendelson, N., Mock, J., & Erbaugh, J. An inventory for measuring depression. *Archives of General Psychiatry 4*: 561-571, 1961.

7. Blaney, P. H. Stress and depression in adults: A critical review. In T. Field, P. McCabe, & N. Schneiderman (eds.), *Stress and coping*. New York: Lawrence Erlbaum, 1984.

8. Bothwell, S., & Weissman, M. M. Social impairments four years after an acute depressive episode. *American Journal of Orthopsychiatry 47*: 231-237, 1977.

9. Carlson, G., & Cantwell, D. Unmasking depression in children and adolescents. *American Journal of Psychiatry 137*: 445–449, 1980.

10. Cofer, D., & Wittenborn, J. Personality characteristics of formerly depressed women. *Journal of Abnormal Psychology 89*: 309–314, 1980.

11. Conners, C. A teacher rating scale for use in drug studies with children. *American Journal of Psychiatry 126*: 152–156, 1969.

12. Crook, T., & Raskin, A. Parent-child relationships and adult depression. *Child Development 52*: 950-957, 1981.

13. Cytryn, L., McKnew, D. H., Bartko, J. J., Lamour, M., & Hamovit, J. Offspring of patients with affective disorders II. *Journal of the American Academy of Child Psychiatry 21*: 389–391, 1982.

14. ______, McKnew, D., Zahn-Waxler, C., & Gershon, E. Developmental issues in risk research: The offspring of affectively ill parents. In M. Rutter, C. E. Izard, & P. B. Read (eds.), *Depression in children: Developmental perspectives*, 1986.

15. Decina, P., Kestenbaum, C., Farber, S., Kron, L., Gargan, M., Sackheim, H., & Fieve, R. Clinical and psychological assessment of children of bipolar probands. *American Journal of Psychiatry 140*: 548–553, 1983.

16. Dohrenwend, B. S., Kransoff, L., Askenasy, A. R., & Dohrenwend, B. P. Exemplification of a method for scaling life events: The PERI Life Events Scale. *Journal of Health and Social Behavior 19*: 205–229, 1978.

17. Endicott, J., & Spitzer, R. A diagnostic interview: the Schedule for Affective Disorders and Schizophrenia. *Archives of General Psychiatry 35*: 837–844, 1978.

18. Garmezy, N., & Rutter, M. (eds.). *Stress, coping, and development in children*. New York: McGraw-Hill, 1983.

19. Guidano, V. F., & Liotti, G. *Cognitive processes and emotional disorders*. New York: Guilford Press, 1983.

20. Hammen, C. L. Predicting depression: A cognitive-behavioral perspective. In P. Kendall (ed.), *Advances in cognitive-behavioral research and therapy* (Vol. 4). New York: Academic Press, 1985.

21. ______, Gordon, D., Burge, D., Adrian, C., Jaenicke, C., & Hiroto, D. Maternal affective disorders, illness, and stress: Risk for children's psychopathology. *American Journal of Psychiatry*, in press.

22. Kanfer, F. H., & Hagerman, S. The role of self-regulation. In L. P. Rehm (ed.), *Behavior therapy for depression*. New York: Academic Press, 1981.

23. Kazdin, A. E., French, N. H., Unis, A. S., & Esveldt-Dawson, K. Assessment of childhood depression: Correspondence of child and parent ratings. *Journal of the American Academy of Child Psychiatry 22*: 157–164, 1983.

24. Klerman, G. L., Weissman, M. M., Rounsaville, B. J., & Chevron, E. S. *Interpersonal psychotherapy of depression*. New York: Basic Books, 1984.

25. Kovacs, M. Rating scales to assess depression in school-children. *Acta Paedopsychiatrica 46*: 305–315, 1981.

26. Lamont, J., Fischoff, S., & Gottlieb, H. Recall of parental behaviors in female neurotic depressives. *Journal of Clinical Psychology 32*: 762–765, 1976.

27. McKnew, D., & Cytryn, L. Historical background in children with affective disorders. *American Journal of Psychiatry 130*: 1278–1279, 1973.

28. Orvaschel, H., Puig-Antich, J., Chambers, W., Tabrizi, M., & Johnson, R. Retrospective assessment of prepubertal major depression with the Kiddie-SADS-E. *Journal of the American Academy of Child Psychiatry 21*: 392–397, 1982.

29. ______, Weissman, M., & Kidd, K. Children and depression: The children of de-

pressed parents, the childhood of depressed patients, depression in children. *Journal of Affective Disorders 2*: 1–16, 1980.

30. ______, Weissman, M., Padian, N., & Lowe, P. Assessing psychopathology in children of psychiatrically disturbed parents: A pilot study. *Journal of the American Academy of Child Psychiatry 20*: 112–122, 1981.

31. Parker, G. Parental report of depressives: An investigation of several explanations. *Journal of Affective Disorders 3*: 131–140, 1981.

32. Piers, E., & Harris, D. *The Piers-Harris Children's Self-Concept Scale*. Nashville TN: Counselor Recordings and Tests, 1969.

33. Poznansky, E., & Zrull, J. P. Childhood depression: Clinical characteristics of overtly depressed children. *Archives of General Psychiatry 23*: 8–15, 1970.

34. Puig-Antich, J., Chambers, W., & Tabrizi, M. A. The clinical assessment of current depressive episodes in children and adolescents: Interviews with parents and children. In D. P. Cantwell & G. A. Carlson (eds.), *Affective disorders in childhood and adolescence*. New York: SP Medical and Scientific Books, 1983.

35. Rutter, M. Longitudinal studies: A psychiatric perspective. In S. A. Mednick & A. E. Baert (eds.), *Prospective longitudinal research: An empirical basis for primary prevention of psychosocial disorders*. Oxford: Oxford University Press, 1981.

36. Sameroff, A. J., Barocas, R., & Seifer, R. The early development of children born to mentally ill women. In N. Watt, E. J. Anthony, L. C. Wynne, and J. E. Rolf (eds.), *Children at risk for schizophrenia: A longitudinal perspective*. Cambridge: Cambridge University Press, 1984.

37. Thoits, P. A. Dimensions of life events that influence psychological distress: An evaluation and synthesis of the literature. In H. B. Kaplan (ed.), *Psychosocial stress: Trends in theory and research*. New York: Academic Press, 1983.

38. Weissman, M. M., & Paykel, E. *The depressed woman: A study of social relationships*. Chicago: University of Chicago Press, 1974.

39. Whalen, C., Henker, B., Collins, B., McAuliffe, S., & Vaux, A. Peer interaction in a structured communication task: Comparisons of normal and hyperactive boys and of methylphenidate (ritalin) and placebo effects. *Child Development 50*: 388–401, 1979.

II

Studies of Psychopathological Groups

7

FAMILY FACTORS IN CHILDHOOD DEPRESSIVE AND SCHIZOPHRENIA-SPECTRUM DISORDERS:
A Preliminary Report

JOAN R. ASARNOW, SHARON L. BEN-MEIR, MICHAEL J. GOLDSTEIN
University of California, Los Angeles

THIS CHAPTER reports preliminary data about family attributes and interaction patterns in families with children who meet DSM-III criteria for major depression, dysthymic disorder, schizophrenia, and schizotypal personality disorder. The study has four major goals: (a) to ascertain whether parental attributes posited as risk factors for these disorders are specific to one class of disorders or are associated with disorder in general; (b) to determine whether these parental attributes are associated with level of impairment or competence across disorders; (c) to provide a descriptive analysis of family interaction patterns that seem to increase and reduce symptomatic behavior in the child and, thus, suggest mechanisms that serve to maintain and/or disrupt deviant child behavior; and (d) to evaluate the extent to which these attributes of the family environment predict the course of childhood-onset depressive and schizophrenia-spectrum disorders from middle childhood to adolescence. This chapter will focus on the first of these aims. We will discuss the rationale guiding the study, provide a brief description of our major procedures, and then present some preliminary findings.

Rationale

The nosological status and predictive validity of childhood depressive and schizophrenia-spectrum disorders have provided much debate. It is only in the past 10 to 15 years that the controversy about the existence of childhood depression receded and a consensus emerged that children do experience depressive episodes similar to those experienced by adults (3, 7, 15–19).

The status of DSM-III-defined schizophrenic and schizotypal disorders of childhood onset is less clear. Because of the controversy regarding the relationship between autism and childhood-onset schizophrenia, many prior studies have not distinguished between autistic and schizophrenic children. Moreover, schizotypal disorders have generally been viewed as adult diagnoses, and there is little information about how these disorders present in childhood. There are also no extant follow-up data on the risk for schizophrenia in children meeting DSM-III criteria for schizotypal personality disorder.

Two major parental attributes were examined in this study: parental communication deviance (CD), which has been posited as a specific risk factor for schizophrenia and schizophrenia-spectrum disorders, and expressed emotion (EE), which has been posited as a nonspecific predictor of the course of psychiatric disorder.

The parental CD index, developed by Wynne and Singer (27, 31), assesses an inability to establish and maintain a shared focus of attention during interpersonal transactions. CD has generally been measured in a nonfamilial context, during administration of a projective test. Additionally, the transactions between the parent and tester have been assumed to reflect transactional patterns that are evident during family interaction. This assumption also is supported by data indicating that, when compared to low-CD parents, high-CD parents of disturbed adolescents fail to focus communication on the discussion topic, fail to share topic-related feelings, and show avoidance and rigidity in their nonverbal affective attitude toward the child (20).

Two major sources of evidence support the hypothesis that CD is a specific risk factor for schizophrenia. First, a number of studies have indicated that CD is more frequent in parents of adult schizophrenics than in parents of normals, or in parents whose offspring presented with nonschizophrenic disorders (26, 29–31). Additionally, results from the UCLA high-risk study indicate that parental CD is more common in the parents of disturbed adolescents who develop schizophrenia-spectrum disorders in young adulthood than in parents whose offspring show other young-adult outcomes (8; see also Chapter 1, this volume).

None of these prior studies examined CD in parents of children meeting

DSM-III criteria for schizotypal or schizophrenic disorders. In a study by Singer and Wynne (25) that used an early version of the CD measures, relatively low levels of CD were found in DSM-II defined childhood schizophrenia. However, most of these children were autistic and would not have met DSM-III criteria for schizophrenia. In contrast, a series of studies by Goldfarb and colleagues (10, 11), demonstrated that mothers of nonorganic DSM-II-defined schizophrenic children showed less clear communication patterns than did parents of autistic-like DSM-II schizophrenic children or normal children. The nonorganic schizophrenic children in these studies may have been comparable to children who would meet DSM-III criteria for schizophrenia. Thus, the Goldfarb et al. data support the hypothesis of disturbed communication in parents of DSM-III-defined schizophrenic children. (For an excellent review, see 6.)

Other research findings, suggest that parental CD may be a more general risk factor. Results from the University of Rochester High-Risk Study indicate that parental CD is associated with low levels of social competence in the biological children of patients with affective and schizophrenic disorders. Additionally, as noted above, although an association is found between parental CD and schizophrenia in adults, high CD is also found in parents of nonschizophrenic offspring (31). These findings are consistent with the hypothesis that CD is a general risk factor for psychiatric disorder and psychosocial dysfunction. The present study evaluated whether high CD is specific to parents of children with schizophrenic and schizotypal disorders, or is a more general characteristic of parents of disturbed children.

The second parental attribute evaluated in this study, expressed emotion (EE), assesses attitudes of overinvolvement, criticism, and hostility expressed by the parent (or key relative) toward the patient. Traditionally, measures of EE have been derived through assessments of EE behavior during the Camberwell Family Interview (CFI), an individual, semistructured interview conducted with the parent (or spouse) shortly after a patient's hospitalization. There is now substantial documentation that EE is a potent predictor of relapse in adult schizophrenic patients during the 9-month period following hospital discharge, and evidence is emerging that supports a similar pattern for adult depressives (28; see also Chapter 10, this volume). High EE in both parents was also found to predict the adult onset of schizophrenia-spectrum disorders in the UCLA high-risk sample of disturbed but nonpsychotic adolescents (see Chapter 1, this volume). A major aim of the present study was to ascertain whether EE would also predict the course of childhood depressive and schizophrenia-spectrum disorders. As a first step in evaluating this question, we examined whether parental EE is associated with patterns of onset, severity of disturbance, and premorbid functioning. Because predictors of onset and premorbid functioning can differ from predictors of prognosis after the disorder has developed (23), longitudinal data on our sample will be obtained to evaluate the prognostic value of EE.

The present report focuses on our initial findings with respect to the relationship between diagnosis, pattern of child-symptom onset, and the parental attributes of CD and EE. Four major questions are addressed.

1. Is parental CD associated with the presence of childhood schizophrenia-spectrum disorders?
2. Is parental EE associated with child diagnosis?
3. Is CD associated with the child's pattern of symptom onset?
4. Is EE associated with the child's pattern of symptom onset?

Methods

Subjects

Children and families were recruited from consecutive admissions to the child psychiatric inpatient units at the UCLA Neuropsychiatric Institute. To be included in the study, children had to meet the following criteria: 7 to 13 years of age; living with parents prior to admission to the hospital; not mentally retarded (Full-Scale WISC-R above 75); no major medical illness; meeting DSM-III criteria for major depression, dysthymic disorder, schizophrenia, or schizotypal personality disorder. The present report provides preliminary data from the first 31 families to participate in the study. Due to the frequency of multiple diagnoses in our sample, it was necessary to establish hierarchical rules for assigning children to primary diagnostic groups. Based on the DSM-III procedure of not diagnosing major depressive disorders when superimposed on schizophrenic disorders, schizophrenia and schizotypal disorders took precedence over depressive disorders. Additionally, because a diagnosis of major depression requires more severe levels of depressive symptoms than dysthymic disorder, major depression took precedence over dysthymic disorder. Operationally, this meant that three children with concurrent schizotypal and dysthymic disorders were grouped in the schizotypal category, and 3 children with major depression superimposed on an underlying dysthymic disorder ("double depression") were grouped in the major depression category. One child who presented with a major depressive picture but also showed some manic symptoms was classified in the major depression group. These rules resulted in the following diagnostic distribution for our sample: schizophrenia (n = 6); schizotypal (n = 10); major depression (n = 11); dysthymic disorder (n = 4). The sample consisted of 8 girls and 23 boys. Twenty-seven children were white, 1 was black, and 3 were of Hispanic descent. Family social class, calculated by the Duncan Socioeconomic Index, ranged from 13.7 to 89.9, revealing a wide range of socioeconomic levels in the sample. WISC-R Full-Scale IQs ranged from 74 to 133, with a mean of 100.55. Fourteen children came from single-parent homes and 17 children came from two-parent homes or homes where the unmarried parent was living with a partner. Four children were residing with adoptive, as opposed to biological, parents. These children included one child with a diagnosis of major depression, one child with a diagnosis of schizophrenia, and two children with schizotypal diagnoses.

Procedures

Diagnostic Assessment

Diagnoses were made by a trained child psychologist or psychiatrist who was blind to the family assessment data. Diagnoses were based on the results of (a) structured interviews conducted with the child using the Schedule for Affective Disorders and Schizophrenia for School-Age Children (K-SADS-E; 22), (b) direct interviews with each parent using a modified version of the Camberwell Family Interview designed to assess all symptoms required to make the target diagnoses (2), and (c) all other information available on the child, including longitudinal observations of the child's clinical status during the course of hospitalization and the results of other interviews conducted during hospitalization. Prior data using similar procedures indicated high interrater agreement on diagnostic judgments, kappa = .82, $p < .001$ (3). For the purpose of this study, we required that two clinicians agree on the child's diagnosis in order for a child to be included in the sample.

Symptom Presentation and Adjustment

Because we were interested in evaluating whether the family measures included in the study were related to the child's pattern of onset of disturbance and general psychosocial functioning, several measures of the child's pattern of symptom development and psychosocial adjustment were obtained. All ratings on these measures were made by a trained rater after reviewing the child's hospital records, cumulative school records, and prior clinical evaluations. First, pattern of onset was classified using the following categories: (a) acute, child was hospitalized within 1 year of the first signs of symptom formation, and (b) nonacute, child showed a pattern of slow decline in adaptive functioning and ultimately required hospitalization. Secondly, premorbid adjustment was rated using Cannon-Spoor's (5) Premorbid Adjustment Scale, modified to include one item from Gittleman-Klein's (9) Asociality Scale. The resulting measure included judgments on the following items: (a) sociability and withdrawal; (b) the number and quality of peer relationships; (c) scholastic performance; (d) social and behavioral adaptation to school; and (e) interests. Ratings for each item were made on a 7-point scale: 0 (ideal adjustment) to 6 (severe impairment in functioning), and an overall percentage, premorbid adjustment score was generated by summing the scores for each item and dividing this sum by the highest possible score. Because these ratings were aimed at assessing the subjects' functioning prior to the onset of disturbance, ratings were made for the period prior to symptom onset. For children who presented with chronic disturbance, ratings were made for the period prior to the onset of the target disorder and hospitalization. Third, ratings on the Children's Global Adjustment Scale (C-GAS; 24) were used to obtain a measure of the severity of disturbance at the time of hospitalization, as well as a measure of the highest level of functioning that the child achieved over the course of his or her development. The C-GAS ranges from 1 to 100 and includes behavior examples that serve as anchor points. Scores above 70 reflect normal adjustment and scores below 40 reflect major impairment. Interrater reliabilities on these measures were consistently above .81 (Pearson correlation coefficients), indicating satisfactory reliability.

Communication Deviance

A measure of communication deviance derived from parents' responses on the TAT (14) was employed. The TAT was administered during the individual parent session after the parent had completed the 5-minute speech sample, CFI, and interaction cue elicitation procedures described below. This administration of the TAT differed from standard TAT procedures in that parents were given minimal prompting (only on the first card). Seven TAT cards were chosen because they elicit familial themes (cards 1, 2, 3GF, 6BM, 7BM, 8BM, and 13MF). Beginning with the instructions, TAT procedures were audiotaped and subsequently transcribed for coding. Coding was conducted using procedures developed by Jones (14). Because of the high rate of single-parent families in our sample, Jones's procedures for classifying CD levels were modified so as not to use criteria that involved combining both parents' data. This resulted in a child being classified as having high family CD only if one or more parents had an elevation on one of two factors: misperceptions or major closure problems. All cases not meeting this criterion were grouped in the low-CD category. Note that this represents a major departure from the Jones criteria, in which elevations on other factors for dual-parent families qualified the family for high-CD status.

Thus, it is possible that some of the families classified as low CD in this sample would have been classified otherwise by the original Jones criteria.

CD coding was completed by a trained rater who was blind to the child's diagnosis and EE status, and had previously demonstrated acceptable reliability. Additionally, to insure adequate reliability of coding throughout the study, TAT transcripts were independently coded by a second rater, and with consistently high reliability.

Expressed Emotion

Expressed emotion ratings were made from our modified Camberwell Family Interview for Children (CFI-C), administered during an individual session with each parent by a trained interviewer. The CFI-C (see 2) is a semistructured, audiotaped interview that focuses on the onset and development of the patient's difficulties and the impact of the patient's behavior on the family environment during the 3 months prior to hospital admission. Administration time is roughly 1½ hours. Modifications to the standard CFI made in the CFI-C primarily involved the addition of items focusing on child behavior (for example, school functioning) and symptoms in order to facilitate diagnostic judgments. Following the interview, audiotapes of the interview were used to rate the number of critical comments, and statements of dislike or resentment about the child by parents. Ratings were also made of the degree to which parents expressed emotionally overinvolved, markedly protective, overconcerned attitudes toward the child, as manifested either in the parents' interview behavior or in their descriptions of events outside of the interview. Ratings of emotional overinvolvement were made using a 6-point scale: 0 (absent) to 5 (extremely high).

CFI scores of 6 or more criticisms and/or ratings of 3 (moderately high) or higher on emotional overinvolvement (EOI) designated a parent as high EE in this study. Although early studies of EE used a cutoff score of 4 EOI for designating relatives as high EE, recent studies (see 4), and the only prior study that evaluated the relationship between EOI and the patient's premorbid adjustment (21), used a cutoff score of 3. Consequently, to provide maximum comparability between the present study and the Miklowitz et al. (21) study, a cutoff score of 3 on the EOI dimension was employed in the present analyses. Parents falling below these cutoff scores (criticism or EOI) were classified as low EE. A family was designated as high EE if either parent was classified as high EE.

EE ratings were made by one of two trained raters from audiotapes of the interviews. Both EE raters had received extensive prior training on rating EE, and had been certified to work independently. In order to receive this certification, each rater had demonstrated a minimum reliability coefficient of .80 in rating the number of critical comments (using Pearson product-moment correlation coefficients) and in judging high versus low emotional overinvolvement (using the phi coefficient). Both raters had had extensive prior experience coding CFI tapes for other studies. Random reliability checks were conducted throughout the course of this study in order to insure against reliability drift, and they indicated continued high reliability.

Family Interaction Procedures

After the individual sessions, the child and his or her parent(s) were brought together for a series of family interaction tasks designed to elicit family interaction patterns in response to three types of situational demands. The interaction tasks included (a) two trials on a family problem-solving task (11), (b) one trial on a modified teaching task aimed at eliciting child and parent responses to achievement situations, and (c) one trial on a modified Family Rorschach task in which families were instructed to "try to have fun" playing a game in which they look at an inkblot together and try to reach a consensus about what it looks like. This modification to the Family Rorschach task was intended as a behavioral challenge to depressed and dysthymic children who, by definition, tend to have difficulty obtaining pleasure from their activities.

Follow-Up Assessment

Four-year follow-up assessments are planned for this sample. Our aims in the follow-up are to evaluate the child's diagnostic status and level of social functioning during the follow-up period. Children and parents will be interviewed using the K-SADS and Social Adjustment Inventory for Children and Adolescents (13).

Major Findings

Preliminary Analyses

Prior to the major data analyses, preliminary analyses were conducted to compare diagnostic groups (children with depressive versus schizophrenia-spectrum disorders), children with high- versus low-CD parents, children with high- versus low-EE parents, and children with acute versus non-acute onset. No between-group differences were found for age, sex, socioeconomic status, or Full-Scale WISC-R IQ. Additionally, there were no significant differences in the number of single- versus dual-parent families as a function of onset type or diagnosis. There was a tendency, however, for children from dual-parent families to be classified as being from high- as opposed to low-CD families (Fisher's exact test, $p < .10$), high EE (Fisher's exact test, $p<.11$), criticism (Fisher's exact test, $p<.14$), and emotional overinvolvement (Fisher's exact test, $p<.05$). This was expected because children from dual-parent families could be classified as belonging to the "high" group based on either mothers' or fathers' scores, whereas children from single-parent homes were classified only on the basis of mothers' scores. Due to this potentially confounding variable, analyses were conducted using both family scores and mothers' scores.

Results

CD and Child Diagnosis

The first major question addressed in the study concerned whether high CD is *specific* to parents of children with schizophrenic and schizotypal disorders, or is a *more general* characteristic of parents of disturbed children. Table 1 shows the distribution of CD by diagnostic group. Inspection of Table 1 reveals a strong association between parental CD and a diagnosis of schizophrenia and schizotypal personality disorders. All of the schizophrenic children and 9 of the 10 schizotypal children had at least one high CD parent. CD was less common in parents of depressed children. Five of the 11 children with major depressive disorder (45.4%) and 2 of the 4 children with dysthymic disorder (50%) had high-CD parents.

Due to the low within-cell expected frequencies, statistical tests of the

TABLE 1

Family Communication Deviance Scores and Diagnosis of Offspring

	Parental Communication Deviance	
Diagnosis of Offspring	**Low**	**High**
Schizophrenia	0	5
Schizotypal*	1	9
Major Depression**	6	5
Dysthymic Disorder	2	2

*Includes three offspring with dual diagnoses of schizotypal and dysthymic disorder.

**Includes three offspring with double depression.

degree of association between CD and child diagnosis were performed using a 2×2 table in which schizophrenic and schizotypal children were combined, and children with major depression and dysthymic disorder were combined. A Fisher's exact test revealed a highly significant ($p < .008$) association between CD and diagnosis. Based on these data, the sensitivity of parental CD as a marker of childhood schizophrenia-spectrum disorders is 93.33% (14/15), the specificity is 53.33% (8/15), and the overall rate of correct classification is 73.33% (22/30). The relationship between CD based on maternal data only and diagnosis was in the same direction but only marginally significant (Fisher's exact test, $p < .08$).

It is important to note that although these data provide strong evidence supporting a link between parental CD and childhood schizophrenia-spectrum disorders, these data also indicate that CD is not specific to schizophrenia-spectrum disorders. The finding that almost half (47%) of the depressed children had high-CD parents led us to examine whether high parental CD was found in a particular subgroup of depressed children. Preliminary analyses indicated that within the depressed group, CD level and onset pattern were not significantly associated with whether the child came from a dual- or single-parent family. Because major depression is viewed as a more severe disorder than dysthymia, we examined whether parental CD was more common in children with major depression than in children with dysthymic disorder. However, as shown in Table 1, relatively comparable proportions of children with major depression and dysthymic disorder had high-CD parents. We then computed a series of t-tests aimed at evaluating whether children within the depressed group with high- and low-CD parents differed on other dimensions of symptomatology and social functioning. These analyses revealed no significant differences between the high- and low-CD groups in severity of dysfunction (C-GAS score) at index hospitalization, highest level of global adjustment achieved, or premorbid adjustment. Similarly, within the depressed group, onset pattern was not significantly associated with parental CD (Fisher's exact test, $p < .18$). It is noteworthy, however, that 80% (4/5) of the depressed children with acute onsets had low-CD parents, whereas only 40% (4/10) of the depressed children with nonacute onsets had low-CD parents. This may reflect a pattern that could be detected with a larger sample size, or with a more differentiated schema for classifying onset.

EE and Child Diagnosis

A second question addressed in the study concerned whether EE subtypes are distributed evenly across diagnostic groups. To evaluate this question, Fisher's exact tests were performed using 2×2 tables comparing the proportion of depressed and dysthymic children relative to schizophrenic and schizotypal children classified as high versus low EE, based on (a) criticisms, (b) emotional overinvolvement, and (c) criticism or emotional involvement. No significant differences as a function of diagnosis were obtained. Similarly, *t*-tests comparing mothers of children with depressive and schizophrenia-spectrum disorders also indicated no significant differences in number of critical comments ($t[24.2]=1.44$, n.s.) or emotional overinvolvement ($t[23.9]=0$, n.s.).

CD and Early Course of Symptom Development

Another aim of this study was to evaluate whether CD and EE are associated with the child's early course of symptom development and onset of disturbance. These analyses were complicated by the fact that there were significantly more acute onsets in children with depressive disorders than in children with schizophrenia-spectrum disorders (Fisher's exact test, $p<.02$), with all of the acute onsets falling in the major depression group. Thus, although a significant relationship was found between CD and onset pattern (Fisher's exact test, $p<.02$), given the relationships between CD and diagnosis and diagnosis and onset, this relationship is strongly influenced by diagnosis. Most (4/5) of the acute onset, major depressive cases had low-CD parents, whereas most (14/15) of the schizophrenic and schizotypal children, who uniformly had nonacute onsets, had high-CD parents.

EE and Early Course of Symptom Development

As noted previously, a major aim of this study was to ascertain whether EE predicted course of childhood depressive and schizophrenia-spectrum disorders. Our first step in addressing this question was to evaluate whether EE was retrospectively associated with the early pre-hospitalization course of illness. Table 2 shows the proportion of children with acute and nonacute onsets whose mothers were classified as high and low in EOI. The distribution for the total sample is shown in Part A (the upper half of the Table), and the distribution for the depressed group is shown in part B (the lower half of the Table). These data reveal a significant relationship between onset pattern and mother's EOI. As shown in Part A, whereas all of the children with acute onset had mothers expressing low levels of EOI, 59% (13/22) of the children with nonacute onset had mothers expressing high levels of EOI (Fisher's exact test, $p<.03$). This relationship is even stronger when only the data for the depressed group (the only group showing variance in onset patterns) is considered. As shown in Part B, the 100% rate of low EOI in mothers of acute cases remains constant. However, roughly 86% (6/7) of the

TABLE 2

Relationship between Child's Onset Pattern and Mother's Emotional Overinvolvement Ratings

A. Total Sample

	Onset Pattern	
Emotional Overinvolvement	**Acute**	**Nonacute**
Low	5	9
High	0	13
Fisher's exact test, $p < .03$		

B. Depressive Disorders Sample

	Onset Pattern	
Emotional Overinvolvement	**Acute**	**Nonacute**
Low	5	1
High	0	6
Fisher's exact test, $p < .01$		

nonacute depressed and dysthymic cases have mothers expressing high EOI (Fisher's exact test, $p < .02$). These data parallel the results of t-tests, indicating significantly higher maternal emotional overinvolvement in nonacute cases than in acute cases.

In contrast to the strong relationship obtained between onset and mother's EOI, onset was not significantly related to mother's criticism level. Additionally, onset was not related to family ratings (including all available parents) for overall EE, EOI, or criticism. These findings indicate that mother's EOI stands out among the other EE ratings as a strong post-dictor of the pattern of onset (chronicity) for these children's disorders, particularly for children in the depressed group.

Discussion

Major findings of this study to date are: (a) communication deviance is significantly more common in parents of children with schizophrenic and schizotypal disorders than in parents of children with major depression or dysthymic disorder; (b) although the relationship between CD and childhood-onset schizophrenia-spectrum disorders is significant, CD is not specific to schizophrenia-spectrum disorders; (c) EE subtype level was not associated with child diagnosis; and (d) the child's pattern of symptom onset was significantly related to the mother's level of emotional overinvolvement, particularly among children with depressive disorders.

These findings have a number of implications for our understanding of childhood-onset schizophrenia-spectrum and depressive disorders. First, the finding that CD was almost uniformly present in parents of children with schizophrenic and schizotypal disorders and less frequent in parents of depressed children provides strong support for the hypothesis that parental CD is a risk factor for schizophrenia-spectrum disorders. Although the present study does not provide a means of ascertaining whether parental CD preceded the onset of child symptoms, or is an index of genetic or psychosocial risk, we do have evidence of a strong concurrent association.

Second, the finding of a comparable high rate of CD in parents of children with schizophrenic and schizotypal disorders suggests similarities and possible continuities between these disorders in childhood. Follow-up data on the rates of subsequent schizophrenia in schizotypal children will be important for further evaluating the relationship between these disorders.

Third, the meaning of high CD in a subsample of depressed children is currently unclear. Our present analyses do not support the hypothesis that CD is associated with greater dysfunction in the depressed sample, although there is a nonsignificant trend for CD to be more common in the nonacute cases. Further research is needed to determine the impact of CD on the development and course of childhood depressive disorders.

Fourth, the finding that mother's EOI was associated with onset provides some evidence of a link between EE attitudes and the early course of childhood depressive and schizophrenia-spectrum disorders. Clearly, however, follow-up data are required to determine the extent to which mother's EOI, other EE dimensions, or other related or unrelated variables predict outcome for our children.

A limitation of this study is that our data do not provide a means of determining whether mother's EOI preceded or was a reaction to the child's developing symptomatology. The present data are consistent with recent findings by Miklowitz, Goldstein, and Falloon (21), which indicate higher EOI in parents of adult schizophrenic patients with poor premorbid adjustment when compared to parents of patients with higher premorbid adjustment. Clearly, if our children were to continue to present with schizophrenic and schizotypal disorders as adults, these children would be among the poorest of the poor premorbid cases. Our data certainly raise the question of whether EOI is a normal maternal reaction to coping with a child who has shown prolonged and severe dysfunction.

In conclusion, our findings to date highlight the potential value of studies of parental communication and affective patterns for increasing our understanding of the development of childhood-onset schizophrenia-spectrum and depressive disorders. It is important to recall, however, that the CD and EE measures employed in this study were not derived from analyses of family interaction patterns. Rather, these measures were derived from interview assessments of individual parents in the child's absence. The CD and EE measures are viewed as "marker variables" that index complex interactional processes. Data clarifying the nature of the interactional processes "marked" by the CD and EE measures are needed. A strong priority for our project will be to evaluate our interactional data with the aim of determining the functional significance of parental communication styles and affective attitudes within the context of parent-child interaction. We will clarify the nature of the child behaviors—in "real time"—that elicit, maintain, and disrupt interactional analogues of these marker variables. Conversely, within the course of our sampling direct family interaction, we will attempt to identify parent behaviors that trigger, escalate, or interfere with symptomatic behaviors. These analyses may help us to elucidate family processes that influence the course of childhood depressive and schizophrenia-spectrum disorders.

REFERENCES

1. Asarnow, J. R. Children with peer adjustment problems: Sequential and non-sequential analyses of school behaviors. *Journal of Consulting and Clinical Psychology 51*: 709–717, 1983.

2. ______. Modified Camberwell Family Interview for Children. Unpublished manuscript, UCLA School of Medicine, Los Angeles CA, 1981.

3. ______, & Carlson, G. A. The Depression Self-Rating Scale: Utility with child psychiatric inpatients. *Journal of Consulting and Clinical Psychology 54*: 491–499, 1985.

4. Berkowitz, R., Kuipers, L., Eberlein-Vries, R., & Leff, J. Lowering expressed emotion in relatives of schizophrenics. In M. J. Goldstein (ed.), *New developments in interventions with families of schizophrenics*. San Francisco: Jossey-Bass, 1981.

5. Cannon-Spoor, H. E., Potkin, S. G., & Watt, R. J. Measurement of premorbid adjustment in chronic schizophrenia. *Schizophrenia Bulletin 8*: 470–484, 1982.

6. Cantwell, D. P., Baker, L., & Rutter, M. Family factors in the syndrome of infantile autism. In M. Rutter & E. Schopler (eds.), *Autism: A reappraisal of concepts and treatment*. New York: Plenum Press, 1978.

7. Carlson, G. A., & Cantwell, D. P. Unmasking masked depression in children and adolescents. *American Journal of Psychiatry 137*: 445–449, 1980.

8. Doane, J. A., West, K. L., Goldstein, M. J., Rodnick, E. H., & Jones, J. E. Parental communication deviance and affective style: Predictors of subsequent schizophrenia spectrum disorders in vulnerable adolescents. *Archives of General Psychiatry 38*: 679–685, 1981.

9. Gittleman-Klein, R., & Klein, D. F. Premorbid asocial adjustment and prognosis in schizophrenia. *Journal of Psychiatric Research 7*: 35–53, 1969.

10. Goldfarb, W., Goldfarb, N., & Scholl, H. The speech of mothers of schizophrenic children. *American Journal of Psychiatry 122*: 1220–1227, 1966.

11. ______, Levy, D. M., & Meyers, D. I. The mother speaks to her schizophrenic child: Language in childhood schizophrenia. *Psychiatry 35*: 217–226, 1972.

12. Goldstein, M. J., Rodnick, E. H., Jones, J. E., McPherson, S. R., & West, K. L. Familial precursors of schizophrenia spectrum disorders. In L. C. Wynne, R. L. Cromwell, and S. Matthysse (eds.), *The nature of schizophrenia: New approaches to research and treatment*. New York: John Wiley & Sons, 1978.

13. John, K., & Davis Gammon, C. Social Adjustment Inventory for Children and Adolescents (SAICA). Unpublished manuscript, Yale University Depression Research Unit, New Haven CT, 1982.

14. Jones, J. E. Patterns of transactional style deviance in the TAT's of parents of schizophrenics. *Family Process 16*: 327–337, 1977.

15. Kashani, J. H., McGee, R. O., Clarkson, S. E., Anderson, J. C., Walton, L. A., Williams, S., Robins, A. J., Cytryn, L., & McKnew, D. H. Depression in a sample of 9-year-old children: Prevalence and associated characteristics. *Archives of General Psychiatry 40*: 1217–1223, 1983.

16. Kaslow, N. J., & Rehm, L. P. Conceptualization, assessment, and treatment of depression in children. In A. E. Kazdin & P. Bornstein (eds.), *Handbook of clinical behavior therapy with children*. New York: Dorsey Press, 1985.

17. Kazdin, A. E., Rancurello, M. D., & Unis, A. S. Childhood depression. In G. D. Burrows & J. S. Werry (eds.), *Advances in human psychopharmacology* (vol. 4). Greenwich CT: JAI Press, in press.

18. Kovacs, M., Feinberg, T. L., Crouse-Novak, M. A., Paulauskas, S. L., & Finkelstein, R. Depressive disorders in childhood. *Archives of General Psychiatry 41*: 229–237, 1984.

19. ______, Feinberg, T. L., Crouse-Novak, M., Paulauskas, S. L., Pollack, M., & Finkelstein, R. Depressive disorders in childhood. *Archives of General Psychiatry 41*: 643–649, 1984.

20. Lewis, J. M., Rodnick, E. H., & Goldstein, M. J. Intrafamilial interactive behavior, parental communication deviance, and risk for schizophrenia. *Journal of Abnormal Psychology 90*: 448–457, 1981.

21. Miklowitz, D. J., Goldstein, M. J., & Falloon, I. R. H. Premorbid and symptomatic characteristics of schizophrenics from families with high and low levels of expressed emotion. *Journal of Abnormal Psychology 92: 359*–367, 1983.

22. Puig-Antich, J., Orvaschel, H., Tabrizi, M., & Chambers, W. J. Schedule for Affective Disorders and Schizophrenia for School-Age Children, Epidemiological Version. Unpublished manuscript, New York State Psychiatric Institute, Department of Child and Adolescent Psychiatry, 1983.

23. Rutter, M., Tizard, J., Yule, W., Graham, P., & Whitmore, K. Isle of Wight studies, 1964–1974. *Psychological Medicine 6*: 313–332, 1976.

24. Shaffer, D., Gould, M. S., Brasic, J., Ambrosini, P., Fisher, P., Bird, H., & Aluwah-

lia, S. A Children's Global Adjustment Scale (CGAS). *Archives of General Psychiatry 40*: 1228–1231, 1983.

25. Singer, M. T., & Wynne, L. C. Differentiating characteristics for parents of childhood schizophrenics, childhood neurotics, and young adult schizophrenics. *American Journal of Psychiatry 120*: 234–243, 1963.

26. ______, & Wynne, L. C. Thought disorder and family relations of schizophrenics: IV. Results and Implications. *Archives of General Psychiatry 12*: 201–212, 1965.

27. ______, & Wynne, L. C. Principles for scoring communication defects and deviances in parents of schizophrenics: Rorschach and TAT scoring manuals. *Psychiatry 29*: 260–288, 1966.

28. Vaughn, C. E., & Leff, J. P. The influence of family and social factors on the course of psychiatric illness: A comparison of schizophrenic and depressed neurotic patients. *British Journal of Psychiatry 129*: 125–137, 1976.

29. Wild, C., Singer, M., Rosman, B., Ricci, J., & Lidz, T. Measuring disordered styles of thinking: Using the Object Sorting Test on parents of schizophrenic patients. *Archives of General Psychiatry 13*: 471–476, 1965.

30. Wynne, L. C., & Cole, R. E. The Rochester risk research program: A new look at parental diagnoses and family relationships. In H. Stierlin, L. C. Wynne, & M. Wirsching (eds.), *Psychosocial intervention in schizophrenia: An international view*. Berlin: Springer-Verlag, 1983.

31. ______, Singer, M. T., Bartko, J. J., & Toohey, M. L. Schizophrenics and their families: Research on parental communication. In J. M. Tanner (ed.), Developments in psychiatric research. London: Hodder and Stoughton, 1977.

8

CONFIRMATORY FEEDBACK IN FAMILIES OF SCHIZOPHRENICS: Theory, Methods, and Preliminary Results*

ARNE HOLTE, LARS WICHSTRØM, KRISTIN Ø. ERNØ, KRISTIN KVESETH
University of Oslo, Norway

According to most psychological theories, personal development evolves through the solving of interpersonal conflicts. The way parents cope with conflicts with their offspring is believed to be of critical importance to the development and maintenance of the child's behavior. Families are able to resolve such conflicts only by means of communication. For a researcher who wants to understand the development or maintenance of dysfunctional behavior, there are two central questions: (a) *What* aspects of communication should be measured? and (b) *How* can we measure them?

Several methods have been developed to detect communication that differentiates families with schizophrenic offspring from families of non-schizophrenic offspring. Some of these methods, such as affective style (AS), communication deviance (CD), and expressed emotion (EE) have been

*The authors wish to express their gratitude to color-chief Urban Willumsen and Einar Hvitt, Ph.D. (engineering), both at the Jotun Fabrikker Company, Sandefjord, Norway, and Professor Lars Sivik, University of Gothenburg, for their assistance in the development of the Color Conflict Method and the calculation of the CIELAB-values; Associate Professor Torbjirn Moum and Research Associate Kristian Tambs, Department of Behavioral Sciences in Medicine, University of Oslo, for statistical consultation; and audiovisual engineer Per Olav Saelid for technical assistance. The research has been funded by a grant from the Department of Behavioral Sciences in Medicine at the University of Oslo, The Norwegian Research Council for Science and the Humanities, and the Anders Jahres Foundation.

discussed elsewhere in this book. Parental communication has been measured by these methods, which have proved to be good "markers" of psychiatric illness in the offspring. Helmersen (8) has recently demonstrated, however, that most of these methods lack the theoretical basis necessary to understand *what* they measure. Because of loose conceptual validity, it is not possible to explain how and why whatever they measure should be related to any particular type of psychiatric disturbance. This raises questions like: What are the critical factors in AS, CD, or EE that are related to schizophrenia? Why does EE have a good predictive validity for relapse not only in schizophrenia, but also in depression, and, as described elsewhere in this volume (see chapters 10 and 11), in onset of mania.

The present chapter addresses the specific relationship between schizophrenia and certain forms of communication in the family. The relationships between measures of parental communication and several psychiatric disturbances definitely are of practical importance. They do, however, contribute little to the theoretical understanding of the relationship between communication and specific psychiatric disturbances. We may conjecture a "missing theoretical link" between the specific aspect of communication to be measured and the particular disturbance to be studied. To be able to draw theoretical conclusions about the significance of communicational factors in the development or maintenance of psychiatric disturbances, however, we need measures of communication that are theoretically based and can be conceptually linked to the specific disturbance in question. In an effort to meet these two requirements, we first present some theoretical arguments that will then lead into our methodological approach.

Theory

Schizophrenia and Reality

Typical of schizophrenic patients is their incapacity to interpret reality. Their ability to differentiate what is "real" or "unreal" has been lost; the distinction between fantasy and the phenomenal world, and the distinction between me and not-me are often confused. Therefore, if schizophrenia is specifically related to any particular types, patterns, or sequences of communication, we would expect it to be related to those aspects of the communication that are involved in the establishment of the distinction between real and unreal, that is, in the definition and maintenance of a common reality.

The Social Construction of Reality

Human action takes place in relation to a social reality. This reality is made of "symbolic matter" (2) and constructed by man himself (3). Social reality is constructed by drawing distinctions (17). By drawing distinctions and labeling the separate parts, categories are established that enable the consequences of an action to be predicted. Being able to predict these consequences reduces anxiety and enables continued action. The distinctions and labels valid in the culture constitute the language. In human beings, language largely replaces the function of instincts in other species. Language structures human action. To learn the language of a culture is to learn a form of life (22). The learning of language or, more precisely, language games (22), implies that the distinctions valid for one particular culture are programmed into the individual. Through the learning of language, the culture is built into the individual, and the individual is built into the culture.

The Quality of Real

As a psychological quality, reality or "real" is that which is perceived to have an existence independent of human action and which can be communicated to others. The quality of real is established when an experience is communicated to another person. That it *can* be communicated, however, must be confirmed by the receiver. This simple feedback process is the core of the continuous negotiation of social reality embedded in all human interaction (16). Social reality is both continuously maintained and broken down by the use of language. The distinctions that constitute social reality stay real and valid only if they are maintained through interaction with others. Therefore, to attain and maintain the quality of "realness", subjective experience must continuously be transformed according to the rules of language and subjected to control by others. Subjective experience that cannot be communicated takes the quality of unreal. In Western industrialized cultures, such experiences are labelled impressions, sensations, perceptions, fantasies, dreams, illusions, hallucinations, feelings, and so on. Definitions of reality do not have to be confirmed explicitly every time they are expressed. As the child grows up, most confirmations are mediated through the consequences of action. Definitions of reality that are never put into practice fade and disappear.

To summarize: to become real, subjective experience must (a) be expressed by a first person (sender) toward a second person (receiver); (b) the first person's action must be received by a second person; and (c) the first person's message must be confirmed by a second person by means of a response directed toward the sender.

Confirmation and Disconfirmation

The interpretation of a message always depends upon the social reality embedded in the context of the message. In human interaction, the sender's action is always a potential context for the receiver's reaction. Confirmation implies that an initial action becomes the context for reaction. Confirmation and disconfirmation refer to the feedback mechanisms in this process. A confirmatory feedback reaction implies that the first person's utterance has been accepted as a valid context for the second person's message. Thus, if two persons disagree, a confirmatory feedback reaction signals that the context for the disagreement has been accepted. Disconfirmation refers to the case where no such signal has been given.

Confirmation may be more precisely defined as a reaction by a second person toward the first person's verbal and nonverbal utterance. From an observer's point of view, this means that the first person can be certain that the second person has understood or accepted the first person's utterance as a valid expression of the first person's experience. This definition implies that the second person signals that the first person's utterance is accepted as a valid context for the second person's utterance, and that the content of the second person's message is thematically congruent with the content of the first person's message (see 14): for example, 1st person: "That man is wearing my hat!"; 2nd person: "No, your hat is on your head!"

For most authors (see 5, 9, 10, 14, 19), the distinction between agreement and disagreement is irrelevant to the determination of confirmation versus disconfirmation. When the family is involved in a conflict between its members, however, it is important for both clinicians and researchers to know if the confirmation takes the form of explicit disagreements or not. In accord with this, we propose to differentiate three *strategies of confirmation: confirmation with agreement, confirmation with neutrality*, and *confirmation with disagreement*.

Disconfirmation may be defined as a reaction by a second person to a first person's utterance, which, from an observer's point of view *neither* explicitly *nor* implicitly indicates whether the second person has understood or accepted the first person's utterance as a valid expression of the first person's experience. Disconfirmation implies that the second person directly or indirectly throws doubt upon the first person's reliability or entitlement to the message expressed. By the act of disconfirmation, the first person's utterance is negated as a valid context for the second person's utterance. A shortcut to the definition of disconfirmation is to say that it refers to an undermining of the other person's definitions of reality: 1st person: "That man is wearing my hat!"; 2nd person: "Have you seen Doctor Rubinstein lately?"

A disconfirmatory feedback reaction may be the response to another person's utterance. In that case, it is labelled *active disqualification of others*. It may also be directed toward one's own utterance. In that case, it is labelled *self-disqualification*. Self-disqualifications and active disqualifications of others may be either *linear* or *paradoxical* (1). Theoretically, this amounts to four different, active strategies or modes of disconfirmation. However, for the purpose of developing a conceptual tool for empirical analysis of disconfirmation, we will not maintain separate categorizations for paradoxical utterances. From our experience, such paradoxical utterances are rare, and when they do occur, acceptable interrater reliability is almost impossible because there are only impressionistic guidelines about how to draw a distinction characterizing the supposedly contradictory context of a message. The "observation of paradoxes" mainly seems to rest upon high-level interpretations.

Hence, we propose to differentiate between three basic, *active* strategies of disconfirmation: *active disqualification of others, linear self-disqualification*, and *egocentric utterance*. Possible paradoxical disqualifications should be included under the category of egocentric utterances—which are not so theoretically pure but are, nevertheless, researchable (1); or they can be classified as active disqualifications of others. However, according to the definition above, all disconfirmations do not have to be uttered actively. The second person may also disconfirm the first person's action *passively* by not reacting. This is a fourth category of disconfirmation, namely, *ignoring*.

The Conceptual System

The following conceptual schema has been constructed in order to analyze the feedback mechanisms involved in the establishment and maintenance of a common reality in social systems.

Strategies of Confirmation

1. *Confirmation with agreement*: The second person takes a position toward the position expressed by the first person. The second person's position is in full agreement with the first person's position: 1st person: "Meryl Streep is a marvelous actress." 2nd person: "Oh, she is fantastic!"

2. *Confirmation with neutrality*: The second person does not take a position. The second person's utterance expresses or clearly implies full

acceptance of the first person's utterance: 1st person: "I am not sure if I want to go to that lecture."; 2nd person: "Well, that is up to you."

3. *Confirmation with disagreement*: The second person takes a position toward the position expressed by the first person. The second person's position is in disagreement with the first person's position. The second person specifies what the disagreement is or why he or she disagrees: 1st person: "T. S. Eliot is an exciting author."; 2nd person: "No, he is too vulgar in my opinion."

Strategies of Disconfirmation

1. *Active disqualification of others*: The second person's utterance throws doubt upon the first person's credibility, status, or competence: 1st person: "I have decided not to be a physician, mother."; 2nd person: "You are still only 23, Jill, and you are not old enough to decide about such an important matter." Or the second person counterdefines the first person's experience ("experiential imperialism"): 1st person: "I am so damned angry with John, I could kill him!"; 2nd person: "No, Jill, I know you better than that. You are really depressed. That's what you really are." Or the second person gives an exaggerated importance to nonessential elements in the first person's utterance and treats them as essential elements (quibbling): 1st person: "Oh Lord, I cannot stand the sight of you, John, when you behave like that."; 2nd person: "Thou shalt not take the name of the Lord thy God in vain!"

2. *Linear self-disqualification*: The second person's utterance contains two or more mutually exclusive messages and a change of mind is not involved: 2nd person: "This soup is too hot—and too cold."

3. *Egocentric utterances*: The second person's utterance, directed toward the first person, is ambiguous or impossible for the first person to understand: 1st person: "What do you want to do?"; 2nd person: "No, that is not possible."; 1st person: "No." In this example, both the second and the third utterances are egocentric.

4. *Ignoring*: The second person does not react toward the first person's utterance when a reaction would have been proper or expected: 1st person: "John, I feel I'm going crazy when you treat me that way!"; 2nd person does not respond. Or the second person reacts with an utterance that clearly does not show that the first person's utterance has registered: 1st person: "I have had a hard day today."; 2nd person: "When does the football match start?" Or the second person interrupts the first person and continues speaking before the first person has completed a meaningful utterance: 1st person: "Would you . . . 2nd person (interrupting): "You should have heard what I heard earlier today!"

Confirmation and Conflict

We introduced this chapter by referring to the fact that most psychological theories relate the development and the maintenance of behavior to the way families communicate during conflicts. One particular kind of conflict is *interpersonal conflict of experience*, which may be defined as a situation in which a first person and a second person have different definitions of what they believe to be the same aspect of reality. As long as the family agrees about reality, or no member is expected to act, then the confirmatory feedback mechanisms are barely activated. If, however, the family is involved in an interpersonal conflict of experience and action is required, the feedback functions are activated. The way the family copes with such conflicts is of crucial importance to the establishment and maintenance of a valid perception of reality that, for example, an offspring can depend upon as a basis for his or her actions.

Confirmation and Schizophrenia

The need for continuous confirmatory feedback and the vulnerability to disconfirmatory feedback varies from individual to individual according to genetic, other biological, psychological, and social factors. However, if the loss of ability to interpret social reality, characteristic of schizophrenic patients, can be related to the feedback mechanism mentioned, it will probably take place in one of three ways—confirmatory feedback may be of low frequency, or disconfirmatory feedback may be of high frequency, or both. Further, we presume that these differences are related to corresponding differences in other aspects of the family's structure and interaction.

Objectives and Design

Figure 1 presents the objectives and the design of the study. The relationships between five "levels" of the family interaction are investigated. These are: 1) *the personality-structure level* as represented by the degree of individuation of the two parents; 2) *the interpersonal-experience level* as represented by the mutual perceptions of the relationship between the two parents; 3) *the communication level* as illustrated in the study by the use of confirmation and disconfirmation in the family; 4) *the interaction level* as illustrated by the types and patterns of cybernetic relationship control (20) in the family; and 5) *the systems level* as represented by the patterns of sequences of confirmatory and disconfirmatory transactions and of cybernetic relationship control transactions in the family. The design is constructed

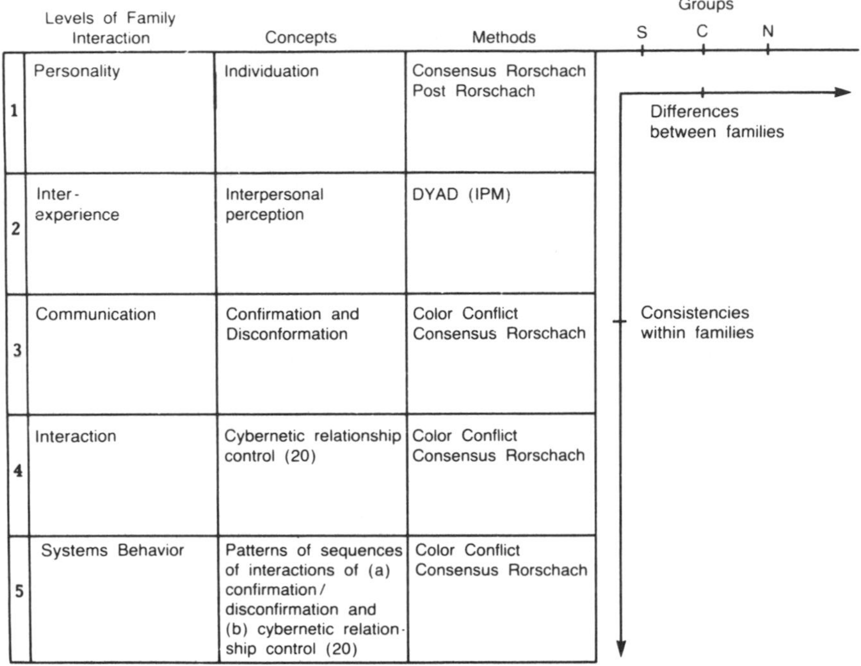

Fig. 1. The experimental design.

for the purpose of detecting (a) theoretical *consistencies within* families across different levels of family interaction (for example, low individuation corresponds to high fusion of interpersonal perception, which corresponds to low confirmation and high disconfirmation), and (b) *differences between* families within each particular level. In this chapter, data on the differences between the families on the communication level are presented.

Method

Sample

The present sample consists of 21 families divided into three groups according to the diagnoses of the index offspring. The groups are: (a) schizophrenia (S), 7 schizophrenics; (b) control (C), 4 schizoaffectives and 3 with borderline personality disorder; and (c) normal (N), 7 with no psychiatric illness among the index offspring or their siblings. All index offspring were

20–35 years of age and were diagnosed separately by the research group, independent of the diagnostic procedures at the institutions of recruitment. The index offspring were interviewed using SADS (6) and diagnosed by two independent judges, one of whom was blind. The offspring of the N-group went through the same procedures as the patients. The RDC (18) was used, supplemented by the DSM-III (1980) criteria for borderline personality disorder. The S-group was also diagnosed according to DSM-III criteria. In order for subjects to be included, the diagnoses by both judges had to be definite and had to coincide. Paranoid schizophrenics (15) and patients with severe alcohol or drug problems as the main diagnosis were excluded. Controls were recruited in the same way as members of the S-group, namely, from psychiatric institutions in the Oslo area. The N-group was recruited through their place of work within the same geographical area as that for S- and C-groups. (It should be noted that the diagnostic groups, included in the C-group in this study, have been classified within the "schizophrenia-group" under the term "schizophrenia-spectrum disorder" in some of the other studies in this volume (chapters 1 and 3).

Procedures

The Color Conflict Method

Confirmation and disconfirmation were assessed by means of the Color Conflict Method (4, 7). The Color Conflict method is a set of situations designed to measure degrees of conflicts between persons. Mother, father, and offspring are seated in a semicircle at separate tables. The index offspring is seated between the parents. A box is placed on the table in front of each subject. Each box contains a book propped at a 45-degree angle. Each book contains 17 separate 15 × 20 cm. colored plates labeled from A to Q. The colors were selected from the National Color System (NCS) "coleur" (hue) no. Y90 R (Red), which varies from light pink through bright red to dark brown. The variations have been arrived at by keeping the hue constant while varying the degree of saturation (the addition of black-white). Thus, from a color-perceptual point of view, only one dimension has been varied. The colors were selected according to the degree of *perceptual* (experiential) differences between them. The perceptual differences between the colors were established by the measurement of CIELAB-values. CIELAB is an internationally accepted standard measurement of reflected light energy from each color under standardized conditions. Based on the measurement of the reflected light energy from each color, the X, Y, and Z-values of the reflected light have been established, and these values symbolize the relative proportions of red, green, and blue, respectively. This was computed into a system of coordinates by means of a high-level equation. Thus, the relative perceptual differences between the colors have been established. Differences below 2–3 CIELAB can hardly be detected by the normal human eye, and can be said to correspond to the psychophysical term "Just Noticeable Difference" (JND). Any observer can identify a difference of 30 CIELAB as a completely different color, that is, as light pink, bright red, or dark brown. Table 1 shows the CIELAB-values.

To avoid pseudoagreements, a reference blackboard was placed three meters away in front of the subjects (see Figure 2). On the blackboard were 32 solid-color plates like those found in the subjects' books. All 17 colors in each book were represented on the blackboard. The blackboard colors were numbered from 1 to 32. To insure that the stimulus material was given under standard lighting conditions constant across all measurements, fluorescent lamps of 5400-Kelvin were placed above and below the reference blackboard and above each box. The instructions were that the subjects had to reach agreement, through discussion, on the color they saw in the book in front of

TABLE 1

The Color Conflict Method

Plate	Color Numbers			CIELAB-values	Conflict level
	Father	Offspring	Mother		
A	1080	1080	1080		Introduction
B	3040	3040	3040		No conflict
C	1070	1070	1070		
D	6020	6020	6015	1.89	
E	2040	2045	2045	4.20	
F	4030	4030	4040	9.51	
G	1030	1020	1030	10.83	Moderate
H	6015	6030	6030	9.53	
I	1055	1040	1055	15.73	
J	2050	2050	2065	17.15	
K	1060	1060	1060		No conflict
L	1070	1050	1050	18.81	
M	3030	3030	3050	17.57	Large
N	2060	2040	2060	18.48	
O	1050	1020	1020	29.20	
P	5020	5020	5050	23.00	Extreme
Q	2070	2030	2030	33.86	

Note: Color numbers are taken from the National Color System; CIELAB-value refers to the difference between deviant and nondeviant colors—the deviant colors are underscored.

Fig. 2. The differences of the change in mean frequencies of *confirmation with disagreement* between the three groups from "no conflict" to "large conflict."

them. The agreed-upon color was then to be communicated to the experimenter by referring to the number of the identical color on the blackboard. The subjects were further told that their books were identical and that the experiment was designed so as to learn more about how different families solve tasks. No time limit was set; the average time taken was approximately 50 minutes, rarely extending to one hour.

The books, however, were *not* identical except for the first three pages and the eleventh page (plates A, B, C, K; see Table 1). With the other thirteen exposures, one of the subjects always had a "deviant" (different) color. We refer to perceptual difference as *the conflict of experience*. The conflict of experience was at first barely noticeable (1.89-CIELAB). Afterwards, it increased progressively. From the CIELAB-values shown in Table 1, four different test conditions may be identified according to the degree of interpersonal conflict of experience involved. These have been labelled: no conflict, moderate conflict, large conflict, and extreme conflict. Each test condition involved three exposures, and the deviant color was systematically shifted among the subjects. At each exposure where a deviance was involved, mother, father, and index offspring received the deviant color once. The degree of the interpersonal conflict, expressed as the CIELAB-value of the deviant color of mother, father and index offspring, was nearly identical at each level of conflict. However, all colors were changed at each exposure. The testing was videotaped. All subjects were tested with the Ishihara colorblindness test before the test procedure. Immediately after testing with the Color Conflict Method, a semistructured, individual interview was conducted with each subject. The purpose of the interview was to assess each subject's confidence in the situation. After the interview, the whole procedure, including the experimental manipulation, was explained to the family.

Because the method is based on standardized, measurable *perceptual* differences, it is possible to study (a) *family reality orientation*, defined as the degree to which the family breaks with reality to maintain its internal organization; (b) *family structure*, defined as alliances in the definitions of reality within the family with regard to an external reality (the stimulus cards); (c) *perceptual dominance*, defined as whose perception of reality carries the most weight when the family is forced to act as an organized unit; and (d) *compromising*, defined as the difference expressed by the CIELAB-value between the stimulus card and the agreed-upon card on the reference board.

The CMCD Coding System

The *Confirmation, Moderate Confirmation, and Disconfirmation Coding System* (CMCD) (11) was constructed to detect and measure confirmatory and disconfirmatory feedback. The system includes criteria and rules for interpretation of the different strategies of confirmation and disconfirmation described above. Three independent raters were used, two of whom were blind as to the diagnostic status of the offspring. The coding was performed directly from videotapes accompanied by transcripts. The estimated mean kappa for categorization of *families* on the CMCD is approximately .95 for all pairs of raters. Mean kappa for the categorization of *single utterances* was .70 for all pairs of raters, and approximately identical for each diagnostic group.[1]

[1]Two revised computer-based editions of the CMCD for interactive coding of dyadic and triadic communication have been constructed as decision-trees, each including 71 different codes. These are now available on disk (CMCD II & III; see 12, 13). Two corresponding systems, *The Cybernetic Relationship Control Coding System* (CRC II, & III; see 20, 21) have been constructed to detect and measure cybernetic relationship control in social systems. These also are available on disk from the authors.

Statistics

A one-way analysis of variance was used to test the differences between the groups at the no-conflict level. An analysis of variance (ANOVA), using the values of each group at the no-conflict level as covariates, was used to test the significance of the differences in the degree of change. Statistically significant differences are expressed as *main effects*, while the covariates refer to the differences in the probability of predicting the frequency at the large-conflict condition, given the frequency at the no-conflict condition. As the groups are still small, our results must be regarded as preliminary until the complete sample is available for statistical analyses. Hence, a ten-percent level of significance was chosen.

Results

This report includes the first results published from our project. We had two specific goals: (a) to detect differences between the families at the *no-conflict* condition (plates B, C, K; see Table 1) and (b) to detect differences between the families at the *large-conflict* condition (plates L, M, N; see Table 1) when the differences at the no-conflict condition have been accounted for. At the large-conflict condition, our main objective was to test the following hypothesis about *differences of strategy*. When the situation is changed from no-conflict (0-CIELAB) to large-conflict (18-CIELAB), families of schizophrenic offspring will react by increasing their frequency of disconfirmatory feedback, whereas families of nonschizophrenic offspring will increase their frequency of confirmation with disagreement. The overall *F*-test at the no-conflict condition was not significant.

Although the no-conflict condition stimulates agreements, the large-conflict condition stimulates disagreements. Figure 2 shows the differences of change of *confirmation with disagreement* as the situation was changed from "no-conflict" (SD = 2.2) to "large-conflict" (SD = 5.8). The largest change was observed in the N-group. The least change was observed in the S-group. The differences between all groups and between the N-group and the S-group were significant (main effects: N vs. S vs. C, $p < .06$; N vs. S, $p < .04$; all covariates n.s.).

The low degree of a change in the frequencies of confirmation may be an indication of a high degree of change in the frequencies of disconfirmation. The highest frequencies of active strategies of disconfirmation were observed in the S-group at both the no-conflict condition (SD = 2.2) and the large-conflict condition (SD = 3.5). Figure 3 shows the differences of the

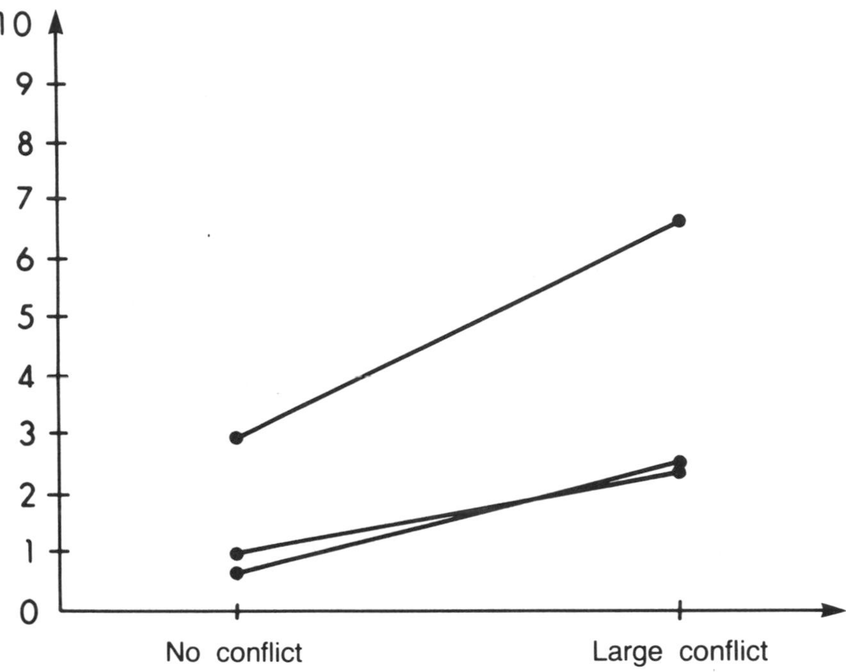

Fig. 3. The differences of the change in mean frequencies of the *active strategies of disconfirmation* (active disqualification, linear self-disqualification and egocentric utterances) between the three groups from "no conflict" to "large conflict."

change in the active strategies of disconfirmation between the groups as the test situation changed. The difference between all groups was significant. The increase of disconfirmation in the S-group was significantly larger than in the N and C groups, and the C-group was similar to the N-group (main effects: N vs. S vs. C, $p<.07$; N vs. S, $p<.02$; S vs. C, $p<.07$; all covariates n.s.). The result observed in the S-group was mainly due to a large increase of active disqualifications of others when the large-conflict condition was introduced (main effect: N vs. S $p<.002$). These disqualifications were directed from the S-group parents toward their schizophrenic offspring (main effects: N vs. S vs. C, $p<.07$; N vs. S, $p<.1$; S vs. C, $p<.09$) and from one parent toward the other parent (main effects: N vs. S vs. C, $p<.08$; N vs. S, $p<.07$). The effect was not due to the behavior of the schizophrenic offspring toward the parents.

Discussion

This study has demonstrated that when confronted with a situation involving an interpersonal conflict of experience, the following was characteristic of the families of schizophrenic offspring as compared to the families of nonschizophrenic offspring. Generally, the different kinds of communication feedback reactions necessary for the maintenance of a common social reality were not adaptive to the changing requirements of the situation. Specifically, families of schizophrenic offspring demonstrated an absence of the expected increase of confirmatory feedback, and a rise of active, disconfirming feedback in their communication. The control group, which included families of borderline and schizoaffective offspring, behaved differently from the families of schizophrenic offspring and were more similar to the families of normal offspring. This was the case particularly with reference to those feedback reactions that are believed to play the most central role in the cognitive breakdown of schizophrenic patients. Hence, the difference between the N-group and the S-group cannot be attributed solely to the fact that the index offspring are psychiatric patients or hospitalized.

The specific relationship demonstrated in the present study between confirmatory and disconfirmatory feedback and "non-spectrum" schizophrenia may be a result of the fact that there has been far less empirical investigation on these feedback mechanisms than on concepts like EE, AS, and CD. In evaluating the present results, however, one should take into consideration the emphasis on the development, refinement, and operationalization of theoretical concepts. This probably is the explanation for our being able to obtain statistically significant results despite our small sample, which again may indicate a strong relationship between the reported observations. We are therefore inclined to conclude that a specific relationship has been detected between schizophrenia and certain feedback mechanisms in the communication of the family.

This research also raises several questions. First, what are the relationships between CMCD and the less theoretically based but empirically more tested measures of AS, CD, and EE? An overlap between a high frequency of disconfirmation and those CD scores that identify disqualifications is likely. Also, the emotional overinvolvement ratings in EE may alternatively be formulated as actively disqualifying statements (AD). However, there is less plausible reason why the EE scores for criticism and hostility should be distinctively related to the development or relapse of schizophrenia. To be sure, the stimulus overload associated with criticism may generate difficulties for schizophrenics, but we doubt that criticism and hostility are more harmful to an offspring who is vulnerable to schizophrenia than they are to others. We would rather take into consideration the *way* that the criticism and hostility is expressed—as confirmatory or disconfirmatory—because this may disturb the child's ability to maintain a firm cognitive grasp of social reality. Thus, we would not expect an overlap between a high disconfirmation score and a high score of hostility or criticism.

With regard to the specific relationship between family communication and the development of, or relapse in schizophrenia, we propose to differentiate between factors specifically related to the disorder (S-factors) and factors that generally seem related to a bad outcome independent of the specific diagnosis (G-factors). So far, disconfirmatory feedback in communication seems to be related to an S-factor. Due to a lack of theoretical foundation before testing was begun, traditional measures like the AS, CD, and EE all seemed to contain a mixture of both S-factor and G-factor items. Therefore, further research based on the CMCD may contribute to the interpretation of findings based on the traditional instruments. Second, the lower frequencies of confirmation with disagreement and the higher frequencies of disconfirmation found in the families of schizophrenics may be indicators of clinically far more significant *patterns* of communication in the family. To answer such questions, sequential analyses will be necessary. Finally, in order to assess a possible etiologic status of disconfirmation versus confirmation, prospective longitudinal studies will be necessary. At present, research in all the three areas mentioned above are in progress.

REFERENCES

1. Abeles, G. Researching the unresearchable: Experimentation on the double bind. In C. E. Sluzki & D. C. Ransom (eds.), *Double bind: The foundation of the communicational approach to the family*. New York: Grune & Stratton, 1976.

2. Becker, E. *The birth and death of meaning: A perspective in psychiatry and anthropology*. New York: Free Press, 1962.

3. Berger, P. L., & Luckmann, T. *The social construction of reality: A treatise in the sociology of knowledge*. Middlesex: Penguin Books, 1966.

4. Blaker, O., Olavesen, B., & Holte, A. The relationship between parents' personality, family interaction and the offspring's personality development. *Journal of the Norwegian Psychological Association 23*: 301–309, 1986; *24*, in press.

5. Cissna, K. L., & Sieburg, E. Patterns of interactional confirmation and disconfirmation. In C. Wilder Mott & J. H. Weakland (eds.), *Rigor and imagination: Essays from the legacy of Gregory Bateson*. New York: Praeger, 1981.

6. Endicott, J., & Spitzer, R. L. A diagnostic interview: The Schedule for Affective Disorders and Schizophrenia. *Archives of General Psychiatry 35*: 837–844, 1978.

7. Hansen, G. K. B., & Wichstrøm, L. *Confirmation, relationship-control and psychopathology*. Doctoral dissertation, Department of Psychology, University of Oslo, 1983 (ISBN 82-569-0650-2).

8. Helmersen, P. Family interaction and communication in psychopathology: An evaluation in recent perspectives. *European Monographs in Social Psychology 34*. London: Academic Press, 1983.

9. Holte, A. Towards a scientific concept of confirmation: I. Specification and criteria. *Journal of the Norwegian Psychological Association 16*: 159–166, 1979.

10. ______. Towards a scientific concept of confirmation: II. Preparations for an empirical study. *Journal of the Norwegian Psychological Association 16*: 199–205, 1979.

11. ______, & Wichstrøm, L. *The Confirmation, Moderate Confirmation and Disconfirmation Coding System (CMCD)*. University of Oslo, Department of Behavioral Sciences in Medicine, P. O. Box 1111, Blindern, 0317 Oslo 3, 1983.

12. ______, Wichstrøm, L., Frysjøenden, G., & Solvang, E. *The Confirmation, Moderate Confirmation and Disconfirmation Coding System: Dyadic Coding (CMCD II)*. (Disk program.) University of Oslo, Department of Behavioral Sciences in Medicine, P. O. Box 1111, Blindern, 0317 Oslo 3, 1986.

13. ______, Wichstrøm, L., Frysjøenden, G., & Solvang, E. *The Confirmation, Moderate Confirmation and Disconfirmation Coding System: Triadic Coding (CMCD III)*. (Disk program.) University of Oslo, Department of Behavioral Sciences in Medicine, P. O. Box 1111, Blindern, 0317 Oslo 3, 1986.

14. Laing, R. D. *The self and others*. London: Tavistock Publications, 1961.

15. Rund, B. R. Communication deviances in parents of schizophrenics. *Family Process 25*: 133–147, 1986.

16. Scheff, T. J. Negotiating reality: Notes on power in the assessment of responsibility. *Social Problems 16*: 3–17, 1968.

17. Spencer-Brown, G. *Laws of form*. London: Allan & Unwin, 1969.

18. Spitzer, R. L., Endicott, J., & Robins, E. Research Diagnostic Criteria: Rationale and reliability. *Archives of General Psychiatry 35*: 773–782, 1978.

19. Watzlawick, P., Beavin, J. H., & Jackson, D. D. *Pragmatics of human communication: A study of interactional patterns, pathologies, and parodoxes*. N. Y.: W. W. Norton, 1967.

20. Wichstrøm, L., Holte, A., & Auråen, A. *The Cybernetic Relationship Control Coding System: Dyadic Coding (CRC II)*. (disk program). University of Oslo, Department of Behavioral Sciences in Medicine, P. O. Box 1111, Blindern, 0317 Oslo 3. 1986.

21. ______, Holte, A. & Auråen, A. *The Cybernetic Relationships Control Coding System: Triadic Coding (CRC III)*. (Disk program.) University of Oslo, Department of Behavioral Sciences in Medicine, P. O. Box 1111, Blindern, 0317 Oslo 3, 1986.

22. Wittgenstein, L. *Philosophische Untersuchungen* (German-English ed.). Oxford: Basil Blackwell, 1968.

9

PARENTAL EXPRESSED EMOTION ATTITUDES AND INTRAFAMILIAL COMMUNICATION BEHAVIOR

KURT HAHLWEG
Max Planck Institute of Psychiatry
Munich, West Germany

KEITH H. NUECHTERLEIN, MICHAEL J. GOLDSTEIN, ANA MAGAÑA
University of California, Los Angeles

JERI A. DOANE
Yale Psychiatric Institute
New Haven, Connecticut

KAREN S. SNYDER
University of California, Los Angeles

ONE CAN now be relatively confident that there is a reliable association between family levels of expressed emotion (EE) and relapse rates in schizophrenic and depressed patients nine months after discharge. With regard to schizophrenia, at least three independent studies (1, 22, 24) have shown that the chance of relapse increases by a factor of approximately four whenever the patient returns to a family environment marked by high levels of criticism and/or emotional overinvolvement. In contrast to the 50–60% relapse rate for a nine-month period among high-EE families, the base rate of relapse in families rated as low on EE is about 15%. Vaughn and Leff (22) and Hooley, Orley, and Teasdale (10) have shown that the EE construct is also a valuable predictor of relapse in depression.

Despite the strong association between EE and relapse, we still know relatively little about how high EE might operate to instigate a return of symptoms in psychiatric patients or how low EE might protect them from relapse (8). Because EE is a measure of relatives' *attitudes* toward the patient expressed within the context of an interview with a mental health professional, we need to know whether these attitudes are also expressed in the face-to-face contact with the patient.

The assumption underlying the EE construct is that there is an association between attitudes and overt interactional behavior of the relatives. Otherwise it would be very difficult to explain how high-EE relatives constitute a form of increased social stress for vulnerable individuals. An approach to investigating the construct validity of EE is to analyze systematically the *behavior* of high- and low-EE relatives when interacting with the patient.

The first to address this question in detail was the research group at UCLA headed by Michael Goldstein. In a series of three studies, the relationship between EE attitudes and direct interactional behavior was assessed by using a standardized situation to elicit interactional behavior, and a coding system that reflected the behavior analogues of EE attitudes (8). In the standardized situation, family members were asked to discuss two emotionally loaded family problems derived from a prior interview, an interaction task developed by Goldstein et al. (3) for a prospective, longitudinal study. The Affective Style (AS) (2) coding system was used to measure specific verbal behaviors of the relatives during this interaction task. The AS system assesses, among other variables, benign and personal criticism, guilt induction, and intrusiveness (a relative speaks as though he or she is an expert on the patient's thoughts, inner states, and motives).

In the first study by Valone, Norton, Goldstein, and Doane (21), 52 families from the UCLA Family Project longitudinal, prospective study were investigated. High-EE parents, who had been classified largely on the basis of the EE criticism criteria, expressed significantly more criticism toward their disturbed but nonpsychotic offspring than did low-EE parents. In the second study by Miklowitz, Goldstein, Falloon, and Doane (14), a sample of 42 families with a chronic schizophrenic member was investigated using the same design. Parents rated high EE, because of criticism in the Camberwell Family Interview (CFI), were distinguished by their frequent use of critical comments during the interaction task, whereas high-EE, over-involved parents used more intrusive, invasive statements.

In the third study by Strachan, Leff, Goldstein, et al. (19), these findings could be replicated in spite of the fact that the study differed in three ways from the Miklowitz et al. (14) investigation: (a) the study was done in Britain; (b) the schizophrenic patients were mostly of recent onset; and (c) the interactional behavior was assessed from dyadic interactions between patient and each relative separately. A special finding was that a critical attitude observed during the CFI was associated with both criticism *and* intrusion, whereas in the more chronic American sample it was associated only with critical behavior.

Another hint that high- and low-EE relatives differ behaviorally comes from a study conducted by Kuipers, Sturgeon, Berkowitz, and Leff (12), in which the rate of relatives' talking and the duration of looking were used as the dependent variables. Although patients did not differ with regard to these variables, high-EE relatives spent more time talking and less time looking at the patient than the low-EE relatives. This study did not examine the content of the verbal interaction, however.

Taking all these findings together, interaction in a high-EE family with a schizophrenic member is characterized by criticism, intrusion, and a high verbal output, while low-EE families interact in a more neutral and calmer way. Interestingly enough, none of these studies showed that low-EE relatives used more supportive, positive statements during the family discussion (18). This finding may be due to the task itself because it was developed to instigate emotionally charged issues or to reflect limitations in the AS coding system, which was specifically designed to capture negative communication behaviors. However, the possibility that the protective value of low-EE behavior should come just from being less critical and more neutral than high-EE relatives is not very convincing. It seems warranted to hypothesize that low-EE families are also more positive, that is, they show acceptance of the patient or have a more constructive approach to solving family problems.

With regard to schizophrenia, two other points are noteworthy. First, while the EE rating is done by taking content *and* tone of voice into account, the affective (nonverbal) climate of the family interaction has not been investigated until now, because the AS coding is done from transcripts. In the Kuipers et al. study (12), duration of looking was coded. Whether this variable reflects affective climate has yet to be shown. Second, except for the Kuipers et al. study, the interactional behavior of the patient has not been investigated.

With regard to depression, first results on these topics are available. Hooley (7) investigated the interaction patterns of 30 depressed patients with spouses who were either high or low EE on the CFI. The interaction task used was a version of Strodtbeck's Revealed Difference Technique (20). The videotaped discussions were analyzed by the KPI (Kategoriensystem für partnerschaftliche Interaktion (5), which will be described later in this chapter.

Results showed that the interaction with a high-EE spouse was more stressful and less rewarding for the patient than interaction with a low-EE partner. In particular, high-EE *spouses* were much more critical, disagreed more, were less positive verbally, and much less likely to accept what their patient-partner said to them than were low-EE spouses. Furthermore, they were much more nonverbally negative and made more negative and less positive statements than their low-EE counterparts. *Patients* interacting with high-EE spouses made fewer accepting, self-disclosing, or agreeing remarks, and were more nonverbally neutral than were patients interacting with low-EE spouses.

When the interactions of high- and low-EE dyads were analyzed using sequential analysis, clear and interesting differences emerged with regard to negative communication patterns. Whenever one partner emitted a negative reaction, this was reciprocated by the other with a high level of conditional probability, resulting in an extended and heated, negative interchange. Low-EE couples, on the other hand, showed virtually no negative escalation, either verbally or nonverbally. Differences between both groups were also found with respect to the control of interaction. It appeared that low-EE patients were more dominant in the interaction, whereas spouses in high-EE dyads were more dominant in that they prolonged negative (and positive) interaction patterns. (For an extended description of the results see 7–10.)

To summarize, clear-cut differences emerged in the behavior of depressed patients and their low- or high-EE spouses. This is true for verbal and nonverbal behavior as well as for the method of analysis—frequency or sequential analysis. Given these results, it seems worthwhile to investigate the interaction patterns of high- or low-EE families with a schizophrenic patient by using the same coding system and statistical methods. The following study was therefore designed to investigate four hitherto unanswered questions:

- Are low-EE relatives of schizophrenic patients more positive-supportive toward the patient while discussing emotionally loaded family problems than high-EE relatives?
- How does the patient contribute to the family interaction?
- Do high- and low-EE families differ in regard to their affective (nonverbal) interactional climate?
- Do high- and low-EE families differ in their interaction patterns when the data are analyzed sequentially?

Method

Subjects

Thirty-four families with a schizophrenic patient were included in the study. Patients were taking part in a longitudinal, prospective project on "Developmental Processes in Schizophrenic Disorders" at UCLA (Principal Investigator, K. Nuechterlein; Co-PI, M. Dawson) and in an accompanying project on "Family Affect and Communication in Schizophrenic Relapse" (Principal Investigator, M. J. Goldstein).

Schizophrenic patients were recruited during their index hospitalization in public hospitals in the western and San Fernando Valley regions of the Los Angeles metropolitan area. Schizophrenic subjects were required to have the following characteristics:

- diagnosis of definite schizophrenia or schizoaffective disorder, mainly schizophrenic by Research Diagnostic Criteria (RDC), based on an expanded version of the Present State Examination administered to the patient and with consideration of any additional data gathered from relatives
- recent onset of major psychosis lasting at least two weeks (first episode not longer than two years before project contact)
- age at project entry between 16 and 45 years
- Caucasian or acculturated Asian or Hispanic in ethnic background

Subjects with any of the following were excluded:

- evidence of an organic central nervous system disorder (for example, epilepsy, traumatic brain injury, infectious or toxic cerebrovascular disease)
- significant and habitual drug or alcohol abuse in the six months prior to the current episode, or past drug or alcohol abuse that may cloud the diagnostic picture
- mental retardation (premorbid IQ less than 70)

This schizophrenic sample was young, with an average age of 22.5 years (SD = 3.6; range = 19 to 32 years). The mean educational level was 11.8 years (SD = 1.5, range = 9 to 15 years). Eighty-eight percent of the patients were Caucasian, 9 percent Hispanic, and 3 percent Oriental. Eighty-two percent of the patients were males. In total, 50 relatives were included in the study. In 59 percent, the family composition was dual-parental, composed of mother, father and patient, while 41 percent were single-parent families, mainly mothers and the patient.

Procedures

Expressed Emotion: CFI

Once the patient had satisfied the RDC criteria, his or her closest relatives were administered the Camberwell Family Interview (23) within one month after hospital admission. CFI audiotapes were rated by trained raters who previously had been certified as reliable in administering and rating the CFI for EE. Interrater reliability coefficients of .85 were satisfying. The raters were not aware of the hypotheses being tested in the present study.

Expressed Emotion: Short Form

Approximately five weeks after hospital discharge, the family was asked to participate in a family discussion. Each relative was first interviewed individually and asked to speak for five minutes—the Five-Minute Speech Sample (FMSS)—about the patient. Later on, utterances were coded from the audiotapes using the guidelines for coding EE from the FMSS (13). Because the FMSS was administered on the same day as the direct family interaction (described below), the FMSS was given at a different time than the CFI. Previous research by Magaña et al. (13) has revealed a substantial relationship between EE classification of the CFI and FMSS when both data sets were collected within two weeks of each other. However, recent data from the developmental processes study has found that when a longer period has transpired, the association is weaker. Interrater reliability coefficients were satisfying and ranged from a kappa of .57 to .80.

Direct Family Interaction

Following the FMSS, each family member was interviewed individually in order to generate problem issues that focused on family conflicts. After an issue had been identified, the interviewer directed the family member to pretend that the person to whom the problem was directed was sitting in the room and to speak about the issue while the tape recorder was running. This audiotape was taken to the respective family member who then listened and was asked to respond. Two issues for each member were generated in this way.

Then the family was brought into the laboratory to listen to the audiotaped statements. The family was directed to discuss the problem for ten minutes, express thoughts and feelings about it, and try to solve the issue while the experimenter was out of the room. After ten minutes, the family was asked to discuss a second problem. One of the issues was generated by the patient and one by a relative. The order of problem-issue presentations was counterbalanced across families (see 14).

Coding System

The behavior of each family member during the videotaped discussions was coded using the KPI (5). The aim of the KPI is to assess empirically the speaker and listener skills that form the basis of communication and problem-solving treatments.

Although the different communication skills (CS) components differ somewhat with regard to content and technique, there are some common assumptions. In general, communication will be enhanced when the family members are using the following skills: (a) speaker skills—use "I" messages, describe specific behaviors in specific situations, and stick to the "here and now"; (b) listener skills—listen actively, summarize your partner's remarks and check their accuracy, ask open questions, and give positive feedback. Family members who employ these skills in turn should avoid blaming, criticizing, and side-tracking, and should increase their mutual understanding. The core skills are reciprocal self-disclosure of feelings, attitudes and thoughts, and accepting (not necessarily agreeing with) the partner's utterances.

Coding Unit

The basic unit is a verbal response that is homogeneous in content without regard to its duration or syntactical structure. For each code, a nonverbal rating is assigned (4, 15). In case of double coding for a speaker, a listening code (LI) with a nonverbal rating is assigned to the listener, thus guaranteeing alternate coding. Alternative codes are necessary when interactions with three family members (mother, father, patient) are scored. The verbal responses of each family member are coded as described. Whenever double coding of mother/father occurs, or both parents are talking to each other, LI plus the nonverbal rating for the identified patient is coded. In case of double coding for the identified patient, LI is coded for the parent to whom the patient is speaking.

Description of Categories

The KPI consists of 11 verbal categories that have been derived primarily from the aforementioned assumptions about effective communication, and they were supplemented by some of the more salient categories and definitions from other coding systems, notably the MICS (11), CISS (4, 15), and KIK (25). In Table 1 the 11 positive, neutral, and negative verbal categories are shown.

All of the content categories described in Table 1 receive a nonverbal rating (see 4, 15). In a hierarchical order, the facial cues of the speaker or listener are first evaluated as positive, negative, or neutral. If the coder is unable to code the utterance as positive or negative, he or she scans the voice tone cues. If the coder is still unable to code the utterance as positive or negative, the body cues are scanned until an appropriate rating can be applied. Full details of the KPI are given in Hahlweg et al. (5). (A coding manual is available from the first author.)

TABLE 1

KPI Verbal Categories

Category	Sub-category	Example
Positive		
1. Self-disclosure (SD)	Expression of feelings	"I'm too angry to listen to you at the moment."
	Expression of wishes	"I'd like to go fishing tomorrow."
2. Positive solution (PS)	Constructive proposals	"I'll do the dishes."
	Compromise	"I'll sweep the floor if you play with the kids."
3. Acceptance of other (AC)	Paraphrase	"You are saying the kids are too young to go to kindergarten."
	Open question	"Are you still upset?"
	Positive feedback	"I liked the way you started the discussion."
4. Agreement (AG)	Direct agreement	"Yes, that is right."
	Acceptance of responsibility	"I know I started the fight."
	Assent	"Yes" or "Okay."
Neutral		
5. Problem description (PD)	Neutral description	"I think we've got a problem with the kids."
	Neutral question	"Did the car break down yesterday?"
6. Metacommunication (MC)	Clarification request	"Would you repeat that, please."
	Topic	"We are really getting away from the issue."
7. Rest (RC)		Inaudible statements or does not fit any other category.

(continued)

TABLE 1

Continued

Category	Sub-category	Example
Negative		
8. Criticism (CRI)	Personal	"You are lazy!"
	Specific	"The car broke down because you forgot to take it to the garage."
9. Negative solution (NS)		"You shouldn't sleep all day!"
10. Justification (JU)	Excuse	"I had too many things to do yesterday."
	Denial of responsibility	"That's not my job."
11. Disagreement (DG)	Direct	"No, that's not true."
	Yes – but	"Yes, you are right, but we don't have the money."
	Short	"No."
	Blocking	"Stop it, I've had enough!"

Psychometric Properties of KPI

Several *reliability* studies in Germany and England yielded satisfactory results. Kappa's were in general well over $K = .80$, showing that the inter-observer agreement is acceptable for frequency and sequential analysis. The discriminant *validity* of the KPI could be established using criterion groups of (a) distressed and nondistressed couples (5) and (b) depressed patients with relatives high and low on EE (7). Results of another study investigating the effects of Behavioral Marital Therapy on the couples' CS showed that the KPI is also a sensitive instrument with which to monitor change after treatment (6).

Reliability of KPI for the Present Study

During his stay at UCLA in 1983–84, the first author, with the assistance of J. Hooley, trained six raters in the use of the KPI. Training was extensive and lasted for about 50 hours. At the end of the training, the raters independently coded five family discussions. Results of the reliability checks are shown in Table 2.

Interrater agreement between the six coders ranged from 71% (JU) to 95.3% (RC). Besides percentage agreement, Cohen's kappa coefficients were computed (see 4). Results were satisfactory, yielding a kappa of .83 for the verbal and a kappa of .84 for the nonverbal codes.

Results

Frequency (Base Rate) Analysis

In a first analysis, correlations were computed between the CFI-EE status of the relative and his or her behavior during both family interactions as coded by the KPI. Results were disappointing because *no* significant correlations were found. Yet, because the CFI was done approximately two months *before* the family interaction, we decided to run analysis using the EE status of each relative as assessed by the 5-minute speech sample (FMSS). As described, this measure was administered just before the family discussion took place.

In Table 3 the correlations of verbal and nonverbal KPI categories with the EE status (1 = low, 2 = high), based on the FMSS, are shown.

In *relatives*, high-EE attitudes based on the FMSS were significantly associated with negative, nonverbal (affective) behavior (NV –, 0.32), personal rejection (CRR, 0.48), specific criticism (CRS, 0.39), and disagreement (DG, 0.23). Low-EE attitudes were associated with positive, nonverbal (affective) behavior (NV +, –0.39), acceptance of partner (AC, –0.36),

TABLE 2
Reliability Coefficients (percentage of agreement) of KPI Verbal and Nonverbal Codes (6 raters)

Code	Frequency	% of Total	% Agreement
SD	258	8.0	88.4
PS	20	0.6	95.0
AC	187	5.8	79.1
AG	463	14.3	92.4
PD	1396	43.2	88.8
MC	89	2.8	85.4
RC	86	2.7	95.3
CRS	175	5.4	81.7
CRR	16	0.5	81.3
NS	12	0.4	91.7
JU	48	1.5	70.8
DG	445	13.8	91.2
NV +	1195	32.2	93.6
NV −	639	17.2	93.7

and positive solution (PS, −0.26). Because most of the relatives were classified as high EE on the basis of the criticism criterion, it is not surprising that the main correlations indicate largely critical behaviors toward the patient by high-EE relatives.

When looking at the *patients*, only one significant correlation emerged. Patients interacting with high-EE relatives were characterized as emitting more justifications (JU, 0.41), that is, excusing one's behavior or denying one's responsibility for the problem during the discussion, than patients interacting with low-EE relatives. Given the high rate of criticism experienced by patients from high-EE families, the pressure for self-justification was obvious.

In order to analyze the data on a family level, KPI frequencies were summed over all family members and correlations were calculated with the family EE status (1 = low, 2 = high). This analysis yielded the highest correlations and the most consistent results. High-EE families are characterized by a negative interaction style in that they show more negative affect and more personal and specific criticism, negative solution proposals, justifications, and disagreements than do low-EE families. The latter are characterized by a positive-supportive style in that they show more positive affect, acceptance of each other, and positive solutions.

TABLE 3

Spearman-Rank Correlations of Verbal and Nonverbal KPI-Categories with EE-Status[1]

KPI-categories		Unit of Analysis Relatives (n = 49)	Patients (n = 34)	Family (n = 34)
Self-Disclosure	(SD)	−.04	−.12	−.05
Positive Solution	(PS)	−.26*	−.17	−.33*
Accept. of partner	(AC)	−.36**	−.08	−.37*
Agreement	(AG)	−.08	−.01	−.02
Problem description	(PD)	.02	.18	.04
Metacommunication	(MC)	.12	.20	.20
Rest category	(RC)	.00	.06	.01
Criticism	(CRI)	.42***	.28(*)	.50***
-specific	(CRS)	.39**	.28(*)	.45***
-rejection	(CRR)	.48***	.04	.42**
Negative Solution	(NS)	.19(*)	.22	.37*
Justification	(JU)	.01	.41**	.32*
Disagreement	(DG)	.23*	.27(*)	.29*
Nonverbal Behavior				
positive	(NV+)	−.39**	−.28(*)	−.38**
negative	(NV−)	.32**	.36*	.32*

Note: Sample: 34 CRC-families with a schizophrenic patient. Task: 20 minutes of family problem discussion.

[1]EE short form based on 5-minute speech sample (13).

(*) = p .10, * = p .05, ** = p .01, *** = p .001

Sequential Analysis

Simply looking at the base rates of families' communication behaviors tells us nothing about the patterns or structure of the familial communication process. Here, the method of choice is to look for probability rules using sequential analysis.

When considering the analysis of longer sequences, one runs into the difficulty that the longer the sequence, the less data are available for analysis. Data reduction is therefore necessary. Thus, the 11 KPI categories were collapsed into three summary codes as follows:

- *Positive Communication*: Self-Disclosure, Positive Solution, Acceptance, and Agreement
- *Negative Communication*: Critique, Negative Solution, Justification, and Disagreement

• *Neutral Information*: Problem Description and Metacommunication

To analyze the data sequentially, the K-Gramm method was used (see 16, 17). The K-Gramm analysis is only possible when dyadic data are available. For triadic families, it is necessary to combine the responses of both parents so that parent-patient dyads are analyzed sequentially. Table 4 demonstrates how the data are analyzed with the K-Gramm method.

For each K-Gramm pattern a conditional probability is computed. Because the number of observations for each family is rather small, results are based on aggregate data. Data are summed across families in each group and the different families are separated by a specific code. Unfortunately, statistical evaluations of the difference between groups are not possible because of the aggregation (see 16, 17). The results must therefore be interpreted descriptively and the data regarded as exploratory.

Families were grouped according to the EE status of the relatives, either as low, mixed, or high EE. Mixed-EE families consisted of those three-member families in which one relative was classified as high and the other as low EE. Because the sample is composed of dual- and single-parent families, the high-EE group is defined as either a dual-parent family where both parents are high EE or a single-parent family where that parent is high EE. Similarly for low-EE families, the analogous patterns were possible.

In the following discussion, positive and negative escalation patterns will be analyzed. The sample sizes were too small to contrast the escalation patterns of dual- versus single-parent families in the high- and low-EE groups.

Negative Escalation

Negative escalation is defined as a sequence of negative communication behaviors (NC, NC, NC, . . .). Figure 1 shows the escalation process for negative verbal behavior in families with low, mixed, and high EE. The conditional probability (in percentages) is given on the ordinate, and the sequence length is shown on the abscissa. Sequence length 1 represents the base rate of negative communication. Examination of Figure 1 shows that about 26% of all verbal behavior emitted by high-EE families is negative. In contrast, about 12% of the behavior of low-EE families is negative (mixed: 11%). In order to explain the Figure, let us consider the high-EE families. Here we see that if partner A shows negative behavior (probability = 26%), the conditional probability that partner B will respond negatively is 41% (sequence length 2). Given that B responds in that way, the probability is .47 that A will again be negative (sequence length 3), and .49 that B will again

TABLE 4

Sequential Analysis Using the K-Gramm Analysis

Behavior sequence (observed):	HDE, WAA, HNI, WCR, HRF, WRF
Sequence length:	
2-Gramm:	p (WAA/HDE), p (HNI/WAA), p (WCR/HNI) . . .
3-Gramm:	p (HNI/HDE, WAA), p (WCR/WAA,HNI) . . .
4-Gramm:	p (WCR/HDE,WAA,HNI), p (HRF/WAA,HNI,WCR) . . .
5-Gramm:	p (HRF/HDE,WAA,HNI,WCR), p (WRF/WAA,HNI,WCR,HRF)

Note: H = husband, W = wife, DE = direct expression, AA = acceptance/agreement, NI = neutral information, CR = critique, RF = refusal.

reciprocate (sequence length 4). This pattern of negative escalation continues and ends at a sequence length of 6 because of lack of further occurrences.

High-EE families show a definite negative escalation process. In contrast, low- or mixed-EE families escalate only briefly up to a sequence length of 3. The escalation process stops because of lack of further occurrences, that is, partner B then emitted either a positive or a neutral statement. Both groups seem to be able to deescalate.

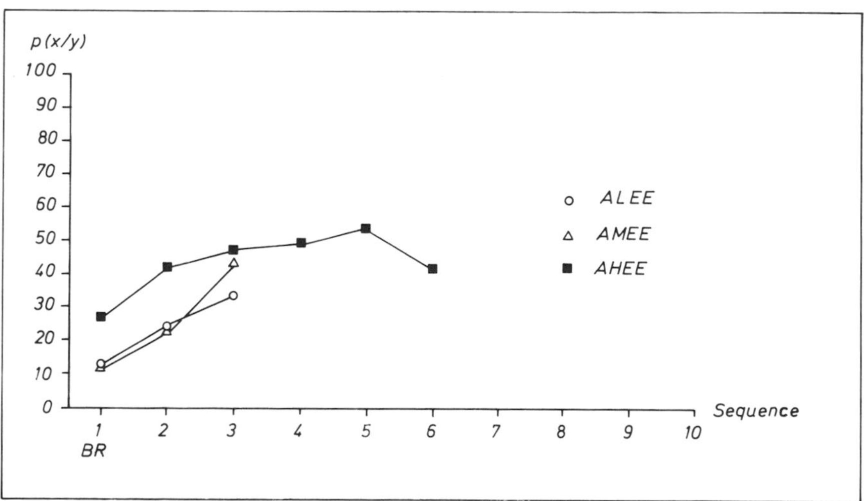

Fig. 1. Negative verbal escalation (ALEE = low EE, AMEE = mixed EE, AHEE = high-EE families). Data points represent alternate partner behaviors.

The escalation process for negative nonverbal behavior is shown in Figure 2. Results are very pronounced for high-EE families. Given that partner B reciprocated negatively in the affective domain (sequence length 2), a long escalation process at a high level of probability is inevitable. Low-EE families show the same tendency to reciprocate; however, the escalation stops at a sequence length of 5. Most interestingly, mixed families, composed of one high- and one low-EE parent, show no escalation tendency.

In Figures 3 and 4 the escalation processes for positive verbal and nonverbal behavior are shown. In general, all families are able to reciprocate positive behaviors. However, high-EE families show the shortest positive escalation patterns.

The Control of Interaction

In the analyses just described, no account was taken of the individual who initiated a particular interaction sequence. In order to investigate the question concerning the control of the interaction—or, stated differently, the question of dominance—it is necessary to consider the behavior of the patient separately from that of the parents. In other words, the data were analyzed according to whether the patient or the parents initiated the particular type of interaction pattern. The results were consistent in that no differences could be found with regard to positive or negative, verbal or nonverbal escalation processes.

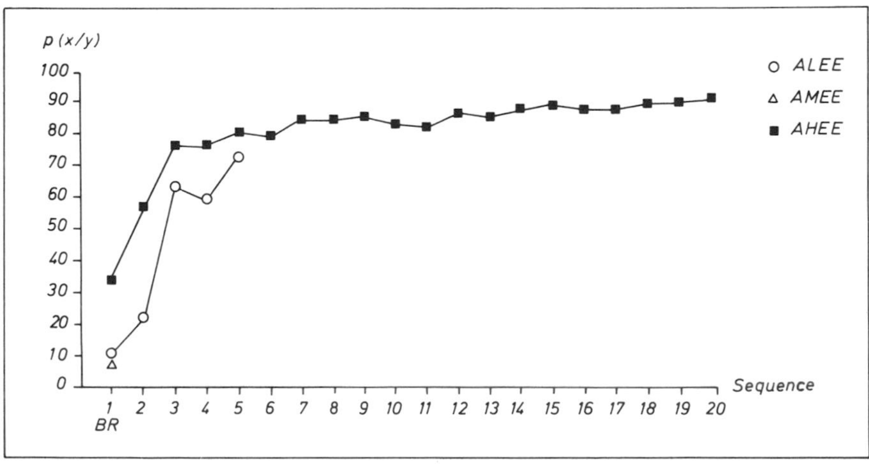

Fig. 2. Negative nonverbal escalation (ALEE = low EE, AMEE = mixed EE, AHEE = high EE families). Data points represent alternate partner behaviors.

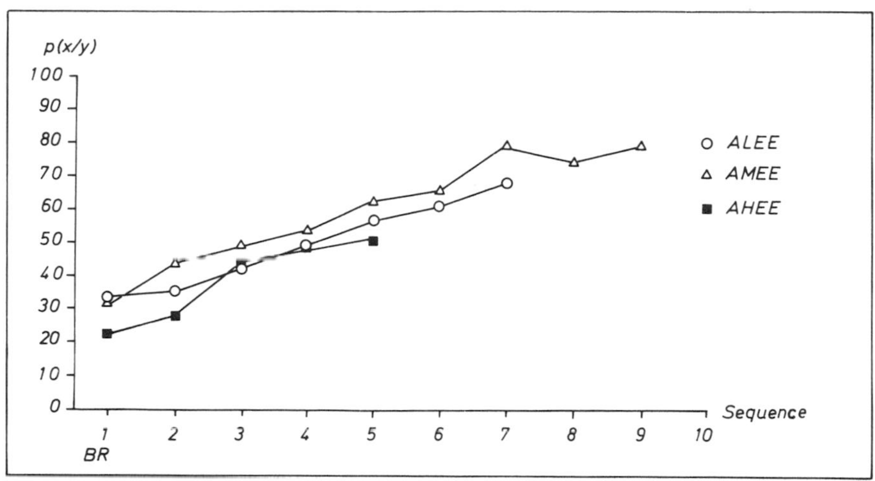

Fig. 3. Positive verbal escalation (ALEE = low EE, AMEE = mixed EE, AHEE = high EE families). Data points represent alternate partner behaviors.

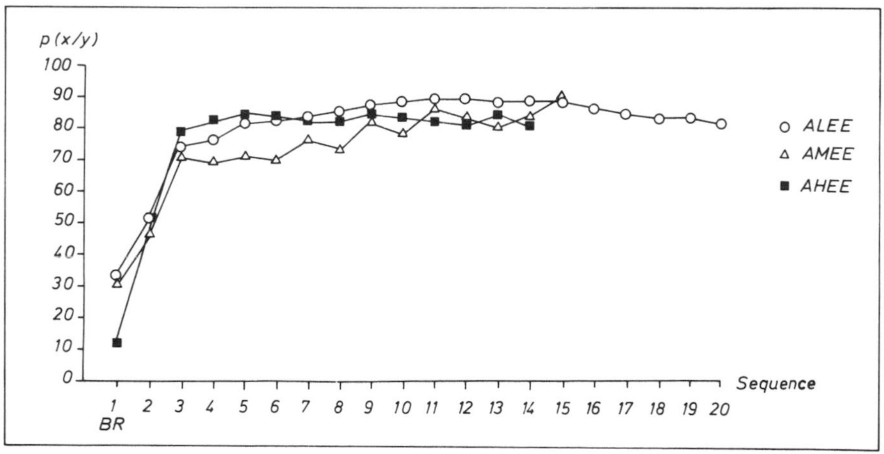

Fig. 4. Positive nonverbal escalation (ALEE = low EE, AMEE = mixed EE, AHEE = high EE families). Data points represent alternate partner behaviors.

In Figure 5, the dominance pattern for nonverbal negative behavior illustrates the findings. In order to keep the Figure distinct, mixed-EE families are omitted. It did not matter who initiated the sequence, whether patient or parent. In high-EE families the negative escalation process was inevitable.

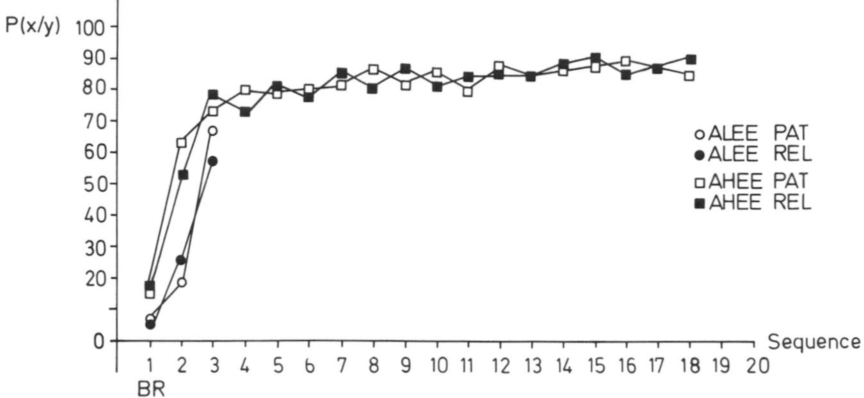

Fig. 5. Dominance pattern with regard to negative nonverbal escalation (ALEE PAT = low EE, patient-initiated sequence; ALEE REL = low EE, relative-initiated sequence; AHEE PAT = high EE, patient-initiated sequence; AHEE REL = high EE, relative-initiated sequence). Data points represent alternate partner behaviors.

Discussion

It is apparent that EE is not a static measure but, instead, seems to be sensitive to changes in the patient. This is at least true for the present study as long as one accepts that EE derived from the 5-minute speech sample is a parallel measure of the CFI-EE. Furthermore, the patients in this study were of recent onset, and it may well be that EE is more stable within families with a more chronic patient population. With recent onset cases, family members are shocked by the occurrence of the first episode and they may express more criticism in the beginning. However, when the patient is in remission, the critical attitude may fade. In contrast, family members of a chronic patient have undergone the experience of a remission being followed by another episode, or even more episodes. Therefore, their critical attitudes may be more stable, an expression of their pessimistic view of the course of illness. Be that as it may, the results of this study have shown that a critical attitude of the relative is associated with specific interactional behaviors of the relatives, patients, and the whole family.

In line with systemic thinking, the results were most clear-cut when the KPI data were analyzed on a family level. During the discussion of family problems, high-EE families are characterized by a negative interaction style in that they show more negative affect, more personal and specific criticism, negative-solution proposals, justifications, and disagreements than do low-

EE families. The latter are characterized by a positive-supportive style in that they show more positive affect, acceptance of each other, and constructive, positive solutions to the family problems under consideration.

These results are in contrast to the studies that did not find any differences between low- and high-EE families in the positive domain using the AS coding system (18). This discrepancy may be explained by the fact that AS was developed to capture predominantly negative behavior whereas the KPI codes are balanced with regard to negative and positive behaviors. In any event, it seems that low-EE families are not just more passive-neutral than high-EE families; instead they are *actively* protecting the patient. They provide a positive nonverbal climate, show concern for the patient, and try to find solutions to problems, thereby reducing family tension.

This is even more apparent when the results of the sequential analysis are taken into account. High-EE families showed destructive and long-lasting, negative escalation patterns, especially in the affective domain, whereas low-EE families were able to deescalate such tension-producing interaction.

The analysis of the dominance patterns revealed that the patient as well as the parents are controlling each other to the same extent. This result points to the need to include the patient in family care because he or she contributes in the same way to the style of interaction. However, it may well be that there are subtle differences in the way in which the parents or the patient contribute to the negative, verbal communication patterns, which are shadowed by the necessity to summarize the KPI codes for sequential analysis. One can infer from the frequency analysis that the negative patterns in high-EE families are characterized not by attack-counterattack (that is, criticism of parents is followed by criticism of patient), but instead by an attack-defensive style (parent is criticizing while patient is excusing himself or herself). This form of defensive communication will most likely result in not solving any problem and in prolonging family tension.

The communication patterns of the mixed-EE families are interesting in that they showed the least likelihood of escalating negatively. One could speculate that the low-EE parent is protecting the patient by intervening in a positive or neutral way whenever there is the danger of a negative escalation. Further analysis may clarify this assumption.

While the results are satisfying, one should not forget that they are far from perfect. The magnitude of the effects reveals that not all of the high- or low-EE families show the respective interaction styles as described. There is a great deal of variability within each group, and there is a definite need to analyze each family separately in order to learn more about the families' "individual differences." Another unsolved issue is that of the predictive validity of the interactional measures with regard to relapse. It may be that a combination of attitude and behavior will result in a better prediction.

To conclude, we have learned more about the attitude-behavior relationship in families with different EE levels but, as is usual in empirical research, we also are puzzled by new, unresolved questions. This augurs well for our meeting again in the near future!

REFERENCES

1. Brown, G. W., Birley, J. L. T., & Wing, J. K. Influence of family life on the course of schizophrenic disorders: A replication. *British Journal of Psychiatry 121*: 241–258, 1972.

2. Doane, J. A., West, K. L., Goldstein, M. J., Rodnick, E. H., & Jones, J. E. Parental communication deviance and affective style: Predictors of subsequent schizophrenia spectrum disorders in vulnerable adolescents. *Archives of General Psychiatry 38*: 679–685, 1981.

3. Goldstein, M. J., Judd, L. L., Rodnick, E. H., Alkire, A., & Gould, E. A method for studying social influence and coping patterns within families of disturbed adolescents. *Journal of Nervous and Mental Disease 147*: 233–251, 1968.

4. Gottman, J. M. *Marital interaction. Experimental investigations*. New York: Academic Press, 1979.

5. Hahlweg, K., Reisner, L., Kohli, G., Vollmer, M., Schindler, L., & Revenstorf, D. Development and validity of a new system to analyze interpersonal communication: Kategoriensystem für partnerschaftliche Interaktion. In K. Hahlweg & N. S. Jacobson (eds.), *Marital interaction: Analysis and modification*. New York: Guilford Press, 1984.

6. ______, Revenstorf, D., & Schindler, L. Effects of behavioral marital therapy on couples' communication and problem-solving skills. *Journal of Consulting and Clinical Psychology 52*: 553–566, 1984.

7. Hooley, J. M. *Criticism and depression*. Unpublished doctoral thesis, University of Oxford, 1984.

8. ______. An introduction to EE measurement and research. In M. J. Goldstein, I. Hand, & K. Hahlweg (eds.), *Treatment of schizophrenia: Family assessment and intervention*. Heidelberg: Springer-Verlag, 1986.

9. ______, & Hahlweg, K. The marriages and interaction patterns of depressed patients and their spouses: Comparing high and low EE dyads. In M. J. Goldstein, I. Hand, & K. Hahlweg (eds.), *Treatment of schizophrenia: Family assessment and intervention*. Heidelberg: Springer-Verlag, 1986.

10. ______, Orley, J., & Teasdale, J. D. Levels of expressed emotion and relapse in depressed patients. *British Journal of Psychiatry 148*: 642–647, 1986.

11. Hops, H., Wills, T. A., Patterson, G. R., & Weiss, R. L. *Marital Interaction Coding System*. Unpublished manuscript, Research Institute, University of Oregon, 1972. (Available from ASIS/NAPS, c/o Microfiche Publications, 305 E. 46th Street, New York NY 10017.)

12. Kuipers, L., Sturgeon, D., Berkowitz, R., & Leff, J. P. Characteristics of expressed emotion: Its relationship to speech and looking in schizophrenic patients and their relatives. *British Journal of Clinical Psychology 22*: 257–264, 1983.

13. Magaña, A. B., Goldstein, M. J., Karno, M., Miklowitz, D. J., Jenkins, J., &

Falloon, I. R. H. A brief method for assessing expressed emotion in relatives of psychiatric patients. *Psychiatry Research 17*: 203–212, 1986.

14. Miklowitz, D. J., Goldstein, M. J., Falloon, I. R. H., & Doane, J. A. Interactional correlates of expressed emotion in the families of schizophrenics. *British Journal of Psychiatry 144*: 482–487, 1984.

15. Notarius, C., & Markman, H. J. The Couples Interaction Scoring System (CISS). In E. Filsinger (ed.), *Assessing marriage*. Beverly Hills CA: Sage, 1981.

16. Revenstorf, D., Hahlweg, K., Schindler, L., & Vogel, B. Interaction analysis of marital conflict. In K. Hahlweg & N. S. Jacobson (eds.), *Marital interaction: Analysis and modification*. New York: Guilford Press, 1984.

17. ______, Vogel, B., Wegener, C., Hahlweg, K., & Schindler, L. Escalation phenomena in interaction sequences. *Behavior Analysis and Modification 2*: 97–116, 1980.

18. Strachan, A. M., Goldstein, M. J., & Miklowitz, D. J. Do relatives express expressed emotion? In M. J. Goldstein, I. Hand, & K. Hahlweg (eds.), *Treatment of schizophrenia: Family assessment and intervention*. Heidelberg: Springer-Verlag, 1986.

19. ______, Leff, J. P., Goldstein, M. J., Doane, J. A., & Burtt, C. Emotional attitudes and direct communication in the families of schizophrenics: A cross-national replication. *British Journal of Psychiatry 149*: 279–287, 1986.

20. Strodtbeck, F. L. Husband wife interaction over revealed differences. *American Sociological Review 16*: 468–473, 1951.

21. Valone, K., Norton, J. P., Goldstein, M. J., & Doane, J. A. Parental expressed emotion and affective style in an adolescent sample at risk for schizophrenia spectrum disorders. *Journal of Abnormal Psychology 92*: 399–407, 1983.

22. Vaughn, C. E., & Leff, J. P. The influence of family and social factors on the course of psychiatric illness: A comparison of schizophrenic and depressed neurotic patients. *British Journal of Psychiatry 129*: 125–137, 1976.

23. ______, & Leff, J. P. The measurement of expressed emotion in the families of psychiatric patients. *British Journal of Clinical and Social Psychology 15*: 157–165, 1976.

24. ______, Snyder, K. S., Jones, S., Freeman, W. B., & Falloon, I. R. H. Family factors in schizophrenic relapse: Replication in California of British research on expressed emotion. *Archives of General Psychiatry 41*: 1169–1177, 1984.

25. Wegener, C., Revenstorf, D., Hahlweg, K., & Schindler, L. Empirical analysis of communication in distressed and nondistressed couples. *Behavior Analysis and Modification 3*: 178–188, 1979.

10

THE NATURE AND ORIGINS OF EXPRESSED EMOTION*

JILL M. HOOLEY
Harvard University
Cambridge, Massachusetts

THE PAST two decades have witnessed a renaissance of interest in the relationship between family factors and psychopathology. Particularly prominent have been studies concerning levels of expressed emotion (EE) in relatives and the relapse rates of their diagnosed family members. Patients who return from the hospital to live with relatives who, during a semi-structured interview, talk about them in a critical, hostile, or emotionally overinvolved way, suffer elevated relapse rates in comparison with patients whose relatives do not express these negative attitudes. This association appears to hold regardless of whether the patient is schizophrenic (7, 40, 43), depressed (25, 40), or manic (Chapter 15 in this volume). Given the practical and theoretical implications of these findings, it is not surprising that EE is now a focus of active research on three continents.

At times, however, it seems that the construct of expressed emotion is in some danger of falling victim to its own success. As EE research gains visibility, it attracts both praise and scrutiny. One current and reasonable observation is that EE researchers have, historically, been preoccupied with demonstrating the predictive validity of EE, with relatively little attention being devoted to analyses of what EE actually indexes, and why it is high only in some families. Although it is true that replication studies have been necessary and desirable in demonstrating the robustness of EE as a predictor of relapse across cultures and diagnostic groups, it is also clear that future replications of the EE-relapse link will be less and less decisive in furthering our understanding of EE, in the absence of theoretical models to account

*Thanks are extended to John Richters and David Funder for their helpful comments on an early draft of this chapter.

for empirical findings. When explicit theoretical models are absent, private assumptions inevitably grow in their place.

This chapter represents a first step toward modelling the nature and origins of EE, with particular emphasis on factors that might engender high levels of criticism in the spouses of psychiatric patients. Through its emphasis on criticism, the chapter focuses on the most important component of the EE index. Through its emphasis on the behavior of spouses, the chapter attempts to explore the link between the constructs of expressed emotion and marital distress. These constructs share much in common, and there is reason to believe that both may be indexing a characteristic of spouse-patient relationships that is crucial to our understanding of psychiatric relapse. Certainly, marital partners represent a high proportion of the relatives of psychiatric patients. Furthermore, there is already a comparatively large body of literature pertaining to marital satisfaction and marital distress, and a well-developed therapeutic technology for implementing change in distressed relationships. Given that most high-EE relatives, particularly high-EE spouses, are rated as high in expressed emotion because they express *critical* rather than emotionally overinvolved (high-EOI) attitudes, high-EE spouses thus represent a potentially valuable population for the study of the critical component of the expressed-emotion index. They also provide a means through which the association between expressed emotion and marital disharmony can be investigated. Following a brief review of some of the important questions that lie ahead concerning EE and relapse, I will focus more narrowly on the elusive question of how and why patient-directed criticism emerges in certain marriages and not in others.

As I will attempt to demonstrate in some detail, the answer to this question may have much to tell us both about the nature of EE and about the paths through which it is linked to psychiatric relapse. The discussion begins with consideration of the link between expressed emotion and marital distress. Attention is then focused on the association between patient symptoms and family stress. Although criticism seems not to be related to type or severity of patient illness, there are other dimensions of psychopathology that may engender high levels of expressed emotion in spouses. Finally, against the backdrop of these observations, an attribution model of expressed emotion is introduced and some recent findings supportive of the model are discussed.

The Nature of Expressed Emotion

Descriptively, the classification of family members as high- or low-EE is based on the substance and tone of their comments about the patient during the Camberwell Family Interview (CFI; see 41). Those who talk about the patient in a critical, hostile, or emotionally overinvolved way are classified as high-EE; those who do not are classified as low-EE. The ease with which the measurement of EE can be described, however, belies the complexity of the underlying construct. Although we can assess expressed emotion in relatives quite reliably, it is still not clear precisely what high-EE represents, why it is such a reliable predictor of patient relapse, or why it is characteristic of certain spouses and not others.

With regard to the first question, what is EE, most researchers have assumed that criticism assessed during the CFI is an indirect measure of criticism directed toward the patient on a day-to-day basis. Although this assumption has only recently received the empirical attention it deserves, it seems warranted on the basis of available data. High-EE relatives are more critical of patients during face-to-face interactions than their low-EE counterparts. Moreover, the patient's diagnosis appears to have little influence on this association. High-EE relatives exhibit critical behavior when interacting with depressed (23), schizophrenic (33; see also Chapter 9, this volume) or "preschizophrenic" (39) individuals.

The second question, why does EE predict relapse has received less empirical attention. While it has been easy for us to assume that high levels of criticism lead naturally to psychiatric relapse, EE is unlikely to support such a straightforward interpretation. On the one hand, it seems reasonable to expect that patients who are criticized often will be subjected to higher levels of stress. In such cases, the diathesis-stress model of psychopathology would predict a higher probability of relapse. On the other hand, it is not obvious that all criticism is equivalently stressful. For some spouses, criticism may be a well-intentioned effort to effect positive change in the patient's functioning. For others, criticism may represent little more than frustration, impatience, and/or a form of retaliation for the patient's misbehavior. At the same time, patient-partners of high-EE spouses may interpret criticism as constructive and supportive, or threatening and stressful—quite aside from the intentions of their spouses.

Recent evidence suggests that high-EE spouses do not consider themselves particularly critical. When the spouses of depressed patients were asked to rate (using a 10-point scale) how critical they were of their patient-partner, the correlation between the spouses' ratings and the actual frequency of critical remarks made during the CFI was .00 (Pearson's r, $n = 23$; see 27). Furthermore, there was only a .27 correlation between the criticism ratings patients assigned to spouses and the frequency of CFI-assessed spouse criticism ($n = 23$, $p > .1$). Patients' subjective perceptions of criticism do not, therefore, mirror the more objective, CFI-based ratings. These subjective appraisals of spouses' criticism are strongly associated with subsequent relapse, however. Indeed, there is some evidence to suggest that perceived criticism ratings explain significantly more of the variance in depressed patients' relapse rates than CFI-based ratings (27). Thus, although EE may seem to lend itself to a fairly straightforward interpretation, a number of important questions remain unanswered.

The third question, why are some spouses critical of their patient-partners and not others, has received perhaps the least empirical attention. Ironically, it is the most interesting in terms of its potential for yielding theoretical and practical insights into the nature of expressed emotion and the causes of psychiatric relapse. Living with a psychiatrically ill individual is not easy. Nonetheless, many families appear to cope quite well with the marked changes in behavior and levels of functioning that typically accompany psychiatric impairment. The remainder of this chapter will thus focus on those dimensions of psychopathology in patients that may be relevant to this issue.

Expressed Emotion and Marital Distress

Expressed emotion may have much in common with the more familiar construct of marital distress. In a recent study of depressed patients and their spouses, for example, Hooley and Hahlweg (24) found that the criticism levels of spouses in the CFI were significantly and negatively correlated with patient reports of marital satisfaction, as assessed with the Dyadic Adjustment Scale (35). That is, depressed patients with critical spouses reported lower rates of marital satisfaction than did patients with low-EE spouses. These data suggest that patient-related criticism expressed by spouses during an interview may be indexing an important aspect of the spouse-patient relationship, which is also indexed by patient-ratings of marital satisfaction.

This interpretation is further supported by analyses of the same sample, which indicated that both spouse EE levels and the marital satisfaction ratings of their patient-partners were equally successful in predicting the likelihood of patient relapse over a nine-month period (27). Patients who lived with low-EE relatives or who reported satisfactory marital relationships were more likely to remain well during follow-up than were patients who lived with high-EE relatives, or whose DAS scores indicated marital distress. Data such as these highlight the potential relevance of marital research to an understanding of what expressed emotion is, how and why it arises, and how it is related to patient relapse.

Why Is Psychopathology Associated with Marital Distress?

Although psychiatric difficulties in general are associated with marital problems and domestic tension, there is currently no clear or consistent evidence to suggest that any one diagnosis is more closely related to family distress than any other. While poor marital quality and depression are frequently linked (8, 10, 45, 46), rates of separation and divorce are also high in couples in which one spouse has a diagnosis of schizophrenia (17), antisocial personality (5), or bipolar disorder (6).

In a similar vein, research on family levels of expressed emotion has demonstrated that the relatives of schizophrenic patients are just as critical as the relatives of unipolar depressives (40) and manic patients (see Chapter 11, this volume). It is also apparent that no reliable association exists between the severity of patients' psychopathology and the extent to which relatives criticize them (7, 25, 33, 40, 43).

This lack of association between family distress (as reflected in high levels of EE or low levels of marital satisfaction) and the severity or diagnosis applied to the patient's disorder raises the question of precisely what it is about psychiatric patients in general (or about the kinds of relatives they have or marry) that accounts for these low levels of domestic harmony.

One currently unexplored avenue of inquiry concerns how relatives attempt to understand the marked behavioral changes that typically accompany psychiatric impairment. In recent years, the role played by causal attributions has led to an increased understanding of marital and other close interpersonal relationships (4, 12, 13, 19, 21, 28, 44). In a related vein, it seems reasonable to suggest that an increased focus on the attributions relatives make about the causes of disruptive behavior in psychiatric patients might yield similar benefits for researchers and clinicians interested in the nature of expressed emotion.

Toward Understanding Expressed Emotion

When faced with the abnormal behavior of a family member, relatives have two choices; they can make either an internal or an external attribution about the cause of the change. The latter involves blaming the illness. The former results in blaming the patient.

Unfortunately for patients, even severe psychiatric difficulties leading to hospitalization are not invariably perceived as manifestations of illness. This point is well illustrated in Clausen and Yarrow's (9) detailed study of the wives of schizophrenics, which represented an early attempt to document the efforts made by these family members to understand and adjust to changes in their disturbed partners' behavior. Although a few wives realized at quite an early stage that their husbands were suffering from serious mental problems, many construed the change in behavior either in terms of a physical problem or else as a weakness of character that was somehow under the control of the patient. Even *after* their husbands had been hospitalized, only just over half of the wives had developed stable interpretations of their husband's behavior that were consistent with an illness attribution.

The ability and/or willingness of family members to accept that a patient is genuinely ill, however, may be of crucial importance in determining their acceptance of and/or tolerance for what is often disturbed and disruptive behavior. As a result of their extensive work with the families of schizophrenics, Vaughn and Leff (41) have suggested that blaming the illness rather than the patient for the behavior changes that typically accompany psychiatric impairment is one attitude that is likely to be associated with a supportive or low-EE home environment. Comments made by low-EE spouses of depressed patients during interviews conducted by the author provide further support for this impression. Low-EE spouses do not doubt the legitimacy of the patient's condition. Furthermore, when potentially disruptive behavior does occur, it is perceived as non-volitional.

> "It wasn't her, it was this illness. I don't think it was her fault because when she's normal she's good."
>
> "She'd wake me up at 1 or 2 a.m. five nights a week. She didn't do it intentionally."

High-EE spouses, in contrast, seem more inclined to make internal attributions about the causes of deviant behavior in their partners. They often express frustration and anger that patients don't do more to help themselves, and they hold them at least partially responsible for their symptoms.

> "There are times when I really felt like shaking him and saying 'pull yourself together!'."
>
> "I feel ever so sorry for him in one way, and then in another way I think no I shouldn't because he did it."

Sometimes, high-EE relatives express doubts about whether the patient is indeed genuinely ill.

> "She has a tendency to walk the way she sees all depressive patients walk in here. I think she's very impressionable."
>
> "To me, she has more of a personality problem than a depressive illness."

The spontaneous comments of high- and low-EE relatives thus suggest that they may be making quite different attributions about the causes of behavior change in patients. Clearly, however, these attributional differences could result from a number of factors. They may reflect personality differences between the relatives themselves. Low-EE relatives may generally be less inclined to make internal attributions about negative behavior irrespective of the form or source of that behavior. Alternatively, these differences in attribution may reflect actual differences in patients' behavior. That is, high-EE relatives may be more inclined to make internal attributions about the causes of disruptive behavior because the behaviors they observe (or do not observe) lend themselves more readily to such attributions. One husband, for example, described how his depressed wife changed her behavior according to circumstances:

> "She was very low—unhappy. And then we were having this party, and she bucked up and perked up for the party, got it all ready. Then afterwards, she deteriorated again and went to bed for a couple of days. But then—this was a few days before Christmas—on Christmas Eve, when she had to play the organ in church, she was up again and played the organ very well. She can pull out of it if she has what she regards as sufficient motivation. She wouldn't necessarily do things which I feel are important—looking after the family. That would be different. But, if she's got to do something—impress I suppose—then she can do it."

Most likely, however, a combination of personality characteristics in relatives and symptom characteristics of the patient act in concert. As one high-EE wife of a hospitalized depressed man said:

> "It's so difficult with an illness like that. If he'd broken his arm you could have said, 'Oh, it's his arm playing him up.' But you couldn't see anything physical. And I'm afraid I'm inclined, well I was, to lose my temper because you just couldn't *see* anything."

The problems relatives face when they try to decide if behavior is illness-related or volitional are made even more difficult by the fact that many psychiatric symptoms (irritability, anorexia, or social withdrawal, to name just three) merely reflect exaggerated or diminished forms of normal behavior. This apparent continuity between "normal" and "deviant" behavior not only creates difficulties for the families of psychiatric patients, but also is a major source of controversy within the field of psychopathology. For relatives, however, one important consequence of this real or apparent continuity is that the causes of many psychiatric symptoms appear ambiguous. This renders attributions of illness less probable, and relatives are likely to be high-EE.

Symptoms that are discontinuous with normal behavior (for example, auditory hallucinations), on the other hand, are much more likely to be viewed as indicative of genuine illness. If these symptoms dominate the patients' clinical picture or are highly salient for relatives, more external attributions about changes in behavior are expected. In such circumstances, family members might well be expected to be relatively sympathetic, tolerant, and low in EE.

As proposed here, the construct of expressed emotion is thus considered to reflect (a) characteristics of relatives (personality factors, attributions about symptoms, coping skills, and so on), (b) characteristics of patients (for example, clinical symptoms and malingering history), and (c) aspects of the pre-illness patient-spouse relationship. Marital quality is particularly important because attributional research has indicated that individuals within distressed relationships are more likely to attribute negative behavior to internal or characterological factors than are individuals whose relationships are not distressed (28). In cases where the pre-illness relationship between the patient and relative has been good, therefore, relatives are more likely to be low-EE regardless of the patients' symptomatology.

If high-EE relatives view the patients symptoms as being (at least to some degree) under voluntary control, it further follows that they may make efforts to change the behaviors they perceive as undesirable. As has been suggested by Hooley (22) and again recently by Greenley (20), high levels of EE may also be marking high levels of social control. Because relatives are rated as critical in EE assessments when they make it clear that there are aspects of the patient's personality or behavior that they do not like, this idea has considerable face validity. Criticism, by its very nature, implies that the relative would like the patient to be different. If relatives (a) desire and (b) consider patients *capable* of change, it is plausible to suggest that high levels of criticism, which occur in the presence of internal attributions of illness, will also be associated with efforts to modify those elements of patients' behavior that are considered aversive.[1]

Insofar as relatives' efforts to modify patients' behavior may sometimes be effective, the model of EE proposed acknowledges that high levels of EE may not invariably be bad. Instead, they may permit some patients to attain higher levels of functioning than they might otherwise. To the extent that psychiatric symptoms are not controlled by patients, however, the coercive

[1]Critical relatives may thus fall into two categories. Some may be critical of patients' behavior but nonetheless accept the uncontrollable nature of the symptoms; these relatives will therefore be critical but not controlling. When criticism and internal attributions coexist, however, social coercion is predicted to result. Under such circumstances, relatives will be both critical and controlling. If social control rather than criticism is implicated in process of patient-relapse, reconceptualization of high levels of EE in the way described provides a potentially important means through which the observation that many patients who live with critical relatives do not relapse can be explained. Although socially coercive tendencies may potentially be gleaned through the recoding of CFI protocols, no data are currently available to address this issue. It is therefore not discussed further.

efforts of relatives are unlikely to lead to major behavioral changes. Two outcomes can result from this. When faced with a patient unresponsive to external demands for change, some relatives may come to accept that the patient is indeed incapable of modifying his or her aversive behavior. This may prompt them to modify their own perceptions about symptom controllability and to accept that the patient is genuinely ill. The model thus provides a mechanism through which high-EE relatives can develop low-EE attitudes as they become more experienced in dealing with the patient and learn more about the nature of his or her psychiatric difficulties.

If, on the other hand, efforts to change patients' behavior fail, and relatives do not modify their attributions, they are likely to continue to be both critical and socially coercive. Over time, as they become increasingly frustrated and aware of their lack of impact on the patient, they may also become hostile.

> "There's no way I can have any influence on it at all. I could walk in, kick the door open, kick the table over and lie on the settee. It would still be exactly the same. If she was going to be in a bad mood she would be. If she was going to be in a good mood she would be. I couldn't affect it in any way."

The model thus provides a mechanism through which the etiology of hostility may also be explained.

Emotional Overinvolvement

Although the main focus of this chapter concerns relatives' expressions of criticism, emotionally overinvolved, self-sacrificing or over-protective attitudes can also result in relatives being rated as high in expressed emotion. At a conceptual level, however, the constructs of criticism and emotional overinvolvement appear to have little in common. They also have different behavioral correlates (32-34). For example, high levels of emotional involvement in relatives are associated with poorer levels of premorbid adjustment in patients and higher levels of residual symptomatology. It is thus possible that this component of the high-EE index is related to relapse primarily through its association with known markers of poor outcome in patients. Because both criticism and emotional overinvolvement are still typically used to provide information about EE levels, however, the question still remains as to how these two principal components of the expressed emotion index can be incorporated into the theoretical schema proposed in this chapter.

It has been argued that if relatives make attributions about psychiatric symptoms in a way that is consistent with a medical model, patients will not be held responsible for their disturbed behavior. To the extent that they are associated with low-EE attitudes in the home, therefore, illness-based attributions are likely to benefit patients. That a medical-attribution bias could actually work to the detriment of some patients, however, is an issue that deserves consideration. It may be possible to have too much of a good thing. For example, a strong acceptance of a medically based interpretation of disturbed behavior may prompt some relatives to become highly concerned and protective of their psychiatrically ill family member. There may thus be a link between high levels of emotional overinvolvement and a strong conviction that a patient is medically ill.

Although this hypothesis is highly speculative at the present time, it does appear to be consistent with Miklowitz et al.'s data concerning the association between premorbid adjustment and emotional overinvolvement. Yet, because emotional overinvolvement is comparatively rare in spouses, little data can be offered here in the service of testing the hypothesis proposed. That positive patient outcomes may not invariably be associated with external attributions of illness, however, is an important issue that deserves future attention from expressed emotion researchers.

The Explanatory Power of The Model

The model of expressed emotion proposed above appears capable of explaining much of what we currently know about expressed emotion. Leff and Vaughn (30), for example, have described the intrusive nature of high-EE relatives and the willingness of low-EE families to respect patients' needs for social distance. These authors also mention the conviction high-EE relatives have that patients can exercise control over symptoms, given the will to do so (30, p. 116). Thus, in many respects, what is being proposed here is not new. It simply represents a framework within which many previously observed characteristics of high- and low-EE families can be organized and understood.

In addition to providing some face validity for model, the current EE literature also lends empirical support to several of its specific predictions. For example, the model predicts that EE levels should not remain constant over time but should instead be responsive to symptom changes in patients. Consistent with this hypothesis are recent data from a West German sample; these indicate that levels of EE in relatives do change over time (14), most typically decreasing subsequent to patients' discharge from hospital (see also 7, and 30, p. 137).

The model further predicts that high levels of EE will be reduced by certain forms of social intervention, particularly those emphasizing the uncontrollable nature of psychiatric symptoms. Here, it is interesting to note that the education of relatives has been viewed for a number of years as an important component in family-based treatments for schizophrenia (18, 29), although the theoretical underpinnings of such an approach have never been precisely specified. Reconceptualization of expressed emotion in terms of illness attributions and social control not only provides this much-needed theoretical framework, but is also consistent with the spontaneous comments of relatives that suggest education facilitates a change in attitudes toward more medically based interpretations of behavior. This is well illustrated by the two remarks below, which are taken from Berkowitz et al. (3). Yet the durability of such attitude changes, and the extent to which they impact on the relatives' actual behavior still remains unclear.

> [mother of patient] "I thought my son was a monster. You helped and showed me it was an illness. That was half the battle, knowing that the poor boy was ill."
>
> [wife of patient] "In the past when John was difficult, I had no idea what was going on. It helps me now to know that he is ill, that he can't help doing or saying things that might be strange. I accept it and let it blow over."

The attributional model of expressed emotion also explains why education about psychiatric symptoms may not be a very successful form of intervention for emotionally overinvolved relatives. Certainly, high levels of emotional overinvolvement appear particularly resistant to modification efforts (29). If emotionally overinvolved relatives *already* hold strong beliefs about the medical basis of psychiatrically disturbed behavior, educational efforts designed to foster the development of illness attributions will only reinforce attitudes the relatives already have. Different intervention strategies may thus be required to modify the two principal components of the high-EE index.

Empirical Support for the Attributional Model

A fundamental assumption of the attributional model described in this chapter is that certain psychiatric symptoms lend themselves more readily to illness-based attributions than do others. It is further assumed that differences in the degree of perceived controllability of symptoms are central to such illness-related or characterological attributions of causality.

Elsewhere (see 22), it has been suggested that behaviors that reflect the distinction between positive and negative symptoms (1, 2, 11) might be particularly worthy of attention in investigations concerned with issues of symptom control. Negative symptoms (for example, self-neglect, alogia, apathy) are likely to be perceived as controllable because they typically involve what is "primarily an absence of normal functions" (38, p. 65). For this reason, it may be difficult for families to accept that negative symptoms which occur in the context of no apparent *physical* inability to speak, move, or engage in appropriate self-care, reflect symptoms of genuine illness. Negative symptoms are therefore predicted by the illness-attribution model to be associated with relatively high levels of family distress.

Positive symptoms, in contrast, reflect behavioral excesses, and are typified by such symptoms as hallucinations, delusions, and bizarre or inappropriate behavior. Because of the essentially florid and unusual nature of positive symptoms, they may be more readily construed as illness-related and beyond voluntary control. Families are thus able to blame the illness rather than the patient for any interpersonal difficulties that develop as a consequence of the symptoms.

But are positive symptoms generally considered to be under less volitional control than negative symptoms? Data recently obtained from a sample of State University of New York college students suggests that they are. In this study, a sample of 73 undergraduates completed a 40-item questionnaire, the Control of Symptoms Schedule (COSS), designed specifically for the purpose of investigating perceptions of symptom controllability. The COSS described a wide range of psychiatric symptoms as well as some symptoms that are more generally viewed as "medical" (for example, backache, asthma, epilepsy, and headache). After reading the definition of each symptom (for example, grandiosity—inflated appraisal of self worth, power, contacts, or knowledge), all subjects rated, using a 5-point scale (1 = no control; 5 = complete control), the extent to which they considered each symptoms to be potentially controllable, that is, the extent to which a patient could reduce or remove a symptom completely if he or she tried hard enough.

Analysis of the students' ratings of the symptoms covered by the COSS revealed that, as predicted, positive symptoms were perceived as being significantly less controllable than negative symptoms. The symptoms that were seen as least controllable were those that reflected more traditional medical problems (backache, headache, epilepsy, and asthma). The sex of the rater did not influence the extent to which the particular symptom groupings were perceived as controllable.

Of all the 40 COSS items rated, epilepsy was perceived as being least controllable (mean controllability rating = 1.45). This was followed by auditory hallucinations (mean controllability rating 2.00), which was the single most uncontrollable psychiatric symptom. At the other end of the scale, self-neglect was perceived as the symptom most under voluntary control (mean controllability rating = 4.30). The results are thus consistent with the view that not all psychiatric symptoms are perceived as equally controllable and that negative symptoms in particular are viewed as more controllable than positive symptoms.

In view of the finding that negative symptoms are perceived as having a stronger volitional component than positive symptoms, it is reasonable to ask whether negative symptom behaviors are also associated with higher levels of family tension. Although the association between positive and negative symptoms and family levels of EE have not yet been systematically investigated, it is worth noting that high levels of EE in the spouses of depressed patients have been shown to be associated with a withdrawn and unexpressive communication style in patients that is essentially "negative" in nature. In a recent study involving face-to-face-interactions with depressed patients, high-EE spouses made more critical remarks to their patient-partners than did low-EE spouses. They also disagreed with patients more and were less accepting of what patients said to them than were their low-EE counterparts (23). Considered together, these data provide concurrent validation for the EE construct in a depressed patient sample.

With reference to the present discussion, however, it is important to note that the high-EE spouses in the study just described were themselves interacting with patients who were quite different from patients who interacted with low-EE relatives. Specifically, patients who interacted with high-EE spouses made fewer self-disclosing remarks. They were also considerably less expressive in their nonverbal behavior than the patients who interacted with low-EE spouses. High-EE spouses therefore had partners who were uncommunicative—both verbally and nonverbally.

Many of the critical comments of spouses who were not videotaped also concerned patients' lack of communication.

> "You couldn't have a conversation with him. He just wouldn't answer you."
>
> "It was a waste of time. You just sat there and talked to yourself for half an hour."
>
> "He'll get very quiet—won't speak. You keep saying 'What have I done? What's happened?' and he'll say, 'Oh, nothing. Nothing'."

Thus, although it is possible that the patients interacting with the high-EE spouses behaved in a neutral and passive way in order to avoid criticism from their partners, it is equally plausible that the high-EE relatives were critical because they had unexpressive and uncommunicative partners. From this perspective, criticism may be viewed as an attempt to get an emotional response from patients.

It is further apparent from interview data that many of the spouses of depressed patients are critical not only of lack of communication in patients but also of other negative symptom behaviors.

> "She wouldn't go out. She just, well, laid in bed for three weeks. Just laid in bed. Wouldn't do a thing. Wouldn't even wash. Never had a wash for a week!"
>
> "Some stupid thing comes on the television and I'll sit there laughing my head off. But not *him*. He'll just sit there, staring into space all the time."
>
> "She has no interests at all. No interests in anything at all. She doesn't read or sew or cook or knit."

Although consistent with the basic ideas proposed in this chapter, the spontaneous comments of high-EE relatives provide illustrations of, rather than support for the model and its associated hypotheses. Recent data concerning the association between psychiatric symptoms and marital adjustment (see 26), however, speak to these issues more directly. Using a large sample of over 100 psychiatric patients, these investigators studied the association between DSM-III diagnosis, predominant symptom profile (positive, mixed, or negative), and self-reported levels of marital distress in the spouses of schizophrenic and affectively disordered patients. Information about psychiatric symptoms was collected by trained interviewers using the Current and Past Psychopathology Scale (CAPPS; see 15, 36). This was also the clinical interview that was used to provide the psychiatric symptoms and symptom descriptions for the Control of Symptoms Schedule, the questionnaire used in the positive and negative symptom controllability rating study described earlier. The use of the CAPPS in both investigations insured that the symptom controllability scores obtained in the earlier study would map as closely as possible onto the symptom groupings derived for the second study. Marital adjustment was measured using the Marital Adjustment Test (MAT; see 31), a widely used self-report inventory of marital satisfaction.

As expected, and in keeping with previous research, the marriages of psychiatric patients were found to be significantly more distressed than the marriages of nonpsychiatric control families matched for SES and family composition. Within the psychiatric group, however, no effect for diagnosis was found. Thus, although the spouses of the schizophrenic patients, the bipolar patients, and the unipolar depressives all reported significantly higher mean levels of marital distress than the controls, no specific diagnosis was more or less associated with spouse-rated levels of marital difficulties.

Reclassification of patients on the basis of their predominant symptom profile, however, did reveal some interesting differences. Spouses of patients whose symptom profile was generally one of positive symptoms were significantly happier with their marriages than spouses married to patients who had a symptom profile that was predominantly negative (mean MAT scores = 99.0 versus 82.9). The mean marital satisfaction score of spouses married to patients with a more mixed symptom profile (neither strongly positive nor strongly negative), on the other hand, fell between that of the positive and the negative symptom profile groups and was not significantly different from either.

The finding that the spouses of positive-symptom patients were significantly happier with their marriages than the spouses of negative-symptom patients is particularly interesting in the light of the fact that positive-symptom patients were rated by clinical interviewers as having significantly *poorer* levels of overall functioning based on the Global Assessment Scale (GAS; see 16). A purely behavioral model does not, therefore, constitute an adequate explanation of the findings. While it is not clear from this study precisely why the spouses of positive-symptom patients should be happier with their marital relationships, the results are nonetheless consistent with the attribution model proposed.

It is interesting to note that in the study investigating students' perceptions of symptom controllability, described earlier, not all positive symptoms were rated as being less controllable than all negative symptoms. Classification of patients according to positive or negative symptom profile is therefore only a crude method of investigating the illness attribution/controllability hypothesis. A necessary next step is to classify patients on the basis of symptom controllability ratings such as those obtained from the earlier investigation, and then to relate the resultant grouping to family levels of EE. This work is now beginning. It is hoped that the results of such investigations will be of value in clarifying the nature and origins of expressed emotion.

Conclusions

In this chapter, it has been proposed that the attributions family members make about the causes of deviant behavior in psychiatric patients may be of potential value in helping us understand more about the expressed emotion construct. Although still highly speculative at this point, it has been suggested that high levels of EE in family members can be interpreted within an illness attribution/symptom controllability framework. Within such a framework, EE can be reconceptualized as a particular form of coercive social control. High-EE attitudes are hypothesized to develop when symptoms are perceived by family members as being to some degree controllable by patients. High-EE relatives will thus be inclined to nag or cajole patients in the service of modifying the undesirable behavior that constitutes the source of their criticism. When these efforts are successful, patients' levels of functioning may improve. To the extent that such efforts fail, relatives may modify their attributions (becoming low EE) or else remain critical and blame the patient for the symptoms exhibited. Under such circumstances, relatives may become hostile.

Because the source of criticism is fundamentally the behavior of the patients, decreases in levels of criticism as symptoms decline are predicted by the model. The model also predicts that levels of EE may be reduced by educating relatives about psychiatric illness, particularly if the uncontrollability of negative symptoms is emphasized. Because internal attributions have been demonstrated to be associated with high levels of marital distress, the model further provides a theoretical basis for predicting that some forms of marital therapy may be effective in reducing EE levels. It also suggests that in cases where the pre-illness patient-spouse relationship is poor, education about symptoms in the absence of marital therapy is unlikely to be successful.

This point is well illustrated by one highly critical spouse, who was himself a consultant, hospital physician. This man refused to accept that his depressed wife had anything physically wrong with her. Instead, he considered her to be a malingerer who liked being in hospital because it allowed her to avoid her responsibilities at home. As far as this spouse was concerned, his wife's current illness was simply another example of her inadequate personality.

Clearly this man did not lack medical education. What he did lack, however, was any affection for his wife ("It's very difficult sometimes even to like her."). In the absence of *motivation* to attribute symptoms to external causes, psychiatric knowledge may confer little benefit. Similarly, if relatives' motivation is high enough, even the most negative symptom profile may be attributed to external factors without explicit information or education about psychopathology being required.

Although the model of expressed emotion described in this chapter has considerable face validity, and appears capable of integrating research findings from a number of different areas, it should be emphasized that it is still essentially untested. The findings presented in support of the model may be consistent with other, alternative interpretations. For these reasons, the model should, at best, be considered only as a potentially valuable, heuristic framework within which much of what we presently know about expressed emotion can be organized. The model is offered here in the service of stimulating future investigations into the nature of expressed emotion. EE is a construct of considerable importance to clinicians and researchers alike. The more we understand about its complex nature, the better able we shall be to help the large numbers of psychiatric patients and their families whose subjective and objective burdens deserve the most effective intervention services possible.

REFERENCES

1. Andreasen, N. C. Negative symptoms in schizophrenia: Definition and reliability. *Archives of General Psychiatry 39*: 784–788, 1982.

2. ______, & Olsen, S. Negative v positive schizophrenia: Definition and validation. *Archives of General Psychiatry 39*: 789–794, 1982.

3. Berkowitz, R., Eberlein-Vries, R., Kuipers, L., & Leff, J. P. Educating relatives about schizophrenia. *Schizophrenia Bulletin 10*: 418–429, 1984.

4. Berley, R. A., & Jacobson, N. S. Causal attributions in intimate relationships: Toward a model of cognitive-behavioral marital therapy. In P. C. Kendall (ed.), *Advances in cognitive-behavioral research and therapy* (Vol. 3). Orlando FL: Academic Press, 1984.

5. Briscoe, C. W., Smith, J. B., Robins, E., Marten, S., & Gaskin, F. Divorce and psychiatric disease. *Archives of General Psychiatry 29*: 119–125, 1973.

6. Brodie, H. K. H., & Leff, M. J. Bipolar depression—A comparative study of patient characteristics. *American Journal of Psychiatry 127*: 1086–1090, 1971.

7. Brown, G. W., Birley, J. L. T., & Wing, J. K. Influence of family life on the course of schizophrenic disorders: A replication. *British Journal of Psychiatry 121*: 241–258, 1972.

8. Bullock, R. C., Siegel, R., Weissman, M. M., & Paykel, E. S. The weeping wife: Marital relations of depressed women. *Journal of Marriage and the Family 34*: 488–495, 1972.

9. Clausen, J. A., & Yarrow, M. R. (eds.). The impact of mental illness on the family. *Journal of Social Issues 11*: (entire issue), 1955.

10. Coleman, R. E., & Miller, A. G. The relation between depression and marital maladjustment in a clinic population: A multitrait-multimethod study. *Journal of Consulting and Clinical Psychology 43*: 647–651, 1975.

11. Crow, T. J. Molecular pathology of schizophrenia: More than one disease process? *British Medical Journal 280*: 1–9, 1980.

12. Doherty, W. J. Cognitive processes in intimate conflict: I. Extending attribution theory. *The American Journal of Family Therapy 9*: 5–13, 1981.

13. ______. Cognitive processes in intimate conflict: II. Efficacy and learned helplessness. *The American Journal of Family Therapy 9*: 35–44, 1981.

14. Dulz, B., & Hand, I. Short-term relapse in young schizophrenics: Can it be predicted and affected by family (CFI), patient, and treatment variables? An experimental study. In M. J. Goldstein & K. Hahlweg (eds.), *Treatment of schizophrenia: Family assessment and intervention*. Berlin: Springer-Verlag, 1986.

15. Endicott, J., & Spitzer, R. L. Current and past psychopathology scales (CAPPS): Rationale, reliability, and validity. *Archives of General Psychiatry 27*: 678–687, 1972.

16. ______, Spitzer, R. L., Fleiss, J. L., & Cohen, J. The Global Assessment Scale: A procedure for measuring overall severity of psychiatric disturbance. *Archives of General Psychiatry 33*: 766–771, 1976.

17. Erlenmeyer-Kimling, L., Wunsch-Hitzig, R. A., & Deutsch, S. Family formation by schizophrenics. In L. N. Robins, P. J. Clayton, & J. K. Wing (eds.), *The social consequences of psychiatric illness*. New York: Brunner/Mazel, 1980.

18. Falloon, I. R. H., Boyd, J. L., McGill, C. W., Razani, J., Moss, H. B., & Gilderman, A. M. Family management in the prevention of exacerbations of schizophrenia. *New England Journal of Medicine 306*: 1437–1439, 1982.

19. Fincham, F., & O'Leary, K. D. Causal inferences for spouse behavior in maritally distressed and nondistressed couples. *Journal of Social and Clinical Psychology 1*: 42–57, 1983.

20. Greenley, J. R. Social control and expressed emotion. *Journal of Nervous and Mental Disease 174*: 24–30, 1986.

21. Holtzworth-Munroe, A., & Jacobson, N. S. Causal attributions of married couples: When do they search for causes? What do they conclude when they do? *Journal of Personality and Social Psychology 48*: 1398–1412, 1985.

22. Hooley, J. M. Expressed emotion: A review of the critical literature. *Clinical Psychology Review 5*: 119–139, 1985.

23. ______. Expressed emotion and depression: Interactions between patients and high versus low EE spouses. *Journal of Abnormal Psychology 95*: 237–246, 1986.

24. ______, & Hahlweg. Interaction patterns of depressed patients and their spouses: Comparing high and low EE dyads. In M. J. Goldstein, I. Hand, & K. Hahlweg, (eds.), *Treatment of schizophrenia: Family assessment and intervention*. Berlin: Springer-Verlag, 1986.

25. ______, Orley, J., & Teasdale, J. D. Levels of expressed emotion and relapse in depressed patients. *British Journal of Psychiatry 148*: 642–647, 1986.

26. ______, Richters, J. E., Weintraub, S., & Neale, J. M. Psychopathology and marital distress: The positive side of positive symptoms. *Journal of Abnormal Psychology 96*: 27–33, 1987.

27. ______, & Teasdale, J. D. Predictors of relapse in unipolar depression: Expressed emotion, marital quality, and perceived criticism, submitted for publication.

28. Jacobson, N. S., McDonald, D. W., Follette, W. C., & Berley, R. A. Attributional processes in distressed and nondistressed couples. *Cognitive Therapy and Research 9*: 35–50, 1985.

29. Leff, J. P., Kuipers, L., Berkowitz, R., Eberlein-Vries, R., & Sturgeon, D. A controlled trial of social intervention in the families of schizophrenic patients. *British Journal of Psychiatry 141*: 121–134, 1982.

30. ______, & Vaughn, C. *Expressed emotion in families*. New York: Guilford Press, 1985.

31. Locke, H. J., & Wallace, K. M. Short marital adjustment and prediction tests: Their reliability and validity. *Marriage and Family Living 21*: 251–255, 1959.

32. Miklowitz, D. J., Goldstein, M. J., & Falloon, I. R. H. Premorbid and symptomatic characteristics of schizophrenics from families with high and low levels of expressed emotion. *Journal of Abnormal Psychology 92*: 359-367, 1983.

33. ______, Goldstein, M. J., Falloon, I. R. H., & Doane, J. A. Interactional correlates of expressed emotion in the families of schizophrenics. *British Journal of Psychiatry 144*: 482-487, 1984.

34. ______, Strachan, A. M., Goldstein, M. J., Doane, J. A., Snyder, K. S., Hogarty, G. E., & Falloon, I. R. H. Expressed emotion and communication deviance in the families of schizophrenics. *Journal of Abnormal Psychology 95*: 60-66, 1986.

35. Spanier, G. Measuring dyadic adjustment: New scales for assessing the quality of marriage and similar dyads. *Journal of Marriage and the Family 38*: 15-28, 1976.

36. Spitzer, R. L., & Endicott, J. *Current and past psychopathology scales (CAPPS)*. New York: Evaluations Unit, Biometric Research, New York State Department of Mental Hygiene, 1968.

37. ______, Gibbon, M., & Endicott, J. Global assessment scale (GAS). In W. Guy (ed.), *ECDEU assessment manual*. Washington DC: Department of Health, Education and Welfare publication (ADM) *76-338*: 583-585, 1976.

38. Strauss, J. S., Carpenter, W. T., & Bartko, J. J. The diagnosis and understanding of schizophrenia: Part III. Speculations on the processes that underlie schizophrenia symptoms and signs. *Schizophrenia Bulletin 11*: 61-69, 1974.

39. Valone, K., Norton, J. P., Goldstein, M. J., & Doane, J. A. Parental expressed emotion and affective style in an adolescent sample at risk for schizophrenia spectrum disorders. *Journal of Abnormal Psychology 92*: 399-407, 1983.

40. Vaughn, C. E., & Leff, J. P. The influence of family and social factors on the course of psychiatric illness: A comparison of schizophrenic and depressed neurotic patients. *British Journal of Psychiatry 129*: 125-137, 1976.

41. ______, & Leff, J. P. The measurement of expressed emotion in the families of psychiatric patients. *British Journal of Social and Clinical Psychology 15*: 157-165, 1976.

42. ______, & Leff, J. P. Patterns of emotional response in the relatives of schizophrenic patients. *Schizophrenia Bulletin 7*: 43-44, 1981.

43. ______, Snyder, K. S., Jones, S., Freeman, W. B., & Falloon, I. R. H. Family factors in schizophrenic relapse: Replication in California of British research on expressed emotion. *Archives of General Psychiatry 41*: 1169-1177, 1984.

44. Weiss, R. L. Strategic behavioral marital therapy: Toward a model for assessment and intervention. In J. P. Vincent (ed.), *Advances in family intervention, assessment and theory* (Vol. 1). Greenwich CT: JAI Press, 1980.

45. ______, & Aved, B. M. Marital satisfaction and depression as predictors of physical health status. *Journal of Consulting and Clinical Psychology 46*: 1379-1384, 1978.

46. Weissman, M. M., & Paykel, E. S. *The depressed woman: A study of social relationships*. Chicago: University of Chicago Press, 1974.

11

THE FAMILY AND THE COURSE OF RECENT-ONSET MANIA*

DAVID J. MIKLOWITZ, MICHAEL J. GOLDSTEIN, KEITH H. NUECHTERLEIN, KAREN S. SNYDER, AND JERI A. DOANE†

University of California, Los Angeles

Yale Psychiatric Institute, New Haven

RESEARCH on the relationship between family interaction and schizophrenia has identified two constructs that appear to predict the onset and course of the disorder. The first, expressed emotion (EE), is a measure of parental emotion *attitudes* expressed about a schizophrenic patient and has been found to be associated with a high probability of patient relapse in the 9 months following hospital discharge (1, 21, 23). The second construct, affective style (AS), refers to the emotional-verbal *behavior* of relatives in direct interaction with a psychiatrically ill family member. AS has been shown to predict relapse in schizophrenic patients and, in one study, was associated with the onset of schizophrenia-spectrum disorders in a cohort of nonpsychotic, disturbed adolescents (4, 5, 7). AS appears to measure, to some extent, the *behavioral* correlates of EE attitudes; high-EE relatives appear to use more critical and/or intrusive, invasive statements in direct interaction with their offspring than do low-EE relatives (13, 19, 20). How-

*This research was supported by a grant from the MacArthur Foundation on Risk and Protective Factors in the Major Mental Disorders, and NIMH grants MH30911, MH08744, MH37705, and MH14584. The authors would like to thank Sibyl Zaden, David Lukoff, Ana Magaña, Portia Loughman, Joe Ventura, Sandra Rappe, and Sandra Malik for their assistance in the study.

†David Miklowitz and Michael Goldstein are affiliated with the Department of Psychology, UCLA, Keith Nuechterlein and Karen Snyder with the Department of Psychiatry, UCLA, and Jeri Doane with the Yale Psychiatric Institute.

ever, the overlap between these two measures of the intrafamilial emotional climate is far from perfect.

Recently, there has been interest in studying the specificity of these negative intrafamilial attributes to schizophrenia. Levels of EE have been found to be similar among parents of schizophrenics and spouses of nonpsychotic, depressed persons (21). Further, levels of EE criticism predict relapse in nonpsychotic depressives, particularly when the criticism threshold for defining high- and low-EE relatives is lowered (10, 21). However, the predictive utility of EE has never been studied in other *psychotic* populations, or in the *parental* families of patients with other disorders. Furthermore, the comparative levels and predictive value of intrafamilial AS have not been investigated in nonschizophrenic populations.

The present study was designed to investigate the applicability of the EE and AS constructs to another psychotic population, bipolar-manic patients. Bipolar disorder, like schizophrenia, is an illness that follows a relapse-remission course, and tends to be quite disruptive to the family environment (3). Although 70% of patients with bipolar disorder show an overall reduction of symptoms in response to lithium (9), at least one study has shown that, despite adhering to recommended lithium regimens during a one-year period, 17% of bipolar patients require hospitalization, and up to 47% require changes in medication regimens due to clinical exacerbations (16). This apparent variability in the course of the disorder suggests that factors other than medication responsiveness or compliance influence clinical outcome, and it is possible that the family environment to which the patient returns following an episode is one such factor.

In the present study, a cohort of recent-onset manic patients and their parental families were compared to a matched sample of families of schizophrenic patients on levels of intrafamilial EE and AS. More importantly, the utility of these constructs in predicting the subsequent course of manic disorder over a 9-month follow-up period was investigated. The relative role of medication compliance in mediating these predictive relationships was examined as well.

Method

Sample Description

Twenty-four bipolar-manic and 45 schizophrenic inpatients participated in the present study. Manic patients were recruited from the adult inpatient wards at the UCLA Neuropsychiatric Hospital. Schizophrenic patients were recruited from the Camarillo State, Olive View, and UCLA Neuropsychiatric Hospitals, and the Harbor General/UCLA Medical Center.

While in the hospital, potential patients were interviewed by a staff psychologist trained in the use of an extended version of the Present State Examination (PSE) (24; also see 14), and were diagnosed using the Research Diagnostic Criteria (RDC; 18). Manic patients had to satisfy the RDC criteria for manic disorder (n = 13), or schizoaffective, mainly affective, manic disorder (n = 11), in order to be included in the study. Schizophrenic patients had to meet criteria for schizophrenic disorder (n = 37) or schizoaffective, mainly schizophrenic disorder (n = 8). These latter two groups were collapsed for data analysis.

Patients had to satisfy the following exclusionary criteria: age between 16 and 45; living with or in significant contact with biological parents and/or stepparents, or married and living with spouse; no evidence of organic impairment or mental retardation; no significant abuse of drugs or alcohol for 6 months prior to hospitalization; not a member of a subcultural or ethnic group that was likely to have a distinctive influence on the validity of certain measures obtained by a collaborative project—Caucasian and acculturated Hispanic and Asian families were included (14); and an initial ward diagnosis of bipolar, schizoaffective, or schizophrenic disorder. In addition, preference was given to patients with illness onset in the 2 years prior to admission.

The manic and schizophrenic patients were matched on several key demographic variables, as indicated in Table 1. Matching was successful on age, family composition, ethnicity, number of prior hospitalizations, illness duration, and prior job history. However, the schizophrenic sample contained a higher proportion of male than female patients than did the manic sample, and manic patients had a younger age of onset, and higher education and social class, than did schizophrenics (for all, $p < .05$).

Diagnostic Reliability

Diagnostic interviewers were trained prior to participation in the study in clinical diagnosis using the extended PSE. In order to work independently, raters had to achieve at least 80% interrater agreement, based on ratings of 10 sample interview tapes, with a criterion judge on the presence or absence of PSE symptoms relevant to the diagnoses in question. Furthermore, a subsample of patients in the bipolar sample were rediagnosed by an independent clinician using case summaries prepared from the diagnostic interviews and other information obtained about the patient. Agreement with the PSE interviewer on diagnoses of manic versus other disorders for the current episode was 100%.

TABLE 1

Comparisons of Recent-Onset Schizophrenic and Bipolar-Manic Patients on Demographic Characteristics

	Schizophrenics (n = 45)		Bipolar-Manics (n = 24)		
Variable	**Mean**	**SD**	**Mean**	**SD**	**p**
Age (years)	22.4	3.45	21.45	3.36	ns
Age of onset (years)	21.44	3.32	19.88	2.64	<.05
Duration illness (months)	10.73	9.03	9.42	6.46	ns
Sex	37 (82%) Male		13 (54%) Male		<.02
	8 (18%) Female		11 (46%) Female		
Ethnicity	41 (91%) Caucasian		22 (92%) Caucasian		ns
	4 (9%) Noncaucasian		2 (8%) Noncaucasian		
Family composition	21 (27%) Single parent		9 (38%) Single parent		ns
	22 (49%) Dual parent		14 (58%) Dual parent		
	2 (4%) Spousal		1 (4%) Spousal		
Education (years)	12.04	1.91	13.17	1.13	<.01
Social class (Hollingshead-Redlich)	2.91	1.18	2.25	1.07	<.05

Procedures

Expressed Emotion

Patients were first interviewed and diagnosed using the RDC while in the hospital. Shortly after the diagnosis was confirmed, the patient's parents or spouse were contacted and asked to participate in the study. If they agreed, each key relative was individually administered the Camberwell Family Interview (CFI; 22) by a trained staff member.

Camberwell scores of 6 or more criticisms, and/or ratings of moderately high (4) or higher on emotional overinvolvement classified a relative as high-EE. Relatives who did not satisfy these criteria were classified as low-EE. A family was considered high-EE when, in the case of dual-parent families, either or both parents satisfied the criteria for individual high-EE status. In the case of single parent or spousal families, the EE status of the family was equivalent to the EE status of the individual relative.

Affective Style

A two-hour family assessment session was conducted with the patient and his or her key relatives (parents or spouse) within three weeks after hospital discharge. The family assessment was composed of three parts: separate individual interviews with the patient and each relative designed to identify problem issues in the family that could subsequently be used to generate family discussions; an interview with the patient that focused on symptomatology experienced during the previous two weeks, with ratings made on an extended version of the Brief Psychiatric Rating Scale (BPRS; 17; see 11); and two 10-minute direct family interaction sequences in which problems identified in the individual interviews were discussed among family members while the experimenter was out of the room. Verbatim transcripts were made from these interactions and relative-to-patient statements were coded on dimensions of affective style (AS).

Families were categorized as negative, mixed, or benign on AS, using criteria developed by Doane et al. (4). Further, in order to assess the cumulative nature of the intrafamilial affective climate, summary scores for each relative were calculated by summing the number of benign criticisms, harsh criticisms (harshly critical and guilt-inducing statements), and neutral intrusive statements made by the relative across both 10-minute interactions. Summary scores for families were calculated by adding together both parents' scores in dual-parent families, whereas individual relatives' scores were utilized for single-parent or spousal families.

Follow-Up Procedures

Longitudinal follow-up data, collected over a 9-month period following hospital discharge, were obtained from patients and relatives in the manic sample. Follow-up of the schizophrenic sample was conducted by a collaborative research team (14) and will not be considered here.

Patients in the manic sample were interviewed on a face-to-face basis every 3 months by an interviewer who was blind to the family assessment data. The interview focused on symptomatology experienced over the previous three months. Patients were then rated on an extended version of the Brief Psychiatric Rating Scale. The scale included the original 18 BPRS items—each rated on a 1 (absent) to 7 (extremely severe) scale—and 7 items that were added to measure other forms of schizophrenic or affective symptomatology: suicidality, self-neglect, bizarre behavior, elated mood, motor hyperactivity, distractibility, and helplessness-hopelessness (11). Furthermore, an abbreviated version of the scale was rated monthly from telephone interviews in order to assess whether a relapse had occurred during the period between face-to-face interviews. One patient refused further participation in the study following the initial 3-month follow-up assessment and was dropped from the longitudinal analyses.

The BPRS interviewer had completed a 3-month training workshop on the administration and scoring of the scale. Reliability for BPRS items, considered individually, averaged .84 (intraclass correlation coefficient; n = 10).

Classification of Outcome

Patients in the manic sample were classified as nonrelapsers, relapsers, or unchanged on the basis of their scores over time on each of ten BPRS "relapse scales": depression, hostility, unusual thought content, hallucinations, conceptual disorganization, suicidality, self-neglect, bizarre behavior, elated mood, and motor hyperactivity. These scales were chosen because they measure core aspects of manic, depressive, and psychotic symptomatology. Patients were classified as *nonrelapsers* (n = 7) if they maintained a state of clinical remission (that is, scores of 3 or below on each of the 10 BPRS relapse scales) or near remission (scores of 4) throughout the nine-month follow-up, or achieved this remitted state after an initial post-discharge phase of severe symptomatology that appeared to represent a continuation of the initial episode. Patients were classified as *relapsers* (n = 14) if they achieved a state of clinical remission for at least one month following discharge and then showed a clear exacerbation of clinical symptoms on one or more of the 10 BPRS relapse scales (a rise to scale points 5 or 6), or were discharged from the hospital in a state of high persisting symptoms (4 or 5 on at least one scale), maintained this state throughout follow-up, and subsequently showed a minimum 2-point increase to scale point 6 or 7 on this same scale. Patients were also placed in this category if they showed a one-point increase on the initially elevated scale and a minimum 2-point increase on a symptomatically related scale.

The final outcome category, *unchanged* (n = 2), consisted of those patients who were discharged in a highly symptomatic state (5 or above on at least one relapse scale) and maintained this clinical state for at least 6 of the 9 months of follow-up. Patients in this category never met the remission or relapse/exacerbation criteria outlined above (15).

Two independent raters classified patients into one of these three outcome categories on the basis of follow-up BPRS data. Agreement on these classifications was .90 ($p < .0001$, kappa statistic).

Medication Compliance

An assessment of the patient's compliance with his or her medication (typically lithium) regimen was conducted for each 3-month interval following discharge. Global ratings were made by two raters on a 7-point scale of compliance (12) on the basis of adherence to lithium and other prescribed medications, for example, neuroleptics. The ratings were based on (a) self-report compliance data, (b) reports obtained from key relatives, (c) reports from the patient's physician, and (d) lithium blood levels (2). Patients were rated as compliant if they missed a maximum of one or two dosages per month for each 3-month period during follow-up. Noncompliant patients were those who missed a minimum of one to two dosages per week during at least one 3-month period. More typically, the latter were taking 50% or less of their medication during follow-up. Interrater agreement on placement into the compliant and noncompliant categories was .92 ($p < .001$), kappa statistic.

Results

The present study addressed two major questions. First, to what degree do negative family communication factors (EE and AS) discriminate families of schizophrenic and bipolar-manic patients? Second, do these family factors predict the longitudinal course of bipolar disorder? These questions will be answered in turn.

In order to evaluate the specificity to schizophrenia of high-EE attitudes and negative-AS behaviors, families of schizophrenic (n = 45) and manic (n = 24) patients were contrasted. In addition, a separate set of analyses was conducted contrasting families of patients from three RDC subgroups (RDC schizophrenics, n = 45; RDC schizoaffective, mainly affective-manics, n = 11; and "pure" RDC manics, n = 13). Both sets of contrasts are reported below. All χ^2 statistics were based on the likelihood ratio method.

Table 2 shows the distribution of high- and low-EE families from the manic and schizophrenic groups. There was no relationship between family EE status and diagnostic group (manic versus schizophrenic comparison: χ^2 [1] = 2.01, $p > .10$; RDC subgrouping: χ^2 [2] = 2.74, $p > .10$). Furthermore, there were no differences in distribution of high- and low-EE individuals when comparing mothers and fathers from the two samples (for all, $p > .10$).

Families were also compared on distribution of Doane's AS profiles (see Table 2). Again, there were no differences among families of manic and schizophrenic patients in distribution of benign, mixed, or negative AS families (χ^2 [2] = .49, $p > .10$; RDC subgrouping: χ^2 [4] = 2.02, $p > .10$). The results were identical when dual-parent and single-parent/spousal families were analyzed separately.

Because the AS profiles are based on a critical incident model, in which the appearance of one or more of the severe, negative-AS codes is sufficient

TABLE 2
Expressed Emotion and Affective Style in Families of Schizophrenic and Manic Patients

Diagnostic Group	EE Status: Low-EE	EE Status: High-EE
Schizophrenic	16	28
Bipolar	13	11
$\chi^2(1) = 2.01, p > .10$		

Diagnostic Group	AS Profile: Benign	AS Profile: Mixed	AS Profile: Negative
Schizophrenic	18	9	15
Bipolar	11	5	6
$\chi^2(2) = .49, p > .10$			

Note: In the schizophrenic sample, one family could not be classified as to level of EE because of unavailability of ratings for one key family member; 3 families in the schizophrenic sample, and 2 in the manic sample refused participation in the direct interaction (AS) procedure.

to classify a family as mixed- or negative-AS, a separate analysis was conducted to determine whether the diagnostic groups differed on the summary scores for families defined earlier: total negative-AS statements, benign criticisms, harsh criticisms, and neutral-intrusive statements.

Results for the critical and intrusive codes are depicted in Table 3. The main effect of RDC subgroup was significant for *total* negative AS-codes (F [2, 61] = 4.73, $p = .01$). Post hoc tests conducted by the Tukey procedure indicated that families of schizophrenics had significantly higher total AS scores than did families of RDC pure manic patients ($p < .05$), with families of RDC schizoaffective-manic patients not differing from either group.

These same intergroup differences were evident for total benign criticisms (F [2, 61] = 3.06, $p = .05$), and for neutral-intrusive statements (F [2, 61] = 4.5, $p < .02$). However, as was indicated when comparing the groups on distribution of the AS profiles, none of the RDC subgroups differed on intrafamilial use of the low frequency, severely critical, or guilt-inducing statements (F [2, 61] = 1.12, $p > .10$). Therefore, it appears that the use by relatives of the lower frequency, more severe AS codes does not distinguish

TABLE 3

AS Total Scores in Families from Three RDC Groups

	Schizophrenics (n = 42)		Schizoaffective-Manics (n = 10)		Pure Manics (n = 12)	
	M	SD	M	SD	M	SD
Total AS	13.83	10.20	9.70	7.21	5.08	3.53
Criticisms						
Benign	5.62	6.13	4.40	2.99	1.42	1.56
Harsh	2.50	3.72	2.40	2.63	0.92	1.51
Neutral Intrusions	5.71	4.00	2.90	3.51	2.75	2.22

families of manic and schizophrenic patients. The groups can be differentiated, however, on total use of the higher frequency, less severe AS codes.

Prediction of Longitudinal Course

The finding that families of manic and schizophrenic patients do not differ on their distributions of high- and low-EE relatives, or mixed/negative versus benign-AS relatives, suggested that these two constructs (EE and AS) might be as useful in predicting the longitudinal course of manic disorder as in predicting the course of schizophrenia. Furthermore, the finding that family EE status (low versus high) and AS profiles (benign versus mixed/negative) were not associated with each other within the manic sample (χ^2 [1] = 0.0, $p > .10$) suggested that the two family attributes might be independently predictive of outcome.

Expressed Emotion

The relationship between levels of intrafamilial EE and clinical outcome (that is, nonrelapsers versus relapsing/unchanged patients) is depicted in Table 4. Family EE status afforded a moderate prediction of outcome (χ^2 [1] = 3.82, $p = .05$) in this sample. Prediction of outcome was actually poorer when the EE criticism cutoff for defining high-EE relatives was lowered to the cutoffs suggested in studies of nonpsychotic depressed patients, that is, 2 or 3 criticisms (10, 21).

Unlike the studies of family EE and schizophrenic relapse, 90% of patients from high-EE homes had poor outcomes, whereas 54% of patients

TABLE 4

Family EE Status and AS Profiles as Predictors of 9-Month Clinical Outcome (Manic Sample)

Family EE Status	No Relapse	Relapse/Unchanged
Low EE	6	7
High EE	1	9
$\chi^2(1) = 3.82$, $p = .05$		
Family AS Profile	**No Relapse**	**Relapse/Unchanged**
Benign AS	5	6
Mixed/Negative AS	1	10
$\chi^2(1) = 3.92$, $p < .05$		
Conjoint Prediction Family Pattern	**No Relapse**	**Relapse/Unchanged**
Low EE/Benign AS	5	1
Negative on one	0	11
Negative on both	1	4
$\chi^2(2) = 15.37$, $p < .0005$		

Note: One subject refused further follow-up after the 3-month longitudinal assessment and was therefore unavailable for the above analyses. In addition, one family participated in the Camberwell Family Interview (EE) procedure but declined to participate in the direct interaction (AS) procedure.

from low-EE homes had poor outcomes, as compared to approximately 56% and 17%, respectively, in schizophrenia studies (23). Therefore, in families of manic patients, high-EE attitudes are almost invariably associated with poor outcomes, whereas a mixed outcome picture is observed in patients from low-EE homes.

EE and Medication Compliance

Medication compliance was not, in itself, a significant predictor of manic outcome (χ^2 [1] = .71, $p > .10$), nor was it related to level of intrafamilial EE or AS ($p > .10$). However, as is noted at the top of Table 5, medication compliance was to some extent a variable mediating the prediction of outcome by intrafamilial EE. As shown, noncompliant patients from high-EE homes were not any more likely to relapse than were compliant patients from these types of homes. This result fails to replicate Vaughn & Leff's (21) finding that, in a schizophrenic sample, regularity of medication was a

TABLE 5

Expressed Emotion, Affective Style, Medication Compliance, and Clinical Outcome in Manic Patients

Expressed Emotion and Medication Compliance	**No Relapse**	**Relapse/Unchanged**
Low EE		
Compliant	3	1
Noncompliant	3	6
High EE		
Compliant	0	3
Noncompliant	1	6
$\chi^2(3) = 6.57$, $p = .09$		

Affective Style and Medication Compliance	**No Relapse**	**Relapse/Unchanged**
Benign AS		
Compliant	3	1
Noncompliant	2	5
Negative AS		
Compliant	0	3
Noncompliant	1	7
$\chi^2(3) = 6.88$, $p < .08$		

protective factor against relapse for patients from high-EE but not low-EE homes. In fact, the reverse was suggested for this sample: Patients from low-EE homes who did not comply evidenced a somewhat higher relapse rate (67%) than did those who complied (25%; χ^2 [3] = 6.57, $p = .09$). Although only a trend is suggested, it appears that for some manic patients, low-EE attitudes in relatives are protective against relapse only when the patient is compliant with his or her medication regimen. When the patient is not compliant, the relapse rates for patients in this group become similar to those noted for patients from high-EE homes.

Affective Style

Table 4 presents the association between family AS profiles and patient outcome. For these analyses, families with mixed-AS profiles (n = 5) were combined with those with negative-AS profiles (n = 6) because of the small number of subjects in these two cells, and because of the finding that mixed- and negative-AS profiles for families did not differ appreciably in several ad-hoc tests of predictive accuracy. As in the case of EE attitudes, AS profiles afforded a moderate prediction of outcome (χ^2 [1] = 3.92, $p < .05$). Once again, negative-AS behaviors were strongly associated with poor clinical outcomes (91% relapsed or unchanged), whereas patients from benign-AS families showed mixed clinical outcomes (55% relapsed/unchanged).

AS and Medication Compliance

The interaction between family AS profiles and medication compliance is depicted at the bottom of Table 5. Once again, a trend was observed for patients from benign-AS families to be at risk for relapse only when they showed evidence of noncompliance (χ^2 [3] = 6.88, $p < .08$). In negative-AS families, medication compliance was not a significant factor mediating the AS-relapse association. Therefore, as in the case of EE attitudes, a benign-AS environment was protective against a poor outcome only when the patient was compliant. However, compliance did not modify the outcomes of patients from negative-AS homes.

Expressed Emotion and Affective Style as Joint Predictors of Outcome

Because family EE status and AS profiles were not correlated in this sample, yet both predicted clinical outcome to a moderate degree, the possibility arose that these two family factors might account for a larger proportion of the variance in outcome if studied as joint predictors. Therefore, families were divided into three groups, as indicated at the bottom of Table 4: low on EE and benign on AS; high-EE *or* negative-AS, but not both; and high-EE *and* negative-AS. The combination of the two predictors accurately identified 91% of the outcome classifications (χ^2 [2] = 15.37, $p < .0005$).

It is noteworthy that the presence of *both* negative attributes in a family constellation did not place the patient at higher risk for a poor outcome than if only one attribute was rated as negative. However, it is clear that data on both family *attitudes* and *behavior* are necessary in order to confidently identify a manic patient who is at risk for a poor outcome.

Intrafamilial EE and AS appeared to be most powerful as joint predictors because they identified patients with different *types* of outcome: High-EE attitudes in relatives were most closely associated with remission-relapse or exacerbation outcomes, but did not predict high persisting symptom or unchanged outcomes. In contrast, negative-AS profiles in families were associated with more severe patient outcomes, that is, high persisting symptoms, with and without exacerbations; but they did not readily predict remission-relapse/exacerbation classifications. It appears, then, that EE and AS are, in a manic sample, two non-overlapping measures of a negative family environment that are associated with different types of clinical outcome for the patient.

Family Attributes and Initial Clinical State

The finding that EE and AS were useful as predictors of the course of the patient's illness suggested the possibility that patients from families rated as negative on these attributes were simply more severely ill to begin with. Perhaps these intrafamilial attitudes and/or behaviors are more likely to persist if the patient returns home from the hospital in a highly symptomatic state. In order to investigate this question, two 2×2 (high/low EE by negative/benign AS) ANOVAs were conducted, with BPRS total scores collected at one and 3 months postdischarge as dependent measures. There were no main effects for either EE or AS, and no interactions between these factors, in accounting for level of residual symptomatology at either the one-month or 3-month follow-up points (for all, $p > .10$). Therefore, it appears that family EE status and AS profiles are not associated with the overall baseline, postdischarge level of symptomatology manifested by the patient.

Discussion

The present study investigated two major questions. First, are families of recently episodic schizophrenic and bipolar-manic patients discriminable on measures of the intrafamilial affective climate, notably parental emotional *attitudes* toward the patient (expressed emotion) and parental emotional verbal behavior during direct family interaction (affective style)? Second, is the variance in these family factors predictive of the *course* of recent-onset mania, as has been found for samples of schizophrenic patients (1, 4, 21)?

The results of this study indicate that parental emotional *attitudes* toward the patient, as measured during hospitalization, do not discriminate these two clinical populations. Distributions of relatives with high- and low-EE attitudes were approximately equivalent in the two populations. These findings replicate those of Vaughn & Leff (21), who reported that levels of EE criticism were similar in parents of schizophrenics and spouses of non-psychotic depressed patients. High-EE attitudes may reflect a general tendency among relatives of psychiatric patients to react negatively to disturbance in an affected family member after the latter has returned home from the hospital.

In contrast, measures of affective verbal *behavior*, as indexed by direct relative-to-patient interaction following discharge, discriminated families of manic and schizophrenic patients. Parents of schizophrenics were found to use more of the high-frequency, situational, less-severe AS code (benign criticisms and neutral intrusions) than did parents of bipolar, particularly, purely manic patients. Families of schizoaffective-manic patients scored intermediately on these AS codes, suggesting the possibility that parental use of these statements may be related to the degree to which schizophrenic-like symptoms are prominent in the offspring.

It is notable that families from the manic and schizophrenic groups did not differ on use of the lower frequency, harshly critical, personal, character-assassinating, or guilt-inducing AS codes. Perhaps these codes measure the more hostile or rejecting emotions that many relatives experience when their offspring or spouse manifests a severe psychiatric illness. It is also possible that the groups did not differ because of the restricted variance of these codes. However, the finding of lack of differences between relatives on these harsh codes supports the use of the AS profile approach (4, 5) for predicting multiple forms of psychiatric outcome, as the distribution of these profiles appears to be equal across families of patients with different forms of psychotic disorders.

A major finding of the present study was that the same family factors that have predictive utility in schizophrenic patients also predict the longitudinal course of patients with recent-onset mania. Both EE and AS were individually, though moderately, associated with clinical outcome at 9-month follow-up. When the two factors were combined, nearly all (91%) of the clinical outcomes were accurately predicted. Therefore, the best predictive fit for this sample was obtained by considering together the role of family affective attitudes and behavior in the longitudinal course of the illness.

It is notable that those AS codes that distinguished families of manic and schizophrenic patients did not have the same predictive value that was obtained with the low-frequency codes, the latter of which did not differ across diagnostic groups. The presence of these more severely critical, hostile, rejecting, or guilt-inducing statements in ongoing family interaction may provide a source of stress for a recently episodic manic patient that may at times exceed his or her coping capacities. It is possible that these statements promote a loss of self-esteem, and fears of loss of emotional ties to relatives, in an emotionally vulnerable patient. The continual exposure to these negative statements over time may lead to chronic feelings of depression or periods of psychosis. Data from the present study cannot unravel the nature of these more complex intrafamilial and intrapsychic factors, but the effect of these intrafamilial behaviors on the ongoing coping strategies of the patient certainly warrants further investigation.

The question can be raised as to whether a negative intrafamilial emotional climate increases the likelihood that a patient will not adhere to his or her medication regimen. However, compliance and family environment were unrelated in this sample. Furthermore, despite the fact that the rate of noncompliance in this sample was very high, noncompliance in itself was not a significant predictor of outcome: Many patients relapsed despite apparently adhering to their drug regimens.

Compliance did appear to modify to some degree the outcomes of patients from low-EE and benign-AS families. Patients in these groups who complied were at relatively low risk for relapse. However, a benign familial environment was not a protective factor against a poor outcome when the patient showed at least one period of noncompliance, and the relapse rates among noncompliant patients from these benign environments were comparable to those for patients from negative family environments.

In contrast, compliance did not protect patients from relapse when the familial environment was characterized by a negative affective climate. Patients from these families were at high risk for relapse even when they complied. It remains possible that some patients in this group who were rated as compliant were actually not taking their medication, or that their drug combinations or dosages were not optimally therapeutic. The present results, however, suggest that negative family environments can be associated with poor outcomes even when the patient is taking medication, as has been found in studies of schizophrenia (21, 23).

General Conclusions and Recommendations for Future Research

Two conclusions can be drawn from the present study. First, families of schizophrenic and manic patients, studied shortly after the patient has returned home from a hospitalization due to an episode of the disorder, are discriminable on certain measures of intrafamilial negative affective expression, notably, critical and intrusive statements that occur with high frequency. Second, measures of negative affective communication that do *not* differ across diagnostic groups, and that have been found to predict the course of schizophrenic illness (family EE status and negative-AS profiles), are also highly predictive of the course of recent-onset mania. These predictive relationships are not readily attributable to intervening factors such as medication compliance or severity of illness at baseline.

The results of the present study need to be replicated in a larger sample of patients. Such a study might help to identify other possible factors—such as genetic history or type of medication regimen—that may mediate these predictive relationships, and to determine whether the association between family factors and illness course remains strong when these factors are independently considered.

A further issue that deserves investigation is whether negative family communication, if modified through psychosocial treatment, leads to a better clinical outcome for manic patients. Family therapy has been found to be very useful in terms of improving the prognosis of schizophrenic patients (6, 8), and it is possible that a family psychosocial intervention that attempts to modify and improve family communication, and encourage medication compliance, may lead to better prognoses for bipolar patients as well.

REFERENCES

1. Brown, G. W., Birley, J. L. T., & Wing, J. K. Influence of family life on the course of schizophrenic disorders: A replication. *British Journal of Psychiatry 121*: 241–258, 1972.

2. Cochran, S. D. Strategies for preventing lithium noncompliance in bipolar affective illness. Unpublished doctoral dissertation, University of California, Los Angeles, 1982.

3. Davenport, Y. B., Adland, M. L., Gold, P. W., & Goodwin, F. K. Manic-depressive illness: Psychodynamic features of multigenerational families. *American Journal of Orthopsychiatry 49*: 24–35, 1979.

4. Doane, J. A., Falloon, I. R. H., Goldstein, M. J., & Mintz, J. Parental affective style and the treatment of schizophrenia: Predicting course of illness and social functioning. *Archives of General Psychiatry 42*: 34–42, 1985.

5. ______, West, K. L., Goldstein, M. J., Rodnick, E. H., & Jones, J. E. Parental communication deviance and affective style: Predictors of subsequent schizophrenia spectrum disorders in vulnerable adolescents. *Archives of General Psychiatry 38*: 679–685, 1981.

6. Falloon, I. R. H., Boyd, J. L., McGill, C. W., Razani, J., Moss, H. B., & Gilderman, A. M. Family management in the prevention of exacerbations of schizophrenia: A controlled study. *New England Journal of Medicine 306*: 1437–1440, 1982.

7. Goldstein, M. J. Family factors that antedate the onset of schizophrenia and related disorders: The results of a fifteen-year prospective longitudinal study. *Acta Psychiatrica Scandinavica 71* (Suppl. 319): 7–18, 1985.

8. ______, Rodnick, E. H., Evans, J. R., May, P. R. A., & Steinberg, M. R. Drug and family therapy in the aftercare of acute schizophrenics. *Archives of General Psychiatry 35*: 1169–1177, 1978.

9. Goodwin, F. K., & Zis, A. P. Lithium in the treatment of mania. *Archives of General Psychiatry 36*: 840–844, 1979.

10. Hooley, J. M., Orley, J., & Teasdale, J. D. Levels of expressed emotion and relapse in depressed patients. *British Journal of Psychiatry 148*: 642–647, 1986.

11. Lukoff, D., Nuechterlein, K. H., & Ventura, J. The expanded Brief Psychiatric Rating Scale manual. (Appendix to Lukoff, D., Liberman, R. P., & Nuechterlein, K. H.

Symptom monitoring in the rehabilitation of schizophrenic patients.) *Schizophrenia Bulletin 12*: 594–602, 1986.

12. Miklowitz, D. J. Family interaction and illness outcome in bipolar and schizophrenic patients. Unpublished doctoral dissertation, University of California, Los Angeles, 1985.

13. ______, Goldstein, M. J., Falloon, I. R. H., & Doane, J. A. Interactional correlates of expressed emotion in the families of schizophrenics. *British Journal of Psychiatry 144*: 482–487, 1984.

14. Nuechterlein, K. H. *Developmental processes in schizophrenic disorders*. NIMH Research Grant MH37705, 1985.

15. ______, Miklowitz, D. J., & Ventura, J. Manual for assessing outcome in schizophrenic and bipolar-manic patients. Unpublished manuscript, 1985. (Available from K. Nuechterlein, Department of Psychiatry, UCLA, 760 Westwood Plaza, Los Angeles CA 90024.)

16. O'Connell, R. A., & Mayo, J. A. Lithium: A biopsychological perspective. *Comprehensive Psychiatry 22*: 87–93, 1981.

17. Overall, J. E., & Gorham, D. R. The Brief Psychiatric Rating Scale. *Psychological Reports 10*: 799–812, 1962.

18. Spitzer, R. L., Endicott, J., & Robins, E. Research diagnostic criteria: Rationale and reliability. *Archives of General Psychiatry 35*: 773–782, 1978.

19. Strachan, A. M., Leff, J. P., Goldstein, M. J., Doane, J. A., & Burtt, C. Emotional attitudes and direct communication in the families of schizophrenics: A cross-national replication. *British Journal of Psychiatry 149*: 279–287, 1986.

20. Valone, K., Norton, J. P., Goldstein, M. J., & Doane, J. A. Parental expressed emotion and affective style in an adolescent sample at risk for schizophrenia spectrum disorders. *Journal of Abnormal Psychology 92*: 399–407, 1983.

21. Vaughn, C. E., & Leff, J. P. The influence of family life and social factors on the course of psychiatric illness: A comparison of schizophrenic and depressed neurotic patients. *British Journal of Psychiatry 129*: 125–137, 1976.

22. ______, & Leff, J. P. The measurement of expressed emotion in the families of psychiatric patients. *British Journal of Social and Clinical Psychology 15*: 157–165, 1976.

23. ______, Snyder, K. S., Jones, S., Freeman, W. B., & Falloon, I. R. H. Family factors in schizophrenic relapse: Replication in California of British research on expressed emotion. *Archives of General Psychiatry 41*: 1169–1177, 1984.

24. Wing, J. K., Cooper, J. E., & Sartorius, N. *The description and classification of psychiatric symptoms: An instruction manual for the PSE and CATEGO system*. London: Cambridge University Press, 1974.

12

ALCOHOLISM AND FAMILY INTERACTION: Clarifications Resulting from Subgroup Analyses and Multi-method Assessments

THEODORE JACOB
University of Arizona, Tucson

DURING the past several decades, family studies of alcoholism have attempted to unravel the complex relationship between family variables and alcohol abuse through various research strategies and theoretical perspectives (13, 17, 20). The major approaches include the investigation of genetic/biological factors that may contribute to the transmission of alcoholism; studies of the personality characteristics of alcoholics and their spouses; and assessment of the psychosocial and psychiatric status of the offspring of alcoholic parents. Most recently, the study of interactions involving alcoholics and their families has become particularly prominent—a research direction based upon the primary contention that an adequate understanding of dysfunctional behavior cannot be achieved independent of understanding the significant interpersonal contexts in which members develop and function.

Application of this perspective to studies of alcoholism has only been attempted in earnest during the past ten years, although results from several of these early studies have been extremely encouraging. In particular, these beginning efforts have focused on transactions between alcoholics and spouses and the processes and patterns of interactions within families containing an alcoholic member. In addition, experimental drinking sessions have been introduced and emergent interactions within these periods have been compared to marital-family interactions that occur when alcohol is not available. The nature of communication patterns, both verbal and nonverbal, characterizing alcoholic-spouse interchanges has also been explored, as has the impact of emergent behavior across several observational settings. Although limited in number and scope, these pioneering efforts have proceeded from an interactional perspective and have introduced promising research strategies and exciting hypotheses regarding the impact of family patterns on the transmission and perpetuation of alcoholism (1–3, 7, 9, 12, 14, 19, 21–23, 28).

My own work in alcoholism research has been closely aligned with this family interaction perspective, and during the past seven years has involved the systematic study of family interaction over a broad range of conditions. The primary objective of this research program is to develop an empirically based understanding of family interactions that characterize families with an alcoholic member, that serve to reinforce and perpetuate cycles of abusive drinking, and that predate and predict the development of abusive drinking in high-risk offspring. To this end, efforts have involved systematic evaluations of intact families containing an alcoholic father and of two, carefully selected control groups—families with a depressed (nonalcoholic) father and families with a nonalcoholic, nondisturbed father. For each family, extensive observation data are obtained within two contexts: (a) the controlled laboratory setting in which major interest is directed toward the impact of alcohol ingestion (drink/no-drink) and family subsystem (marital, parent-child, and parent-parent-child) on patterns of Personal Evaluation, Problem Resolution, and System Organization; and (b) the natural home setting in which attention is focused on issues related to the quantity, quality, and organization of marital, parent-child, and sibling interaction.

The focus of this chapter will be limited to the laboratory interactions of approximately 105 families—35 with an alcoholic husband, 35 with a depressed husband, and 35 normal controls. Given the range of materials to be presented, only the marital interaction data will be discussed.

Laboratory Methods

Subject and Subject Recruitment

Our primary recruitment strategy has been newspaper advertisements and the payment of subjects involved in the project. All participating families must satisfy the following selection criteria: (a) both parents are currently living together, and the family contains at least one child between 10 and 18 years of age living at home; (b) no wife has a current, major psychiatric or alcohol abuse disturbance; (c) no child shows a current, major psychiatric or cognitive disturbance; (d) no family member is currently in psychiatric treatment; (e) neither parent has any significant medical problem for example, liver disease, seizure disorder, or brain damage, or is currently involved in a regimen of prescribed or nonprescribed medication that could cause adverse side effects when alcohol is consumed.

The next step in the screening procedure involves extended telephone and in-person interviews and the completion of various self-report questionnaires by each spouse. Most importantly, the Schedule for Affective Disorder and Schizophrenia (SADS) is administered to each spouse in order to determine whether or not subjects meet the required Research Diagnostic Criteria, or RDC (18). In order to be accepted into the alcoholic group, the father must satisfy RDC for alcoholism as well as show disturbance in at least three of four domains specified by Feighner and his colleagues (5): medical problems, social problems, control problems, and prior identification of alcohol-related problems. Of particular importance, alcoholic subjects are excluded if they meet the RDC for Major Depressive Disorder. In contrast, depressed subjects must satisfy RDC for Major Depressive Disorder and must not satisfy criteria for Alcoholism. Normal controls are included only if no RDC can be assigned.

Observation Procedures

The major purpose of the first laboratory session is to acclimate the family to the experimental setting in order to minimize potential observer effects. During the second and third meetings, after completing several additional questionnaires and warm-up tasks, four combinations of the three family members are separately engaged in videotaped discussions (mother-father-child, mother-father, mother-child, father-child). Discussion topics are based upon items from the Revealed Difference task, adapted from Strodtbeck (24), and the Areas of Change Questionnaire by Weiss (27), in order to maximize personal relevance and investment. Only analyses of the ACQ-generated discussions of personally relevant problem areas will be described in this chapter.

Experimental Drinking

The second and third laboratory sessions are parallel in terms of the four combinations of family members discussing topics. The only difference between these two meetings is the availability of alcoholic beverage to the parents in one session but not in the other.

Most experimental drinking studies in the extant literature have assessed alcohol's impact on perceptual-motor functions and affective states. In contrast, few studies have attempted empirically based assessments of alcohol's effects on interpersonal patterns in general and marital/family interaction in particular. Most relevant to the current effort are the observations of Steinglass (23) about intoxicated and sober states, which suggest that behavior during periods of drinking can have "adaptive" consequences for the individual and his or her social context, which, in turn, may actually reinforce the cycle of abusive drinking. According to Steinglass, problems can arise at the individual, intrafamilial, or family/environmental level, and alcoholism can provide a temporary solution to these problems. In this respect, Steinglass suggests that alcoholism can have adaptive consequences for the family—consequences that serve the common purpose of temporarily restoring equilibrium in family life. "For example, in some families, equilibrium is restored by increasing interactional distance (the drinker goes off to drink in the basement), or diminishing physical contact (the nonalcoholic spouse refuses to have sex with someone, who is drunk), or reducing tension in the family (family members' usual patterns of behavior are less tension provoking than unique patterns); whereas in other families, alcohol might be associated with closer interactional distance (the nonalcoholic makes contact by fighting after the alcoholic spouse has been drinking), disinhibition (the use of alcohol permits ritualized sexual behavior), or maintaining distance from the social environment (the alcoholic's fights with neighbors when drunk)" (23, pp. 300–301).

A major implication of this model is that variation in drinking patterns can play a central role in adaptive and disruptive marital states and ultimately in the maintenance of heavy drinking—an assumption of major significance in theoretical developments linking interpersonal variables to dysfunctional behavior, and of potential importance to the development of family-oriented treatment and prevention programs. Notwithstanding these implications, it must be acknowledged that this model has received most of its support from theoretical and clinical-anecdotal reports of alcoholic-spouse interaction (15). Clearly, considerable empirical data are needed in order to provide stronger evidence for the validity of this model.

Our experimental drinking procedure involves a general expectancy that is communicated to families. Throughout the screening process and during the laboratory meetings, it is indicated that we are trying to learn more about alcohol use and family relationships, and that we pursue this objective through questionnaire data, daily drinking reports, and the videotaped discussions with and without alcohol consumption. The key aspect of the instructional set related to the laboratory drinking procedure involves a strong general expectancy induction—that is, we certainly expect that alcohol can and does have important effects on family relationships although we are uncertain about the direction of such effects. With this understanding as a general context, we then encourage participants to drink as much alcohol as they would normally consume in a social setting outside of the laboratory situation.

Data Reduction Procedures

The laboratory data are coded with a modification of Weiss's Marital Interaction Coding System (10, 26). Our version of the MICS is a 20-code rating system that is focused on three dimensions of observed interaction: Personal Evaluation, Problem Resolution, and System Organization. The first and second domains overlap with two, seemingly universal dimensions (6, 25) of interpersonal behavior concerned with issues of affect expression and solidarity, on the one hand, and skill performance and problem solving on the other. Personal Evaluation is measured by such codes as "criticize," "negative response," and "put down," as well as an agreement ratio (Agrees divided by Agrees plus Disagrees). Problem Resolution is measured by such codes as "assent," "solution," "command," and "consequential thinking." System Organization, the third dimension of interest, is focused on system properties related to issues of interactional structure and patterning. Following Gottman (8), assessment of System Organization will involve sequential analysis procedures whereby the interrelated concepts of reciprocity, rigidity, and predictability will be addressed. Only aggregate analyses will be discussed here.

Laboratory Interactions: Results and Discussion

Although definitive analyses of this data set have not yet been completed, one outcome seems quite clear—alcoholic-spouse interaction is not only more negative and less constructive in general, but increasingly so during the drinking session. Most strikingly, the differences between alcoholic and comparison groups in terms of affective state can be accounted for almost entirely by the marked increase in negative communication that occurs during the drinking session.

On the one hand, such findings seem reasonable and expectable in light of the large clinical literature in the alcoholism field that has often and vividly described alcohol's deleterious impact on family life in which conflict, dissatisfaction, and dissension are the norm (13, 15). Given the great disturbance and disruption that is often brought on during states of heavy drinking and intoxication, the presence of alcohol and the engagement in drinking (even within the relatively restricted and "safe" confines of the interaction laboratory) could be providing powerful discriminative stimuli for both spouses, which, in effect, communicates the expectancy that the subsequent interchanges will be aversive and punishing. Acting on this expectancy (or as some would prefer to describe it, responding to this "setting event"), the interaction comes to manifest lower rates of positive and higher rates of negative exchange.

But there may be other ways to view this outcome that are more germane to a family interactional perspective. Gorad (7), for example, has suggested that alcoholics exhibit a "responsibility avoiding" communication style, which becomes exaggerated in interactions with intimates and during periods of drinking and intoxication. In essence, the alcoholic is sending two messages—one indicating some negative, nasty, or deviant act, and the other (more precisely, a qualification of the first message) indicating that "I am not responsible for what I say or do. I am under the control of the alcohol." In so doing, the alcoholic exerts great control over relationships to the extent that actions can be enacted for which he or she cannot be held responsible—that is, one acts but avoids responsibility for one's actions. The core aspect of this theory—that the alcoholic can attribute deviant behavior to the alcohol and therefore avoid personal responsibility for any actions—has also been discussed in the social labeling literature, and has often been referred to as "deviance disavowal" or "timeout" (16).

With regard to present findings, one might conjecture that, in effect, the alcoholic can attribute his or her nastiness to the alcohol. To the extent that this occurs (and the spouse accepts this attribution), periods of drinking allow for the expression of negative affect toward the relationship and spouse that would be more difficult to express if one were going to be held accountable for these behaviors. As such, the context of drinking enables the alcoholic to express strongly held feelings that otherwise could only be given partial expression.

Although present findings are interesting and consistent with various clinical and theoretical expectations, several critical variables have not yet been examined nor have key statistical analyses been performed. For example, all analyses reported thus far have been based on rate variables—measures that do not provide direct information about whether or not the couple exhibits any patterning or sequencing in their ongoing dialogues. Furthermore, and of particular relevance to the current presentation, our alcoholic couples represent a rather heterogeneous group in which subjects vary considerably along several potentially critical dimensions. Given the great within-subject variance associated with many of the dependent variables, it would seem critical to identify subgroups that are associated with different family patterns and that exhibit different styles of interchange during drinking periods. Several lines of research relevant to typology development are currently underway, one of which suggests that drinking style and location may be critical variables for partitioning heterogeneous groups; and if this partitioning is undertaken, resultant subgroups can be extremely important in clarifying the interdependencies between alcohol and family process.

Drinking Style and Location: Impact on Marital Interaction

Several years ago, we began examining various report data gathered during the course of the study. In the process, we conducted assessments of the relationship between several drinking variables and measures of individual and marital adjustment. The results of these initial analyses were quite remarkable, indicating that alcoholic husbands who consumed large amounts of alcohol in the past month had wives who (a) obtained relatively low scores on various MMPI scales, (b) obtained relatively low scores on the Beck Depression Inventory, and (c) reported relatively greater marital satisfaction on the Locke-Wallace Marital Adjustment Test and on the Dyadic Adjustment Scale. Most importantly, categorizing subjects into steady versus binge drinkers and then analyzing each group separately revealed a striking outcome; most correlations between alcohol consumption scores and the symptom and marital satisfaction measures were nonsignificant for the binge drinkers but highly significant and consistent for the steady drinkers (12).

Although various explanations of this outcome were considered, our interest in the interactional aspects of the family lead to the following working hypothesis: Marital/family relationships are more satisfying during high versus low consumption periods, and these consequences serve to maintain or perpetuate drinking to the extent that (a) the alcoholic's behavior is more predictable when he is consuming alcohol at a high rate than when he is not drinking, (b) the experience of stress in family life is minimized during periods of high consumption, and (c) the family has adapted to and incorporated high-rate drinking into family life.

Despite the provocative nature of these preliminary findings, several important limitations were evident. Of particular importance, the sets of measures on which analyses were conducted were of a cross-sectional, retrospective nature. As such, we could only say that alcoholics who consumed relatively large quantities of alcohol had wives who reported relatively few psychiatric symptoms and high marital satisfaction. To conclude that the variables in question are related to one another over time, one would have to assess drinking, psychiatric symptoms, and marital satisfaction on a day-to-day basis, and to examine the actual covariation among these variables.

In our first attempt to assess these day-to-day covariations, a small group of drinkers ($n = 8$) who previously participated in the core study was recruited (4). The study was restricted to steady drinkers because only this group exhibited a significant association between alcohol consumption and marital stability in the original study. Because drinking location (in-home versus out-of-home) was correlated with the binge-steady categorization, our original findings could have resulted from differences on either or both dimensions. To assess this issue more systematically, half of the selected subjects were in-home and half were out-of-home drinkers.

Procedurally, the eight couples were asked to provide daily records regarding alcohol consumption, psychiatric symptomatology, and marital satisfaction ratings over a 90-day period. Analyses involved specification of the univariate Auto Regressive Integrated Moving Average (ARIMA) model for each variable in the study and the various bivariate ARIMA models specifying the relationship between the variables of interest—in particular, the husband's alcohol consumption and wife's satisfaction ratings and daily symptom scores.

Univariate ARIMA Models

Of particular interest were the univariate models involving the daily drinking behavior of our alcoholic subject. Most of the *in-home drinkers* consumed alcohol at a fairly consistent and predictable level, the only exception being Husband 4, a "mixed-location" drinker whose pattern appeared more similar to husbands in the out-of-home group. In contrast with the in-home drinkers, the *out-of-home drinkers* demonstrated much greater variability in their consumption patterns. Of particular note, three of the four out-of-home drinkers had seasonal (that is, 7-day fluctuations) ARIMA models.

Bivariate ARIMA Models

In the *out-of-home group*, the most striking finding was a negative relationship between alcohol consumption and the wives' marital satisfaction ratings at various lags for all four couples. As noted, three of the four out-of-home drinkers had weekly drinking patterns, and *all* wives of these drinkers had a *five*-day lagged, negative relationship with the alcohol consumption; that is, five days after husbands' drinking, wives' marital satisfaction ratings decreased. In these cases, the husband typically drank most heavily on the weekend, and his wife's marital satisfaction decreased on Thursday. In the context of this cycle, it appears as if the wife's decline in marital satisfaction ratings reflects her *anticipation* of the husband's drinking by *two* days. It should be noted that this is *not* to say that the wife's marital dissatisfaction *causes* the husband's alcohol consumption (there is no support for that direction of effect) but, rather, that her marital dissatisfaction reflects an anticipatory phenomenon.

In the *in-home group*, two of four couples replicated the original cross-sectional findings quite clearly; that is, alcohol consumption was associated with an increase in marital satisfaction. A third couple exhibited no relationship of any of the assessed variables, a finding that perhaps represents a statistical expression of total disengagement in the marriage. The final couple produced a positive relationship between husband's alcohol consumption and spouse's symptomatology ratings three days later—a finding that is opposite in direction to that obtained with the original cross-sectional findings, but similar to the time-series findings for the four out-of-home drinkers. It is of interest to note that in Couple 4, although the husband was categorized as an in-home drinker, based upon his Marlatt Questionnaire data, he was actually a "mixed-location" drinker; as such, the positive relationship between consumption and symptomatology is more consistent with the four out-of-home drinkers than with the three in-home drinkers.

To replicate and extend these cross-sectional and longitudinal findings, efforts of the past two years have involved the collection of data on a large, heterogeneous sample of married alcoholics. From all couples, we collected the same drinking personality, and marital measures as obtained in the original study. Because of the large sample size, we can now cross-classify drinkers in terms of drinking style (binge, steady) and primary drinking location (in-home, out-of-home) in order to assess the original cross-sectional findings more carefully. In addition, 32 couples (eight binge in-home, eight binge out-of-home, eight steady in-home, and eight steady out-of-home) will be conducted through the 90-day longitudinal assessment, providing a sizeable sample on which to evaluate the stability of our preliminary findings.

Alcoholism Subgroups and Laboratory Interaction

In overview, both the correlational and time-series analyses indicate the importance of defining more homogeneous subgroups within the larger sample of alcoholics. Two consequences of this subgrouping process are most important: (a) the family's response to the alcoholic's drinking is quite different depending upon the subgroups assessed, and (b) one's conclusions regarding the consumption/family stability relationship becomes increasingly refined (and complex) as additional methodologies are brought to bear on this issue. Notwithstanding the need to underscore the tentative nature of conclusions in light of small samples and preliminary analyses, an interesting "picture" seems to be coming into focus.

First, the family's response to the binge drinker is clearly different from that to the steady drinker (and in particular, the steady in-home drinker). For binge drinkers, the drinking does not seem to result in any adaptive or positive consequences for the family at all, with the exception of a deviance-disavowal perspective allowing for expression of deviant behavior with fewer sanctions. For these individuals, drinking most often takes place out of the home, and the variability in type and quantity of beverage consumed is significant. Compared with steady drinkers (steady in-home drinkers in particular), binge drinkers are clearly more disturbed and disruptive as indicated by higher MMPI elevations (especially of the 498 pattern), higher rates of previous marriage and divorce, and more psychopathology in addition to the alcoholism. Furthermore, the binge (B) group reported greater social impairment associated with their drinking (for example, higher frequencies of missed work, missed meals, fights, reckless driving, and physical abuse of spouse) and lower levels of marital satisfaction. In essence, then, it would appear that binge drinkers are involved in more sociopathic behavior, show more disturbed relationships in domains other than the marital relationship, and engage in a pattern of drinking that is unpredictable, at times chaotic, and certainly not incorporated into in-home, family life.

At the other end of continuum, the steady in-home (SI) drinkers appear to experience the least disruption in their lives as a result of the drinking, and at least in some cases seem to experience positive benefits associated with drinking. That is, it is the SI group that shows the strongest correlations between amount consumed and marital satisfaction ratings of the wife. In addition, for two of the three clearly defined SI drinkers conducted through the time-series analysis, there was substantial support for the drinking/family stability relationship—that is, *drinking resulted in increases in marital satisfaction*. Compared with the B drinkers, the SI drinkers seem to be least affected by the alcohol abuse and least impaired generally, as reflected in lower MMPI elevations (the mean MMPI profile for the SI groups is in the nonclinical range), relatively high marital satisfaction scores, and relatively low levels of social impairments related to drinking.

The third group—steady out-of-home drinkers (SO)—seems to fall somewhere between the B and SI groups in terms of associated background profile, although the relatively small samples that we are analyzing make strong statements about group differences unwarranted. In general, however, the SO drinkers seem to be different from the SI group insofar as alcohol's impact on family relationships, and more closely resemble the B group in terms of drinking variability, wives' marital satisfaction ratings, and increased psychopathology.

And now for the final question: What outcomes would be obtained from the laboratory interaction data if we were to re-analyze these data taking into account the dimensions of drinking style (B, S) and primary drinking location (I,O)? Based on the original cross-sectional study, the preliminary replication and refinement of these relationships, and the intriguing time-series analyses, we would expect that our direct observations of alcoholic families in the interaction laboratory would yield subgroup differences that are (a) different than would be obtained without these subgroupings, and (b) consistent with the patterns we are beginning to discern from the cross-sectional and longitudinal data.

For these within-group analyses, we began with 37 alcoholic couples who were subsequently divided into the two major subgroups of B (n = 14) and S (n = 22). In addition, a three-group analysis was conducted in order to tease out any interactional differences between in-home versus out-of-home steady drinkers and to limit B drinkers to only out-of-home drinkers. Although sample sizes of these three subgroups were admittedly small—10 BO, 9 SI, 11 SO—we hoped that findings could add further clarity to the Binge/Steady typology.

Negativity

For both the two-group (B,S) and three-group (BO, SI, SO) analyses, there was clear support for differences in negativity. For the two-group analysis, the B couples exhibited higher rates of negativity than S couples, and the locus of this difference resulted from major differences between husbands' scores—that is, B drinkers were significantly more negative than S drinkers, whereas the wives of B and S drinkers were more similar to one another. The three-group analysis yielded a borderline significant effect indicating that both SI and SO drinkers reflected substantially less negative affect and communication than B drinkers.

Problem Solving

With the two-group analysis, we find dramatic differences in problem solving as a function of drinking condition and group status. Specifically, couples in the S group become *more* problem-focused and instrumental in the drinking session whereas couples in the B group become *less* task-focused and less instrumental in the presence of the alcohol. Although the three-way interaction involving Group, Condition, and Member was not significant, inspection of cell means suggested that it was the spouse in the B group who decreased her task-directed activity as much or more than the drinker himself.

Positivity

The positivity index provided the most dramatic effect of all. For the three-group analysis, the G X C interaction indicated that the SI drinkers became significantly more positive in the interaction during the drink versus no-drink session whereas both the B and the SO drinkers showed little change in positivity across the drinking and no-drinking conditions. (It is to be noted that both the alcoholics and their spouses in the SI group become more positive in the drinking condition.)

In summary, for the B group, communications are generally negative and aversive. The locus of the negativity seems to reside in or to be expressed by the B drinker rather than by his wife, and we see interactions becoming increasingly negative in the drinking session. Simultaneously, these couples show a decrease in problem-solving efforts during the drinking session, with the suggestion that the wife shows the more dramatic reduction in task focus. One implication that might be read into these data is that negativity (especially the husband's) during the drinking session leads to an increase in off-task talk, especially by the wife. That is, the alcoholic's increasing anger and criticism results in the wife "backing off" from direct attempts to deal with areas of conflict—a sequence that would suggest a coercive control mechanism at the center of this mode of relating. His nastiness is reduced if she withdraws from attempts to change his behavior. This mechanism is not the same as, but it seems consistent with the deviance-disavowal explanation of aggressive behavior and its resulting in fewer negative sanctions if the person is seen to be drinking or under the influence of alcohol. That is, the wife "backs off" from the arguments or does not counterattack because of the futility of dealing with the husband when he is drinking or under the control of the alcohol. On the other hand, we could entertain a negativity accelerating process underlying the obtained findings in which cycles of negative reciprocity are of high strength and long duration. Other analytic procedures obviously will be needed in order to determine which of these processes is operating.

For the SI group, communication is much less negative than for the B groups in general. In fact, the rate of Negativity for the SI husbands equals that for the Depressed and Normal husbands. Although there is some increase in negativity in going from the no-drink to the drink condition, it is quite moderate in comparison with the negativity change we see in the B groups. Furthermore, Problem Solving actually improved somewhat as a function of the drinking condition and, as we saw, Positivity increased dramatically during the drinking session. Given this pattern of outcomes, we can entertain the hypothesis that alcohol facilitates more problem-focused behavior that is experienced as—or which is in the context of—a clearly positive mood.

Finally, the SO group appears to be the least stable type that we have examined so far, sometimes appearing more similar to the B drinkers and at other times operating more like the SI drinker. Obviously, our small sample analyses must be followed by larger sample designs so that issues of stability and strength of findings can be determined more confidently than is presently possible.

Future Directions

Present findings, although provocative, are still of a preliminary nature and must be interpreted cautiously. In the months ahead, many important questions must be addressed in order to gain further understanding of relationships involving alcoholism subgroups and patterns of marital and family interaction. Several directions for promising future efforts can be noted.

First, we must determine if our laboratory findings hold up under closer scrutiny. In particular, we have been analyzing data involving relatively small samples, so that issues of reliability and stability are of considerable concern. Analyses planned during the next year will capitalize on increasingly larger samples that are now being collected.

Second, all analyses conducted thus far have been based upon simple rate measures and have not directly examined actual interactions—patterns of mutual or reciprocal influence—in a direct manner. A major analytic effort of the next year, therefore, will involve application of sequential analysis procedures to our laboratory data in an effort to identify and document changes in contingencies occurring between members. In this regard, we hope to examine direction-of-effect issues by means of sequential analysis procedures in a manner analogous to use of the time-series methods with our longitudinal data collections, as previously described. Of particular importance to hypotheses raised in regard to steady in-home drinkers (SI), we will want to assess differences in wives' contingent responses to husbands during the drink versus no-drink session. That is, beyond overall increases in positivity and problem solving that are seen in moving from the no-drink to drink session, is there any evidence that the wife actively responds to these changes contingently and sequentially?

Third, the theoretical and empirical links between variations in drinking style and location and psychopathological syndromes certainly deserve further attention. For the B group, sociopathy seemed to be a major, associated psychopathology or psychopathological style. For the SI, the personality/psychopathology concomitants were less clear, although there were suggestions that dysthymia or personality disorder may be an important correlate of SI status. If so, it is possible that this group includes an overrepresentation of anxious/inhibited men who are unassertive and passive, who reflect deficits in social skills (particularly in their expression of personal views and feelings), and who overcome these deficits by use of alcohol and are subsequently reinforced by the family's response to changes in their behavior. As a variation on this theme, alcohol's disinhibiting effects may allow for the expression of positive and tender feelings that are lacking during nondrinking (sober) times, and reinforced when expressed.

Fourth, the drinking style and location variables must be more precisely defined and more fully understood. As previously noted, our definition of binge and steady drinking was based on relatively simple questionnaire responses, and further work will certainly need to clarify the specific meanings and referents for these terms. Even among steady drinkers, there is great variability in pattern and amount of consumption, as was seen in the further differentiation of the SI and SO groups which were quite different in consistency of drinking as well as drinking cycles (weekend heavy drinking generally superimposed on a daily-consumption pattern). For our Binge drinkers, there was a wide range of "styles," from several long binges in a year separated by relatively long periods of abstinence, to many periods of heavy, out-of-control drinking separated by several days to several weeks.

Finally, the need to examine the unique nature of our sample and associated findings is of major importance and is, in fact, being pursued at the present time in several directions. First, another sample of 50 male alcoholics is being recruited and conducted through the same procedures, as well as groups of female alcoholics and female depressives. Together with the home observations on the core samples and the new samples, attempts to corroborate and elaborate on our preliminary interaction findings can be pursued. Second, an independent sample of married alcoholics, larger (n = 160) and more heterogeneous than that seen in the core study, has been collected during the past two years. Analyses of these data should allow for important replications and extensions of many of the key, cross-sectional and longitudinal findings reported thus far.

REFERENCES

1. Becker, J. V., & Miller, P. M. Verbal and nonverbal marital interaction patterns of alcoholics and nonalcoholics. *Journal of Studies on Alcohol 37*: 1616–1624, 1976.

2. Billings, A., Kessler, M., Gomberg, C., & Weiner, S. Marital conflict-resolution of alcoholic and nonalcoholic couples during sobriety and experimental drinking. *Journal of Studies of Alcohol 3*: 183–195, 1979.

3. Davis, P., & Stern, D. *Typologies of the alcoholic family: An integration*. Unpublished manuscript, University of Pennsylvania Wharton School of Finance and Commerce, 1980.

4. Dunn, N. J., Jacob, T., Hummon, N., & Seilhamer, R. A. Marital stability in alcoholic-spouse relationships as a function of drinking pattern and location. *Journal of Abnormal Psychology 96*: 99–107, 1987.

5. Feighner, J. P., Robins, E., Guze, S. B., Woodruff, R. A., Winokur, G., & Munoz, R. Diagnostic criteria for use in psychiatric research. *Archives of General Psychiatry 26*: 57–63, 1972.

6. Foa, V., & Foa, E. *Societal structures of the mind*. Springfield IL: Charles C. Thomas, 1974.

7. Gorad, S. L. Communicational styles and interaction of alcoholics and their wives. *Family Process 10*: 475–489, 1971.

8. Gottman, J. M. *Marital interaction: Experimental investigations*. New York: Academic Press, 1979.

9. Hersen, M., Miller, P., & Eisler, R. Interaction between alcoholics and their wives: A descriptive analysis of verbal and nonverbal behavior. *Quarterly Journal of Studies on Alcohol 34*: 516–520, 1973.

10. Hops, H., Wills, T., Patterson, G., & Weiss, R. *Marital Interaction Coding System*. Unpublished manuscript, University of Oregon Research Institute, 1972.

11. Jacob, T. Family interaction in disturbed and normal families: A methodological and substantive review. *Psychological Bulletin 82*: 33–65, 1975.

12. ______, Dunn, N., & Leonard, K. Patterns of alcohol abuse and family stability. *Alcoholism: Clinical and Experimental Research 7*: 382–385, 1983.

13. ______, Favorini, A., Meisel, S., & Anderson, C. The spouse, children and family interactions of the alcoholic: Substantive findings and methodological issues. *Journal of Studies on Alcohol 39*: 1231–1251, 1978.

14. ______, Ritchey, D., Cvitkovic, J., & Blane, H. Communication styles of alcoholic and nonalcoholic families when drinking and not drinking. *Journal of Studies on Alcohol 42*: 466–482, 1981.

15. ______, & Seilhamer, R. A. The impact on spouses and how they cope. In J. Orford & J. Harwin (eds.), *Alcohol and the Family*. London: Croom Helm Ltd., 1982.

16. MacAndrew, C., & Edgerton, R. B. *Drunken comportment: A social explanation*. Chicago: Aldine, 1969.

17. Orford, J., & Harwin, J. *Alcohol and the family*. London: Croom Helm Ltd., 1982.

18. Spitzer, R. L., & Endicott, J. *Research Diagnostic Criteria (RDC) for selected groups of functional disorders* (3rd ed.). Biometrics Research: New York State Psychiatric Institute, 1977.

19. Steinglass, P. The simulated drinking gang: An experimental model for the study of a systems approach to alcoholism: I. Description of the Model; II. Findings and implications. *Journal of Nervous and Mental Disease 161*: 100–122, 1975.

20. ______. The conceptualization of marriage from a systems theory perspective. In T. Paolino & B. McCrady (eds.), *Marriage and marital therapy*. New York: Brunner/Mazel, 1978.

21. ______. The alcoholic family in the interaction laboratory. *Journal of Nervous and Mental Disease 167*: 428–436, 1979.

22. ______. A life history model of the alcoholic family. *Family Process 19*: 211–226, 1980.

23. ______. The impact of alcoholism on the family. *Journal of Studies on Alcohol 42*: 288-303, 1981.

24. Strodtbeck, F. L. Husband-wife interaction over revealed differences. *American Sociological Review 16*: 468–473, 1951.

25. Triandis, H. Some universals of social behavior. *Personality and Social Psychology Bulletin 4*: 1-16, 1978.

26. Weiss, R. *Marital interaction coding systems, MICS-II: Training and reference manual for coders*. Unpublished manuscript, University of Oregon, 1979.

27. ______. *The Areas of Change Questionnaire*. Marital Studies Program, University of Oregon, Department of Psychology, 1980.

28. Wolin, S., Bennett, L., Noonan, D., & Teitelbaum, M. Disrupted family rituals: A factor in the intergenerational transmission of alcoholism. *Journal of Studies on Alcohol 41*: 199-214, 1980.

III

Marital Interaction Research

13

DIFFERENCES BETWEEN HUSBANDS AND WIVES:
Implications for Understanding Marital Discord

CLIFFORD I. NOTARIUS
DAVID S. PELLEGRINI
The Catholic University of America
Washington, D. C.

SINCE the turn of the century, the stability of marriage has decreased dramatically in Western society. Few who consider marriage today can be unaware of the chance that they will have first-hand experience with separation, divorce, remarriage, and life in a blended family. For example, the yearly divorce rate in the United States presently stands at 4.9 per 1,000 individuals, with 1,165,000 divorces granted in the 12-month period ending April, 1985 (28). Although this represents a slight attenuation in the divorce rate since the beginning of the decade, we can now expect approximately 40–45% of those married in the last ten years eventually to divorce.

The *structure* or form of marriage also has undergone considerable transformation in the last century. These transformations reflect historical changes in the sociocultural context in which marriages are embedded. For example, the industrial revolution ushered large numbers of women into the labor force for the first time. As a result, women gained "a power based on the production of economic resources independent of the husband" (42, p. 29). These new economic realities, together with expanding expectations fostered by feminism, eroded traditional role divisions in marriage (41). Whereas, prior to this point, women were largely restricted in marriage to subservient or complementary roles, new marital forms emerged in which women and men could establish equal roles.

Thus, although divorce rates were lower in previous eras, one cannot assume that this was due to greater domestic felicity. Increased employment opportunities in recent years may simply have provided women with the personal and financial resources necessary to terminate unhappy unions. Clearly, though, even the current divorce rate represents only a proportion of the population of couples who experience marital distress, because years of conflict frequently precede a couple's decision to divorce, and it does not invariably result in divorce, perhaps especially when children are involved.

Although not without controversy and ambiguities (see 39), an abundance of evidence documents the enormous costs and wide-ranging deleterious effects of marital discord and disruption, not just for marital partners (especially husbands), but also for their offspring (10). For example, a variety of surveys consistently link marital status (married, divorced, widowed, separated, and never married) and the distribution of psychopathology in the population (see 7). When psychopathology is indexed by admission rates to private or public hospitals, the married show the lowest rate while the divorced or separated have the highest (2). The widowed and the never married have inpatient rates between the married and the divorced, but their relative standing varies across surveys and by sex. Bloom, Asher, and White (2) reported that the ratio of inpatient admission rates for those divorced and separated to those married was between 7 : 1 and 22 : 1 for males, and between 3 : 1 and 8 : 1 for females. These trends, slightly attenuated, were also found for admissions to public outpatient clinics where the ratio of those divorced or separated to those married ranged between 4 : 1 and 9 : 1 for males, and between 3 : 1 and 6 : 1 for females. In summarizing their thorough review, Bloom et al. (2) concluded:

> First, regardless of type of facility or sex, admission rates are highest for those with disrupted marriages; second, males with disrupted marriages have substantially higher admission rates than females; and third, regardless of sex or type of facility, where rates have been separately calculated, rates for separated persons are notably higher than those for divorced persons. [p. 870]

Similar studies are available linking marital status to the distribution of physical illness in the population. For example, Verbrugge (46) reported that the divorced and separated are less healthy, across a variety of indices, than are the single and the married. Bloom et al. (2) similarly reported lower illness susceptibility among the married as compared with other groups.

Given the turmoil that affects present-day marriage and the costs that attend marital dissatisfaction and dissolution, it may seem somewhat surprising that marriage has survived as a lifestyle of common choice. As evidence of this, consider the fact that the current 12-month marriage rate remains relatively constant at 10.4 per 1,000 individuals (28). Even more striking is the fact that most people who get a divorce choose to remarry; indeed, half of these remarriages take place within 36 months of divorce (4).

This brief review, then, poses several questions of considerable theoretical and clinical relevance. *First*, given the evolution of marriage over the last fifty years, we can ask: What functions does marriage currently promise to fulfill for its partners that help to maintain its popularity? A number of investigators (see 44, 45) have argued that marriage serves the needs of men more than the needs of women. While there is, indeed, some evidence for such inequity, we might still wonder if the functions of a *successful* (mutually satisfying) marriage differ for men and women and, if so, are these functions mutually exclusive or incompatible. Recent writings by Gilligan (13), Rubin (38), and others, suggest such fundamental, seemingly incompatible differences between men and women.

A *second* critical question concerns how we can account for the fragility of the marital relationship. Earlier on we noted that contemporary marriage is often established in the context of equality between husband and wife. A defining feature of such a marriage is the couple's commitment to companionship as a primary relationship goal. Marital satisfaction within a companionship marriage largely will be a function of the partners' ability to meet each other's needs and desires and to resolve relationship problems effectively.

Unlike earlier marital forms that provided partners with role prescriptions for the expected behaviors of husbands and wives, contemporary marital styles more typically require partners to negotiate individual resolutions to the mutual tasks of family life. Thus, marriage has altered in response to changes in the broader sociocultural context. New skills may now be required of couples to meet successfully the challenges presented by newly evolving relationship forms or structures. If these evolving relationship forms have contributed directly to the sharp increases in the divorce rate in recent years, perhaps it is because many couples have failed to learn the communication and problem-solving skills that such marriages undoubtedly require to be successful (33). Assuming that there are a set of relationship skills vital to the successful contemporary marriage, we wonder if these skills are differentiated by gender (see for example 20, 29). Alternatively posed, it is important to ask if there are particular skill deficits in husbands and/or wives that are remediable in the interest of enhancing stability and satisfaction in present-day marriage. We will address these questions in the sections that follow.

Perspectives on Husband and Wife Differences

Among the first models of family functioning to posit different styles for wives and husbands was the sex-role differentiation theory of Parsons and Bales (34). This model held that the husband's behavior within a marriage was more task-oriented or instrumental whereas the wife's behavior was more emotion-oriented or expressive. Although data in support of this model have been hard to come by (see below), two current writers, from different disciplines, have refueled the debate on inherent differences between men and women in their needs and interpersonal styles.

Gilligan (13), in her popular text, *In a Different Voice*, argues that the sexes are exposed to two different pathways of identity formation. Girls are responsive to a "world of relationships and psychological truths where an awareness of the connection between people gives rise to a recognition of responsibility for one another" (p. 30). Boys, on the other hand, are "fascinated by the power of logic" and rational thought. Whereas girls are said to rely on communication to negotiate conflicts in a world of enduring social relationships, boys are believed to rely on rationality to resolve interpersonal dilemmas in a world that prizes independence and autonomy. These divergent developmental pathways are hypothesized to result in strikingly different needs, styles, and desires in relationships between men and women. Because men develop within the context of separation, they react to attachment and intimacy as a threat; because women develop within the context of relationship, they react to separation and isolation as a threat.

Rubin (38), who, like Gilligan, drew on the work of Chodorow (5), extends the tenets of Gilligan's arguments and makes explicit the consequences of early developmental patterns upon marital partners. From interviews with husbands and wives, men and women, Rubin portrays modern spouses as "intimate strangers." Wives seek an intimacy grounded in communication and open sharing of thoughts, feelings, desires, and events; while husbands seek an intimacy grounded in proximity and shared activities. Given these opposing styles, wives complain:

> I can't stand that he's so damned unemotional and expects me to be the same. He lives in his head all the time, and he acts like anything that's emotional isn't worth dealing with. . . . I'm the one who tries to get things going. I'm always doing my bla-bla-bla number, you know, keeping things moving along and alive around here. But he's the original Mr. Shutmouth most of the time. [38, pp. 73–75]

Husbands have the reciprocal complaint:

> She wants to talk about something that worries her — maybe something between us — but it makes me nervous so I don't want to hear about it. As soon as she starts talking about her worries, she exaggerates the problem, and all of a sudden, we've got a big nut on our hands. Who needs it? [38, p. 76]

These portrayals of husbands and wives, provocative as they are, are based on interview data and cannot provide a basis for valid conclusions about actual behavioral differences between partners. Yet, it is the behavioral patterns of husbands and wives that are the key to understanding any effects spouse differences may have upon relationship functioning (see 35). The complaints stated above may stem not from different needs in husbands and wives, but from the social interaction processes through which spouses attempt to service what may be similar needs.

Not only is the identification of behavioral differences generally beyond interview methodology, it also should be noted that Gilligan and Rubin, in particular, may have exerted considerable bias (however inadvertent) in their selection and presentation of material pertinent to differences in the way in which men and women reason about relationships. Readers are provided with abstracted and, at times, rewritten vignettes to convey "fairly represented" situations, but not ones that are "actual or descriptive of any individual" (38). Because whole interviews are not provided, we cannot know if certain (inconsistent) responses were omitted nor the extent to which spouses were less consistent than it appeared.

Rubin's analysis is itself without internal consistency at times. She writes of a wife who, comparing her husband to her son, says: "He just wants me to be there to listen to him . . . He doesn't want conversation, he just wants to talk." When expressing her needs, this wife reports: "I try to tell him that I don't want it to be all on his timetable. Why doesn't he care about me and my timetable; why doesn't he ask about how I'm feeling or what I'm thinking?" (p. 78). Note the similarity between the wife's critique of what the partner wants and his perceived attempts to get it and what is being asked for by the wife from the partner, that is, validation. It may be that both husband and wife are in need of the same response from the other and that a focus on interview data may obscure this fact behind stereotyped response hierarchies.

Indeed, a number of theorists (for example, 6, 9) have suggested that validation is but one form of social support sought by men and women alike in their personal relationships with others. The provision of social (especially emotional) support through an intimate, confiding relationship with a spouse may be the primary function of a successful marriage, serving to maintain the physical and psychological well-being of partners presumably, in part, through its positive effects on self-esteem (3). The availability of spousal support may play a particularly critical role in buffering marital partners from the otherwise deleterious effects of threatful life events and difficulties (3, 8, 27).

Interestingly, while a wide range of studies suggest that men and women alike suffer from the absence of a supportive (that is, intimate and confiding) relationship with a spouse (26, 37, 47), cultural norms may make it more difficult for men to admit to needs for intimacy (23) and thus, perhaps, to seek openly to fulfill such needs. At the same time, men are more likely than women to rely exclusively on their spouses as confidants, being more isolated from and less intimate with relatives, friends, and coworkers (11). Thus, men may be more vulnerable to the disruption of a marital relationship, having fewer alternative outlets for emotional support (44). On the other hand, men appear to be more likely than women to report having sufficiently supportive relationships with their spouses (see 45). That is, while there may be no sex differences in the supportive function of a successful marital relationship, self-report data suggest that men may be more successful in obtaining emotional support from their spouses than in providing it to them. While the latter findings are generally consistent with clinical anecdotes (for example, 25), it seems reasonable to question the extent to which they are concordant with actual patterns of interaction between husbands and wives. To address this important issue, we will turn to a selective review of the interactional studies of distressed and nondistressed marriages.

Husband and Wife Differences in Marital Interaction

As noted above, one of the early models guiding the initial studies of interaction in couples was Parsons and Bales's (34) sex-role differentiation theory, which held that men were more instrumental and task-oriented while women were more expressive and concerned with emotions. In one of the first sophisticated studies of marital interaction, Raush, Barry, Hertel, and Swain (36) found no support for Parsons and Bales's predictions. These authors concluded that sex-role differentiation theory could be safely called dead! Yet significant (though small) differences between husbands and wives did emerge from their data. Raush et al. found that husbands made more attempts to resolve conflict and to restore harmony in the relationship, whereas wives displayed more negatively toned behaviors such as rejection and personal attack. When husband and wife were confronted with an issue to discuss, wives appeared "to behave in ways designed to enforce their own point of view" (p. 144), while husbands showed "relatively greater concern for actually resolving the problem and keeping the relationship harmonious" (p. 144).

Schaap (43), studying Dutch couples, found that wives displayed more "put downs" and more negative affect, while husbands made more comments suggesting withdrawal from conflict (for example, statements irrelevent to the current topic of discussion, "I don't know" responses to questions, or no response) and showed more positive affect. Margolin and Wampold (24) found wives to display more smiling and laughing, complaints, and criticisms than husbands. Husbands, on the other hand, offered more excuses for their behavior. Hahlweg et al. (19), using the Kategoriensystem für partnerschaftliche Interaktion (KPI), found that wives showed more self-disclosure, more criticism, and less justification than husbands. These sex differences were similar in distressed and nondistressed couples.

In a study of interaction in nondistressed couples using the Couples Interaction Scoring System (CISS; 32), Notarius and Johnson (31) found wives (when speaking) to display less neutral and more negative behavior than their husbands. Wives showed nearly three times as much negative-speaker behavior than did their husbands. Husbands and wives did not differ in the display of positive-speaker behavior. Wives were also observed to display over three times as much negative-listener behaviors compared to husbands. Notarius and Johnson also found spouse differences in reciprocity patterns. Wives reciprocated their husbands' positive and negative behaviors, while husbands did not reciprocate their wives' positive and negative behaviors. Instead, husbands responded with neutral behavior to their wives' positive behavior and showed no consistent response to their wives' negative behavior. These results suggest that husbands are less overtly responsive to the ongoing interaction than are wives. This tendency may lead wives to feel that their messages are not heard or are not sufficiently considered.

If responsiveness to another is reduced to component skills, then the skills of encoding (sending) and decoding (receiving) interpersonal messages are certain to be critical (see 29). Encoding can be viewed as an expressivity construct combining the extent of expression with the quality of the expression. Accurately decoding another's message and accompanying nonverbal cues is perhaps a first step to responding appropriately to another. For example, failure to receive a negatively intended message may leave the sender feeling misunderstood or ignored, and may result in the sender increasing the stimulus value of the message in order that it be registered. Even with accurate decoding by the receiver, the sender might still be prodded in this direction if the receiver failed to signal that a negatively intended message was received (that is, if the receiver failed to validate the speaker's message). Several studies have considered encoding and decoding among distressed and nondistressed couples; these will be briefly reviewed as they pertain to spouse differences.

Encoding and Decoding Skills

Noller (29) undertook perhaps the most systematic examination of this topic. With respect to spouse differences in encoding, Noller's findings are consistent with the large body of interaction studies (19, 24, 31) in that wives were observed to send more negative and more positive messages than husbands. Examination of the quality of expression revealed that wives were more adept than husbands at sending positive messages whereas both spouses were equally competent at sending negative messages. Noller suggests that wives may be more facile at communicating affection and appreciation in a marriage. In contrast, there were generally few overall decoding differences between husbands and wives.

Noller also examined encoding and decoding resources as a function of marital satisfaction. Here spouse differences were sharpest for distressed husbands. In a distressed relationship, husbands tended to be (a) poor senders, especially of positively toned messages, (b) poor receivers of wives' messages, and (c) less aware of the quality of their encoding. Distressed wives were marked by their unjustified confidence in their (incorrect) decoding of their husbands' messages. Noller (29) suggests these distressed wives "may be less likely to admit the possibility of misunderstandings occurring because of their decoding" (p. 178). To round out the picture, in distressed relationships *both* husbands and wives tend to be (a) more negative in their interactions, (b) less positive, (c) more likely to send inconsistent messages, and (d) less able to predict if their partner will accurately decode their message.

The differences that exist betweeen distressed and nondistressed spouses, then, point toward deficits in distressed husbands. This conclusion is more directly supported by Gottman and Porterfield's (17) study of encoding and decoding within spouse and stranger dyads. Husband and wife marital satisfaction was found to be correlated with the husband's ability to accurately decode his wife's nonverbal messages. The poor decoding performance of distressed husbands was apparently not due to wives' sending ability; strangers had no difficulty accurately receiving wives' messages. Moreover, this poor decoding performance was restricted to the receipt of messages from partners; distressed husbands accurately decoded stranger-encoded messages. Thus, the results locate a decoding deficit in distressed husbands that appears to be *relationship specific*.

Because it seems that distressed husbands have a performance rather than a skill deficit, it is intriguing to speculate as to its origin. Gottman and

Porterfield (17) proposed that it may be traced to a cognitive bias whereby distressed husbands perceive their wives' expressions as irrational and therefore insignificant. As this occurs, they may cease to decode effectively their wives' nonverbal behavior. We offer another explanation for these findings: Distressed husbands' decoding deficits may be secondary to *escalating negative affect*, which is characteristic of distressed marital interaction. Thus, as negative affect exchange escalates in the relationship, distressed husbands may begin to attend less to their wives and thereby to be less effective in decoding their wives' nonverbal behavior, but not that of strangers. Obviously, the need for longitudinal data is apparent in testing such a model. In general, the cross-sectional studies we have reviewed cannot provide us with evidence to ascertain the extent to which observed differences between distressed husbands and wives predate distress and may be causally related to dysfunction or follow as consequents of marital dissatisfaction.

"Insider-Outsider" Studies of Marital Interaction

Although not all studies support a decoding deficit among husbands in distressed relationships (see 40), several related studies are consistent with such a finding. One study, undertaken by Floyd and Markman (12) compared spouses' evaluations of partners' behavior ("insider" ratings of message impact) with observer ratings based on the same behavior sample ("outsider" ratings). For nondistressed couples, Floyd and Markman found no difference between observers' and spouses' ratings of partners' behavior. However, in distressed couples, a large discrepancy was observed between distressed husbands' average impact ratings of their wives' behavior and observers' average ratings of this behavior. Distressed husbands' average ratings of their spouses were dramatically more positive than were observers' average ratings. Such a finding would be expected if these distressed husbands were inaccurately decoding their wives' messages, as suggested by both Noller's (29) and Gottman and Porterfield's (17) results.

In a recently completed study, Notarius, Benson, Vanzetti, et al. (30) replicated and extended Floyd and Markman's findings. Using a similar paradigm, a large discrepancy was again found between distressed husbands' average subjective ratings of their wives' behavior and observers' average ratings of this behavior, with the husbands' ratings being far more positive than the observers' ratings. This replication provides some degree of confidence in the identified pattern. However, mean ratings averaged across an entire interaction cannot inform us about the nature of any relationships between spouse and observer codings on each particular conversational exchange or "floor switch." Comparison of spouse and observer ratings, with the floor switch as the unit of analysis, has particular relevance to enhancing our understanding of reciprocity patterns in distressed and nondistressed relationships. *Negative affect* reciprocity is perhaps the single most telling signature of distressed marital interaction.

In the study mentioned above, Notarius et al. (30) had spouses and observers continually rate the affective impact of each partner's behavior during both a high-conflict and a low-conflict problem-solving discussion. These ratings were used to examine the associations among speakers' antecedent behaviors, listeners' subjective evaluation of these behaviors, and listeners' consequent responses. Hierarchical log-linear procedures were applied to cross-classification tables examining husbands' and wives' consequent responses separately. In each case a model was sought to account for the associations present in each table. These associations can be gauged from the expected frequencies, odds, and odds ratios generated by the preferred models, portrayed in Tables 1 and 2.

For example, Table 1 considers the associations among observer coding of wives' antecedent behaviors, husbands' subjective evaluation or receipt of these messages, and observer coding of husbands' consequent responses. The preferred model allowed for the direct association between (a) couple status and wives' antecedent behavior, (b) wives' antecedent behavior and husbands' subjective evaluation of that behavior, (c) husbands' subjective evaluation and husbands' response, and (d) wives' antecedent behavior and husbands' response. Table 2 considers the associations among observer coding of husbands' antecedent behavior, wives' subjective evaluation of these messages, and observer coding of wives' consequent responses. The preferred model for these data again incorporated direct associations between antecedent behavior and subjective evaluation and between subjective evaluation and response. However, the preferred model here also established a relationship between couple status and subjective evaluation and a three-way interaction among couple status, observer coding of husbands' antecedent, and observer coding of wives' response.

Perhaps the most striking feature of Table 1 is the *equivalent behavioral patterns that were displayed by distressed and nondistressed husbands* in response to each type of antecedent behavior. Differences in the frequencies of distressed and nondistressed husbands' positive, neutral, and negative responses appeared to be due to the differences in the observer coding of their wives' antecedent behaviors. Observers were 5.5 times as likely to code distressed wives' antecedents as negative relative to neutral or positive than they were to code nondistressed wives in this way.

Table 2 further captures the rather striking differences between distressed and nondistressed wives. Consider, for example, the situation wherein husbands' antecedents were coded as positive by the observers *and* were

TABLE 1

Expected Frequencies, Odds, and Odds Ratios Associated with Husbands' Response

Couple Status	Observer Coding of Wives' Antecedent	Husbands' Subjective Coding of Antecedent	Observer Coding of Husbands' Response			Odds		Odds Ratio
			+	0	–	– :0& +	0& + : –	Dist:Nondist
Distressed	+	+	7.6	4.2	1.2		9.8	1.0
	+	0	.9	1.0	.4			
	+	–	1.2	.5	1.0			
	0	+	9.1	8.6	1.3		13.6	1.0
	0	0	3.0	5.7	1.4		6.2	1.0
	0	–	1.2	.8	.9			
	–	+	11.3	8.7	11.6	6		1.0
	–	0	3.6	5.7	11.5	1.2		1.0
	–	–	4.6	2.4	24.6	3.5		1.0
Nondistressed	+	+	29.3	16.0	4.7		9.6	
	+	0	3.4	3.7	1.7		4.2	
	+	–	4.7	1.8	3.9		1.7	
	0	+	16.2	15.3	2.4		13.1	
	0	0	5.3	10.2	2.4		6.5	
	0	–	2.1	1.4	1.6			
	–	+	5.5	4.2	5.7	.6		
	–	0	1.8	2.8	5.6	1.2		
	–	–	2.2	1.2	12.0	3.6		

Note: Odds were calculated only when there were 9 or more exchanges within a given row. Odds for distressed and nondistressed couples were equivalent under the accepted model and appear slightly different due to rounding error.

TABLE 2

Expected Frequencies, Odds, and Odds Ratios Associated with Wifes' Response

Couple Status	Observer Coding of Husbands' Antecedent	Wives' Subjective Coding of Antecedent	Observer Coding of Wives' Response			Odds		Odds Ratio
			+	0	–	– :0& +	0& + : –	Dist:Nondist
Distressed	+	+	13.8	4.1	6.9		2.6	.19
	+	0	1.1	1.6	1.3			
	+	–	1.1	1.2	2.8			
	0	+	2.1	4.4	9.4		.7	.17
	0	0	.4	4.0	4.1		1.1	.26
	0	–	.5	3.6	10.6		.4	.25
	–	+	1.1	2.7	10.4	2.7		3.00
	–	0	.2	2.9	5.3	1.7		1.31
	–	–	.7	6.3	33.3	4.8		1.50
Nondistressed	+	+	31.4	11.6	3.1		13.9	
	+	0	5.3	9.5	1.2		12.3	
	+	–	1.3	1.9	.7			
	0	+	13.9	8.0	5.2		4.2	
	0	0	5.4	15.4	4.7		4.2	
	0	–	1.6	3.6	3.2		1.6	
	–	+	5.6	1.1	6.1	.9		
	–	0	2.6	2.5	6.5	1.3		
	–	–	1.9	1.4	10.5	3.2		

Note: Odds were calculated only when there were 9 or more exchanges within a given row.

received as positive by his wife. Nondistressed wives were 5.3 (13.9/2.6) times as likely as distressed wives to offer their husbands a positive or neutral as compared to a negative response. Thus, the nondistressed wives promoted positive reciprocity at a rate 5 times that of distressed wives. Similar patterns were observed when husbands' antecedents were coded as neutral. Distressed wives were far more likely to display a negative response relative to a positive or neutral response than were nondistressed wives.

Data in Tables 1 and 2 also permit an evaluation of negative reciprocity among distressed and nondistressed spouses. When observers coded an antecedent as negative and when spouses received that antecedent as negative, nondistressed husbands and wives and distressed husbands were each about 3.5 times as likely to give a negative response relative to a positive or neutral response. Distressed wives, however, were about 5 times as likely to give a negative response relative to a positive or neutral response.

Two factors may be operating within distressed relationships to account for the pattern of findings. First, it may be that distressed wives were biased toward negative behaviors. This may account for wives' greater negativity in several of the studies reviewed above. Perhaps wives have more to be upset about in a marital relationship (18). Second, distressed wives may be "prodded" toward negativity by having relatively unresponsive partners. Assuming that marital tensions characterize distressed relationships, it is notable that the interaction style of distressed and nondistressed husbands was quite similar. In the presence of relationship difficulties, the responses of distressed husbands may appear to their wives as disengagement or minimizing of relationship difficulties. In response, these wives may escalate their negativity in order to get through to their husbands. Distressed wives may find it frustrating to be confronted with a partner who is responding positively but who has failed to acknowledge or to validate relationship difficulties. Obviously, this speculation goes far beyond the data at hand and could be confirmed only with content coding of the interaction.

Commentary

Interactional studies to date have provided a fairly consistent picture of behavioral differences between husbands and wives. Most of these differences are evident across distressed and nondistressed marriages. Wives appear to engage in more behavior that is negatively valenced than do husbands. These behaviors include more criticism, rejection, personal attack, and complaints. Distressed wives appear particularly prone to view their husbands' behavior negatively and to respond in kind. Distressed husbands, on the other hand, behave in ways that appear to reflect an insensitivity to their wives' behavior. They inaccurately decode their wives' nonverbal behaviors, but not that of other women, suggesting a specific withdrawal from their wives. Distressed husbands also receive their wives' behavior more positively than that same behavior is rated by observers; this tendency may be the result of emotional withdrawal, of attempts at emotional control, or both.

Although spouse differences are often not large, they are still likely to have a large impact on couple functioning. Comparison of marital interaction in distressed and nondistressed couples also reveals differences that are more subtle than dramatic (32). It seems somewhat surprising that subtle interactional differences can be associated with the level of subjective distress reached by a couple in conflict. Yet this is exactly what we would argue; *subtle interactional differences played out over the myriad of interactions required of intimate living can shape the subjective outcomes of marriage in a powerful way.*

Given the nature of spouse differences, an interactional scenario between husbands and wives might have these elements. Given either a decoding deficit or a perceived need for emotional containment, husbands are likely to communicate an inattention or insensitivity to wives' behavior. Whether this is due to husbands' disposition, a response to the interactional system with their wives, or some kind of interaction between the two is currently unknown. Wives are likely to interpret husbands' neutral behavior as unresponsiveness, and they appear to attribute it to husbands being "unemotional." Feeling unresponded to, wives seem locked into negative behaviors as they seek a sign of understanding from husbands. The net effect of these different styles is likely to leave both partners feeling ignored, unvalidated, and in need. To the extent that emotional support is a key relational element for men and women alike, both partners are thus likely to experience relational dissatisfaction and distress, with the increased vulnerability to psychological and physical illness that may accompany such distress and discord.

Because the culture places emphasis on the inexpressive male as the primary contributor to the above scenario (see 1), it is important to distinguish between a lack of emotional *expression* and a lack of *emotion*. Are husbands unfeeling? In the study by Notarius and Johnson (31) cited above, electrodermal responding was monitored throughout the interactional tasks. At those times when the speaker was coded negative (using CISS), and the listener was observed to be nonreactive, husbands were showing *more* electrodermal activity than wives. This finding, indicative of greater sympathetic arousal in husbands, suggests that husbands are reactive to the interactional stream and are not "unemotional," even though they may appear to be "inexpressive."

In a recent study, Levenson & Gottman (22) provided provocative data that also support physiological responsiveness in husbands. In this three-year prospective study, the greater the physiological arousal displayed by husbands and wives prior to and during a conversation with their spouses, the more their respective marital satisfaction declined three years later. Among these husbands and wives, decline in marital satisfaction was also predicted by less positive and negative affect from husbands as well as by a *decreased* likelihood for husbands to respond negatively to their wives' negative messages. Thus, if we accept physiological arousal as some measure of emotionality, it is clearly not the case that husbands are not feeling, though it does appear that they are less behaviorally responsive to their wives. Levenson and Gottman also found that more positive affect from wives and more negative affect reciprocity in their response to husbands' behavior were also important antecedents of relationship decline. However, more negative affect in wives' behavior was not predictive of relationship decline, perhaps because wives appear to show more negative behavior in general.

Directions for Future Study

A number of avenues of investigation seem promising for the future in light of the preceding review. First, it seems useful to explore marital and family interaction data for spouse differences. Not only will this help to extend our understanding of distressed and nondistressed marriage, it may also contribute to our understanding of family systems marked by psychopathology. Additionally, it will be useful to examine marital and family interaction patterns elicited by a variety of tasks, not just problem-solving ones. Most of the interactional data we have reviewed were based on problem-solving discussions. Would a different pattern of characteristics emerge during nonproblem interactions, such as when one spouse seeks support from a partner? In general, task effects have not received sufficient consideration by either interactional researchers or interview investigators (see 38). There is a clear need for longitudinal data to explore the onset of the observed behavioral differences between husbands and wives. Do husbands and wives bring predispositions to a relationship that shape interactional patterns from the inception of the relationship? Alternatively, do differences more regularly emerge as a product of interactional tendencies that destine couples to reciprocal relationship roles? How do distressed and nondistressed couples differentially adjust to these components of relationship formation? Finally, are there differences as yet unrecorded by our observational systems that distinguish the interaction styles of husbands and wives and that promote their divergent behaviors? For example, a husband interviewed by Rubin (38) described his wife's behavior as follows: "As soon as she starts talking about her worries, she exaggerates the problem, and all of a sudden we've got a big nut on our hands" (p. 76). Do some men and women have different styles of discussing problems that predispose them to conflict? Hoffman (21) has offered the perspective that males are oriented toward "instrumental ameliorative action" while females are oriented toward imagining themselves in others' places. If these are taken as goals guiding dyadic behavior, the husband's attempts at problem solving may be quite frustrating for both him and his wife. His attempts at problem solving for his partner, who seeks less problem solving and more emotional support, may leave him feeling helpless and his wife feeling unloved.

While we may not yet fully understand the nature of the interactional differences between husbands and wives, the pattern of results to date have clear implications for enhancing clinical interventions with distressed couples. At an interactional level, husbands and wives must come to understand the impact of their respective behaviors on the other (see 16). A wife's negativity appears to promote her husband's withdrawal, thus having the opposite impact than she intended. The husband's withdrawal may promote his wife's increased negativity, thus having the opposite impact than he intended. This dysfunctional cycle without clear cause and effect must be disrupted. At a cognitive level, it may be useful to disrupt husbands' attributing wives' expressivity to irrationality and wives' attributing husbands' lack of responsiveness to unemotionality, as exemplified in wives interviewed by Rubin (38). As we have argued, the emotional needs of wives and husbands appear more similar than dissimilar. Clinically, a shift in goals may be quite useful, as is often the case when spouses are encouraged to validate their partners' feelings. The frequency with which spouses have difficulty with this intervention and immediately try to offer problem solutions suggests that there may be some utility in pursuing this line of inquiry into the relationship between interpersonal goals and interactional behaviors during problem discussions.

REFERENCES

1. Balswick, J. O., & Peek, C. W. The inexpressive male: A tragedy of American society. *Family Coordinator 20*: 363–368, 1971.

2. Bloom, B. L., Asher, S. J., & White, S. W. Marital disruption as a stressor: A review and analysis. *Psychological Bulletin 85*: 867–894, 1978.

3. Brown, G. W., & Harris T. *Social origins of depression: A study of psychiatric disorder in women*. New York: Free Press, 1978.

4. Cherlin, A. J. *Marriage, divorce, remarriage*. Cambridge: Harvard University Press, 1981.

5. Chodorow, N. *The reproduction of mothering: Psychoanalysis and the sociology of gender*. Berkeley: University of California Press, 1978.

6. Cobb, S. Social support as a moderator of life stress. *Psychosomatic Medicine 38*: 300–314, 1976.

7. ______, & Jones, J. M. Social support, support groups and marital relationships. In S. W. Duck (ed.), *Personal relationships 5: Repairing personal relationships*. London: Academic Press, 1984.

8. Costello, C. G. Social factors associated with depression. *Psychological Medicine 12*: 329–339, 1982.

9. Dean, A., & Lin, D. The stress-buffering role of social support: Problems and prospects for systemic investigation. *Journal of Nervous and Mental Disease 165*: 403–417, 1977.

10. Emery, R. E. Interparental conflict and the children of discord and divorce. *Psychological Bulletin 92*: 310–330, 1982.

11. Fischer, C. S., & Phillips, S. L. Who is alone? Social characteristics of people with small networks. In L. A. Peplau & D. Perlman (eds.), *Loneliness: A sourcebook of current theory, research, and therapy*. New York: John Wiley & Sons, 1982.

12. Floyd, F., & Markman, H. Observational biases in spouse observation: Toward a cognitive/behavioral model of marriage. *Journal of Consulting and Clinical Psychology 51*: 450–457, 1983.

13. Gilligan, C. *In a different voice*. Cambridge: Harvard University Press, 1982.

14. Gottman, J. *Marital interaction: Experimental investigation*. New York: Academic Press, 1979.

15. ______, Notarius, C., Gonso, J., & Markman, H. *A couple's guide to communication*. Champaign IL: Research Press, 1976.

16. ______, Notarius, C., Markman, H., Bank, S., Yoppi, B., & Rubin, M. E. Behavior exchange theory and marital decision making. *Journal of Personality and Social Psychology 34*: 14–23, 1976.

17. ______, & Porterfield, A. Communicative competence in the nonverbal behavior of married couples. *Journal of Marriage and the Family 4*: 817–824, 1981.

18. Gove, W. R. Sex, marital status, and mortality. *American Journal of Sociology 79*: 45–67, 1973.

19. Hahlweg, K., Reisner, L., Kohli, G., Vollmer, M., Schindler, L., & Revenstorf, D. Development and validity of a new system to analyze interpersonal communication: Kategoriensystem für partnerschaftliche Interaktion. In K. Hahlweg & N. Jacobson (eds.), *Marital interaction: Analysis and modification*. New York: Guilford Press, 1984.

20. Hall, J. Gender effects in decoding nonverbal cues. *Psychological Bulletin 85*: 845–857, 1978.

21. Hoffman, M. L. Sex differences in empathy and related behaviors. *Psychological Bulletin 84*: 712–722, 1977.

22. Levenson, R. W., & Gottman, J. M. Physiological and affective predictors of change in relationship satisfaction. *Journal of Personality and Social Psychology 49*: 85–94, 1985.

23. Lynch, J. J. *The broken heart: The medical consequences of loneliness*. New York: Basic Books, 1977.

24. Margolin, G., & Wampold, B. Sequential analysis of conflict and accord in distressed and nondistressed marital partners. *Journal of Consulting and Clinical Psychology 49*: 554–567, 1981.

25. ______, & Weinstein, C. D. The role of affect in behavioral marital therapy. In A. Aronson & L. Wolberg (eds.), *Group and family therapy 1982: An overview*. New York: Brunner/Mazel, 1983.

26. Miller, P. McC., & Ingham, J. G. Friends, confidants and symptoms. *Social Psychiatry 11*: 51–58, 1976.

27. Murphy, E. Social origins of depression in old age. *British Journal of Psychiatry 141*: 135–142, 1982.

28. National Center for Health Statistics. Births, marriages, divorces, and deaths for March, 1985. *Monthly Vital Statistics Report 34* (3): DHSS Publ. No. (PHS) 85-1120. Hyattsville MD: Public Health Service, 1985.

29. Noller, P. *Nonverbal communication and marital interaction*. Oxford: Pergamon Press, 1984.

30. Notarius, C., Benson, P., Vanzetti, N., Sloane, D., & Hornyak, L. Behavioral and phenomenological determinants of interaction in distressed and nondistressed married couples, submitted for publication.

31. ______, & Johnson, J. Emotional expression in husbands and wives. *Journal of Marriage and the Family 44*: 483–489, 1982.

32. ______, Markman, H. J., & Gottman, J. M. Couples Interaction Scoring System: Clinical implications. In E. E. Filsinger (ed.), *Marriage and family assessment: A sourcebook for family therapy*. Beverly Hills: Sage Publications, 1983.

33. ______, & Pellegrini, D. Marital processes as stressors and stress mediators: Implications for marital repair. In S. W. Duck (ed.), *Personal relationships 5: Repairing personal relationships*. London: Academic Press, 1984.

34. Parsons, T., & Bales, R. F. *Family socialization and interaction process*. Glencoe IL: Free Press, 1955.

35. Patterson, G. R. Stress: A change agent for family process. In N. Garmezy & M. Rutter (eds.), *Stress, coping, and development in children*. New York: McGraw-Hill, 1983.

36. Raush, H. L., Barry, W., Hertel, R., & Swain, M. *Communication, conflict, and marriage*. San Francisco: Jossey-Bass, 1974.

37. Roy, A. Vulnerability factors and depression in men. *British Journal of Psychiatry 138*: 75–77, 1981.

38. Rubin, L. *Intimate strangers: Men and women together*. New York: Harper & Row, 1983.

39. Rushing, W. A. Marital status and mental disorder: Evidence in favor of a behavioral model. *Social Forces 58*: 540–556, 1979.

40. Sabatelli, R., Buck, R., & Dreyer, A. Nonverbal communication accuracy in married couples: Relationship with marital complaints. *Journal of Personality and Social Psychology 43*: 1088–1097, 1982.

41. Scanzoni, J. *Sexual bargaining: Power politics in American marriage*. Englewood Cliffs NJ: Prentice-Hall, 1972.

42. ______. A historical perspective on husband-wife bargaining power and marital dissolution. In G. Levinger & O. C. Moles (eds.), *Divorce and separation: Context, causes, and consequences*. New York: Basic Books, 1979.

43. Schaap, C. *Communication and adjustment in marriage*. Netherlands: Swets & Zeitlinger B. V., 1982.

44. Stroebe, M. S., & Stroebe, W. Who suffers more? Sex differences in health risk of the widowed. *Psychological Bulletin 93*: 279–301, 1983.

45. Vanfossen, B. E. Sex differences in the mental health effects of spouse support and equity. *Journal of Health and Social Behavior 22*: 130–143, 1981.

46. Verbrugge, L. M. Marital status and health. *Journal of Marriage and the Family 41*: 267–285, 1979.

47. Wandersman, L., Wandersman, A., & Kahn, S. Social support in the transition to parenthood. *Journal of Community Psychology 8*: 337–342, 1980.

14

DETECTION OF CONFLICT PATTERNS IN COUPLES*

ANDREW CHRISTENSEN
University of California, Los Angeles

BRET and Rachel don't agree about money. They both work full time and contribute their earnings to a joint account. They each draw freely from this account to pay for joint and individual expenses, but one draws more freely than the other. Rachel wants to save as much as possible so they can purchase a home. While Bret agrees with this long-term goal, he wants to satisfy many immediate desires for items related to his "high-tech" hobbies.

Rachel often proposes that they make up a budget or at least discuss the problem. Bret alternatively resists the suggestion or appeases Rachel with a vague reply, "That might be a good idea." But they never make up a budget or have a calm discussion of the problem. Instead, they argue about the problem, usually after Rachel becomes aware of a recent purchase by Bret. Rachel questions the need and use for the purchase, criticizes Bret for his lack of restraint, and attacks his loyalty to the long-term goal of a home. Bret defends the purchase, himself, and his loyalty, although he occasionally offers the feeble counterattack that Rachel doesn't support him and his interests.

Bret has tried to avoid open confrontation by disguising his purchases. He often hides the purchases from Rachel by paying for them in cash, by giving misleading information about their usefulness in his work and the discounts he obtained, and by sneaking them into the house. Rachel has meanwhile become more suspicious of Bret, often interrogating him about

*I express my gratitude to the following people for providing the data indicated: Jeff Ball and Diana Crampton for the community sample, Megan Sullaway for the medical stress sample, and Gayla Margolin for the anger and violence sample.

his purchases and the large withdrawals from the automatic teller. Occasionally she even examines his home office or the den for evidence of new acquisitions.

To understand and intervene in marital conflicts such as this, we need information on at least three aspects of the conflict: the *topic* of the conflict, the *structure* of the conflict, and the *interaction process* that occurs during the conflict. The topic of the conflict refers to the manifest issue over which there is disagreement, in this case, money. The distinction between structure and interaction process comes from the theoretical work of Kelley (13), who contrasts the interdependence structure of a conflict with the actual interaction between the participants. This distinction is similar to Deutsch's (8) distinction between objective conflict and experienced conflict, and to Peterson's (18) distinction between conflict of interest and open conflict. The structure of a conflict refers to features of the people and situation that occasion the conflict; it represents the predicament that the couple faces. The interaction process refers to the actual behavior of the participants; it represents their efforts to handle the predicament. In Bret and Rachel's conflict about money, structure refers in part to their differing goals for their income. Rachel wants to save a larger portion of it for a home while Bret wants to use a larger portion of it for current interests. Structure also refers to aspects of their financial situation, such as their relatively equal earning power and their equal access to money (their "joint" account). In essence, the structure of a conflict defines the problem that the participants face. In contrast, interaction process refers to how a couple "solves" this problem, that is, how they behave with each other in the face of that problem. In this case, interaction process refers broadly to Rachel's criticism, interrogation, and pressure for a budget, and to Bret's defensiveness, evasiveness, and avoidance.

How can we best assess these three aspects of marital conflict? We can efficiently discover the topics of conflict simply by asking the participants. Relationship satisfaction inventories, such as the Dyadic Adjustment Scale (21), list areas of disagreement that can be checked by spouses. Observational studies of marital conflict often ask couples about conflict areas or have them check off their conflicts from a list of common conflicts. While we could theoretically observe couples over a period of time to discover their topics of disagreement, observation seems clumsy and inefficient compared to simply asking them.

The assessment of the structure of conflict presents similar considerations. Participants can often tell us about the predicament they face in reference to a specific area of disagreement. Some questionnaires, such as the Areas of Change Questionnaire (25), directly ask about the nature of the conflict and the direction of changes each would like in the other, and thus provide relevant information about the structure of the conflict. However, in some cases, participants are unclear as to what their goals are and what a conflict is really about. Observation presents only an indirect means of assessing the structure of conflict. During a conflict discussion, partners usually do not explicitly state what their predicament involves, although it can often be inferred.

The assessment of the interaction process presents a compelling case for observational analysis. Couples are unaware of many of their behaviors during conflict, particularly molecular behaviors. Rachel doesn't realize that the volume and pitch of her voice rises during conflict. Bret doesn't realize that he frowns and looks down frequently during conflict. Couples are probably also unaware of the sequencing of their behavior. Even if Rachel and Bret were aware of their respective behavior changes during conflict, they might not be aware that a change in Rachel's voice is usually followed by Bret's frowning. Furthermore, awareness does not insure accurate reporting. The difficulties in recall and the distortions that mar self-report data in general are likely to operate during marital conflict (23). These problems may be even more intense during an emotionally charged situation such as marital conflict.

Despite these strong arguments for the study of marital conflict through observation, and despite the important advances that have taken place (see 11), observational strategies have inherent limitations because of several features of marital conflict. First, a number of marital couples avoid open discussion of conflict areas. If we conduct home observations and wait for a natural occurrence of conflict discussion, we may have to wait forever. If we, as researchers, ask them to discuss a conflict area, we may precipitate behavior that never occurs naturally. Second, marital conflict often occurs in physical settings not accessible to observers or replicable in the laboratory. People often argue in their bedrooms. They often argue when they are away from their homes, for example, in their cars, while shopping, or while trying to have fun. Third, and perhaps more importantly than physical setting, marital conflict is usually initiated by events that are unlikely to occur under observation or be replicated in the laboratory. In his empirical analysis of marital conflict, Peterson (18) examined detailed records written by husbands and wives about conflictual interactions. He classified the precipitating events for conflicts into four categories: criticism, illegitimate demand, rebuff, and cumulative annoyance. These precipitants for conflict differ dramatically from the typical laboratory instruction to discuss a current conflict. Furthermore, couples are unlikely to engage in behaviors such as illegitimate demand and rebuff when under observation, that is, when and if we attempt to elicit the behaviors in the laboratory or wait for their occurrence in the home. Fourth, the course of marital conflict does not lend itself to observation. Conflicts often do not occur in circumscribed periods or settings. A conflict begun in the morning at the breakfast table may continue in the car on the way to work and be resumed in the evening at bedtime. Furthermore, it may be referred to periodically after that. In work by Margolin and myself (16), which examined daily records of conflict, we found that an occurrence of marital conflict at any point in the day increased the probability of marital conflict later that same day, and at the same time the next day.

Because of these features of marital conflict, observational approaches will never be able to capture the naturalistic phenomenon and, as it were, to "bring it home alive." Certainly, observational approaches have provided revealing and provocative information about marital conflict, but this information must be supplemented by data from the participants themselves.

My students and I have examined broad interaction patterns in couples by asking them to respond to descriptions of typical patterns. We constructed a questionnaire that consists of a series of paragraphs describing a number of hypothetical interaction patterns generated on the basis of the clinical literature, personal clinical experience, and pilot work with couples. In creating these descriptions of interaction sequences, we tried to avoid presenting either participant in a more favorable light, and to avoid gender stereotyping by using "A" or "B" to refer to the participants. For example, an interaction pattern that we have labeled "demand/withdraw" is illustrated below:

> Sometimes A wants more of B's attention and B reacts by withdrawing from A. Possible examples:
>
> 1. A might try to get more contact with B by being unusually affectionate, or outgoing, or demanding. B may react by initiating less contact, by replying with very short answers, or by being preoccupied. A then tries harder to get attention.
> 2. When A asks for more attention, B sometimes feels "crowded." A may feel hurt or confused by B's lack of response.

After each pattern description, respondents indicate how frequently this pattern occurs in their relationship and who plays each of the indicated roles (A or B).

The first study (22) examined interaction patterns in a sample of 50 college student couples in long-term dating relationships. Of the 12 patterns investigated, three were found to correlate significantly with relationship dissatisfaction. The demand/withdraw pattern described above, a relationship versus work-oriented pattern in which partners show unequal attention to the relationship, and an emotional/rational pattern in which one partner emphasizes rational argument while the other emphasizes feelings, occurred more frequently in the dissatisfied relationships.

The second study (7) examined 21 interaction patterns in a community sample of 61 married couples. Fifteen of the patterns were significantly correlated with marital dissatisfaction, including the three from the first study. Five of the patterns were strongly correlated ($r > .50$) with dissatisfaction: (a) the demanding/withdrawing pattern, (b) a critical/hurt pattern in which one partner criticizes the other who responds by feeling hurt, (c) an engaging/avoiding pattern in which one partner tries to discuss relationship difficulties while the other tries to avoid those issues, (d) a role-changer/role-stabilizer pattern in which one partner wants to change marital roles while the other resists, and (e) flirtatious/jealous pattern in which one partner is flirtatious and attention-seeking while the other is jealous and angry.

On the basis of evaluations of this research by reviewers and colleagues, and on the basis of couples' reactions to the questionnaire, Megan Sullaway, my colleague and former student, and I completely revised this instrument. First, we rewrote the pattern descriptions so that they more clearly assessed interaction sequences. In the earlier questionnaire, descriptions of interaction sequences were intermingled with descriptions of desire and intent (for example, "A *wants* more of B's attention" in the example above), which I have called the structure of the conflict. Ideally, items on an interaction questionnaire would focus more purely on interaction process (for example, on the demanding and withdrawing reactions in the example above). Second, we revised the questionnaire to remove the confusing use of A and B. Although we had used these terms to maintain neutrality with respect to the gender of the roles assessed, the couples who completed the questionnaire found this usage confusing. Third, we revised the questionnaire so that one participant was not described as the initiator while the other was described as the reactor (for example, in the pattern description above, "B reacts by withdrawing"). Finally, we revised the questionnaire to specify more clearly the context of these patterns, that is, during periods of disagreement. As an example of our revisions, consider the demand/withdraw item above. Two of the items used to assess this pattern on the revised questionnaire are listed below. The likelihood of each is rated by both partners.

During a discussion of a relationship problem:

1. Husband nags and demands while wife withdraws, becomes silent, or refuses to discuss the matter further.

2. Wife nags and demands while husband withdraws, becomes silent, or refuses to discuss the matter further.

In this chapter, I will present recently collected data on this revised questionnaire. The purposes will be to (a) examine interpartner agreement on interaction patterns, (b) examine the association between conflict structure and interaction patterns, and (c) examine the association between relationship satisfaction and both conflict structure and interaction patterns.

Methods

Subjects

Four samples of married or living-together couples participated in the research. The community sample included 55 couples who were solicited through advertisements and announcements. The medical-stress sample included 32 couples who had at least one pre-teenage, diabetic child and who were solicited through physicians and diabetic organizations. The distressed sample included 24 couples who sought therapy for relationship problems. In addition, there were 31 couples who volunteered for a project comparing couples with anger and violence problems to couples without these problems. These groupings of subjects will not be important for the current investigation; we will examine data across the entire sample of 142 couples.

Couples were primarily young, well-educated, and middle-class. The mean age of the males was 35.6 (SD = 9.4); the mean age of the females was 33.5 (SD = 8.8). Eighty-seven percent of the males and eighty percent of the females had at least some college education. Mean family social status, as measured by the Hollingshead (12) four-factor index of social status, was 50.1 (SD = 10.8). Fifty-four percent of the couples had children while 46 percent were childless.

Assessment Instruments

Dyadic Adjustment Scale

This relationship satisfaction inventory (see 21) is based largely upon the Marital Adjustment Test (15) but, unlike the Marital Adjustment Test, was constructed for the assessment of unmarried as well as married couples, and is scored in a nonsexist fashion.

Relationship Issues Questionnaire

Christensen and Sullaway (6) developed this questionnaire in order to assess desires for intimacy and satisfaction with the power distribution in the relationship. Both theoretical (4, 14) and empirical analyses (26) suggest that intimacy and power are two central dimensions in close relationships. We assumed that different preferences for intimacy level and power-sharing present common yet significant occasions for conflict of interest within couples.

This study focused only on the intimacy questions. We created two subscales measuring, respectively, differences in desired levels of intimacy between partners and the direction of this difference. Thus, the Difference in Desired Intimacy subscale consisted of two items that asked respondents to rate the extent to which their relationship was characterized by different needs for independence and intimacy, while the Independence Versus Intimacy subscale consisted of two items rating female desires for independence/intimacy, which were subtracted from two items rating male desires for independence/intimacy. Thus, positive values indicate that the male wants greater independence while the female wants greater intimacy; negative values indicate the reverse.

Communication Patterns Questionnaire

Christensen and Sullaway (5) developed this questionnaire in order to assess interaction patterns during periods of disagreement. The items are classified under three sequential periods: (a) "When some problem in the relationship arises" (four items ask about discussion or avoidance of the issue), (b) "During a discussion of a relationship problem" (twelve items ask about behaviors such as blaming, negotiating, criticizing, defending, demanding, and withdrawing), and (c) "After a discussion of a relationship problem" (eleven items ask about behaviors such as withholding and reconciliation, and reactions such as guilt and understanding). Some items assess symmetrical patterns ("both members blame, accuse, and criticize each other") while other items assess asymmetrical patterns ("husband criticizes while wife defends herself"). All items are rated on 9-point scales that range from "*un*likely" to "likely."

For purposes of this study, three subscales were created: (a) Mutual Constructive Communication consists of five items assessing mutual discussion of problems, expression of feelings, negotiation of solutions, understanding of views, and resolution of problems; (b) Demand Withdraw Communication consists of six items assessing asymmetrical behaviors in which one partner presses the other to discuss a problem and then criticizes, nags, and makes demands on him or her, while the other tries to avoid discussion of the problem, tries to defend himself or herself, and withdraws, becomes silent, or refuses to discuss the matter further; and (c) Demand Withdraw Roles consists of the same six items as the Demand Withdrawn Communication subscale, but ratings of the male were subtracted from ratings of the female so that positive values indicate female demands while male withdraws, and negative values indicate the reverse.

Demographic Questionnaire

A demographic questionnaire assessed variables such as age, occupation, and number of children. As a measure of differential power, the social status of male and female was separately computed, based on their individual educational and occupational positions (see 12). The female's score was then subtracted from the male's score to create the variable Status Difference.

Procedures

Males and females in each couple completed the questionnaires independently. All participants were asked to answer each item, whether it referred to male's behavior, female's behavior, or their mutual behavior. Couples also participated in a variety of other assessment procedures not relevant to this study.

Results

Reliability

We intended the Relationship Issues Questionnaire and the Communication Patterns Questionnaire to assess not just males' and females' perceptions but also "objective" features of their structure and interaction process. If males and females demonstrate independent agreement in their reports, then we may argue that their assessments provide an objective account. Others could argue that agreement indicates only shared misperceptions and delusions, but we will ascribe greater validity to the couple's shared views. Of course, if couples do not agree within themselves, then we cannot assume an "objective" view.

In our analyses, we will use the mean of male and female responses rather than their individual responses as data because the mean of two raters provides a more reliable estimate than either of their individual ratings. We must therefore assess the reliability of this mean rating rather than the reliability of the male or female individual rating. A Pearson product-moment correlation coefficient would, for example, assess the reliability of the

TABLE 1

Between-Partner Agreement on Structural, Process, and Satisfaction Variables

Variables	Uncorrected Pearson Correlation	Corrected Pearson Correlation[a]	Intraclass Correlation
Structure			
Difference in Desired Intimacy	.47	.64	.64
Intimacy versus Independence[b]	.39	.56	.56
Process			
Mutual Constructive Communication	.69	.82	.80
Demand-Withdraw Communication	.57	.73	.73
Demand-Withdraw Roles[c]	.58	.74	.74
Satisfaction			
Dyadic Adjustment Scale	.75	.86	.85

Note: All values are significantly greater than zero, $p<001$.

[a]Spearman-Brown correction was applied to the raw correlations.

[b]Computed so that positive values indicate male wants greater independence while female wants greater intimacy; negative values indicate the reverse.

[c]Computed so that positive values indicate female demands while male withdraws; negative values indicate the reverse.

individual ratings but underestimate the reliability of the mean rating. However, either the Spearman-Brown correction of the Pearson correlation coefficient (19) or the intraclass correlation coefficient (20) can be used to indicate the reliability of a mean rating.

Our criteria for acceptable levels of agreement between male and female were: (a) statistically significant levels of agreement ($p<.001$) between male and female on individual items, and (b) corrected correlation coefficients or intraclass correlation coefficients of .5 or greater on any subscale. One item on the Independence Versus Intimacy Subscale did not meet the first criterion and was excluded. All subscales met the second criterion, as indicated in Table 1.

Structure, Process, and Satisfaction

Table 2 provides an intercorrelation matrix of the three process variables, the two structural variables, and the mean DAS score. As expected, Difference in Desired Intimacy between partners was negatively and significantly correlated with Mutual Constructive Communication ($r=-.52$, $p<.001$), positively correlated with Demand Withdraw Communication

TABLE 2

Intercorrelation of Structural, Process, and Satisfaction Variables

Variables	1.	2.	3.	4.	5.
Structure					
1. Difference in Desired Intimacy					
2. Intimacy versus Independence[a]	.16				
Process Variables					
3. Mutual Constructive Communication	−.53*	−.02			
4. Demand-Withdraw Communication	.48*	.13	−.59*		
5. Demand-Withdraw Roles[b]	.17	.39*	−.17	.04	
Satisfaction					
6. Dyadic Adjustment Scale	−.56*	−.07	.79*	−.55*	−.12

[a]Computed so that positive values indicate male wants greater independence while female wants greater intimacy; negative values indicate the reverse.

[b]Computed so that positive values indicate female demands while male withdraws; negative values indicate the reverse.

$*p<.001$

($r=.48$, $p<.001$), but uncorrelated with Demand-Withdraw Roles. Thus, when males and females want different levels of intimacy, one is liable to be demanding while the other is withdrawing, and their constructive communication is negatively affected. The difference in level of intimacy desired does not, of course, predict what roles each will play in the interaction. However, the structural variable of Intimacy Versus Independence does predict Demand-Withdraw Roles ($r=.39$, $p<.001$). When the female wants a closer relationship while the male wants more independence, the female more likely will be demanding while the male more likely will be withdrawing, and vice versa.

Difference in Desired Intimacy, but not Intimacy Versus Independence, was negatively correlated with the Dyadic Adjustment Scale ($r=-.55$, $p<.001$, and $r=-.07$, n.s., respectively). Thus, a difference in what the male and female want from the relationship bodes poorly for relationship satisfaction, but the specific direction of this difference is irrelevant to their satisfaction.

The process variables of Mutual Constructive Communication with Demand-Withdraw Communication were, as expected, correlated with the Dyadic Adjustment Scale, the former positively ($r=.79$, $p<.001$), the latter negatively ($r=-.55$, $p<.001$). These two variables were also correlated with each other ($r=-.58$, $p<.001$). Demand-Withdraw Roles was uncorrelated with each of the other two process variables.

Power and Gender

The structural variable of Intimacy Versus Independence and the process variable of Demand-Withdraw Roles were both created by taking the difference between male and female scores. One might hypothesize an effect of gender and power on these scores. As expected, the mean of Intimacy Versus Independence (mean $= .849$, $t = 3.77$, $p < .001$) was significantly greater than zero, indicating that men generally wanted greater independence while women generally wanted greater intimacy. Likewise, the mean for Demand-Withdraw Roles (mean $= 2.377$, $t = 4.37$, $p < .001$) was significantly greater than zero, indicating that women were more likely to demand while men were more likely to withdraw. The power variable of Status Difference was not significantly correlated with either variable.

Discussion

A number of clinical theorists have identified a dysfunctional pattern of interaction similar to what we have called a "demand-withdraw" pattern. Watzlawick, Beavin, and Jackson (24) described a nag-withdraw pattern of interaction; Fogarty (10) described an interaction sequence in which one partner is a "pursuer" and the other a "distancer"; Napier (17) described the "rejection-intrusion pattern," in which one partner clasps and clings to a retreating mate; Wile (27) argued that the "demanding-withdrawn" polarization is one of the three major troubled patterns of couple interaction. While each of these descriptions is unique, they all point to a pattern in which one member pressures the other, who pulls back.

This study has demonstrated that (a) interaction sequences like the "demand-withdraw" pattern can be assessed through questionnaire measures with moderate reliability; (b) these interaction sequences may be strongly related to relationship satisfaction; and (c) they may be associated with structural features of the relationship. Specifically, the data reveal a strong connection between the "demand-withdraw" pattern and relationship satisfaction and a strong connection between the "demand-withdraw" pattern and a structural asymmetry in the level of intimacy and independence desired in the relationship. Furthermore, the nature of the structural asymmetry (who wants independence and who wants more closeness) predicts the roles in the interaction sequence (who demands and who withdraws).

Early psychoanalytic views of marital discord implicated individual psychopathology in marital partners as the causative factor. While acknowledging that individual psychopathology may create marital discord, contemporary theory suggests that marital discord may develop without any psychopathology in either husband or wife. For example, DSM-III (1) defines a condition of "marital problem" when there is marital discord not due to a mental disorder.

If psychopathology is not creating discord, then what is? Social learning theory argues that skill deficits account for relationship distress (see 3). Partners may lack, for example, the communication skills to discuss and resolve their differences. This approach stands in marked contrast to the commonsense view that incompatible differences account for marital discord. This commonsense view, which is present in legal thinking (for example, irreconcilable differences as grounds for divorce), implicates neither sickness nor deficits in the marital partners, but simply describes them as being too different to get along. Each of these two views is limited. The social learning view ignores the mate selection process and any differences between mates other than their skill level. On the other hand, the incompatibility model ignores the developmental history of the relationship: that the members of the couple chose one another, that they did so out of love, and that they spent some period, often years, being satisfied with each other. How did incompatibility develop from such auspicious beginnings?

Skill deficits and incompatibility are probably both involved, interactively, in marital discord. The greater the differences between partners, the more difficulty they will have communicating constructively. The poorer the communication between partners, the greater the likelihood that their differences will become accentuated (through lack of understanding and polarization of positions). In contrast, the fewer the differences between partners, the greater the chances are for constructive communication. The greater the constructive communication, the higher the likelihood that partners will understand and compromise their differences. The present data are consistent with these speculations. Couples who had Differences in Desired Intimacy were more likely to show Demand-Withdraw Communication but less likely to show Mutual Constructive Communication. Likewise, couples who engaged in Mutual Constructive Communication were less likely to have Differences on Desired Intimacy, whereas couples who engaged in Demand-Withdraw Communication were more likely to have Differences on Desired Intimacy.

The findings from this study must, of course, be qualified because they are correlational results. For example, I would like to argue that the "demand-withdraw" pattern occurs, in part, when partners have different needs and preferences for intimacy and independence and when they have insufficient skills to negotiate these differences. I would also argue that these different needs and preferences result, in part, from socialization experiences that are gender-related. However, one could argue from the data that both the "demand-withdraw" pattern and the relationship structure are dictated by gender differences. Women want more intimacy and press for that interactionally; men want greater independence and withdraw from the relationship to achieve it. Perhaps the use of causal modeling in a larger data set will illuminate these connections.

We achieved higher levels of interpartner agreement in this study than in previous studies (7, 23). Probably our greater success resulted from the revision of the questionnaire, which clarified several items and removed the confusing use of A and B to designate partners (see above), and from our combining items into subscales. Reliability usually increases with a larger number of raters and a larger number of items. However, the levels of agreement are still below that usually required in observational research. Given the extensive data documenting poor agreement between partners, even when reporting on objective events in the recent past (see 22), I doubt that these levels can be improved a great deal. Currently, one of my students and I are attempting to improve reliability on these questionnaires by an exercise that focuses the couple on their interactions prior to completing the measures. However, the improvement, if any, is liable to be modest. We may have to accept a moderate level of agreement and realize that, as a result, weak effects may escape our detection. However, we can reassure ourselves that, unless a systematic bias is discovered, the effects we do discover with these measures will be robust.

Of what relevance is this research to the topic of this book: family research and psychopathology? I have talked much about marital conflict but little about psychopathology. However, the quality of the marital relationship is directly related to the emotional well-being and psychopathological status of the participants in that relationship (see 2). Undoubtedly, the causal effects are reciprocal. Marital stress affects emotional well-being and vice versa. Second, the quality of the marital relationship directly affects the emotional well-being of the offspring of that marriage (see 9). Parents affect more than each other by the quality of their interaction; children are the unfortunate victims of marital conflict. Thus, any contribution to our understanding of marital conflict also contributes to our understanding of individual emotional disorder.

Furthermore, I plan to extend this methodology to the analysis of family interaction patterns. Parents and children could respond to descriptions of common family interaction sequences in the same way that couples have in this research. For example, items might describe alliance patterns in which one child is more closely attached to one parent than the other, control patterns in which one parent regularly dispenses punishment while the other indulges the children, or communication patterns in which one parent communicates to the children through the other parent. Certainly, there would be limits on what kind of patterns could be assessed. It is doubtful, for example, that communication deviance could ever be assessed by questionnaires. Furthermore, assessment of family interaction patterns presents greater complexity because of the additional person or persons involved. Intrafamilial agreement may be even harder to achieve. But my guess is that an extension of this methodology to family interaction would be worth the effort. We might be able to tap interaction sequences that contribute to individual psychopathology in the participants.

In addition, I would like to develop a structured interview for the assessment of interaction patterns. The convenience of questionnaires is seductive; but the flexibility of an interview, even when structured, may be more informative. My ideas for this kind of interview are still in the formative stages. However, I envision a series of questions, centered around areas of disagreement between the couple or within the family, that would investigate the process of conflict resolution from awareness of disagreement to its resolution.

I am often struck with how little research exists on the instrument that clinicians use most often—the interview. When couples or families come to me for treatment, I assess the structure and process of their conflicts through a clinical interview. While I also observe their interaction and have them complete questionnaires, I generally put more weight on the clinical interview. I would venture that most marital and family therapists do likewise. Yet we have no systematic procedures for interviewing couples and families.

My argument for the interview is not based simply on its prevalence; common usage does not validate an assessment instrument. Rather, I see no alternative than to ask participants about their interaction. As I discussed in the introduction, family conflict (particularly marital conflict) does not lend itself easily to naturalistic observation; it too often occurs out of our reach, either practically or ethically. After years of looking for, and detecting natural occurrences of family interaction, I concluded that observation, even naturalistic observation, could provide only one part of the picture. We must *ask* participants about their interaction in order to get a complete description. In the investigation of marital and family conflict, the star witnesses must be family members. They were present at the scene of every conflict.

REFERENCES

1. American Psychiatric Association. *Diagnostic and statistical manual of mental disorders* (3rd ed.). Washington, DC: American Psychiatric Association, 1980.

2. Bloom, B. L., Asher, S. J., & White, S. W. Marital disruption as a stressor: A review and analysis. *Psychological Bulletin 85*: 867–894, 1978.

3. Christensen, A. Intervention. In H. H. Kelley, E. Berscheid, A. Christensen, J. H. Harvey, T. L. Huston, G. Levinger, E. McClintock, L. A. Peplau, & D. R. Peterson, *Close relationships*. New York: W. H. Freeman, 1983.

4. ______, & Arrington, A. Research issues and strategies. In T. Jacob (ed.), *Family interaction and psychopathology: Theories, methods, and findings*. New York: Plenum Press, 1987.

5. ______, & Sullaway, M. Communication patterns questionnaire, unpublished, 1984. (Available from A. Christensen, Department of Psychology, University of California, Los Angeles CA 90024.)

6. ______, & Sullaway, M. Relationship issues questionnaire, unpublished, 1984. (Available from A. Christensen, Department of Psychology, University of California, Los Angeles, CA 90024.)

7. ______, & Sullaway, M., & King C. Dysfunctional interaction patterns and marital satisfaction, submitted for publication.

8. Deutsch, M. *The resolution of conflict*. New Haven: Yale University Press, 1973.

9. Emery, R. E. Marital turmoil: Interpersonal conflict and the children of discord and divorce. *Psychological Bulletin 92*: 310–330, 1982.

10. Fogarty, T. F. Marital crisis. In P. J. Guerin (ed.), *Family therapy: Theory and practice*. New York: Gardner Press, 1976.

11. Gottman, J. M. *Marital interaction: Experimental investigations*. New York: Academic Press, 1979.

12. Hollingshead, A. B. *Four-factor index of social status*. Privately published, 1975. (Available from author, Department of Sociology, Yale University, 1965 Yale Station, New Haven CT 06520.)

13. Kelley, H. H. *Personal relationships: Their structure and processes*. Hillsdale NJ: Lawrence Erlbaum, 1979.

14. ______, Berscheid, E., Christensen, A., Harvey, J. H., Huston, T. L., Levinger, G., McClintock, E., Peplau, L. A., & Peterson, D. R. *Close relationships*. New York: W. H. Freeman, 1983.

15. Locke, H. J., & Wallace, K. M. Short marital adjustment and prediction tests: Their reliability and validity. *Marriage and Family Living 12*: 251–255, 1959.

16. Margolin, G., & Christensen, A. Everyday conflict in distressed and nondistressed families, submitted for publication.

17. Napier, A. Y. The rejection-intrusion pattern: A central family dynamic. *Journal of Marriage and Family Counseling 4*: 5–12, 1978.

18. Peterson, D. R. Conflict. In H. H. Kelley, E. Berscheid, A. Christensen, J. H. Harvey, T. L. Huston, G. Levinger, E. McClintock, L. A. Peplau, & D. R. Peterson. *Close relationships*. New York: W. H. Freeman, 1983.

19. Prinz, R., & Kent, R. Recording parent-adolescent interactions without the use of frequency or interval-by-interval coding. *Behavior Therapy 9*: 602–604, 1978.

20. Shrout, P. E., & Fleiss, J. L. Intraclass correlations: Uses in assessing rater reliability. *Psychological Bulletin 86*: 420–428, 1979.

21. Spanier, G. B. Measuring dyadic adjustment: New scales for assessing the quality of marriage and similar dyads. *Journal of Marriage and the Family 38*: 15–28, 1976.

22. Sullaway, M., & Christensen, A. Assessment of dysfunctional interaction patterns in couples. *Journal of Marriage and the Family 45*: 653–660, 1983.

23. ______, & Christensen, A. Couples and families as participant observers of their interactions. In J. Vincent (ed.), *Advances in family interaction, assessment, and theory* (Vol. 3). Greenwich CT: JAI, 1983.

24. Watzlawick, P., Beavin, J. H., & Jackson, D. D. *The pragmatics of human communication: A study of interactional patterns, pathologies, and paradoxes*. New York: W. W. Norton, 1967.

25. Weiss, R. L., & Birchler, G. R. Areas of change, unpublished questionnaire, 1975. (Available from R. L. Weiss, Department of Psychology, University of Oregon, Eugene OR 97403.)

26. Wiggins, J. S. Circumplex models of interpersonal behavior in clinical psychology. In P. C. Kendell & J. N. Butcher (eds.), *Handbook of research methods in clinical psychology*. New York: John Wiley & Sons, 1982.

27. Wile, D. B. *Couples therapy: A nontraditional approach*. New York: John Wiley & Sons, 1981.

15

THE PREDICTION AND PREVENTION OF MARITAL DISTRESS: A Longitudinal Investigation

HOWARD J. MARKMAN, S. WAYNE DUNCAN, RAGNAR D. STORAASLI, PAUL W. HOWES
Center for Marital and Family Studies
University of Denver, Colorado

FIGURES from the United States government indicate that although the divorce rate has steadily fallen since its peak in 1980, approximately four out of ten first marriages still end in divorce (42). These rates translate into over one million divorces each year and directly involve an estimated one million children each year (8, 16). Despite the severe negative consequences of divorce and the marital conflict that both precedes and follows it (7, 13, 23), there is virtually no longitudinal research that sheds light on the causes of marital distress, nor are there well-evaluated programs to prevent the development of marital problems, as compared to treating problems after they occur (20, 36). The current research program, by combining a longitudinal study of couples with a long-term evaluation of a prevention program, was designed to begin providing both theoretical and practical information on this important problem.

Do Communication Problems Cause Marital Distress?

There has been an increasing number of cross-sectional investigations comparing the problem-solving interaction of distressed and nondistressed couples, the results of which have supported a cognitive-behavioral model of marriage (see 4, 17, 18, 26). These studies have demonstrated that distressed compared to nondistressed couples use more negative verbal and nonverbal communication (as rated by themselves or observers) and report more problems and less satisfaction with their marriages. However, because these studies are cross-sectional in nature, they allow inferences only about concomitants rather than determinants of marital distress. Our research during the last ten years has been designed to test longitudinally the hypothesis that dysfunctional communication precedes and may cause marital problems.

Our first investigation indicated the importance of early interaction patterns for later relationship satisfaction. Specifically, the more positively couples rated each other's interactions before marriage, the more satisfied they were $2^{1}/_{2}$ and 5 years later (30, 31). These findings have been recently replicated using different measures of interaction (25). While these results were important and supported cognitive/behavioral theories of marital distress, we perceived the need to replicate and extend the study using observer-based as well as self-report measures of communication with a larger, more heterogeneous sample. These were the primary objectives of the current investigation.

How is Spouse Mental Health Related to Marital Distress?

Although this chapter focuses primarily on the results of the interactional analyses we have made, we are also beginning to examine the contribution of various personality factors to later relationship satisfaction and outcome. Earlier work has examined, for instance, the contribution of maternal personality and attitudes toward child care on the *mother's* subsequent mental health, (see 9), but only recently have investigators begun to explore the role of personality characteristics in couples' adjustment to a significant life transition, such as the transition to parenthood (see 2, 21). With our research, we are now able to begin tracing longitudinally the impact of individual personality organization and functioning on marital interaction, which provides important data for identification of proximal and distal contributors to marital distress. Of particular interest is the role of the spouse's level of psychological adjustment in predicting future marital satisfaction. Many investigations have demonstrated a covariation between spouse functioning and marital quality (13). This is summarized by the statement that happy people tend to have happy marriages and that happy marriages tend to produce happy people (60). However, few longitudinal data are available to address the question of which comes first. The current investigation provides the opportunity for us to shed some light on this important question.

Can We Prevent Marital Distress?

The results from our previous research provide the link between longitudinal research and preventive intervention with couples. These findings indicate that unrewarding interaction patterns *preceded* the development of relationship dissatisfaction and that early signs of impending distress were potentially recognizable in premarital interaction, *independent* of the couple's premarital relationship satisfaction and problems (31, 32). Both clinical and research experience suggest that once dysfunctional interaction patterns form, they are hard to modify (41, 43, 52, 54). The fact that communication deficits may be apparent *before* marriage suggests that couples might benefit from training early in their relationship in skills traditionally taught in many forms of marital therapy as a preventive strategy, rather than waiting until severe marital conflict develops. It is thought that the points in a couple's relationship when they are most amenable to intervention are transition periods. During such times, the couple encounters new situations and role demands for which they may be unprepared, which makes them more amenable to interventions that help them to cope with changes (6). For marital problems, the logical time for intervention is before the couple is married, that is, during the transition to marriage.

In this longitudinal study, couples were randomly assigned to a preventive intervetion program, Premarital Relationships Enhancement Program (PREP) or to a control group. The prevention program was designed to improve communication and problem-solving skills because deficits in these areas have been linked to future marital problems. Thus, another major objective of our research was to conduct a well-controlled, *long-term* evaluation of an empirically based premarital prevention program that we had developed previously (34, 39, 40).

To summarize, the goal of this chapter is to provide a general overview of our work described in greater detail in various other articles now in preparation. In the first section of this chapter, we briefly review the rationale underlying the research program on the prediction and prevention of marital distress. Then we provide an overview of the research design, followed by a presentation and discussion of our findings four years into the project. Finally, we consider future directions of our research and the implications of our findings for future work in marital communication, marital distress, and mental health.

Method

Subjects

The subjects were 135 couples planning marriage for the first time, one group (n = 73) recruited during the first year of the project (Year1) and one group (n = 62) recruited during the second year (Year 2). Because there were no major differences between the two groups of couples in demographic characteristics and patterns of results, groups are combined in this study unless otherwise noted. The average age of the subjects when they entered the study was 23.3 for females and 24.1 for males; 65% were formally engaged. Couples were predominantly white and middle-class. They had know one another for an average of 2½ years, and 41% were living together.

Procedures

Couples were recruited through community-wide publicity (for example, newspaper stories, radio announcements) that requested couples who were planning marriage to participate in a study on relationship development. Couples were required to be planning marriage (although they did not have to be formally engaged), and it had to be the first marriage for both partners. They were informed that participation required completing, at the minimum, three two-hour sessions over a period of 8 to 10 weeks, for which they would be paid $25. At this time, couples were not informed about the possibility of participating in an intervention program. The rationale for the recruitment strategy was to obtain a no-intervention control group necessary to evaluate the long-term, preventive effects of the program. Couples who specifically requested intervention were referred to a treatment agency and were not included in the study. There were five procedural phases to the first stage of the present project: Pre-assessment, Intervention, Post-assessment, 1½-year Follow-up (Follow-up 1), and 3-year follow-up (Follow-up 2).

Pre-assessment

In the pre-assessment phase, couples participated in two laboratory sessions during which they were interviewed, completed a battery of questionnaires, and then completed two interaction tasks under two conditions. The order of the tasks and conditions was randomized. The two tasks were: (a) discussion of vignettes from the Inventory of Marital Conflicts (IMC) (47) and (b) discussion of their most important relationship issues (19). In one condition, described below, couples used the "communication box" to make ratings (38). In the other condition, the couples talked without using this procedure. At the end of the second pre-assessment sesssion, the couples assigned to the intervention group were invited to participate in a premarital, preventive intervention program. Couples who declined were scheduled for the post-assessment session. Couples included in the control group were not informed about the intervention program and were scheduled for the post-assessment sesssion. During the time the experimental group participated in the intervention, the control group received no contact.

The program was offered to 86 couples; 33 (39%) completed the program, 43 (51%) declined the program, and 9 (11%) partially completed the program. The major reason couples stated for declining the program was the lack of time. In fact, over 85% of the decliners initially accepted the program and then claimed that they were too busy.

Intervention Program

The goal of our intervention program (PREP) is to modify or enhance dimensions of the couple's relationships (for example, communication and problem-solving skills) that have been linked to effective marital functioning by research and theory. In contrast to couple's therapy, the PREP program is future-oriented and does not directly focus on current problems. The program involves five meetings that lasted approximately 3 hours each. A trained consultant works with each couple throughout the program. Each session is devoted to one or two major content areas: Session 1 – Communication Skill Training I; Session 2 – Communication Skill Training II; Session 3 – Behavior Change; Session 4 – Examining Expectations; Session 5 – Relationship and Sexual-Sensual Enhancement.

Post-Assessment and Follow-Ups

Approximately eight weeks after the pre-assessment phase, all couples participated in a post-assessment session. In this session couples again completed the questionnaires included in the pre-assessment battery and engaged in another series of problem-solving interactions during which they evaluated the positivity of their interactions using the communication box. Approximately 1½ years later, couples participated in the first follow-up session. This session was similar to the post-assessment session. Finally, approximately 1½ years after Follow-up 1, couples participated in the second follow-up session, which was similar to the previous ones.

The inventories completed independently by both partners at each procedural phase included the following: premarital or marital forms of a Relationship Satisfaction Test (29, 30), Sexual Dissatisfaction Scale (60), Relationship Problem Inventory (27), and Rubin's Love Scale (56). The Symptom Check List, Revised (SCL-90) (11) was completed at the pre- and follow-up 2 assessment. This measure reflects psychological adjustment along nine primary symptom dimensions and provides an index of overall psychological adjustment.

Three communication measures reported in this chapter of the couple's interaction were used throughout the study; however, only two are considered in the current chapter:[1] (a) the communication box (38), used to obtain couples' self-ratings of the pleasingness of their partner's statements; and (b) the Communication Skill Test (14), an economical behavioral observation system developed specifically to evaluate changes in communication skill usage. The coding unit is a speech unit, and each receives a rating on a scale ranging from 1 to 5, from deficits to skills, and representing the degree to which the subject uses such behaviors.

Results and Discussion

We begin by *briefly* presenting the findings on relationship status, problem areas, and sex and time differences. We then present the results addressed to the question of predicting future relationship functioning. Finally, we present the data on the short- and long-term effects of the PREP program.

Relationship Status

At 1½-year follow-up, 20% of the couples were still planning marriage, 63% were married, 17% had broken up before marriage, and .06% (one couple) were divorced. The attrition rate was less than 5%. The vast majority (85%) of the couples were planning to have at least one child, and 81% were planning to have children within the next 5 years. At 3-year follow-up, 7% of the couples were still planning marriage, 65% were married, 19% had broken up before marriage and 2% were separated or divorced. The attrition rate was 7%.

[1]The third is the Couples Interaction Scoring System (CISS) (17,18,44), revised for the purposes of the present study.

Time and Sex Differences

Significant time and sex differences emerged on the relationship satisfaction and problem intensity variables. Relationship satisfaction declined significantly over time: Time 1 = 125.4, Time 2 = 124.9, Time 3 = 122.0, Time 4 = 115.1 ($F = 9.48$, $p < .001$). Problem intensity decreased from times 1 to 3 and then increased from Time 3 to 4: Time 1 = 186.9, Time 2 = 161.3, Time 3 = 157.0, Time 4 = 209.7 ($F = 4.17$, $p < .05$). Females, as compared to males, had higher relationship satisfaction scores over time: female mean = 123.1, male mean = 120.6 ($F = 3.53$, $p < .10$); females also had significantly lower problem intensity scores over time: female mean = 170.0, male mean = 187.3 ($F = 4.17$, $p < .05$).

Prediction of Relationship Functioning

This section examines the extent to which couples' Time 1 (pre-assessment) communication patterns are related to future relationship functioning. To test the hypothesis that higher levels of communication ratings would be positively related to future relationship quality, we first defined the construct of relationship quality as consisting of the combination of the relationship satisfaction and problem intensity measures. We then entered, as predictor variables, communication box ratings, relationship satisfaction, problem intensity, love scores, and individual functioning (measured by the SCL-90) from Time 1 into a series of canonical correlations. Time 3 and 4 relationship satisfaction and problem intensity were entered as the outcome variables. Table 1 presents the results separately for PREP, control, and decline groups, as well as for all groups combined.

The first major finding is that, taken together, the predictor variables account for approximately 45% of the variance in Time 3, and 34% in Time 4 relationship quality (ranging from 39–65% for each group). These findings are among the highest reported in the literature (17) and are consistent with previous findings that assessment of relationship variables such as communication and conflict provide the best predictors of marital distress (25, 30, 31).

The second major finding is that the results of the first three years of the project have only partially replicated our earlier studies' findings (30, 31). The multiple correlations for all couples satisfaction and problem intensity are presented in Table 1. The results indicated a weak to moderate relationship that declines over time. The findings were in contrast to our earlier research that found communication ratings to be an increasingly strong predictor of future relationship satisfaction. We then examined the correlations for each group separately. As seen in Table 1, the expected

TABLE 1

Squared Canonical Correlations (Percent Variance Accounted for) between Time 1 and Time 3 and 4 Measures

	Relationship Quality			
	Time 3		Time 4	
	Self[b]	Couple[c]	Self[b]	Couple[c]
All Groups				
All predictors	.47	.45	.34	.34
Communication box	.14	.13	.07	.07
Relationship satisfaction	.41	.39	.28	.26
Problem intensity	.32	.31	.20	.20
Love	.10	.06	.04	.06
SCL90	.08	.08	.16	.15
PREP				
All predictors	.48	.51	.42	.48
Communication box	.34	.30	.24	.31
Relationship satisfaction	.27	.33	.24	.29
Problem intensity	.31	.39	.16	.22
Love	.12	.09	.03	.03
SCL90	.06	.08	.21	.21
Control				
All predictors	.56	.51	.39	.43
Communication box	.19	.19	.11	.06
Relationship satisfaction	.54	.50	.33	.40
Problem intensity	.34	.29	.21	.17
Love	.15	.08	.08	.17
SCL90	.20	.22	.20	.15
Decline				
All predictors	.45	.41	.65	.53
Communication box	.07	.11	.17[a]	.17[a]
Relationship satisfaction	.25	.16	.47	.38
Problem intensity	.35	.31	.12	.14
Love	.04	.01	.02	.02
SCL90	.05	.00	.04	.02

[a]Communication box is in opposite direction as compared to other groups.

[b]Correlations are between each individual's scores on the predictor variables and each *individual's* scores on the outcome measures.

[c]Correlations are between each individual's scores on the predictor variables and the *couples'* scores on the outcome measures.

relationship between communication ratings and later relationship quality emerged for the PREP group ($R^2 = .34$, .24 for years 3 and 4, respectively) and to a lesser extent for the control group ($R^2 = .19$, .11, for years 3 and 4, respectively). In contrast, the decline group showed the opposite pattern, with higher levels of communication ratings associated with *lower* levels of future relationship functioning ($R^2 = .07$, .17, for years 3 and 4, respectively).

How can we understand the differences in the pattern of correlations for the decline as compared to the PREP and control groups? We began by assuming that the correlational differences were related to the reason the couples declined the PREP program. Analysis of Time 1 data on relationship satisfaction, feeling of love, and so on, revealed that decline males held much more positive views of the relationship compared to PREP and control males. There were no such differences for females. Floyd and Markman (14) found that distressed husbands rated their wives' communication significantly more positively than did observers' ratings. It was as if the husbands were screening out their wives' negativity, likely leading to increased negativity from the wife and increased distancing and withdrawal from the relationship by the husband.

If the decline males' high scores represent positive perceptual bias and/or relationship withdrawal, then we can speculate that they would not make a commitment to work on their relationship by accepting the intervention program. Consequently, the assessment of the decline males' reaction to their partners' communication may not provide a valid index of the nature and quality of their relationship. (Correlations between communication box ratings and relationship quality for the decline group males were essentially zero.) In contrast, the PREP couples who chose to participate in the intervention program emphasizing communication skills are more likely to view communication as central to their relationship. As a result, communication measures for these couples should provide a more valid "window" on their perceptions of the nature and quality of their relationship. In fact, the communication box ratings for PREP couples were the most highly correlated of all the groups with their subsequent relationship satisfaction ratings. However, our interpretations are speculative, and additional analyses will be conducted to address the hypotheses we have generated.

The results for the PREP and control couples are generally consistent with the hypothesis that the quality of the couples' premarital interaction is etiologically related to future satisfaction. These findings add to the growing body of literature linking quality of communication to future marital functioning. The results also indicate that other factors (for example, conflict and initial adjustment) account for considerable variance in future levels of relationship quality. However, at least for some couples, communication quality becomes more important relative to other factors over time. This explanation assumes that the patterns of interaction identified at Time 1 remained relatively constant throughout the study. While there is some evidence suggesting that couples' communication styles are constant over time (52), this question will be examined with multiple measures of communication in the current logitudinal study.

A competing explanation of the preliminary results is that the quality of the interaction is not the primary determinant of marital distress, but provides a global summary of other factors that influence relationships. While we examine below the effects on relationship quality of one noninteractional characteristic (individual adjustment), we will be examining others as our research continues (for example, social support, stress, and commitment). There is growing evidence, though, that the quality of the couple's interaction is the most proximal cause of marital distress (46).

Despite the promising findings, there are two important limitations that will be addressed as the project continues. First, couples in the study are still in the early stages of marriage and hence still generally happy. The findings need to be generalized to more severely distressed couples and those who go on to become divorced. Second, careful observation of communication patterns was made in the present study, and we have not yet conducted sequential analyses of the interaction sequences related to outcome. Our previous research has indicated that distressed couples get stuck in "cross-complaining loops" while nondistressed couples are able to get out of such negative cycles (45). Therefore, a major future objective is to identify the specific interaction patterns that are associated with the erosion of satisfaction.

Correlates of Psychological Adjustment

While there is growing evidence that relationship variables such as couple communication and conflict are better overall predictors of future marital distress, there is also support in the literature that individual psychological adjustment is predictive of future relationship functioning. In fact, our analyses of Time 1 data revealed that scores on the SCL-90 accounted for approximately 20% of the variance in relationship quality 3 years later at the Time 4 assessment. Thus, some support is provided for the hypothesis that individual psychological adjustment affects future relationship functioning. As the project continues, we will be examining different causal links between relationship and individual variables and marital quality. Some of our preliminary results have already shed additional light on the relationship between these variables.

For example, when zero-order correlations for Time 1 SCL-90 and Time 4 Locke-Wallace scores are examined separately for males and females (regardless of group), different patterns emerged than when gender was combined. For males, the higher the Time 1 SCL-90, the lower the Time 4 relationship satisfaction ($r = -.44$, $p < .05$); however, for females this relationship is nonsignificant. Cross-sectional correlations at Time 4 also show a stronger relationship between these variables for males than for females. These results support a hypothesis that it is the male's, rather than the female's psychological stability that has the greater impact on relationship satisfaction. This finding suggests that clinicians and researchers may need to give special consideration to the male's level of psychological adjustment in developing and implementing premarital prevention programs.

When the SCL-90 subscales are examined separately for males and females, the same patterns emerge. Overall, there is stronger negative relationship for males' Time 1 subscale scores and Time 4 marital satisfaction. The one exception is depression, which shows a moderate and significant negative relationship with concurrent and future relationship satisfaction for both males and females ($r = .35$). That female depression, as opposed to other subscales, shows a strong relationship to marital satisfaction is consistent with frequently reported findings that depression is more common among married women (51). However, our data are inconsistent with the position that marriage serves as a protective factor against depression in men. In fact, depression in males is more strongly related with relationship satisfaction than any other SCL-90 subscale. Space does not permit speculation on the many possible reasons that could account for these findings. Indeed, any conclusions must be tempered until the data are further analyzed. Our preliminary results suggest, however, that with the exception of depression, relationship satisfaction appears to be more reactive to males' as compared to females' level of psychological adjustment.

We have also examined the impact of Time 1 relationship satisfaction on future individual adjustment in order to begin addressing the question of whether individual psychological problems are antecedent or consequent to relationship problems. Correlations between Time 1 Locke-Wallace scores and Time 4 SCL-90 future individual adjustment begin to address the question of whether scores indicate that higher levels of relationship satisfaction are predictive of lower levels of psychological problems and depression in particular. This relationship appears to be stronger for males ($r = .35$, $p < .001$) than for females. Thus, our findings indicate that premarital relationship satisfaction is related to future individual adjustment and premarital individual adjustment is related to future marital satisfaction. While this appears to be particularly true for males, sex differences emerge when premarital individual adjustment is compared with problem intensity ratings.

Correlations between Time 1 problem inventory and Time 4 SCL-90 scores indicate a moderate association between premarital problems and overall future psychological adjustment. However, in contrast to findings with the Locke-Wallace, this relationship is stronger for females ($r = .47$, $p < .001$) than for males ($r = .24$, $p < .01$). In general, females tended to show stronger positive correlations between Time 1 problem intensity ratings and specific SCL-90 subscales than did males. The strongest relationships were found on the depression, hostility, and psychoticism subscales. These results are consistent with findings of Weissman and Paykel (62) who found that interpersonal alienation and hostility typified the relationships of depressed women. In addition, they support well-documented findings that women are more likely to report relationship difficulties (in this case, premarital problems) prior to depression (48). In any event, while relationship satisfaction appears more predictive of males' future psychological adjustment, level of premarital problems seem to be a better predictor for females. Thus, having a good premarital relationship appears to serve as a protective factor against future psychological problems in general, and depression in particular.

Finally, we have looked at correlations between communication box ratings and SCL-90 scores in order to assess the relationship between couples' communication and individual adjustment. No longitudinal relationship between these variables was found. Cross-sectional correlations at Time 4 revealed no significant correlations for females, but there was a moderate relationship between more positive ratings of communication and higher psychological adjustment for males. These results suggest that, for males, communication may be the mechanism or "transmission medium" that connects marital distress with some forms of personal maladjustment.

The causal links between relationship quality, communication, and psychological adjustment are obviously complex. Our data suggest that the quality of the premarital relationship impacts future individual adjustment and that premarital individual adjustment affects future relationship quality. As sequential analysis data become available in the near future, we will be able to examine more fully various etiological models relating communication and relationship variables to certain types of psychological problems, and vice versa. An examination of correlations between communication box ratings and SCL-90 scores separately for PREP, control, and decline groups are suggestive of the importance of couples' communication interaction in predicting later psychological problems. For PREP, correlations between Time 1 communication box ratings and SCL-90 scores are positive or essentially zero. In contrast, the pattern for the control and decline groups reveals consistent weak to moderate negative correlations between communication box ratings and SCL-90 scores. Thus, the PREP couples may be benefiting from better communication and problem-solving skills and are thus less likely to experience significant future maladjustment, while control and decline couples, without the benefit of the PREP skills training program, are more likely to experience individual mental health problems related to these skill deficits.

Evaluation of the Premarital Relationship Enhancement Problem (PREP)

Relationship Stability

The relationship status of each group of couples (PREP, control, decline, incomplete) was evaluated at each follow-up point. At Follow-up 1 only one PREP couple (3%) had dissolved their relationship, while 16% of the control group, 21% of the decline group, and 66% of the incomplete group had done so. A chi-square test with Yates' correction indicated that the dissolution rate for PREP couples was significantly lower when compared to the rate of the other three groups combined (χ^2 [1] = 5.2, $p < .05$. At Follow-up 2, 9% of the PREP group, 22% of the control group, 23% of the decline group, and 66% of the incomplete group had dissolved their relationship. A chi-square test in the Yates' correction indicated that there was a trend for the dissolution rate of PREP couples to be lower than the other 3 groups combined ($\chi^2 = 3.44$, $p < .10$).

These findings indicate that PREP couples are more stable than the other three groups. It is not clear if one of the effects of PREP is increased stability or if factors that were related to the couple accepting and completing PREP were also related to increased stability. If PREP did in fact contribute to increased stability, the mechanism of this effect is still unknown. For example, does the improved relationship satisfaction experienced by PREP couples lead to increased stability, or does the program lead to increased commitment to the relationship, which in turn leads to increased stability?

The very high rate of breakup *before* marriage of couples who started but did not complete the PREP program also deserves comment. One possible explanation is that these couples may have been more distressed than the PREP group and their participation may have been viewed as a last resort to save a failing relationship. The Time 1 relationship satisfaction data, which indicate that the incomplete group had lower levels of relationship satisfaction than the other groups, lends support to this hypothesis. The program may have helped the couples clarify their feelings about the relationship and thereby facilitated the breakup. This raises the issue of how to evaluate the meaning of relationship breakup. Should breakup be considered a negative outcome, or is it positive in the sense that the couple decided to get out of a bad relationship before potentially inflicting harm on children and/or themselves?

It should be noted that the differential breakup rates actually work *against* finding significant differences at follow-up between PREP and the control and decline groups. This stems from the likelihood that couples with the poorest scores on the relationship functioning measures have dropped out of the study. Thus, the mean scores for the decline and control groups are inflated as these couples break up and drop out of the study. The lower functioning PREP couples, however, seem to be staying together and "weathering the storm."

Relationship Functioning

Overview of data analysis: In order to evaluate the effects of the program, a series of 3 × 2 (group × sex) analyses of covariance (ANCOVA) were conducted with pretest measures as the covariate. The factors were group (PREP, control, decline),[2] and sex (male versus female). Group was treated as a between factor and sex was treated as a repeated factor to take into account the dependencies between male and female scores from the same couple, as recommended by Kraemer and Jacklin (28). The major dependent measures at each point in time were relationship satisfaction (Premarital Adjustment Test), problem intensity, and communication positivity (communication box). In addition, an assessment of communication skills (as measure by the CST) was available for the pre/post and pre-follow-up comparisons for a subset of PREP and control couples, and the sexual dissatisfaction scale was available for Year 2 couples.[3]

Short-term effects: The Year 1 PREP (n = 17), compared to the control (n = 17) group, significantly increased their level of communication and problem-solving skills as measured by the CST (F [1,13] = 4.63, $p < .05$)

[2]Although couples were initially matched, maintaining the matched set for the purposes of longitudinal data analyses was not practical because too many cases would be lost. In addition, the decline group could not be compared to match sets of control and PREP couples. Incompleters were included in the decline group in the PREP evaluation analyses but not the correlational analyses.

[3]In order to increase homogeneity of the PREP group, four couples were omitted from the main set of analyses because their premarital relationship satisfaction scores were very low (both partners scored below 115) and widely divergent from the other couples. The results, therefore, should not be generalized to premarital couples with relatively severe relationship problems. Premarital intervention programs, such as PREP, are not designed for "distressed" relationships, and other interventions are needed for these couples. Omitting these couples from the analyses provides a better understanding of the impact of the intervention on couples who are the intended targets. Preliminary analyses indicate that the PREP groups show more powerful positive changes, as compared to the control-decline group, when these four distressed couples are omitted from the analyses. This is consistent with evidence in the prevention literature that target-subjects who are the best adjusted at the onset show the strongest preventive effects (22).

(14). The results of the 2×2 ANCOVAs for the other dependent variables indicated no significant differences between groups. These results are summarized in Figures 1 through 4.

The finding that PREP couples were learning and using the skills taught in the program is very important in that effective skill-training programs must demonstrate that participants learn the skills being taught. Because the goals of the PREP program are long-term in nature, the general lack of post-differences was not a major concern. Nevertheless, the program does enhance premarital relationship satisfaction for Year 1 couples and enhances sexual functioning for Year 2 couples (this was not assessed at pretest for Year 1 couples). In another PREP evaluation study, Blew and Trapold (5) found that intervention couples had higher levels of communication box ratings and relationship interaction, compared to waiting-list and attention-placebo control groups.

Longer-term effects: Because the goals of prevention programs are necessarily long-term in nature, the ultimate test of their effectiveness with couples requires longitudinal designs comparing experimental and control groups over time. This is one of the basic objectives of the current project.

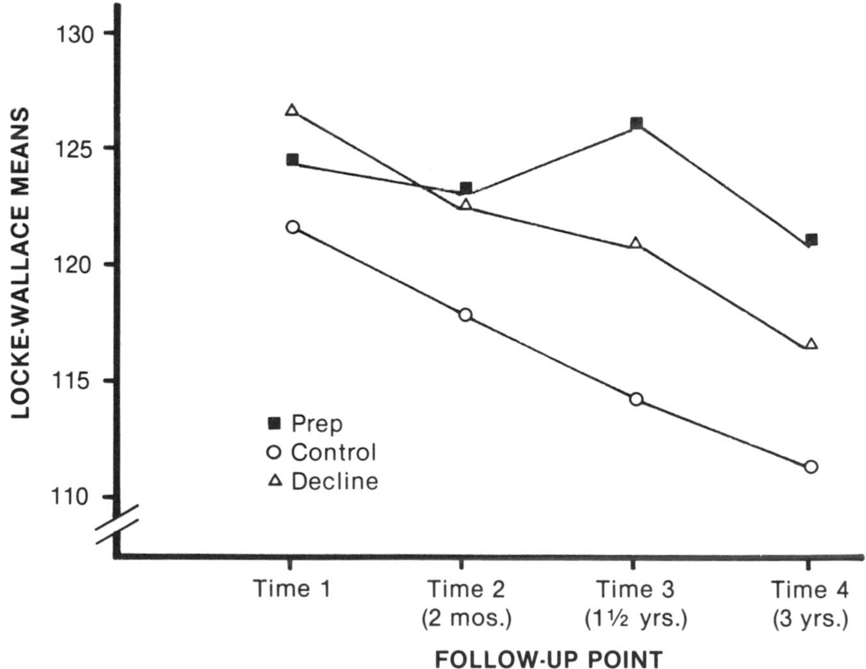

Fig. 1. Locke-Wallace means by group and time.

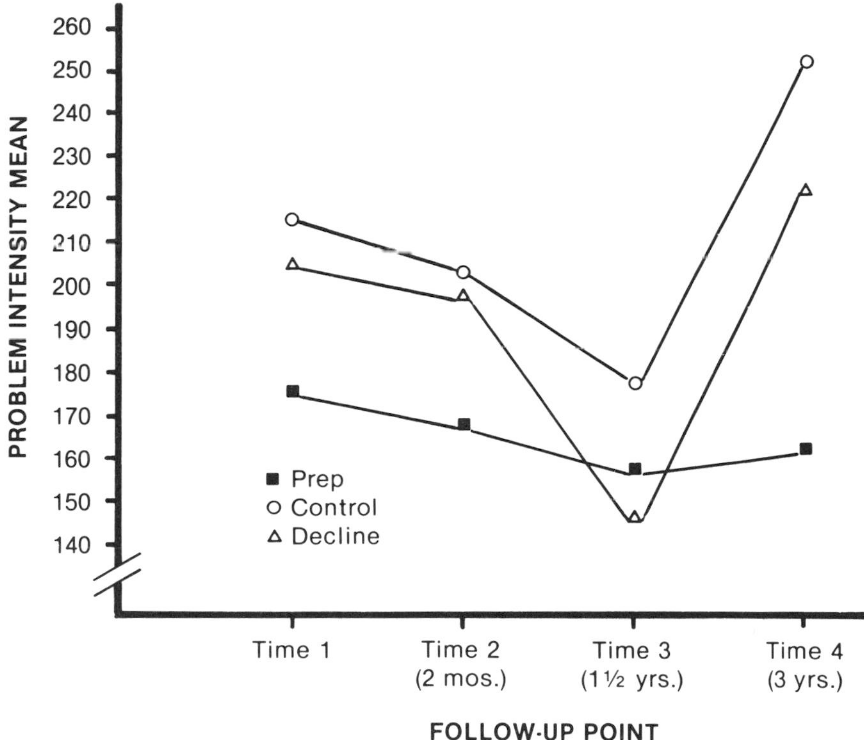

Fig. 2. Problem intensity by group and time.[4]

[4]Because Problem Intensity means at Time 1, Time 2, and Time 3 are based on 10 problem category ratings, while Time 4 is based on 11 ratings, Time 4 means are slightly inflated. However, this should not affect interpretation of between-group differences.

The short-term results presented above do not directly address the question, "Are we preventing marital and family distress?" The answer to this critical question is starting to emerge from follow-up phases of the project. The results at Follow-up 1, summarized in Figures 1-4, indicate that the PREP subjects, as compared to control and/or control and decline groups, were significantly more satisfied with their relationships (F [1,75] = 3.25, $p < .05$) and had higher communication ratings (F [1,60] = 3.87, $p < .095$). There are no differences on the other measures. Thus, consistent with its long-term preventive goals, the PREP program has stronger effects at Follow-up 1 than at post-test. These findings replicated and extended a previous study, which found that at the 1½-year follow-up (Time 3), PREP couples were more likely to maintain a stable relationship and less likely to experience a decline

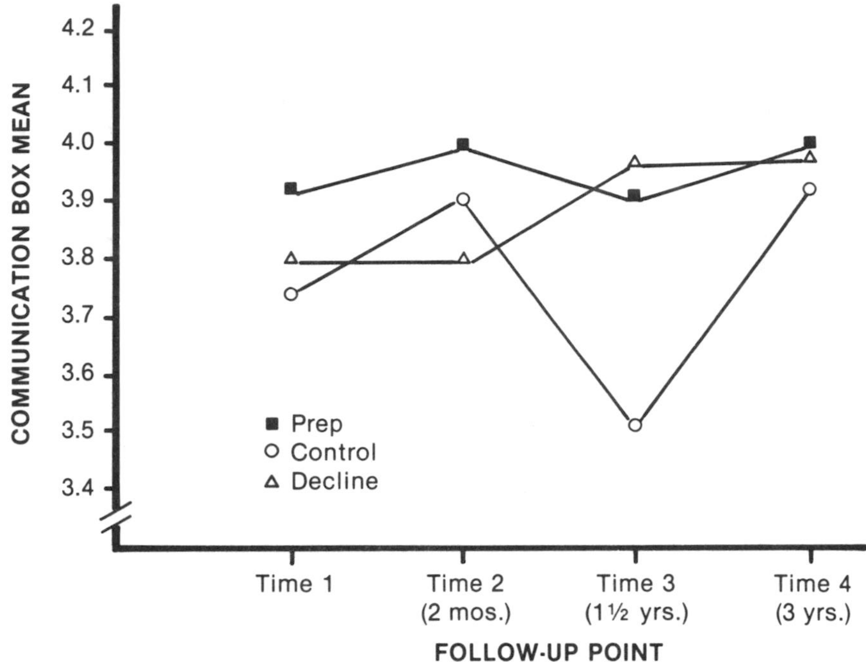

Fig. 3. Communication box means by group and time.

in relationship satisfaction from post-test to follow-up (33). In the current study, PREP males maintained their gains in communications skills, but females showed a tendency to lose some of their advantage over the controls.

The results at Follow-up 2 (Time 4), presented in Figures 1-4, indicate that the PREP, as compared to the control and decline groups, were more satisfied with their relationships (F [1,65] = 4.121, $p < .05$) and tended to report lower levels of sexual dissatisfaction (F [1,18] = 3.44, $p < .10$) of problems (F [1,61] = 2.86, $p < .10$). Thus, the relationship satisfaction differences at Follow-up 1 are being maintained at Follow-up 2, while the communication rating differences are not. Differences appear to extend to other areas of relationship functioning, problem intensity, and sexual functioning.

To summarize, the PREP evaluation results provide preliminary evidence for the possibilities of preventing marital distress through a cognitive-behavioral intervention program. The results indicate that we are increasing or preventing a decline in: (a) couples' satisfaction with their interactions, (b) use of communication and problem-solving skills, (c) global relationship satisfaction, (d) problem intensity, and (e) sexual functioning. These results are consistent with the preventive objective of the prevention program. It is

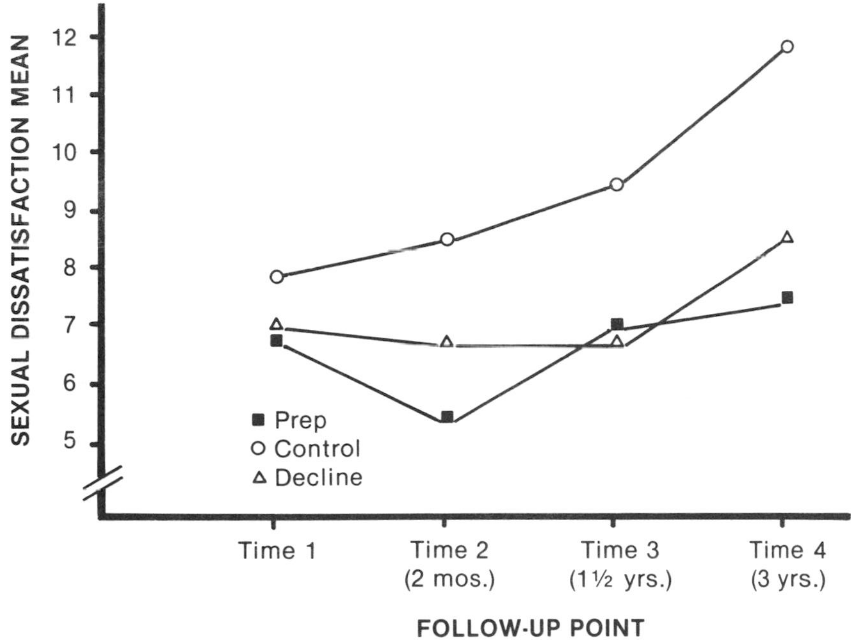

Fig. 4. Sexual dissatisfaction means by group and time (Year 2 only).

interesting to note that the pattern of findings indicates that the best possible outcome from prevention programs with premarital couples may be to provide the communication and problem-solving skills necessary to help them maintain high levels of functioning, that is, to prevent a decline in satisfaction.

Although the initial results have been promising, longer-term follow-up is necessary because the goals of primary prevention programs (for example, preventing marital dissolution and promoting marital satisfaction) are necessarily long-term in nature in that it sometimes takes years for these problems to appear. At the very least, these findings provide an optimistic perspective as we continue with our work.

Future Directions: Marital Communication, Marital Distress, and Mental Health

The work that we have presented provides some understanding of the development of marital distress when particular attention is given to the role of communication factors. Such longitudinal research is clearly essential in that it allows us to begin unraveling cause-effect relationships and in planning intervention programs for premarital couples or those couples in the early stages of marriage. Our future work will continue to examine the factors related to marital distress and dissolution. It is possible that factors that are important in marital distress *early* in a relationship—such as those examined in this chapter—may be quite different from those important later on. Thus, it will be essential to continue the study of these factors over time in order to ascertain their relative contributions across different developmental epochs.

Of particular value, though, will be the opportunity afforded by the longitudinal data to study various aspects of individual and family functioning in those families experiencing marital discord and/or divorce. Such work will be important because of the mental health problems associated with divorce for adults, for example, depression and suicide, and for children, for example, depression and conduct disorder (7, 62). Reviews of the many empirical studies have identified *marital conflict* as the likely underlying cause of the negative effects of divorce on children (13, 57). Thus, over time we will have the opportunity to study the consequences of marital discord for children and their parents and the processes by which these consequences are brought about. We plan to do this in several ways and will briefly describe them.

With the present rate of divorce in the United States, it is expected that an increasing percentage of "nonintervention" couples will experience marital distress, and that some percentage of the "intervention" couples will as well. Because we will have followed these couples over time, we will be able to trace behaviorally and by self-report measures changes in the family's functioning that we would expect to be related to mental health problems and the development of psychopathology. For instance, increased negative interaction cycles often characterized distressed marriages (see 18, 31, 54), and family members report increased conflict duirng the period preceding and during divorce (23, 24). Thus, the substantial amount of interactional data on couples as well as their own reports of conflict and discord in their families will provide useful windows on their functioning, allowing us to trace patterns of interaction over time with specific couples and allowing us to search for specific patterns across couples. To our knowledge, such longitudinal data from the time of the couple's engagement have not been available before. Thus, the opportunity to trace such patterns over the early stages of marriage and at least through the seventh year of marriage (our current time-line for the study) should provide important insights into not only the early precursors of marital dissatisfaction and distress but also the concomitants.

Additionally, for many couples with children (about 22% in our most recent follow-up assessment), we will have extensive data on the children's development and the nature of the parent-child relationships during the time of decreasing marital satisfaction (10, 12, 49, 53, 55). Such information will permit us to examine the impact of marital discord on the nascent parent-child relationship, consider interaction patterns that reflect changes in the marital relationship, and look more closely at process dimensions that are often implicit in the description of children from divorced families. Given the extensive data we have on marital communication, it will be especially important to examine the impact of decreasing marital satisfaction on a couple's interaction and communication with their children. Thus, we will be focusing on more subtle outcomes of marital distress than simply the rate of marital dissolution. The use of sequential analyses of both marital and parent-child interaction will permit a micro-level analysis that should prove useful in delineating the mechanisms by which certain conditions (for example, maternal depression) have their effects. Such conditions may not be related to the emergence of psychopathology at that particular point, but may place the child or parent at risk for later difficulties (58, 59). Of course, not all of our families will be involved in the parent-child research components of the study and, thus, some families who experience discord/divorce will not be represented in such analyses. Nevertheless, careful study of a small group of families can be highly informative and generative for future research.

During the coming years, it is likely that we will attempt to follow up couples and families in the study who experience divorce. Such follow-ups will likely involve the assessment of individuals whom we have studied previously in interaction with their new spouse/partner. Also, if children are present, it is likely that we will study their adjustment and functioning as well. Such work should help us understand longer-term impacts of marital distress on children and on the subsequent intimate relationships of adults. This research will undoubtedly be difficult to do logistically, but its importance is clear, given the high rate of remarriage in the United States and the high incidence of problems in remarriages.

Another important aspect of this future research is the opportunity it provides to test different models of the relationship among such variables as spouse communication, marital distress, adult mental health problems, and child mental health problems. The presence of longitudinal data should provide useful information about causal influences. For example, one key model that will be examined is the impact of the preventive intervention: Does communication skills training in the premarital period lead to better interaction between spouses, improved marital functioning, and then better child and spouse functioning? Various paths of influence can be considered and tested with the data available from this study. Such work will be helpful in theory development and in developing better targeted intervention programs. The causal chains are likely to be quite complex, and various competing hypotheses and models will need to be considered carefully. Yet, the extensiveness of our data on these couples and their communication patterns should provide a fruitful starting point for this work. This research should provide additional insights into the role of marital, personality, and communication factors in the development of psychopathology.

REFERENCES

1. Aldous, J. Family interaction patterns. *Annual Review of Sociology 3*: 105–135, 1977.

2. Belsky, J. *A path analysis of the multiple determinants of parenting*. Paper presented at the Society for Research in Child Development meeting, Toronto, April, 1985.

3. ______, Gilstap, B., & Rovine, M. Stability and change in mother-infant and father-infant interaction in a family setting: One to three to nine months. *Child Development 55*: 692–705, 1984.

4. Birchler, G. R., & Webb, L. J. Discriminating interaction in behaviors in happy and unhappy marriages. *Journal of Consulting and Clinical Psychology 45*: 494–495, 1977.

5. Blew, A., & Trapold, M. Fixing what isn't broken: Methodology and ethical considerations in premarital interventions. Paper presented at the Annual Meeting of the Association for the Advancement of Behavior Therapy, Los Angeles CA, November, 1982.

6. Bloom, B. *Community mental health: A general introduction*. Monterey CA: Brooks-Cole, 1977.

7. ______, Asher, S., & White, S. Marital disruption as a stressor: A review and analysis. *Psychological Bulletin 85*: 867–894, 1978.

8. Cherlin, A. J. *Marriage. divorce, remarriage*. Cambridge: Harvard University Press, 1981.

9. Cohler, B. J., Weiss, J. L., & Grunebaum, H. U. Child-care attitudes and emotional disturbance among mothers of young children. *Genetic Psychology Monographs 82*: 3–47, 1970.

10. Cowan, C., & Cowan, J. Preparation for parenthood. *Marital and Family Review 3*: 5, 1978.

11. Derogatis, L., Lipman, R. S., & Covi, L. SCL 90: An outpatient psychiatric rating scale (A preliminary report). *Psychopharmacology Bulletin 9*: 13–27, 1973.

12. Duncan, S. W. Marital functioning and couples adjustment to early parenting. Paper presented at the Biennial Meeting of the Society for Research in Child Development, Toronto, April, 1985.

13. Emery, R. Interparental conflict and the children of discord and divorce. *Psychological Bulletin 92*: 310–330, 1982.

14. Floyd, F., Markman, H. An objective coding system for evaluating communication and problem solving skills. *Journal of Consulting and Clinical Psychology 52*: 97–103, 1984.

15. Gibson, H. B. Early delinquency and relation to broken homes. *Journal of Child Psychology and Psychiatry and Allied Disciplines 10*: 195–204, 1969.

16. Glick, P. C., & Norton, A. J. Number, timing, and duration of marriages and divorces in the United States: June 1975. In U.S. Bureau of the Census, *Current Population Reports*, Series p-20:297. Washington DC: U.S. Government Printing Office, 1976.

17. Gottman, J. *Marital interaction: Experimental investigations*. New York: Academic Press, 1979.

18. ______, Markman, H. J., & Notarius, C. I. The topography of marital conflict: A sequential analysis of verbal and nonverbal behavior. *Journal of Marriage and the Family 39*: 461–478, 1977.

19. ______, Notarius, C. I., Markman, H. J., Banks, D., Yoppi, B., & Rubin, M. E. Behavior exchange theory and marital decision making. *Journal of Personality and Social Psychology 34*: 14–23, 1976.

20. Hahlweg, K., & Markman, H. J. The current status of the outcome of behavioral marital interventions: An interaction perspective. Paper presented at the Annual Meeting of the American Association of the Advancement for Behavior Therapy, Washington DC, December, 1983.

21. Heinicke, C. M. Pre-birth couple functioning and the quality of the mother-infant relationship in the second half of the first year of life. Paper presented at the Society for Research in Child Development meeting, Toronto, April, 1985.

22. Heller, K., & Monahan, J. *Psychology and community change*. Homewood IL: Dorsey Press, 1977.

23. Hetherington, E. M. Children and divorce. *American Psychologist 20*: 30–40, 1979.

24. ______, Cox, M., & Cox, R. Family interaction and the social emotional and cognitive development of children following divorce. In V. Vaughn & T. Brazelton, *The family: Setting priorities*. New York: Science and Medicine, 1979.

25. Huston, T., personal communication, March, 1984.

26. Jamieson-Darr, K. The prediction of relationship satisfaction from couples' communication: A competency-based model. Unpublished doctoral dissertation, University of Denver, 1984.

27. Knox, D. *Marriage happiness*. Champaign IL: Research Press, 1971.

28. Kraemer, H., & Jacklin, C. Statistical analysis of dyadic social behavior. *Psychological Bulletin 86*: 217–224, 1979.

29. Locke, H., & Wallace, K. Short marital adjustment and prediction tests: Their reliability and validity. *Marriage and Family Living 21*: 251–255, 1959.

30. Markman, H. J. The application of a behavioral model of marriage in predicting relationship satisfaction of couples planning marriage. *Journal of Consulting and Clinical Psychology 4*: 743–749, 1979.

31. ______. The prediction of marital distress: A five year follow-up. *Journal of Consulting and Clinical Psychology 49*: 760–762, 1981.

32. ______. The longitudinal study of couples' interaction: Implications for cognitive/behavioral, social exchange, and social skills models of relationship development. In K.

Hahlweg & N. Jacobson (eds.), *Marital interaction: Analysis and modification*. New York: Guilford Press, 1984.

33. ______, Floyd, F., & Dickson-Markman, F. Toward a model for the prediction and prevention of marital and family distress and dissolution. In S. Duck (ed.), *Personal relationships 3: Dissolving personal relationships*. London: Academic Press, 1982.

34. ______, Floyd, F., Stanley, S., & Jamieson, K. A cognitive/behavioral program for the prevention of marital and family distress: Issues in program development and delivery. In K. Hahlweg & N. Jacobson (eds.), *Marital interaction: Analysis and modification*. New York: Guilford Press, 1984.

35. ______, & Jamieson, K. A premarital version of the Couples Interaction Scoring System (PCISS). Unpublished manuscript, University of Denver, 1981.

36. ______, Jamieson, K., & Floyd, F. The assessment and modification of premarital relationships: Implications for the etiology and prevention of marital distress. In J. Vincent (ed.), *Advances in family intervention, assessment, and theory*. Greenwich CT: JAI Press, 1983.

37. ______, & Notarius, C. Issues in behavior observation of family interaction and psychopathology. In T. Jacob (ed.), *Family interaction and psychopathology: Theories, methods, and finding*. New York: Plenum Press, 1987.

38. ______, & Poltrock, S. A computerized system for recording and analysis of self-observations of couples' interaction. *Behavioral Research Methods and Instrumentation 14*: 186–190, 1982.

39. Minton, B., & Markman, H. J. A model for how church/synagogue and mental health professionals can work together to enhance marital and family relationships. Paper presented at Nebraska Symposium on Building Family Strengths, Lincoln, 1982.

40. ______, & Markman, H. J. How church/synagogues and family professionals can work together to enhance marital and family relationships. In G. Rowe, J. DeFrain, H. Lingren, R. MacDonald, N. Stinnet, S. Van Zandt, & R. Williams, *Family strengths 5: Continuity and Diversity*. Newton MA: Education Development Center, Inc., 1984.

41. Minuchin, S., Rosman, B. L., & Baker, L. *Psychosomatic families: Anorexia nervosa in context*. Cambridge MA: Harvard University Press, 1978.

42. National Center for Health Statistics. Births, marriages, divorces, and deaths for November, 1982. *Monthly Vital Statistics Report 34* (No. 5), DHHS, (PHS) 83-1120. Hyattsville MD: Public Health Service, 1985.

43. Notarius, C. I., Krokoff, L., & Markman, H. J. Analysis of observational data. In E. Filsinger & R. Lewis (eds.), *Assessing marriage: New behavioral approaches*. Beverly Hills CA: Sage, 1981.

44. ______, & Markman, H. J. The Couples Interaction Scoring System. In E. Filsinger & R. Lewis (eds.), *Assessing marriage: New behavioral approaches*. Beverly Hills CA: Sage, 1981.

45. ______, Markman, H. J., & Gottman, J. The Couples Interaction Scoring System: Clinical issues. In E. Filsinger (ed.), *Marital measurement sourcebook*. Beverly Hills CA: Sage, 1983.

46. ______, & Pellegrini, D. Marital processes as stressors and stress mediators: Implica-

tions for marital repair. In S. Duck (ed.), *Personal relationships, Vol. 5: Repairing personal relationships*. London: Academic Press, 1984.

47. Olson, D. H., & Ryder, R. G. Inventory of Marital Conflicts (IMC): An experimental interaction procedure. *Journal of Marriage and Family Living 32*: 433–448, 1970.

48. Paykel, E. S., Myers, J. K., Diendelt, M. N., Klerman, G. L., Linenthal, J. J., & Pepper, M. P. Life events and depression: A controlled study. *Archives of General Psychiatry 21*: 753–760, 1969.

49. Pederson, F. Research issues related to fathers and infants. In F. Pederson (ed.), *The father-infant relationship*. New York: Praeger, 1980.

50. Power, M. J., Ash, P. M., Schoenberg, E., & Sorey, E. C. Delinquency and the family. *British Journal of Social Work 4*: 17–38, 1974.

51. Radloff, L. S. Risk factors for depression: What do we learn from them? In M. Guttentag, S. Salasin, & D. Belle (eds.), *The mental health of women*. New York: Academic Press, 1980.

52. Raush, H. L., Barry, W. A., Hertel, R. K., & Swain, M. A. *Communication conflict and marriage*. San Francisco: Jossey-Bass, 1974.

53. Reiss, R. *The family system in America*. Chicago: Henry Holt, 1971.

54. Revenstorf, F. D., Hahlweg, K., & Schindler, L. Interaction analysis of marital conflict. In K. Hahlweg & N. Jacobson (eds.), *Marital interaction: Analysis and modification*. New York: Guilford Press, 1984.

55. Rollins, B., & Galligan, R. The developing child and marital satisfaction of parents. In R. Lerner & G. Spanier (eds.) *Child influences on marital and family interaction: A life-span perspective*. New York: Academic Press, 1978.

56. Rubin, Z. Measurement of romantic love. *Journal of Personality and Social Psychology 16*: 265–273, 1970.

57. Rutter, M. Protective factors in children's responses to stress and disadvantage. In M. W. Kent & J. E. Rolf (eds.), *Primary prevention of psychopathology: III. Promoting social competence and coping in children*. Hanover NH: University Press of New England, 1980.

58. ______. Stress, coping and development: Some issues and some questions. *Journal of Child Psychology and Psychiatry 22*: 323–356, 1981.

59. ______. The developmental psychopathology of depression: Issues and perspectives. In M. Rutter, C. E., Izard, & P. B. Read (eds.), *Depression in young people: Clinical and developmental perspective*. New York: Guilford Press, 1986.

60. Snyder, D. *Marital Satisfaction Inventory*. Los Angeles: Western Psychological Services, 1979.

61. Strean, H. *Resolving marital conflicts: A psychodynamic perspective*. New York: John Wiley & Sons, 1985.

62. Weissman, M. M., & Paykel, E. S. *The depressed woman: A study of social relationships*. Chicago: University of Chicago Press, 1974.

16

APPLICATION OF MARITAL RESEARCH AND METHODOLOGY TO THE STUDY OF THE FAMILY*

DONALD H. BAUCOM
TAMARA GOLDMAN SHER
University of North Carolina
Chapel Hill

ALTHOUGH the fields of marital and family research are often assumed to be united, in reality, investigators who focus on the marital dyad are frequently not fully informed of progress being made by researchers who focus on the entire family, and vice versa. This is clearly unfortunate because there are many issues that are important to both fields, and findings in one field often can help to guide workers in related areas of investigation. The purpose of this chapter is, first, to focus on methodological issues of importance to both fields. The second purpose is to discuss some of the recent major findings in the field of marital interaction and to assess their utility for future research in the area of individual psychopathology and family functioning. Although there are many areas of family and individual psychopathology that have been investigated, the domain of expressed emotion (EE) has received much attention and yielded many important findings. Therefore, EE will be used as an example of how marital findings can be applied to study the family, but the issues discussed will hopefully have applicability to other areas of family research.

*Preparation of this article was supported in part by a National Institute of Mental Health Grant MH37118.

Models of Family Functioning

One major conceptual issue that has corresponding methodological implications deals with how data from more than one family member are to be treated so as to represent a couple or family. That is, in most investigations information is gathered from several family members. Yet the investigator wishes to use this multisourced information to make a statement about the family as a unit. How this task is accomplished will greatly affect the results of any investigation. Furthermore, different strategies for handling data from different family members make different assumptions about how to conceptualize the meaning of a family.

Although multiple measures are often gathered on each family member, for the sake of simplicity the following discussion will assume a single measure on each person. The issue becomes, then, how to combine these measures across family members. Three different major strategies have been employed for this purpose: linear approaches, configural approaches, and the maintenance of individual scores. Linear approaches involve some version of adding or subtracting the scores of the various family members in order to derive a family score. Configural strategies consider the pattern of scores shown by the various family members, and the family is represented in terms of this pattern. Finally, it is possible not to represent the family as a unit but, rather, to retain the scores of the individual family members and observe relationships between separate family member scores and some criterion, such as the individual pathology of one family member.

Linear Approaches

The simplest linear model is the *additive model.* In this approach, scores from various family members are added together or averaged, and this average score represents the couple or family. The additive model has been the usual model of choice in marital investigations. In fact, in a recent review of marital treatment outcome investigations, Baucom and Hoffman (6) found that all controlled outcome studies have used this model. That is, the husbands' and wives' scores are added together, and treatment results are presented for the couple. Whereas the simplicity of this strategy is appealing, it makes a major assumption about couples that the investigator should recognize. This approach assumes that one spouse's low score on a variable can be compensated for by the other spouse's high score on that same variable. As an example, consider the variable of marital adjustment in which a score of 100 for an individual is the cutoff for differentiating distressed from nondistressed, with scores above 100 representing greater marital adjustment. A couple with one spouse greatly distressed (60) and the other spouse with a high level of marital adjustment (140) would be represented by the *additive model* as a couple at the cutoff point for marital adjustment, $(60+140)/2=100$. Similarly, a couple in which each spouse had a cutoff score of 100 each would be represented in the additive model with a couple's score of 100. Therefore, within the additive model these two couples would be seen as identical. This might be appropriate under some circumstances, but numerous differences would likely be obvious to anyone who observed the two couples. Therefore, the additive model should be reserved for those situations in which there is either a theoretical or empirical basis for allowing the scores of one family member to linearly compensate for the scores of the other family member(s).

A second linear model is the *difference model*, which involves subtracting the score of one family member from another member's score. In the marital field this means that one spouse's score will be subtracted from the other partner's score. If more than two family members are considered, then some logic will have to dictate whose scores are to be subtracted. The difference model is not used as widely in marital research, but it is appropriate when there is reason to believe that discrepancies in scores are important. For example discrepancies could be indicative of an imbalance within the couple on the variable of interest, and imbalances could be of theoretical importance when studying couples and families. Again, the difference model makes a major assumption about couples and families: that discrepancies or imbalances are all that arc of importance. For example, a couple with adjustment scores of 80 and 60 has a difference score of 20; a couple with scores of 130 and 110 also has a difference of 20. The first couple is clearly distressed whereas the second couple is clearly nondistressed. Representing the two couples with the identical score of 20 loses potentially important, discriminatory information about the level of functioning on the variable under investigation.

A third linear approach is a combination of the two previously discussed models: the *sum plus difference model*. In this approach, a couple is represented by the sum of the two spouses' scores and the difference between the two spouses' scores. Such a model is appealing because it retains information about (a) level or elevation and (b) discrepancy. However, when considering a couple, this approach results not in a single score but in two scores: the sum and the difference. This is a problem if the investigator wishes to represent the couple with a single score for certain types of data analysis.

Whereas the sum plus difference is still not extremely complex when considering a couple, the situation becomes dramatically more complex when an entire family is considered. For a family with a father, mother, and three children, the sum is easily obtained by adding the scores of the five family members together. However, some strategy must be developed in order to obtain difference score(s). Should each family member's score be subtracted from the father's score? If so, are these four difference scores retained or are they averaged to provide an average of the differences scores? There is clearly no single answer; instead, the research model will have to provide guidance on how to create appropriate difference scores. It is clear that as the family size increases, the issue of how best to conceptualize the family can quickly become complex.

Configural Models

Whereas linear models are based on addition and subtraction of family members' scores, configural models take the *pattern* of scores of family members into account in deriving a score or category for representing the family. Configural models appear to take one of two forms in family research. We have called these two forms the "*family representative*" *model* and the "*family typology*" *model*. The family representative approach considers the scores of the various family members and, according to some criterion, selects the score of one family member to represent the family. This approach assumes that the presence or absence of some criterion or an extreme score best captures the essence of the family. One example of the family representative model is what we have previously entitled the "*weak link*" *model* (3, 7). The name derives from the adage that a chain is no stronger than its weakest link. Thus, when considering maritally distressed couples, one approach is to use the scores of the more distressed spouse as representative of the couple. Baucom and Mehlman (7) hypothesized that the weak link model might be useful in predicting which couples would remain married after undergoing behavioral marital therapy. Considering spouses' scores at the end of marital therapy, they compared all of the models discussed thus far to determine which approaches best predicted maintenance of the relationship six months later. The results indicated that the weak link model was the best predictor of relationship maintenance.

Whereas the family representative model has the potential to portray meaningful aspects of a family's functioning, it also can lead to an oversimplification in representing the family. Once a given member is chosen as the family representative, the scores of the other family members are ignored, and possible moderating or compensating effects of other family members are lost.

The second configural model, the family typology model, involves retaining scores from all of the family members of interest and using these scores to categorize or label the family. It differs from the representative model in that the representative model considers all family members' scores initially but is defined finally in terms of only one family member's score. The family typology model continues to include the various members' scores in the definition of the family type. For example, Schaap (47) used the marital adjustment scores of both husband and wife to develop a three-category system of marital distress. If both spouses scored in the distressed range on an adjustment scale, the couple was referred to as distressed. If one spouse was distressed and the other nondistressed, the couple was viewed as mixed. If both spouses scored in the nondistressed range, the couple was labeled nondistressed.

The strength of the family typology model is that it can retain information about the various family members in categorizing the family. However, this strength can also become one of its weaknesses. As the number of family members increases, the number of combinations of scores becomes large. Consequently, the number of categories or types can become overwhelming. Any investigator attempting to develop a typology must confront the difficult issue of how many categories to form, such that the members of a single category are somewhat homogeneous yet the number of categories is not impractical. A second potential limitation of the family typology approach is that it typically is employed to form categories, and quantitative aspects of the data become lost.

Individual Members' Model

A third approach to handling data from several family members is to make no attempt to combine the data to represent the family. Instead, the data from each family member is kept separate, and the relationship of each family member's score to some criterion is established. For example, the investigation by Baucom and Mehlman (7), which attempted to predict maintenance of marital relationships after marital therapy, also explored the usefulness of the individual member's model. The results indicated that the wives' scores at the end of treatment predicted continuation of the relationship; however, the husbands' scores were not significantly related to relationship maintenance. Furthermore, the wives' scores predicted better than the additive model. That is, when the husbands' and wives' scores were added together and relationship maintenance was predicted, the predictability was not as strong as when the wives' scores alone were considered. The inclusion of the husbands' scores actually added error to the prediction!

The individual member's model is appropriate when there is no desire to describe the family as a unit. Of course, individual scores from various family members can be included in some analyses. For example, in the Baucom and Mehlman study (7), the husbands' and wives' scores could be entered as separate variables into a multiple regression equation to predict relationship maintenance. This approach should not be confused with what has been referred to as the additive model. In the additive model, the scores are added together and entered as a single variable. Entering the husbands' and wives' scores separately into a multiple regression equation is mathematically equivalent to entering the sum and difference, as described earlier. This equivalence points out that the various models discussed are not mutually exclusive, and as one model is built upon, it may become redundant of another model.

Summary

As should be obvious from the above discussion, there is no correct way to portray marital and family data. However, as should also be apparent, the various models make different assumptions about the ways in which relationships operate. The purpose of this discussion is not to promote a specific model, because different models are likely to have differential utility in various contexts. Instead, our hope is that investigators will become mindful of the assumptions they are making when they employ various models and be certain that they wish to make those assumptions.

Having described various models and some examples of their use in marital research, we turn now to an examination of the EE literature to clarify how various models have been used in this area of investigation. This has already been a fruitful area of research that has demonstrated levels of predictability rarely achieved in the marital, family, or psychopathology fields. Our hope is that with increased attention to the ways in which families are defined in this area of investigation, perhaps the level of predictability will increase even further.

Expressed Emotion and Family Models

As discussed earlier, linear approaches have been the models of overwhelming choice in the marital field. Yet when one turns to the EE literature, one finds linear models to be essentially absent. This lack of use of linear models has likely resulted from methodological considerations related to the samples included in these studies. In their early influential paper, Brown, Monck, Carstairs, and Wing (14) explored the relapse rate of male schizophrenics who returned to their homes after being hospitalized. Because some of these men returned to live with their wives, there was only one other adult living in the home. Thus, no linear approach was appropriate because the scores of only one person were being considered. Many adult

TABLE 1

Models of Marital and Family Functioning

Type	Definition	Representative Applications from Marital Literature	Representative Applications from EE Literature
Linear Models			
Additive Model	Scores from individuals are summed or averaged	Almost all marital treatment studies use couples' scores based on sum or average of two spouses' scores	Not employed
Difference Model	Scores from individuals are subtracted from each other	Predict level of adjustment and behaviors based on discrepancies between spouses in desire for intimacy	Not employed
Sum + Difference Model	The sum across individuals' scores and the differences between individuals' scores are determined	Studies that investigate whether both elevation and imbalances between spouses are important	Not employed

Configural Models			
Family Representative Model	Family member with most extreme score meeting some criterion represents the family	Weak link model – use scores of more distressed spouse to represent couple	Major model employed in EE research: – Use EE score of adult female family member – Use EE score of person having most contact with patient – Weak link – if either parent scores high on EE, family is high EE
Family Typology Model	Pattern of scores from family members used to define types or categories	Form 3-category system of marital distress based on whether both, one, or neither spouse is distressed	Form 3-category system of EE based on whether both, one, or neither parent is high on EE
Individual Members' Model	No attempt made to represent family as such; each family member's scores are retained	Predict marital stability from wives' marital adjustment scores	Predict physiological reaction of patient to family member with a given EE level

schizophrenics live with their parents, and Brown et al.'s sample also included male schizophrenics who returned to live with their parents after hospitalization. In this instance, Brown et al. assessed the EE level of the "closest female." Although no explanation is given for this approach, it likely resulted from an attempt to keep constant the sex of the family member whose EE was being assessed. In terms of the models discussed above, this is an example of the family representative approach, with the criterion being the EE level of the closest female. Whereas their decision is defensible from a methodological perspective, it meant that the levels of EE expressed by significant males living with the patient were considered to be of no consequence. Such an assumption clearly warranted empirical investigation, and almost all subsequent investigators have included the EE level of significant males in their explorations of EE. However, the work by Brown and his associates seems to have set a precedent for a focus on configural models to the exclusion of linear models.

Just as the above investigation employed a family representative, configural model, the majority of subsequent investigations also used a family representative model, although the basis for choosing the family representative has varied among studies. One approach used to select the family representative has been to assess the EE level of the relative who is in high face-to-face contact with the patient (see 32, 49). Unfortunately, the basis for defining high face-to-face contact was not defined in these investigations. More importantly from the standpoint of family models, this particular application implicitly made the assumption that the person who has more contact with the patient is the person whose EE will have the greatest impact on the relapse of the patient. Whereas this is certainly possible, it may be that sheer amount of time together is not the critical variable. Perhaps the level of EE of the person whom the patient considers most significant in his or her life is even more critical. Relevant to our presentation, these investigations made a crucial assumption about what is important in the family (amount of contact with patient as a basis for defining it as a high- or low-EE family), but justification for that assumption was at no point addressed in the studies.

Perhaps the most frequently used family model in the EE literature is a variant of the weak link model discussed above. Investigators have worked on the unstated assumption that the emotional climate of the family is no better than that of the most negative family member. In investigations in which a patient returns to live with both parents, this has been operationalized by assessing the EE level of both parents. If either parent scores high on EE, then the family is designated as a high-EE family. Both parents must score low for the family to be categorized as low on EE (see 2, 13, 33–37, 49–51, 55, 57). Because it has been the most frequently used model, some empirical exploration of the weak link model seems crucial. Valone et al. (54) report that Vaughn, Leff, and associates have found that the presence of a single high-EE family member predicts patient relapse as well as the presence of both parents who are high on EE. At present, however, empirical findings in this area have not been published. Also, as will be seen below, recent work suggests that the constellation of family members' EE scores are important, casting some doubt on the weak link model assumptions. Of course, this issue is moot if almost all families have all high-EE family members or all low-EE family members. Again, this issue has rarely been addressed in the literature, so the consistency of EE scores across family members within the same family is unknown.

More recently, other models have begun to be investigated in the EE field. Goldstein and his associates have placed major emphasis on a family typology model. Essentially, they have assessed the EE level of both parents and developed a three-category system based on combinations of these scores. Both parents can score high on EE; both parents can score low on EE; or one parent can score high while the other parent scores low (21, 22, 45, 53). Similarly, Doane and her colleagues (15) developed a measure of affective style (AS) similar in concept to EE, but based on actual interactions between patients and family members rather than on interviews. Doane et al. also constructed a three-category system based on both parents' communication: benign (neither parent had negative codes); intermediate (one or both had negative, but at least one parent had one supportive statement); and poor (both negative, no supportive statements).

The fruitfulness of this typological approach is becoming apparent. For example, Norton (45) found that adolescents received widely varying diagnoses (when followed up to five years later) as a function of the EE patterns shown by their parents during the initial assessment period. Among families with both parents high on EE, 91% of high-risk adolescents received schizophrenia-spectrum diagnoses five years after EE was assessed. When both parents were low, only 10% of the adolescents received a schizophrenia-related diagnosis; and when one parent was high and one was low on EE, 25% of the adolescents received a schizophrenia-spectrum diagnosis. Note that this last group would have been designated as high-EE families using the frequently employed weak link model because each of these families contained one family member with a high EE score. Similarly, Valone et al. (54) found that these three different groups of EE families demonstrated different communication patterns when interacting with adolescents considered to be at high risk for the development of schizophrenia-spectrum disorders.

Finally, the individual members' model is being investigated in EE research. For example, Miklowitz et al. (44) and Valone et al. (53) used this approach in assessing communication patterns and physiological effects of families on patients. In these two studies the behavior or effects of individual parents were under consideration. Therefore, there was no need to categorize the *family* as a high or low EE but, rather, high- and low-EE *individuals* could serve as the focus.

All of the above studies have provided meaningful contributions to the literature, but it is unclear why one study adopts one model and another study adopts another model. On some occasions there might be good reasons for adopting one model over the other; at such times, it is the responsibility of the investigator to clarify why a particular family model was selected. Otherwise, at our present state of knowledge, further exploration of various family models in the EE literature as well as in other marital and family fields might be useful.

Implications of Marital Findings for Studying the Role of the Family in Individual Psychopathology

Investigations focusing on the marital dyad and studies on the larger family system have led to major advances in our knowledge of intimate relationships in recent years. Often, however, findings in one area have not maximally benefitted investigators in the other area. The purpose of the remainder of this chapter is to mention briefly some of the major recent findings from studies of distressed married couples, and to suggest how such results might benefit research on the family *and* individual psychopathology. A number of variables have been found to be important in marital adjustment, and it is likely, although not necessarily the case, that some of these same variables will also influence the individual psychological functioning of various family members.

Studying How People Think about Each Other in the Family

Behavioral investigators have learned that in order to understand marital relationships more fully, a focus on couples' behavior must be broadened to include an examination of the way that couples think about the relationship and about their partners. In particular, increased attention has been given to couples' attributions and expectations. Behavioral therapists have realized that teaching couples to alter behavior without taking into account their attributions for changes in partners could easily undermine what appeared to be productive behavioral changes. For example, if a wife changes an annoying behavior during treatment after many years of the behavior, the husband may make various attributions for her change. If he believes that she has changed because she wishes to improve their relationship and make him happier, then her change will likely have a positive impact on him. If, however, he concludes that she has changed only to please the therapist, then he may dismiss her change as unimportant or even become angry that she changed for the therapist but would not change for him despite his repeated requests.

Although attributions have been discussed on a number of different dimensions, perhaps the ones receiving most investigation thus far in the marital field are: source, stable/unstable, global/specific, and control. Source is related to an internal/external dimension and involves an explanation of who or what is responsible for an event. For example, a given marital event might be attributed to oneself, one's partner, the relationship, and/or outside circumstances. We have employed Doherty's term, "source" (16), rather than internal/external, because the latter term has typically been construed as involving a single dimension. However, recent research we have conducted suggests that it is preferable not to attempt to align all of these various sources on a single dimension (9). The stable/unstable dimension refers to the extent to which the cause is perceived to be changeable in the future (60). The global/specific dimension refers to the extent to which the attribution will affect numerous aspects of the relationship or will affect few aspects of the relationship (1). Control refers to the extent to which the person viewed as responsible can choose to behave in a given way.

In recent years, a number of theoretical papers have been written about the role of attributions in marital distress (4, 11, 16, 19). In addition, several empirical investigations have been conducted relating various attributional dimensions to marital distress (8, 9, 20, 31, 32, 38, 46, 52). Overall, these studies support the hypothesis that marital adjustment is related to couples' attributions for marital events in that the attributions reflect the general emotional tone of the spouse toward the relationship. More specifically, distressed spouses show a tendency to make attributions that minimize the importance of their partners' positive behavior and maximize negative behaviors. Nondistressed spouses make attributions that have the opposite impact.

More important for the current discussion is the number of research strategies that have become available for assessing attributions. First, self-report questionnaires have been developed that present hypothetical marital situations and ask the respondent to make attributions for why his or her partner might act as described in the vignettes (8, 20). The respondent evaluates the attribution along several of the dimensions discussed above. Similarly, Baucom et al. (9) developed a self-report questionnaire in which the respondent makes attributions for marital events that actually have occurred during the previous 24 hours. Thus, using the above questionnaires, different persons can be asked to make attributions for the same events and for events specific to their own relationships. Pretzer et al. (46) have constructed a different type of attribution questionnaire that does not ask the respondent to rate specific events. Instead, it asks the respondent to make assessments of the partner's motivations in the marriage and provides indices of the extent to which the respondent believes that the partner desires to make the respondent feel bad. In addition, Holtzworth-Munroe and Jacobson (27) have developed a coding system in which trained observers rate attributions made by spouses during interactions between the partners. Thus, there are now strategies in which respondents clarify their attributions on a number of dimensions and strategies, and outside observers rate these attributions on various dimensions. The situations being rated include both hypothetical and actual events, and assessments are made from both self-report inventories and from behavorial interactions between the spouses.

Continuing with our examples from EE research, it appears that a focus on attributions might advance our knowledge and understanding of EE in that part of the operational definition of EE involves attributions. One major component of EE is criticism about the patient, and many criticisms involve attributions. For example, if a relative states about a patient, "He stays in bed all of the time because he is lazy and does not want to assume responsibilities like the rest of us," the relative is making an attribution about the patient's behavior. In addition, if the relative notes a negative behavior of the patient but sees himself or herself as responsible for the patient's undesirable behavior, then the statement is not scored as a criticism contributing toward a high EE score. In this case, criticisms are defined according to the source of attributions. Consequently, attributions are inherent in the very definition of EE, and a more systematic focus on the types of attributions made by relatives for the patients' behavior may provide greater clarification of one major aspect of EE.

Although not inherent in the definition of EE, additional findings also suggest that attributions are important in understanding the family environment of families assessed for EE. Vaughn and Leff (56) have suggested that one difference between low- and high-EE families is that the latter families believe the patient has control over his or her symptoms, thus implicating the attributional dimension of control as important. Similarly, many of the treatment programs based on EE research involve an educational component about schizophrenia and help relatives understand to what extent and how quickly various behaviors and symptoms are likely to change for the patient; that is, they provide a major focus on the stability dimension of attributions (see 10, 18, 23).

The above discussion suggests that assessing family members' attributions in greater detail seems warranted in EE investigations. Although the specific contents may have to change, many of the self-report inventories developed for the assessment of attributions among distressed couples could provide a format for similar instruments for use in EE research. Similarly, the observational coding system developed for assessing attributions from interaction sequences may be useful when observing interactions of patients and family members. This coding system is not focal to marital distress, so few if any changes might be needed for applications to EE research.

A second area receiving increasing attention in the marital literature involves the expectations that spouses have of each other and their relationship. Actually, the term "expectations" is used in two different ways in discussing marital relationships. First, it is used to refer to what one believes *will* happen in the future—a prediction. Thus, one might expect that one's spouse will never alter a certain behavior. Second, expectations refer to what one believes *should* occur, or the way things should be—"I expect you to be here when you say you are going to be here." Recent marital investigations and clinical observations indicate that both of these expectations are related to marital adjustment. Maritally distressed individuals appear to predict that their partners will behave in negative ways. Also, distressed individuals often have unreasonably high expectations of how their partners should behave or what their marital relationships should offer. Edelson and Epstein (17) have developed a relationship beliefs questionnaire that assesses both forms of expectations.

The area of expectations also appears to be an important aspect of EE-related phenomena. Hooley (29) has suggested that high-EE families might have higher expectations of patients that could promote stress and contribute to patient relapses; yet these higher expectations may lead to higher levels of functioning between psychotic episodes. In addition to criticisms, the second major component in the current definition of EE is emotional overinvolvement of the family member in the patient's life. Emotional overinvolvement can be related to level of expectations in at least two different ways. First family members might become overinvolved because they expect that the patient will be able to do little for himself or herself; consequently, overinvolvement could result from predictions of low functioning for the patient. On the other hand, overinvolvement could result from a family member's belief that the patient should be able to function at a high level and will be able to do so with intense assistance of the family member. Thus, high expectations involve both "shoulds" and predictions. Whereas two very different sets of expectations could lead to emotional overinvolvement, they seem to result in two different kinds of behaviors by family members. The low level of expectations seemingly leads to attempts to overprotect or infantilize the patient, whereas the high expectations likely lead to attempts to push the patient to be more self-sufficient and achieving. The important point is that emotional overinvolvement is a broad construct that may result from a number of different expectations, be related to a number of different emotions, and result in widely varying behaviors. A more detailed focus on expectations both as shoulds and predictions can perhaps help us to understand more clearly how family members' attitudes play a role in various EE-related phenomena.

Communication

Quality of communication is clearly related to marital discord, and much progress has been made in recent years in developing observational coding systems and sophisticated data analysis, as well as self-report inventories to assess communication among married couples (see 5 for a literature review of communication in marriage). In addition, the important role of cognitive processes in communication is now being investigated. In a longitudinal study, Markman (41, 42) has demonstrated the importance of how couples interpret their own and their partners' communication. He initially recruited engaged couples who were presumably happy with their relationships and who intended to marry in the near future. He asked each couple to have a conversation and to evaluate the communication. After one person spoke, that person rated the *intent* of his or her communication on a positive to negative dimension. The partner simultaneously rated the *impact* of that communication on the same negative to positive dimension. Although intent ratings made prior to marriage did not predict subsequent marital adjustment, initial impact ratings were highly predictive of marital adjustment two and five years later.

Furthermore, other investigations have indicated that how couples rate their own communication is not highly correlated with how trained observers rate the same communication (25, 39, 40, 63). Therefore, it is important not to assume that trained observers' ratings of a communication are an index of the emotional impact of the communication on the listener. One of the major focuses in studying the role the family plays in individual psychopathology has been to investigate how the family's communication might influence the development, maintenance, or exacerbation of an individual's symptoms. In order to do so, it seems important to evaluate how the patient perceives communication from family members. At present, there are at least two methods for evaluating the intent and impact of specific communication sequences. Markman and Floyd (43) have developed a communication box for this purpose. One spouse speaks and then each person presses one of five buttons to rate either the intent or impact of the communication.

Weiss et al. (63) have employed a video reconstruction technique for similar purposes. A communication sequence is videotaped, and afterwards the couple is shown the videotape and asked to rate each communication in the sequence.

The implications of the cognitive components of communication are important for the study of EE. One way in which EE may affect a patient's status is during direct communication between family members and the patient. Strachan, Goldstein, and Miklowitz (48) report on three investigations they have conducted to address this issue. For example, Miklowitz et al. (44) found that family members scoring high on EE during an interview do demonstrate similar behavior when interacting directly with the patient, as based on raters' evaluations of the communication. However, not all patients coming from high-EE families relapse. As Hooley (29) has suggested, perhaps these latter patients do not view their family's communication as aversive. Given the above strategies for assessing impact, the research methodology now exists to address this issue.

Intent/impact ratings may also be helpful in differentiating types of high-EE families and in designing intervention for these families. For example, many families who have been categorized as high EE based on frequent criticisms are likely to have negative intent in their critical comments, along with negative impact. Families with such intent need to change their affective attitude toward the patient in a more positive direction, and treatment can be oriented in that direction. However, some high-EE families categorized on the basis of emotional overinvolvement may have many positive feelings toward the patient. That is, the intent of their communication may be positive, but the impact of it on the patient may be negative. Support for this idea is provided by Brown et al.'s (13) finding that families high on emotional overinvolvement were also often high on warmth. Intervention with such families might focus on teaching them alternative ways to be helpful to the patient.

More generally, one assumption appears to be that the EE expressed in an interview when the patient is absent is also communicated to the patient. Perhaps the patient's assessment of the communication from the family member is at least, if not more important than an outsider's evaluation of the family member's communication. Combining assessments from both perspectives can provide maximum clarity about the communication process in the family.

Investigations within the marital field have also helped to make clear that there is no single definition of positive and negative communication. The most widely used observational coding system for marital interactions is the Marital Interaction Coding System (MICS; 62). Hahlweg and his colleagues (26) have noted that at least seven different strategies have been employed to group specific MICS codes into larger negative and positive summary codes. Clearly, one's definition of negative and positive communication will affect the results of a study. EE includes three types of communication expressed by a relative in an interview setting: (a) criticism; (b) hostility; and (c) emotional overinvolvement. All three of these have been interpreted as negative communications. However, these are not the only negative communications. For example, a person can deny responsibility, disagree, and so on. What is focal about the three negative components of EE is that they are all negative communications focused on the patient. Brown et al. (13) hypothesized that the schizophrenic is highly sensitive to the social environment and has an optimal level of arousal. High-EE families were believed to create too high a level of arousal for the patient. Results of EE investigations seemed to suggest that it was the negative aspects of EE that were crucial to predicting relapse. What has not been demonstrated is whether it is the particular negative components currently defined within EE that are important or whether other types of negative communication would have the same impact on the patient. In essence, one must ask if the findings suggest that schizophrenics who live with families who have negative communications are more likely to relapse, or whether the negative communications specific to EE are what impact the patient. In observing the interaction between relatives and depressed patients, Hooley and Hahlweg (30) found that the presence or absense of sustained *positive* communication was what differentiated high-EE from low-EE relatives; thus, the potential importance of positive communication must not be ignored. Related to the intent/impact issue, perhaps living in a family in which the schizophrenic frequently perceives the communication of a family member as negative, regardless of its content, increases the likelihood of relapse.

Additional findings within the marital area point to some of the situation-specific parameters of communication. For example, some studies clearly indicate that to whom a married individual speaks greatly shapes his or her communication (see 12, 58, 59). Generally, married individuals speak more negatively to their spouses than they do to strangers. Also the type of task or the focus of the conversation affects the observed communication (12). Therefore, in trying to understand a family's communication, one must consider carefully who is included in a conversation and the focus of the interaction.

EE is assessed in an interview with the patient's relative and with the patient absent. One very obvious hypothesis is that EE reflects the way in which the family member communicates with the patient. In order to address this issue, direct communication with the patient must be observed and such investigations have recently been performed (15, 21, 22, 28, 30, 44, 54). The results of these investigations only generally support that EE is related to how family members talk with patients. Some high-EE families do not communicate negatively with patients, and perhaps these are the patients who do not relapse. After all, EE is not an assessment of how family mem-members interact *with* patients, and some families classified as high EE, based on CFI interviews, can be viewed as test misses in that EE ratings did not assess actual communication with patients. One may expect direct observations of communication between family and patient to be a more valid assessment than interviews with the patient absent. There are now some available data on this issue.

Recently Goldstein (22, 24) has predicted the development of schizophrenia-spectrum disorders using EE, AS—the EE-oriented measures obtained from direct interaction between patient and family (15), and Singer and Wynne's (64) communication deviance (CD). He found that the best predictors of the development of schizophrenia-spectrum disorders were AS and CD; EE did not add significant predictability after AS and CD were considered. However, EE was not assessed using the standard Camberwell Family Interview, so the results cannot be generalized.

Noncommunication Behavior

Whereas one interpretation is that EE is an indirect assessment of actual family communication, another possibility is that the negative feelings and attitudes expressed in interviews are demonstrated in ways other than direct communication with the patient. That is, some family members may have negative feelings about a patient that they are willing to discuss with a professional in an interview context, but they do not communicate these same feelings and attitudes when speaking directly to the patient. Yet these feelings might be demonstrated in other ways. Findings from the marital area suggest that this is quite possible. At times, marital researchers tend to equate the terms "communication" and "behavior," yet it is obvious that couples behave toward each other in ways that do not involve speech. Although one could argue that any behavior has a communicational aspect, at present we are distinguishing between conversations and the other behaviors in which couples engage, such as mowing the lawn, washing clothes, going to the movies, and so on. Results from marital investigations indicate that positive and negative communications as rated by outside observers do not correlate highly with the frequency of positive and negative noncommunication behavior that couples experience on a daily basis (39). Consequently, in order to understand the emotional climate that a spouse or family member experiences, it is not enough to observe the family communicating with each other. Other behaviors must also be assessed.

One frequently used instrument in the marital field is the Spouse Observation Checklist (61). It consists of approximately 400 behaviors in which a spouse might engage on a daily basis. Each spouse completes the form, checking those behaviors that the partner has engaged in during the past 24 hours. In addition, the respondent rates each behavior as having a positive or negative impact. Whereas the accuracy of the retrospective reports has at times been questionable, the SOC provides one strategy for attempting to assess noncommunicational behaviors that occur in the natural setting.

The application of this marital finding (that observed communication is not highly correlated with noncommunicational behavior) to EE research is hopefully apparent. Different families may learn different ways to express their attitudes and feelings toward the patient. Unless the various behavioral strategies available to a family are taken into account, then hypotheses about a single class of behaviors from high-EE families may be disconfirmed or only weakly supported. In essence, negative emotion expressed in an interview may be demonstrated in a number of ways in the family's daily life, and EE research is likely to benefit to the extent that it is able to make these differentiations.

Summary

Our hope is that some of the conceptual issues currently being addressed in the marital field and some of the empirical findings in marital research can be of help in considering the role of the family in individual psychopathology. More specifically, the assumptions underlying the various models of the family must be examined in more detail and investigators should not continue with a given model simply because it has become the norm for that particular area of research. From the marital area, there is increasing evidence of the importance of certain variables in relational distress, and systematic approaches to the assessment of these variables is underway. Among these are the increasing focus on cognitive variables, including attributions and expectations. The cognitive and communicational approaches are being bridged with the exploration of the perceived intent and impact of communication as evaluated by the couple. We have stressed the importance of situation-specific parameters of communication, and the varying definitions given to negative and positive communication must be considered in interpreting findings. Finally, the need to assess noncommunicational behavior is discussed.

In attempting to demonstrate how these marital findings may be of use to the family field, we have focused on the area of expressed emotion. This is not because EE research is in great need of shifts in direction. To the contrary, EE research appears to hold even greater potential for an understanding of the role of the family in individual psychopathology. Our intent is to show how even a productive research approach can perhaps be strengthened by taking into account findings from related areas of investigation. A close analysis of any other subfield of investigation within the marital/family area is equally likely to show the benefits of such cross-fertilization.

REFERENCES

1. Abramson, L. Y., Seligman, M. E. P., & Teasdale, J. D. Learned helplessness in humans: Critique and reformulation. *Journal of Abnormal Psychology 87*: 49–74, 1978.

2. Anderson, C. M., Hogarty, G., Bayer, T., & Needleman, R. Expressed emotion and social networks of parents of schizophrenic patients. *British Journal of Psychiatry 144*: 247–255, 1984.

3. Baucom, D. H. Conceptual and psychometric issues in evaluating the effectiveness of behavioral marital therapy. In J. P. Vincent (ed.), *Advancements in family intervention, assessment, and theory: Research annual* (Vol. 3). Greenwich CT: Jai Press, 1983.

4. ______. Attributions in distressed relations: How can we explain them? In S. Duck & D. Perlman (eds.), *Heterosexual relations, marriage, and divorce*. Newbury Park CA: Sage Publications, 1987.

5. ______, & Adams, A. Assessing communication in marital interaction. In K. D. O'Leary (ed.), *Assessment of marital discord*. New York: Lawrence Erlbaum, in press.

6. ______, Hoffman, J. A. The effectiveness of marital therapy: Current status and application to the clinical setting. In N. S. Jacobson & A. S. Gurman (eds.), *Clinical handbook of marital therapy*. New York: Guilford Press, 1986.

7. ______, & Mehlman, S. K. Predicting marital status following behavioral marital therapy: A comparison of models of marital relationships. In N. S. Jacobson & K. Hahlweg (eds.), *Marital interaction: Analysis and modification*. New York: Guilford Press, 1984.

8. ______, Sayers, S. L., & Duhe, A. *Assessing couples' attributions for marital events*, submitted for publication.

9. ______, Wheeler, C. M., & Bell, G. *Assessing the role of attributions in marital distress*. Paper presented at the 18th Annual Convention of the Association for the Advancement of Behavior Therapy, Philadelphia, November, 1984.

10. Berkowitz, R., Eberlein-Vries, R., Kuipers, L., & Leff, J. P. Educating relatives about schizophrenia. *Schizophrenia Bulletin 10*: 418–430, 1984.

11. Berley, R. A., & Jacobson, N. S. Causal attributions in intimate relationships: Toward a model of cognitive behavioral marital therapy. In P. Kendall (ed.), *Advances in cognitive-behavioral research and therapy* (Vol. 3), 1984.

12. Birchler, G. R., Weiss, R. L., & Vincent, J. P. Multimethod analysis of social reinforcement exchange between maritally distressed and nondistressed spouse and stranger dyads. *Journal of Personality and Social Psychology 31*: 349–360, 1975.

13. Brown, G. W., Birley, J. L. T., & Wing, J. K. Influence of family life on the course of schizophrenic disorders: A replication. *British Journal of Psychiatry 121*: 241–258, 1972.

14. ______, Monck, E. M., Carstairs, G. M., & Wing, J. K. Influence of family life on the course of schizophrenic illness. *British Journal of Preventive Social Medicine 16*: 55–68, 1962.

15. Doane, J. A., West, K. L., Goldstein, M. J., Rodnick, E. H., & Jones, J. E. Parental communication deviance and affective style: Predictors of subsequent schizophrenia spectrum disorders in vulnerable adolescents. *Archives of General Psychiatry 38*: 679–685, 1981.

16. Doherty, W. J. Cognitive processes in intimate conflict: I. Extending attribution theory. *American Journal of Family Therapy 9*: 3–13, 1981.

17. Eidelson, R. J., & Epstein, N. Cognition and relationship maladjustment: Development of a measure of dysfunctional relationship beliefs. *Journal of Consulting and Clinical Psychology 50*: 715–720, 1982.

18. Falloon, I. R. H., Boyd, J. L., McGill, C. W., Razani, J., Moss, H. B., & Gilderman, A. M. Family management in the prevention of exacerbations of schizophrenia: A controlled study. *New England Journal of Medicine 306*: 1437–1439, 1982.

19. Fincham, F. D. Attributions in close relationships. In J. Harvey & G. Weary (eds.), *Contemporary attribution theory and research*. New York: Academic Press, 1985.

20. ______, & O'Leary, K. D. Causal inferences for spouse behavior in maritally distressed and nondistressed couples. *Journal of Social and Clinical Psychology 1*: 42–57, 1983.

21. Goldstein, M. J. Family factors that antedate the onset of schizophrenia and related disorders: The results of a fifteen-year prospective longitudinal study. Paper presented at the Regional Symposium of the World Psychiatric Association, Helsinki, Finland, June, 1984.

22. ______. The UCLA Family Project. Paper presented at the High Risk Consortium Conference, San Francisco, April, 1985.

23. ______, & Kopeikin, H. S. Short- and long-term effects of combining drug and family therapy. In M. Goldstein (ed.), *New developments in intervention with families of schizophrenics*. San Francisco: Jossey-Bass, 1981.

24. ______, & Strachan, A. M. In M. J. Goldstein, I. Hand, & K. Hahlweg (eds.), *Treatment of schizophrenia: Family assessment and intervention*. Heidelberg: Springer-Verlag, 1986.

25. Gottman, J. M. *Marital interaction: Experimental investigations*. New York: Academic Press, 1979.

26. Hahlweg, K., Schindler, L., Revenstorf, D., & Brengelmann, J. C. The Munich marital therapy study. In K. Hahlweg & N. S. Jacobson (eds.), *Marital interaction: Analysis and modification*. New York: Guilford Press, 1984.

27. Holtzworth-Munroe, A., & Jacobson, N. S. Spontaneous Attribution Coding System (SACS). Unpublished material obtainable from Department of Psychology, Seattle WA 98195.

28. Hooley, J. M. Interactions involving high and low EE relatives: A behavioral analysis. Paper presented at the Schloss Ringberg EE Conference, Munich, June, 1983.

29. ______. Expressed emotion: A review of the critical literature. *Clinical Psychology Review 5*: 119–139, 1985.

30. ______, & Hahlweg, K. Interaction patterns of depressed patients and their spouses: Comparing high and low EE dyads. In M. J. Goldstein & K. Hahlweg (eds.), *Treatment of schizophrenia: Family assessment and intervention*. Heidelberg: Springer-Verlag, 1986.

31. Jacobson, N. S., McDonald, D. W., Follette, W. C., & Berley, R. A. Attributional processes in distressed and nondistressed married couples. *Cognitive Therapy and Research 9*: 35-50, 1985.

32. Kelley, H. H. *Personal relationships: Their structures and processes*. Hillsdale NJ: Lawrence Erlbaum, 1979.

33. Kuipers, L., Sturgeon, D., Berkowitz, R., & Leff, J. Characteristics of expressed emotion: Its relationship to speech and looking in schizophrenic patients and their relatives. *British Journal of Clinical Psychology 22*: 257-264, 1983.

34. Leff, J. P. Schizophrenia and sensitivity to the family environment. *Schizophrenia Bulletin 2*: 566-574, 1976.

35. ______, Kuipers, L., Berkowitz, R., Eberlein-Vries, R., & Sturgeon, D. A controlled trial of social intervention in the families of schizophrenic patients. *British Journal of Psychiatry 141*: 121-134, 1982.

36. ______, & Vaughn, C. The interaction of life events and relatives' expressed emotion in schizophrenia and depressive neurosis. *British Journal of Psychiatry 136*: 146-153, 1980.

37. ______, & Vaughn, C. The role of maintenance therapy and relatives' expressed emotion in relapse of schizophrenia: A two-year follow-up. *British Journal of Psychiatry 139*: 102-104, 1981.

38. Madden, M. E., & Janoff-Bulman, R. Blame, control, and marital satisfaction: Wives' attributions for conflict in marriage. *Journal of Marriage and the Family 44*: 663-674, 1981.

39. Margolin, G. A multilevel approach to the assessment of communication positiveness in distressed marital couples. *International Journal of Family Counseling 6*: 81-89, 1978.

40. ______. Relationships among marital assessment procedures: A correlational study. *Journal of Consulting and Clinical Psychology 46*: 1556-1558, 1978.

41. Markman, H. J. The application of a behavioral model of marriage in predicting relationship satisfaction for couples planning marriage. *Journal of Consulting and Clinical Psychology 47*: 743-749, 1979.

42. ______. Prediction of marital distress: A 5-year follow-up. *Journal of Consulting and Clinical Psychology 49*: 760-762, 1981.

43. ______, & Floyd, F. Possibilities for the prevention of marital discord: A behavioral perspective. *American Journal of Family Therapy 8*: 24-48, 1980.

44. Miklowitz, D. J., Goldstein, M. J., Falloon, I. R. H., & Doane, J. A. Interactional correlates of expressed emotion in the families of schizophrenics. *British Journal of Psychiatry 144*: 482-487, 1984.

45. Norton, J. P. Expressed emotion, affective style, voice tone and communication deviance as predictors of offspring schizophrenia spectrum disorders. Unpublished doctoral dissertation, University of California, Los Angeles, 1982.

46. Pretzer, J., Epstein, N., & Fleming, B. The marital attitude survey: A measure of dysfunctional attributions and expectancies, submitted for publication.

47. Schaap, C. *Communication and adjustment in marriage*. Lisse: Swets & Zeitlinger, B. V., 1982.

48. Strachan, A. M., Goldstein, M. J., & Miklowitz, D. J. Do relatives express their expressed emotions? In M. J. Goldstein, I. Hand, & K. Hahlweg (eds.), *Treatment of schizophrenia: Family assessment and intervention*. Heidelberg: Springer-Verlag, 1986.

49. Sturgeon, D., Kuipers, L., Berkowitz, R., Turpin, G., & Leff, J. Psychophysiological responses of schizophrenic patients to high and low expressed emotion relatives. *British Journal of Psychiatry 138*: 40–45, 1981.

50. ______, Turpin, G., Kuipers, L., Berkowitz, R., & Leff, J. Psychophysiological responses of schizophrenic patients to high and low expressed emotion relatives: A follow-up study. *British Journal of Psychiatry 145*: 62–69, 1984.

51. Tarrier, N., Vaughn, C., Lader, M. H., Leff, J. P. Bodily reactions to people and events in schizophrenics. *Archives of General Psychiatry 36*: 311–315, 1979.

52. Thompson, S. C., & Kelley, H. H. Judgments of responsibility for activities in close relationships. *Journal of Personality and Social Psychology 41*: 69–477, 1981.

53. Valone, K., Goldstein, M. J., & Norton, J. P. Parental expressed emotion and psychophysiological reactivity in an adolescent sample at risk for schizophrenia spectrum disorders. *Journal of Abnormal Psychology 93*: 448–457, 1984.

54. ______, Norton, J. P., Goldstein, M. J., & Doane, J. A. Parental expressed emotion and affective style in an adolescent sample at risk for schizophrenia spectrum disorders. *Journal of Abnormal Psychology 92*: 399–407, 1983.

55. Vaughn, C. E., & Leff, J. P. The influence of family and social factors on the course of psychiatric illness: A comparison of schizophrenic and depressed neurotic patients. *British Journal of Psychiatry 129*: 125–137, 1976.

56. ______, & Leff, J. P. Patterns of emotional response in relatives of schizophrenic patients. *Schizophrenia Bulletin 7*: 43–44, 1981.

57. ______, Snyder, K. S., Freeman, W., Jones, S., Falloon, I. R. H., & Liberman, R. P. Family factors in schizophrenic relapse: A replication. *Schizophrenia Bulletin 8*: 425–426, 1982.

58. Vincent, J. P., Friedman, L. C., Nugent, J., & Messerly, L. Demand characteristics in observations of marital interaction. *Journal of Consulting and Clinical Psychology 47*: 557–566, 1979.

59. ______, Weiss, R. L., & Birchler, G. R. A behavioral analysis of problem solving in distressed and nondistressed married and stranger dyads. *Behavior Therapy 6*: 475–487, 1975.

60. Weiner, B. *Achievement motivation and attribution theory*. Morristown NJ: General Learning Press, 1974.

61. Weiss, R. L., Hops, H., & Patterson, G. R. A framework for conceptualizing marital conflict. In L. A. Hamerlynck, L. C. Hardy, & E. J. March (eds.), *Behavior change: Methodology, concepts, and practice*. Champaign IL: Research Press, 1973.

62. ______, & Summers, K. J. Marital Interaction Coding System—III. In E. E. Filsinger (ed.), Marriage and family assessment: A sourcebook for family therapy. Beverly Hills: Sage Publications, 1983.

63. ______, Wasserman, D. A., Wieder, G. R., & Summers, K. Subjective and objective evaluation of marital conflict: Couples versus the establishment. Paper presented at the Annual

Meeting of the Association for the Advancement of Behavior Therapy, Toronto, November, 1981.

64. Wynne, L. C., Singer, M. T., Bartko, J. J., & Toohey, M. L. Schizophrenics and their families: Research on parental communication. In J. M. Tanner (ed.), *Developments in Psychiatric research*. London: Hodder & Stoughton, 1977.

Name Index

Italicized page numbers refer to bibliographies at the end of each chapter.

Subject Index